D0210997

GREAT SOULS: SIX WHO CHANGED THE CENTURY

GREAT SOULS: SIX WHO CHANGED THE CENTURY

DAVID AIKMAN

WORD PUBLISHING

Nashville·London·Vancouver·Melbourne

WORD PUBLISHING
1998

Library of Congress Cataloging-in-Publiscation Data
Aikman, David, 1944–
Great souls : six who changed the century / by David Aikman.
p.   cm.
"Personal character profiles of: Billy Graham, Mother Teresa,
Aleksandr Solzhenitsyn, Pope John Paul II, Elie Wiesel,
Nelson Mandela."
ISBN 0-8499-0965-1
1. Biography—20th century.   ¾. Title
CT120.A43 1998
97-32773 920.'009'04–dc21
CIP

Printed in the United States of America.
8 9 0 1 2 3 4 5 9 BVG 9 8 7 6 5 4 3 2 1

CONTENTS

ACKNOWLEDGMENTS

MANY PEOPLE ARE INVOLVED in the making of a book, and this has certainly been true of *Great Souls*.

I owe Michael Schick a debt of gratitude for introducing me to the idea of a TV series on prominent figures of our era. Although that project is not yet up and running, the concept sparked ideas in me of which this book is a result. I would like to thank Joe Cosby of Cosby Speakers Bureau for suggesting that books sometimes precede television and for specifically proposing the inclusion of Mandela.

My editor, Lela Gilbert, offered wise and very helpful guidance at various points in the writing of the book. She also carried out some of the early research for the project. Pam Tuben saved my neck when editing deadlines were imminent and there were still numerous facts and references that needed checking. Her hard and rapid work was invaluable.

I am very grateful to Lee Gessner, Senior Vice President and Deputy Publisher for his patience when the original publishing schedule slipped by because the book was not yet ready. Nelson Keener, formerly of Word, was a friendly contact in the early stages of discussion of the book. I owe great thanks to my agent at the William Morris Agency, Debra Goldstein.

In Moscow and the U.S. the Solzhenitsyn family was helpful and gracious in arranging my interview with Aleksandr Solzhenitsyn for both television and the book. I am grateful to them for their kindness.

My family put up with my disappearances for long—and no doubt exasperating—periods in "the dungeon" of my home basement office while I wrote away. I am deeply grateful to my two daughters, Abbie and Amanda, for their encouragement, and above all for the sweet presence in my life of my wife, Nonie, throughout the project.

I'm particularly grateful to the late Kip Jordan, former Publisher and Senior Vice President of Word Publishing. His kindness to me personally, his generosity of spirit, and his vision for God's kingdom will always be an inspiration to me. With the greatest of affection and respect, I dedicate this book to his memory.

THE LIFE OF A FOREIGN CORRESPONDENT is a rich array of experiences. It can be adventurous and exciting, covering wars or great upheavals in the lives of nations. It has moments of long folly, waiting for hours outside the door of some obscure foreign ministry for a bureaucrat to come out and issue a platitude. There is often pathos, listening to the anguish of those made homeless by the harsh ebb and flow of ethnic strife, or sometimes literally stumbling upon their bodies. And there are the moments of exhilaration: a horse ride in Mongolia, an elephant ride in Burma, or a soaring helicopter tour of Jerusalem. One has surely found a great profession when he can ask rhetorically, as every foreign correspondent has done at some point or other: "And they pay me for this?"

If it is seldom the life of glamour depicted in countless movies and novels, some of the stereotypes, like most stereotypes, have a grain of truth to them. I have certainly met men (and a few women) propping up dingy bars in exotic parts of the world between bouts of adventure and genuine danger. There are the proverbial war-junkies, grinning hacks from a dozen newspapers and magazines around the world—the electronic media tends to take itself more seriously—who show up in Beirut or Beijing or Bosnia and specialize in gallows humor.

Virtually every correspondent is grateful for the opportunity to occasionally be an eyewitness to huge tectonic movements of history: for example, the wars in the Middle East, the collapse of Communism, the massacre in Beijing, the Gulf War. I myself was blessed by the privilege of being present at some strategic moments during these crises.

Despite the drama of unfolding historical events, I think many reporters, when they reflect on the most exciting aspects of their careers, will recall the amazing people they have met—and sometimes come to know—as readily as the circumstances they may have covered. This has certainly been true for me. I have met a few villains, the senior Khmer Rouge leader Khieu Samphan, for example, who rationalized to my face the killing fields of Cambodia in 1975 (the victims were "war criminals"). But what remain in my mind at a far deeper level are my encounters, in different parts of the world, with a few people of truly extraordinary moral stature.

Historians, political scientists, and sociologists have for decades been at loggerheads over the significance of individuals in the course of great historical developments. Sometimes the debate is a crude argument between the "great leader" approach to history or the "historical forces" approach—a debate unlikely ever to be ultimately resolved. What has struck me as a reporter for most of my adult life, however, is the capacity of individual human beings again and again to rise above their times and their circumstances to change, if only just a little, the direction of the human tide. How else is one to explain Boris Yeltsin standing atop a tank outside the Russian Parliament in 1993 and turning back, at first single-handedly, a coup against democracy itself? Or Nelson Mandela, one of our Great Souls, transforming what seemed an almost certain blood-bath in South Africa into a change of government described by much of the world as "a miracle"?

The six people I have profiled in this book have all exerted a phenomenal, and unquestionably beneficial, influence on the human race during this century. I met four of them in the course of my reporting as a foreign correspondent: Mother Teresa, Billy Graham, Aleksandr Solzhenitsyn, and Elie Wiesel. I selected the other two, Nelson Mandela and Pope John Paul II, because they stood out so significantly that I could not seriously profile the first four without including them also.

I realize that not all of these six will appeal equally to all people. They do not even agree with one another on some very important human issues.

What all of them certainly would agree on, however, is that individual people still count enormously, indeed infinitely, in our sometimes fearfully crowded world. They would also affirm that there are qualities of virtue throughout the human race that transcend politics, race, culture, language, epoch, or inherited religious background.

One of the greatest Christian writers in the twentieth century, C. S. Lewis, made the point forcefully in his short work *The Abolition of Man*. Lewis, a Protestant Englishman, embraced a wholly orthodox, biblically based Christian view of the human condition. Yet he felt compelled to point to what he believed were universal ideas of right and wrong found among such diverse cultural groups as Greeks, Chinese, Indians, Hebrews, Anglo-Saxons, Babylonians, Norse, and ancient Egyptians. Writing not as a theologian at all, but as a cultural anthropologist, Lewis even used a Chinese term, the "Tao" (or *dao* in modern Chinese), to denote what he thought were six transcendent moral or ethical principles of virtually all major global cultures: the law of beneficence; duty to family; the law of justice; good faith and veracity; the law of mercy; the law of magnanimity.[1]

Amid the clamor over "culture wars" and arguments over the best laws for governing society as we head toward a new millennium, this notion of transcendent moral principles is often overlooked. In the United States, people of both liberal and conservative philosophical and political persuasion sometimes deny to those of differing viewpoints the virtue of moral behavior. At its most harmless, such an attitude of mind is merely parochialism; at its worst, it is bigotry. The assumption (usually by conservatives) that a person who holds tolerance as a very high virtue is unlikely to esteem highly the virtues of personal morality is as mistaken as the belief (usually among liberals) that people of deeply orthodox religious conviction are themselves incapable of tolerance. In fact, a former professor of mine subtitled one of his graduate school courses, "The more orthodox, the more tolerant," in order to make this second point.[2]

Social liberals and social conservatives will always pillory each other on what constitutes an acceptable social lifestyle, especially in the area of sexual behavior. They will fight tooth and nail in politics over which policies are most likely to bring about their very differing visions of the good life for the nation or the global community. But ancient qualities like courage (especially in overcoming great adversity), truthfulness (especially in the face of powerfully entrenched lies), and compassion (especially when the price to act it out is very high) resonate consistently in the hearts of all human beings from one generation to the next.

The word *great* has many different definitions, but among them are "prominent, renowned . . . eminent, distinguished . . . lofty, noble, magnanimous . . . assiduous, persistent . . . wonderful, admirable."[3] The list could go on. In a thesaurus, under *magnanimous,* one also finds "great of heart or soul."[4] As for *soul,* we learn that it is, among other things, "a person's total self in its living unity and wholeness . . . man's moral and emotional nature as distinguished from his mind or intellect."[5] A *Great Soul,* therefore, as we define it in this book, is "someone of preeminent attainment characterized by one or more character qualities of greatness." Each of the people profiled in this book fits that description, but for reasons that are, in every instance, different from the others.

In the case of each of the Great Souls, there is at least one biography available, and sometimes several, which are very good. The profiles I have written, though, are not designed to unearth previously unknown facts or statements—although this may occur. My intention is to make a different point: In a remarkable way, the life of each of them, as it has been lived out, has demonstrated one overriding human quality, or preoccupation, or virtue, more than any other. And that virtue has been expressed for the entire human race so vividly that its importance is likely to resonate not just into the next millennium, but for as long as the human race continues to survive and keep records of its history.

What was it about Mother Teresa that caught the imagination of the entire world? Or about Solzhenitsyn that seemed to provide the catalyst for the demolition of Marxist-Leninist Utopianism as a plausible future for the human race? Or about Elie Wiesel that forces us, again and again, to address the profundity of evil of which the human race, under the Nazis, showed itself so capable? Or about Billy Graham that has made the salvation of the human soul an issue of extraordinary urgency across the world for five decades? Or about Nelson Mandela that turned his most intransigent adversaries—even his jailers—into supporters of his particular social and political visions? Or about Pope John Paul II that has saved the papacy from becoming just an emblem of archaic spirituality, instead transforming it into a vital debating chair for global issues that are entirely contemporary? At least in part, the answers to these questions can be found in the virtues or lifelong preoccupations especially characteristic of their lives, which I have attached to the six Great Souls:

Billy Graham	*Salvation*
Nelson Mandela	*Forgiveness*
Aleksandr Solzhenitsyn	*Truth*
Mother Teresa	*Compassion*
Pope John Paul II	*Human Dignity*
Elie Wiesel	*Remembrance*

All six of the Great Souls in this book have had enormous, perhaps in some instances incalculable, impact on their own societies or on the world as a whole. Four of them, Mother Teresa, Nelson Mandela, Aleksandr Solzhenitsyn, and Elie Wiesel, have been awarded Nobel Prizes in recognition of their achievement. The other two, Billy Graham and Pope John Paul II, are so universally recognized that not even the Nobel award could add to their accomplishment or fame.

The selection, inevitably, has been subjective. Other names might have been added to the list: Václav Havel, the Czech playwright and dissident who led his country out of the collapse of Communism in 1989 into a new era of democracy and, above all, national truthfulness; Aung San Suu Kyi, the courageous Burmese oppositionist who won the Nobel Peace Prize in 1991 for her principled stand against her nation's military dictatorship; or the Dalai Lama, perhaps, another Nobel Peace Prize laureate, for his own leadership of a national struggle to ensure the continued survival of Tibetan civilization.

In the end, however, the selection of the six boiled down to four elements. First, they had to be people who lived in the second half of the nineties decade, as the book was being written. Second, they had to have had an impact on the world well beyond their own nation of origin. Third, it was important to me that I had either met them or would have a good chance of meeting them as the book proceeded. Fourth, they needed to have been known and recognized as truly outstanding human beings even by those who did not agree with their views.

They are all, in varying degrees, "famous," and in measurable ways three have been publicly defined as "admirable." *Good Housekeeping* magazine, for example, has been polling its readers each year since 1969 on the most admired men and women of the world. By 1996, Mother Teresa had been listed eighteen times, Billy Graham, fifteen, and Pope John Paul II, fourteen times. Solzhenitsyn was virtually a household name in the world in the 1970's, and Mandela today elicits global adulation. Only Elie Wiesel is less widely known, by and large.

Yet fame was certainly not the principal criterion of selection. If it had been, Oprah Winfrey, the late Princess Diana, or even Dennis Rodman might have been in the book, for all three also have either appeared at different times in the *Good Housekeeping* top ten or are seldom out of the public eye for more than a few weeks at a time. Other candidates might have included Madonna or Michael Jackson, whose American and global recognition far exceeds that of, say, Elie Wiesel. But as we shall see, with no disrespect for the pop stars mentioned, there is a disproportionately greater moral impact from the life and work of Elie Wiesel than from the lives and ideas of Michael Jackson, Madonna, and virtually any other list of entertainers and "personalities" one could assemble on a large sheet of paper. The Great Souls selected for this book were all remarkable for their combination of character, conviction, and ideas that contributed to their global prominence and the power of their influence.

They were also chosen because most people, however diverse their political and cultural points of view, would select at least three or four of them if asked to come up with their own list. Liberals, for example, would almost certainly agree to the inclusion of Nelson Mandela and Elie Wiesel, and many would include the late Mother Teresa too. Conservatives would likely agree to Billy Graham, Aleksandr Solzhenitsyn, and Pope John Paul II. Many liberals would feel uncomfortable with the inclusion of John Paul II, and many conservatives with the addition of Nelson Mandela. Yet while people might disagree with some of the social and political ideas of these six individuals, most fair-minded individuals would find it difficult to take issue with the particular moral excellence epitomized by each.

Famous as these six are, not a single one of them is a "celebrity," a term perceptively defined by the historian Daniel Boorstin as "a person who is well-known for his well-knownness."[6] "In the past," Boorstin explained, "a man's name was not apt to become a household word unless he exemplified great-ness in some way or other." The twentieth century, he said, has increasingly confused celebrity worship and hero worship. "We have willingly been mis-led into believing," he suggests, "that fame—well-knownness—is still a hallmark of greatness," a problem that has been made worse by the fact that a celebrity is almost by definition "morally neutral."[7]

There are some striking points in common in the lives of these Great Souls. Three (Mandela, Graham, and Solzhenitsyn) were born in the same year, 1918, a watershed year of the century, when World War I came to an end and with it collapsed two major European empires, the Russian and the Austro-Hungarian. Three of the Great Souls spent time in prison; Nelson Mandela, twenty-seven years, much of it on the notorious, high-security Robben Island, off the South African coast. Solzhenitsyn was in the infamous Soviet Gulag camp system eight years. Elie Wiesel spent the shortest time imprisoned, from May 1944 until his liberation on April 10, 1945, but it was in the heart of the worst prison system of all, the Nazi concentration camps of Auschwitz and Buchenwald.

Four of the Great Souls came from Eastern Europe and Russia: Mother Teresa from Skopje in Macedonia (though she was Albanian by birth), Solzhenitsyn from Russia, Pope John Paul II from Poland, and Elie Wiesel from Romania. Three of these either fought the Nazis (Solzhenitsyn), was arrested by them (Wiesel), or lived under Nazi occupation (John Paul II). Two had deeply unhappy marriages that led to divorce (Solzhenitsyn and Mandela), two had, and continue to have, successful marriages (Graham and Wiesel), and two took vows never to be married at all (Mother Teresa and John Paul II). As far as I have been able to determine, each of the Great Souls has met at least one of the others, the pope has met four of them, but Billy Graham is the only one who has met them all.

Whether they have met or not, these extraordinary people have some interesting qualities or attributes in common. First, each demonstrated phenomenal self-discipline from an early age and continued to show it throughout his or her life. Second, five of the six (all except Wiesel, whose Jewish faith was sorely tested by the Holocaust) came to be convinced— though not in identical ways—that their lives had been touched by a divine calling, a calling so unique that only a personal God could have envisaged it, engineered the circumstances of it and communicated it, and then provided the strength and energy necessary to carry it out. Five of the six Great Souls came from different traditions within Christendom: Mother Teresa and Pope John Paul II from Roman Catholicism, Solzhenitsyn from Russian Orthodoxy, Billy Graham from the Southern Baptists, and Nelson Mandela from Methodism. Elie Wiesel came from a devout Orthodox Jewish family with strong connections to the Hasidic tradition.

None of the six Great Souls were ever, or are today, perfect. Even

Mother Teresa was criticized for administrative and other failings. Besides, just as most virtues have a corresponding vice ready to trap the unwary, so some of these people, at times, have crossed the thin line that separates single-mindedness from selfishness, self-confidence from arrogance, decisiveness from arbitrariness, skepticism from querulousness, moral scrupulousness from self-righteousness. But the border-crossing, when it occurred, was never permanent. Virtue, after all, often consists not so much in the absence of fault altogether as in the speed and grace with which fault is recognized and corrected.

Like most readers of biographies throughout history, I have always personally been inspired by the lives of great people. It is hard not to be energized by the stories of how individuals have risen above adversity or suffering, or have maintained a purity in the face of great temptation. Our age, with its habit of instantly judging a man or woman's life based on the fragmentary and proverbial sound bite, is often impatient with detail, nuances, depth. It takes a certain generosity of spirit too—sadly a rare virtue in our age—to admire the moral quality of a person when one disagrees with his or her ideas.

In my experience, that generosity of spirit is nevertheless almost always rewarded. I have repeatedly been delighted to find large kernels of decency and integrity in the lives of people with whom, on political issues in particular, I have strongly disagreed. In his illuminating work *On Character*, James W. Wilson notes that observations about character "are, or should be, statements about morality; saying that someone has good character is fundamentally different from the assertion that someone can hit a good curve ball, play a good chess game, or sing a Mozart aria."[8] If you don't like the word *morality*, how about *virtue*? This fine and ancient descriptive, after decades of neglect, is beginning to return to proper usage thanks to writers like Gertrude Himmelfarb and William Bennett.[9]

Virtue—striking, dazzling, inspiring—is found abundantly in the lives of each of these Great Souls, though not at all in the same manner. I know that I was influenced in my own life in the course of writing this book, a point that even my most astute critic of all, my dear wife, noticed. It seems that, being as close as I was to these admirable people through my writing, I could not help but unconsciously seek to emulate them. James Wilson has something else very interesting to say in this respect:

Mankind's moral sense is not a strong beacon light, radiating outward to illuminate in sharp outline all that it touches. It is, rather, a small candle flame, casting vague and multiple shadows, flickering and sputtering in the strong winds of power and passion, greed and ideology. But brought close to the heart and cupped in one's hands, moral sense dispels the darkness and warms the soul.[10]

There is much "flickering and sputtering" in the lives of these six Great Souls. But oh, how they have warmed my soul. I hope, in a similar way, that they will warm yours too.

CHAPTER 1

BILLY GRAHAM: SALVATION

"I am going to preach a gospel not of despair but of hope—hope for the individual, for society and for the world."

—BILLY GRAHAM, LONDON, 1954

HE WAS HUNKERED DOWN LOW—as low as a six-foot two-inch man can hunker down—in a plastic airport chair in the modest-size airport waiting area. He wore a nondescript tweed jacket and sweater, and pants that looked as though they had met up at different times with brushwood along the pathways in the North Carolina mountains. But it was the hat that struck me: one of those carelessly shapeless cloth hats that fishermen and hunters wear. It covered at least some of his forehead and the mane of white hair at the back of his head—a sort of halfhearted attempt to avoid being recognized by travelers passing through the small airport.

The oddest thing was that he needn't have showed up at all. I was coming to interview him, the most famous evangelist in the world, not the other way around. I could have taken a cab to the Cove, his office headquarters in Montreat, North Carolina, or rented a car. But he had come in person, with his driver, to meet yet another journalist fascinated to delve into the heart and soul of Billy Graham.

As we drove back to his Montreat office of the Billy Graham Evangelistic Association, I was fascinated, as so many reporters have been, by his capacity for interest in other people. In the car, over lunch, during the interview, and afterward, Graham unconsciously conveyed his phenomenal ability to put people at ease, to converse with you as comfortably as he would with a long-time neighbor.

I had met him and his wife, Ruth, before, offering some small suggestions as he planned what became his 1988 visit to China. I had been in the comfortable, country-style log cabin atop a hill near Montreat. Even then, what came across from both Grahams was an air of comfortable normality, made spicier, perhaps, by Billy Graham's capacious anecdotal memory of the prominent people he has encountered over the years, and rendered stimulating by the enormous experience of the world that he has gathered in his travels.

I had also met him a decade and a half before that when he was in Hong Kong preparing for the 1975 crusade. I interviewed him at the time in the Sheraton Hotel, Kowloon; though, as with Mother Teresa, I must have failed to draw from him anything that my editors considered newsworthy. "I would have studied more and spoken less," Graham said when I asked him if he would have changed anything in his career. "I would have spent more time with my family." That seemed like something close to a confession, so my editors at least graciously included this snippet of *mea culpa* in the "People" section of the magazine. But Graham also spoke in passing of the burdens imposed upon him by his sheer fame. "I'm constantly surrounded by people," he said. "I'm never alone." Paradoxically, he felt that this perpetual fame had become a prison for him, preventing him from keeping in touch with ordinary people. "I can't go to New York without the police taking the next room in the hotel," he complained.

"What advice would you give to Christians?" I asked back in 1975. "Study the Word," he replied. "Memorize Scripture, and get ready for persecution." Persecution? There didn't seem much likelihood of that taking place imminently, at least not in the United States. But in the fall of 1975, just months after the horrendous American humiliation in abandoning South Vietnam, there were grounds for believing that Soviet global power was in the ascendancy to an extent that could threaten the freedom of Christians in many countries. Ironically, though Graham's concerns about a Soviet preeminence proved happily unfounded, his worries about Christian persecution were well ahead of their time. Not until 1997 did American Christians—partly with the friendly goading of sympathetic Jews—wake up to the massive degree of persecution taking place against Christians around the world.[1]

Billy Graham has been described in innumerable articles and books as "charming," and it is true. But his is not the charm of the maître d' in an elegant restaurant, or a polished protocol officer in some diplomatic service or other. There is an innocence to it, a sincerity that catches you off guard. How can a man who has been an intimate friend of presidents, monarchs, popes, and prime ministers be both thoughtful and respectful to people with whom there is not likely to be any long-term connection? Graham has many times spoken of "integrity" as being the highest honor that he would wish to have attributed to him after his death. In his capacity to relate with equal warmth and sincerity to the high and the low, the fiercely antagonistic and the unctuously friendly, he attained it long ago.

Graham has been hurt by people he was close to, and betrayed by a handful over the years. But what seems to have protected him from bouts of vindictiveness—the common refuge of the deeply offended—has been a resurgent humility and a genuine sense of wonder at the heights to which, for nearly half a century, he has been elevated. Billy Graham has somehow managed to remain over those years, in part, an innocent North Carolina country boy, prankish, and having fun. He seems amazed at all he sees in the big city, and still fearful of putting a foot wrong.

"I wish I could go to heaven right now," he told Paula Zahn of CBS television a few years ago. "My greatest fear is that I'll do something or say something that will bring disrepute on the Gospel of Christ before I go."[2] The remark is totally typical of Graham, as typical as the airport welcome of an unimportant visitor.

Graham's innocence is all the more surprising in light of what he has been exposed to. In the past half-century, because of his worldwide fame and friendship with major world leaders, he has in a sense acquired a penthouse view of many of the major developments around the globe. From these leaders, he has often received something of a running commentary on events by those who have actually influenced them. No other human being this century, living or dead, has had such intimate conversations with so many of the age's powerful and famous, from Winston Churchill to Mikhail Gorbachev, from Generalissimo Chiang Kai-shek to Queen Elizabeth of England, from Pope John Paul II to North Korea's fiery Communist leader Kim Il Sung.

Throughout this period, Graham has served as an unofficial pastor to ten American presidents in succession and, in a major way, to the American people as a whole. When presidents die, or terrorist catastrophes like the 1995 Oklahoma City bombing occur, Americans turn instinctively to Billy Graham for spiritual solace. Former Texas governor John Connally said of him, "Billy Graham is more than a preacher, more than an evangelist, more than a Christian leader. In a greater sense, he has become our conscience."[3] Former President George Bush has called Graham "America's pastor."[4] Numerous others have simply dubbed Graham "the Protestant pope."

Pope or pastor, confidant of presidents or evangelist, Graham's popularity among ordinary Americans has been astounding—measured statistically—for four decades. Since the 1950's, he has appeared in the annual top ten listing of "the most admired American" in polls organized by the Gallup organization thirty-seven times, and for seventeen of those times he has been in the top four of the list. For three years in a row Graham was top of the *Good Housekeeping* poll of "The Most Admired Men," and for a total of fourteen times he was in the top ten. When *Ladies Home Journal* conducted a survey in 1978 in the category "achievements in religion," Graham was second; the winner was God. *Life* magazine listed him as one of the one hundred most important Americans of the twentieth century. In the Nixon presidential archives there is a letter to former President Nixon from a woman requesting the president's assistance in obtaining an appointment with Billy Graham.[5]

Globally, statistics of popularity are harder to gauge, since many countries forbid any kind of popularity survey (their own leaders might not fare so well). It is reasonable to say, though, that no American has been held in higher esteem around the world than Graham on a consistent basis for the past four decades, and almost certainly no American's name is as well known. At the headquarters of the Billy Graham Evangelistic Association in Minneapolis, letters have been delivered from around the world with the simple address, "Billy Graham, U.S.A." or—entertainingly, no doubt, for the post office—"Belly Grayem, Menihapuls, Menisoldiem."

Graham has preached during his five-decade global ministry to more people in person than anyone else in history, around 210 million, with some 2.8 million people responding to his invitation to "come forward" as "inquirers." With his satellite broadcast called "The Billy Graham World Television Series" in April 1996, it was estimated that as many as 2.5 billion people in more than 160 countries may have heard Graham's Easter Sunday sermon, which was translated into forty-eight languages. Once again, the numbers dazzle. Since the beginning of Christianity there has never been a larger number of people to hear the gospel message on one particular day. *Decision* magazine, which Graham founded in 1960, is published each month, and reaches some two million readers in 163 countries, the most widely distributed religious magazine in the world—and, of course, ever.

Graham's tangible accomplishments have been documented assiduously by the Billy Graham Evangelistic Association, the organizational base of his ministry since 1950. He founded the magazine *Christianity Today* in 1957, and within a year of start-up, it had outstripped in circulation its rival, more liberal periodical, *Christian Century*. For the past four decades it has continued to be perhaps the most influential single magazine for Protestant Christians of any theological persuasion in the U.S. He started World Wide Pictures, a motion picture production company that in 1994 alone screened its movies, through videos, in some 350 churches in the U.S. and Canada. The viewing audience was estimated at close to four million, perhaps small potatoes for the general motion picture industry, but big-time exposure for any Christian organization.

Graham's weekly *Hour of Decision* radio program, started in 1950, is now broadcast by more than one thousand stations around the world. His newspaper column, "My Answer," is carried by papers across the U.S. with a combined circulation of seven million readers. He has written seventeen books, all of them best-sellers, and some of them setting publishing records immediately after their release. *The Jesus Generation*, published in 1971, sold 200,000 copies in the first two weeks, while *Angels: God's Secret Agents*, published in 1975, well before the current angels fad, sold one million copies in the first ninety days and was the best-selling new book in the U.S. for that year. *How to Be Born Again* (1977), had a first printing of 800,000 copies, the largest in publishing history at that time. *Approaching Hoofbeats: The Four Horsemen of the Apocalypse* (1983) was for several weeks on the *New York Times* best-seller list, as indeed were two of his other books. His 1953 book *Peace with God* sold more than two million copies and has been translated into thirty-eight languages.

Graham's list of major national and international awards is so numerous and weighty that it defies enumeration except in the most outstanding cases. It includes the Congressional Medal of Freedom, Clergyman of the Year Award, the Freedom's Foundation Distinguished Persons Award (several years), the Gold Medal Award of the National Institute of Social Science, the Horatio Alger Award, the Templeton Prize for Progress in Religion, and the Sylvanus Thayer Award from the United States Military Academy. Jewish organizations have awarded Graham the Torch of Liberty Plaque (the Anti-Defamation League of Baha'i Brith), the First National Interreligious Award (the American Jewish Committee), and the Jabotinsky Centennial Medal (the Jabotinsky Foundation). Roman Catholics have honored him with the Franciscan International Award.

In May 1996, the U.S. Congress honored Graham with the highest award ever conferred on private U.S. citizens not serving in the armed forces, the Congressional Gold Medal. Only 114 of these medals have been awarded since 1776, when the first such medal was given to George Washington. President Clinton signed into law the legislation enacting this honor. The citation recognized both Grahams, Billy and his wife, Ruth, for their "outstanding and lasting contributions to morality, racial equality, family, philanthropy and religion." Numerous universities have conferred on Billy Graham an honorary doctorate. The only major international award that Graham has never been awarded is the Nobel Peace Prize.

These are the obvious reasons for Billy Graham's inclusion among our Great Souls. But it is the intangible aspect of Graham's achievement that, in so many ways, is more remarkable. No other Protestant leader of this or any century has so successfully articulated the central features of the Christian doctrine of eternal salvation and at the same time mobilized global Protestant Christianity in pursuit of them. Graham has been able to do this, moreover, by persuading a very wide variety of Christian groups, from liberal to extremely conservative, that their differences on particular doctrines and practices are less important than what they hold in common.

He has done even more than this. In focusing on the core of Protestant Christianity—justification by faith on the authority of the Bible—he has also built hitherto nonexistent bridges to the Roman Catholic world and to the Eastern Orthodox traditions, both of which have traditionally had uneasy, often hostile, relationships with Protestants. For many years, his crusade organizers have invited Roman Catholic churches to be partners in preparatory prayer, counseling of the "inquirers" who "come forward" at the crusades, and follow-up discipling of them within their own churches. He himself has frequently observed that he has more in common in his beliefs with orthodox Catholics than with some modernist Protestants. "Now I have reconciled in my mind," he told me in 1990,

> that God has his people in all kinds of places and all kinds of churches and groups. I have found many people in the Roman Catholic church, both clergy and laity, who I believe are born-again Christians. They may hold different theological views than I hold, but I believe they are in the body of Christ. So I consider them my brothers and sisters in Christ.[6]

No one has yet satisfactorily defined a sort of "generic" Christian faith, a nondenominational essence of Christian belief to which virtually all Christians, of whatever background, can give their assent. If any Christian leader of this century, however, has exemplified both in belief and behavior what Christians can constructively agree upon doctrinally and how they should live out their faith amid a variety of challenges, Billy Graham has probably come the closest to doing so.

Graham's exemplary warmth toward Catholics, without his giving up any core Protestant beliefs, may have done more to heal the wounds of the great Protestant-Catholic schism of the Reformation than the actions of any other Christian in the past five hundred years. Reinhold Niebuhr was one of the first Protestant theologians to acknowledge this. Speaking of Graham, he said, "This handsome, youthful, modest, and obviously sincere evangelist is better than any evangelist of his kind in American history." In 1964, the late Cardinal Cushing of Boston added, "I only wish we had half a dozen men of his caliber to go forth and do likewise."[7]

Niebuhr's and Cushing's comments were courageous as well as generous when they uttered them. The Catholic-Protestant divide at that time in the U.S. was still great: a "mixed marriage," until the 1960's, was a term largely used to refer to a Catholic-Protestant marriage union, not to an interracial marriage. In addition, before the great Roman Catholic conciliar movement known as Vatican II in the early 1960's, there was little Roman Catholic inclination as a whole to seek common ground with Protestants. Graham's consistency, sincerity, and generosity of spirit to the Catholics nevertheless reaped rich fruit some two decades after these qualities first became evident.

Billy Graham did not formally meet any pope until 1981, when he was received in Rome by Pope John Paul II for half an hour. Their conversation ran the gamut of inter-Christian affairs: interchurch relations, contemporary moral issues, evangelism, and the emergence of Evangelicalism around the world. After it was over, Graham bubbled with a characteristically unrehearsed enthusiasm about the meeting. "We had a spiritual time," he said. "He is so down-to-earth and human, I almost forgot he was the pope."[8]

What he did not say, and what he did not in fact reveal until several years later, was exactly how warm the meeting had been. By the late 1980's, the theological conservatism and yet broad human interests of Pope John Paul II had made themselves clear to everyone. Graham himself had met the pope a second time and had also come to know some of the Vatican officials close to him. Yet it was nearly a decade after this meeting before he was willing to risk mentioning in public an important detail of his papal meeting that he had not told anyone earlier. During their 1981 meeting, he said, the pope had reached across and grabbed him by the thumb (in some Graham versions it was by the lapels), drawn Graham close to him, and said with great intensity, "We are brothers."[9] In 1981, it might have been embarrassing for the pope if Graham had revealed this. It certainly would have raised some hackles among many evangelical Protestants.

Graham accomplished three things that, in retrospect, will be seen as his most significant contributions to the development of global Christianity in the twentieth century. The first was to establish Evangelicalism—or as it became known at the time, the "New Evangelicalism"—as the most dynamic, and indeed the dominant movement within late twentieth-century Protestantism, not just in the U.S., but globally. The second was to reach out inclusively and in a spirit of brotherhood well beyond the usual confines of Protestants to Christians of all traditions throughout the world. The third achievement was to demonstrate that a person could associate with the rich, the powerful, and the successful in their own settings, and yet still maintain a life of modesty and moral purity. In these three areas of accomplishment—all for the sake of communicating the message of salvation to the world—Graham has demonstrated that he is a Great Soul.

COWS, PRANKS, AND A HAYLOFT IN CHARLOTTE

Graham's small-town origins are so well known they are almost the stuff of legend. His grandfather was a Confederate veteran who died in 1910, before Billy's birth, with a Union bullet from Gettysburg in his leg. He was a man with a broad, patriarchal beard, habits of drinking and swearing, and a reluctance to pay his bills. His two sons, William Franklin Graham and Clyde Graham, built up a three-hundred-acre farm a few miles outside Charlotte, in the rich, red North Carolina soil. Graham's father, William Franklin Graham, inherited the farm. He was a successful dairy farmer who had been among the first to use electricity in the area. He and his wife, Morrow, were not wealthy, but they lived well by the standards of the time. William Franklin Graham Sr. even managed to augment the family income by occasional real estate deals and the skillful purchase and resale of cars from time to time.[10] He didn't drink, but he smoked the odd cigar.

The parents of William Franklin Graham Jr., Billy Graham's formal name, were Presbyterians of strong faith and clear moral decency. At the age of eighteen, Billy's father had experienced the Christian phenomenon of "new birth," or knowledge of Christ's forgiveness from sins, at a Methodist chapel called the Planck Meetinghouse. He had even been told by an old preacher that he might himself become a preacher of the gospel. He didn't, and the fervor of his initial moment of conversion does not seem to have been maintained throughout his life.[11] But the family was upright in its practices, holding family prayers every evening, saying grace before every meal, and limiting work on Sundays to as little as was absolutely necessary to maintain the running of the farm. In practice, this meant milking and feeding the cows.

Billy's mother, Morrow, never had any dramatic experience of conversion to Christ, but later told friends, "I couldn't tell you the day or the hour when I was converted, but I knew I was born again." She believed very much in the importance of memorizing Scripture verses, and would recite verses to her children as she gave them their baths. She would also expect them to memorize a verse each day—from the King James Version of the Bible, of course—before they went off to school or out to play. On Sundays, the family would travel to Charlotte to attend the Associate Reformed Presbyterian Church, a strict Calvinist congregation that believed in the literal truth of the Bible and subscribed to the historical Westminster Confession of Faith.[12]

Billy Graham was born into this family November 7, 1918, one year to the day after the Bolshevik Revolution had overturned an incipient democracy in Russia (the czar had actually been deposed in April), and just four days before the armistice that brought World War I to an end. He was the oldest of four siblings, Catherine, Melvin, and Jean, the youngest, who was born fourteen years after Billy. By all accounts it was a happy but well-disciplined childhood, with Billy several times getting a good hiding by belt from his father and/or by hickory switch from his mother across his backside.

"Billy was rowdy, mischievous," one older relative has recalled. "But on the other hand, he was soft and gentle and loving and understanding. He was a very sweet, likable person."[13] He was a prankster who would cut off the school bus's external gas valve just before getting off the bus at his own home, but he seemed to lack any personal malice. Early on he exhibited a strong tendency to like people from the moment of meeting them.[14]

Graham's father apparently wanted the boy to succeed him in running the family farm, and as soon as he was physically up to it, Billy added various chores around the farm to his normal childhood obligations of homework for school and helping keep up the house. He rose before dawn to feed and milk the cows, then worked in the fields or did more work with the cows on returning from school. But at about the age of eleven, he developed a passion for reading, spending long hours around the farm, sometimes in the hayloft, devouring Tarzan or biographies, or the stories of missionaries in distant lands. He was not an especially gifted child at school, but his curiosity about the world outside the mountains of North Carolina and his fascination with meeting, and listening to, new acquaintances seem to have been ignited at this time.[15]

As he grew into his teens, Billy rose rapidly in height toward his full stature of six feet two inches. He was a healthy, lanky, energetic teenager with an eye for the girls and a thoroughly normal liking for driving cars as fast as possible. He would often drive his father's car along the country roads, sometimes in the company of school girlfriends, no doubt trying to impress them by roaring around curves in the road at hair-raising speed. He once got the car stuck in the mud, to the fury of his father. But Graham's attraction to the girls, by today's standards, was remarkably innocent. By his own testimony—and no one has ever suggested this was anything but the truth—he was never more physical with any of the girls than simple kissing.[16]

Reading in his spare time, infatuation almost on a weekly basis with some female classmate or other, delight with baseball and occasional Walter Mitty fantasies about playing in the big leagues—these seemed to be preoccupations of young Billy Graham as he approached his mid-teens. As to any religious sentiment, he appears to have had none. While he respected his parents and their daily devotions, emphasis on Scripture memorization and church attendance, he reports no early glimmering of the religious future in store for him.

His mother, at the urging of her sister Lil Baker, had begun to attend a Bible study group in 1933 and read the evangelical writings of several famous preachers of the day. She also began to pray more and to attend Bible studies at the Plymouth Brethren Church, whose English founder, John Nelson Darby (1800–1882), had combined a zealous Evangelicalism with teachings on biblical prophecy and its fulfillment that became known as "dispensationalism."

Frank, Billy's father, was badly injured in a freak accident when the mechanical saw sent a block of wood smashing into the side of his face. His head injuries were serious, and the surgeons who attended him evidently believed he might die. The accident, however, had occurred just a few weeks after Morrow's renewed interest in the Bible and in prayer, and she was able to gather her friends to batter the gates of heaven to prevent this from happening. She went to her bedroom and "just laid hold of the Lord," she was to say later. "I got up with the assurance that God heard my prayer."[17] Frank recovered and came to believe, along with Morrow, that God had truly intervened in their lives. Morrow was clearly becoming more devout in her faith than before. As for the young Billy, he was busy admiring the girls and sowing his wild oats in teenage pranks. His parents' newfound seriousness about religion, he thought, was just "all hogwash."[18]

"I GUESS THEY ARE JUST SOME FANATICS"

Charlotte had the reputation of being one of the most heavily church-attended cities in the United States. The visit of evangelist Billy Sunday there in 1924 had shaken up its spiritual complacency and was remembered by many. But the Wall Street crash of 1929 and the following Great Depression had hit the city's economy hard. Businesses and banks were collapsing, as they were elsewhere in the nation, unemployment was soaring, and church attendance hadn't done much to raise the city's spirits.

One of the consequences of Billy Sunday's visit had been the emergence of a group of men, mostly in the business community, who decided to commit themselves on a regular basis to pray for Charlotte. Discouraged by what they saw happening in their community and by the gloomy attitude to life that came in its wake, they set aside a day of prayer and fasting in the spring of 1934. The location they selected was one of the pastures of farmer Frank Graham, and it was to his property that they drove their cars one morning in May 1934.

Inside the Graham home, to support what the men were doing, Morrow organized her own group of female Bible students and prayer warriors as well. As the sense of fervor rose among the men outside, one man's prayer seemed to soar out from among that of the others. It was the leader of the group, Vernon Patterson, and he was pleading with God in a loud voice that "out of Charlotte the Lord would raise up someone to preach the Gospel to the ends of the earth."

The story may have been embellished once Billy Graham's true fame was becoming obvious decades later. But that something of this sort did indeed happen has not been disputed. Whether one believes in prayer or not, the "coincidence" of that gathering, its location, and what was to happen in the life of Franklin Graham's son is certainly, well, unusual.[19]

As for Billy Graham himself, when he came home from school, the large group of cars and the men standing or kneeling in their shirts struck him as merely eccentric. A school friend asked what the group was all about. Billy replied, "Oh, I guess they are just some fanatics who talked Dad into letting them use the place."[20] But the one-day meeting had some dramatic consequences in the short as well as the long term. In the late summer, the same group of businessmen sponsored the construction of a pine-and-steel-framed tent in Charlotte. With it went an invitation to a fiery, itinerant preacher named Mordecai Ham.

A man given to challenging local clergy to abandon formalism or listlessness in their approach to the gospel, Ham was not a popular visitor to many city communities, particularly among the clergy that he delighted to rant against for their shortcomings. He was a Fundamentalist, for one thing, intolerant of shades of opinion less theologically conservative than his own. He was also occasionally given to remarks of racist and anti-Jewish unpleasantness—as were many Fundamentalists of that time. Not surprisingly, the local ministerial leadership of Charlotte declined to support his presence in their city either by endorsement or by encouraging their congregations to attend. Nevertheless Ham's mini-crusade went ahead. For some eleven weeks, from September into late November, every night he preached his sermons on the need for repentance and conversion.

What was *Fundamentalism*, a word sometimes erroneously used to denote everyone and everything of orthodox, historic Christian belief? Fundamentalists were originally Protestants who strongly resisted the late nineteenth-century Protestant trend of rejecting the truth of the Bible. These strongly opinionated believers adopted the name after publication during 1909–15 of a series of twelve pamphlets defending traditional Christian Orthodoxy on the Bible and other Protestant faith issues, called "The Fundamentals."

The term "Evangelicalism" has generally been used to refer to the emphasis on preaching the Christian message to nonbelievers and to the need for a personal experience of salvation through a process (preferably quite brief and entirely conscious) of commitment to Jesus Christ. By the 1920's and 1930's, however, Fundamentalism had become a distinct and recognizable subgroup within Evangelicalism. It stressed legalistic definitions of behavior that outlawed such things as dancing, attending movies or the theater, drinking any kind of alcohol—even, in some cases—reading a novel. It was often xenophobic and intolerant of other nationalities or religions, especially of Roman Catholicism and Judaism, not to mention Islam or belief systems even farther removed from the Protestant sources of American culture.

Billy Graham's conversion to ardent Christian belief took place during a revival crusade of a talented Fundamentalist preacher. But while Billy himself, in his early years as an evangelist, embraced many of the beliefs of Fundamentalists, over his lifetime of preaching the gospel around the world he shed virtually all of those aspects of Fundamentalism that could fairly be identified as having specific American cultural roots.

After an initial reluctance to attend Ham's meetings, Billy's parents had begun attending nightly, urging their children to come as well, but not forcing Billy to do so. The young man was openly skeptical of what was going on in the Ham "tabernacle," perhaps even antagonistic. Revival meetings like Ham's tended to be melodramatic and highly emotional, with choirs singing hymns that focused on the dire plight of those who did not repent of their sins and accept Christ, and the soul's bliss of those who did.[21] Ham was a full-throated champion for the prohibition of liquor, a constant theme of Christian evangelical meetings at the time, especially since Prohibition had been repealed just one year earlier, in 1933.

One of Frank Graham's tenants, Albert McMakin, had himself been converted a few months before this at preparatory meetings for Ham's revival. The owner of a dilapidated truck, he used it night after night to drive to the crusade both blacks and whites whom he wanted to see converted. Billy Graham himself had no interest in attending, but Ham had become controversial by alleging moral depravity among students at Charlotte's Central High School. Billy was certainly intrigued by this. Still, it may have been McMakin's offer to drive his truck to Ham's sermons that finally got him to Ham's meetings.[22]

Graham began to drive to the Ham "tabernacle" on a nightly basis, making sure at first that he sat at the back of the tent. Ham's sermons had a way of quickening the conscience of anyone who listened attentively, and it was not long before Graham himself began to be affected by it. The preacher's words, he was to recall later, "had an almost embarrassing way of describing your sins and shortcomings and demand, on pain of divine judgment, that you mend your ways." He added: "As I listened, I began to have thoughts I had never known before."[23]

To avoid the chance that Ham's eyes might fix on him at some particularly painful moment of moral revelation, Graham joined the choir, which sat behind the preacher. With him were two brothers who were to become intimate friends and close collaborators with him once his own career as an evangelist gathered momentum—Grady Wilson and T. W. Wilson. Their father had been part of the earnest prayer meeting on Frank Graham's farm earlier in the year.[24]

It is not known exactly how many evenings of Ham's fire-and-brimstone preaching Billy Graham attended. But as October and November passed, something clearly was changing within Billy's own heart. No longer skeptical or mocking, Billy Graham was obviously wrestling, in full awareness of the implications for his own life, with whether or not to "hit the sawdust trail" himself, as the jargon of revival meetings had it. (The phrase derived from the practice of spreading sawdust on the floor of tent meetings to reduce the noise of chairs being moved and hobnailed boots shuffling in and out of the rows.) Almost as if Ham could read his thoughts, Billy felt that Ham had been speaking to the sin in his own life. He was aware of how radical a change would take place in his life if he "went forward," as the phrase had it, when the preacher made his altar call.

The decision came on the night of November 6, 1934, the day before Billy's sixteenth birthday. As the choir sang, "Almost persuaded . . . Almost— but lost!" Graham got up from his seat near the front of the tent and moved forward to where others professing their conversion were standing. Grady Wilson went forward too. "I didn't have any tears, I didn't have any emotion," Billy said later.

> I didn't hear any thunder, there was no lightning. I saw a lady standing next to me and she had tears in her eyes and I thought there was something wrong with me because I didn't feel worked up. But right there, I made my decision for Christ. It was as simple as that, and as conclusive.[25]

There is no evidence that anything major or visible happened to Graham after this "decision." He told his delighted parents that night, but it took a while for anyone to see what, if anything, had happened within him. Over several weeks, some said his behavior was "nicer" than it had been before, but when he wanted to join a group of young Evangelicals calling themselves the Life Service Band, he was turned down by them on the grounds of being "too worldly." He still liked the company of pretty girls, and he wasn't yet aware of any call on his life to Christian evangelism.[26]

POOR BAPTIST PREACHER

Graham graduated from high school in the spring of 1936. College beckoned in the fall, but in the meantime, money needed to be made. Billy and the Wilson brothers took a job in the summer as Fuller Brush salesmen, achieving great success in door-to-door sales throughout the Carolinas. By the end of the summer he was the best-selling salesman in North and South Carolina, netting some $50 to $75 a week (a huge income in those days, when an office clerk's or secretary's job would be $12 on average). Along the way, Billy showed an interest in the work of some of the traveling evangelists who passed through the towns where he happened to be. After being goaded by one evangelist into joining him for a visit to the city jail to preach to the prisoners, he suddenly found himself asked to give his testimony. The story has become a classic in virtually all Graham biographies. "I'm glad to see so many of you out this afternoon," he said in a nervous rush of words as he began his story.[27]

By the end of the summer of 1936 it was time to enroll in college. Frank Graham had decided to send Billy to Bob Jones College, a Fundamentalist institution in Cleveland, Tennessee, whose rigid discipline, the father felt, would provide Billy with training suitable for any future career. The college drove its students hard in classwork, but was rigidly legalistic in virtually every aspect of daily life. Dating was forbidden under any circumstances with one exception—fifteen minutes of carefully chaperoned conversation in a place on campus designated for such meetings. Physical contact of any kind with the opposite sex, even holding hands, was against the rules.

Despite having become a Christian two years earlier, Billy barely lasted the fall semester in this stern environment, racking up demerits close to the level where expulsion was automatic. He chafed under the stiff, dogmatic structure of the educational system. He was also suffering from allergies, flu, and what was probably depression resulting from the regimented way of life.

Doctors recommended a warmer climate with plenty of sunshine. During the semester after Christmas in 1936, Billy's discussion of other college options with fellow students led to a confrontation with the formidable Dr. Bob Jones. "Billy," he warned, in yet another meeting that has become a classic Graham biographical example of misjudgment by others, "if you leave and throw your life away at a little country Bible school, the chances are, you'll never be heard of. At best, all you could amount to would be a poor Baptist preacher somewhere out there in the sticks."[28]

Undeterred by such dire warnings, Graham enrolled at the Florida Bible Institute, certainly a small Bible school, with only thirty men and forty women students. It was located on the premises of a former country club, built in elegant Spanish-colonial style, in Clearwater, Florida. The college still exists, but today operates under the name Trinity College.

It was not just the warm sunshine that appealed to Graham. (Whether influenced by this college experience or not, Graham has generally enjoyed vacationing in warm places, preferably with a beach as well.) In stark contrast to the fierce regimentation of Bob Jones College, the Florida Bible Institute seemed to encourage students to allow the Holy Spirit to work His way in their lives without precise preplanning.

The college environment certainly invited healthy outdoor activities with plenty of time for personal reflection and prayer. There were opportunities for swimming and tennis, and for canoeing in the Hillsboro River. Billy Graham seems to have been a popular student there, with his outgoing, generous personality, a penchant for flashy clothes, and a high energy level. But there was clearly more to him than congeniality, good looks, and an active outdoors life. One man who thought so, at any rate, was the academic dean of the school, the Reverend John Minder. As warmhearted as Dr. Bob Jones had been stern, Minder, one evening at an Easter vacation retreat, invited the young Billy Graham on the spur of the moment to preach in a small Baptist church in the community of Bostwick, in northeast Florida.

He had nervously assembled detailed notes from a sermon book that would enable him, if necessary, to preach four forty-five-minute sermons. But shaken almost to desperation by the ordeal of actually preaching to a group of ordinary people, he rattled through the notes of all four sermons in less than eight minutes. "Nobody has ever failed more ignominiously" in a first sermon, he has said since then.[29] But Minder saw in Graham the core of something both powerful and unusual in a Christian young man. He invited Billy to become youth director at the Tampa Gospel Tabernacle, and Graham did so until his graduation three years later. Under Billy's energetic leadership, the youth group grew and thrived.[30]

The Florida Bible Institute may have been a lot more congenial to Billy Graham's temperament, but it was no party school. Students were under curfews at night and dating was highly circumscribed. In any event, Billy and most of the students were earnest in their desire to live morally pure lives, including the proscription of premarital sex. It was probably not surprising, therefore, that his idealism and yet his vigorous masculinity led him to quickly fall in love with an attractive female student, Emily Cavanaugh, and actually to propose to her when he was just eighteen. He asked her to marry him during the summer vacation of 1937 and she accepted, after several months of thinking it over, in February 1938. It was unlikely that they would marry for three or four years.

In May of that year, Emily told Graham that she wasn't sure anymore. She asked that he pray about whether it was the right thing to do. He did so on a daily basis until, one evening that month, the prayer seemed obviously answered, even if not in the way he had probably imagined. Emily told him that she was in love with a senior classman. She returned the engagement ring.

It was a devastating blow for Billy. But it may have been instrumental in turning his heart more zealously to try to divine God's plans for his life. It was around this time that he seems to have sensed a calling to preach to very large groups of people. "Billy, God has called you to preach," he was often told by Brunette Brock, secretary to the college's president.[31] Later on, he spoke of pacing the golf course or the still-uncompleted streets of the town of Temple Terrace, wrestling with God, and with God's purpose in his life, in deep prayer.

A major turning point seems to have taken place in March 1938, when he had been in Florida a year. He returned from one of his long walks tense, with a feeling that God wanted him not just to be a pastor, or a Bible teacher, but something far more on the front line of Christian work. God was calling him to be an evangelist. He said later, "I now had a purpose, an objective, a call. That was when the growing up began, and the discipline to study."[32]

Around midnight one fresh spring evening in 1938, Billy confronted the very inhibitions against God's calling that Moses had used in the Bible. The young man discovered an even more powerful conviction: God Himself wanted Graham to be an evangelist whether he was equipped to be one or not. As he later described it, a moment came when he knelt down on the grass by the eighteenth green, close to the main entrance of the Bible Institute, and prayed a prayer of relinquishment to God's calling on him: "All right, Lord, if you want me, you've got me. I'll be what you want me to be and I'll go where you want me to go."[33]

He had, in fact, already been practicing the physical process of evangelistic preaching, calling upon the woods and nearby creeks to repent, testing what it might feel like to be speaking to big crowds. He had also tried street preaching, with sometimes uncomfortable results. Two or three other students would accompany him into Tampa, and gather on a street corner or some other public place. Once, a saloon owner on Franklin Street, irate because his potential customers were being scared away, ordered him to stop preaching, and when he didn't, knocked him down into the mud. "I got my clothes messed up," he remembers. "I remembered the words of Jesus, and felt that I was suffering for Christ's sake. It was quite tactless the way I went about it, zeal with no knowledge; but those experiences helped develop me."[34] In Venice, he offered his first, full-fledged invitation. He asked those in the congregation who felt so led to come forward, thus expressing their need for conversion. Amazingly, thirty-two people in an audience of barely one hundred did so. The Sunday school superintendent observed, "There's a young man who is going to be known around the world."[35]

It was during this time that salvation became the predominant theme of Graham's life. "I had one passion," he has said of this period, "and that was to win souls. I didn't have a passion to be a great preacher; I had a passion to win souls."[36] He was left in charge of the Tampa Gospel Tabernacle for six weeks while John Minder was in California, and his reputation as a powerful evangelist, however ill-formed, flamboyant, and unpolished, had steadily trickled out to a growing number of churches. Meanwhile, in the belief that personal decisions bring men and women to Christ, regardless of the issue of "election" or "predestination," he joined the Southern Baptists. He was ordained by them, with his parents' approval, in 1939.

War clouds, meanwhile, were gathering over Europe. To those who focused on biblical prophecy as keenly as the Fundamentalists did, the sense of impending, nation-shaking disasters over the horizon was palpable. At Billy's Florida Bible Institute, class valedictorian Vera Resue expressed the firm belief that the times called for God to raise up some new great Christian leader in the mold of Luther or the brothers John and Charles Wesley. "The time is ripe for another Luther, Wesley, Moody," she said. "There is room for another name in this list."[37]

However much Billy Graham yearned to see people converted, he was deeply conscious of his need for more education. One day in the spring of 1940, a group of tourists connected with Wheaton College in Illinois, the evangelical college founded by Jonathan Blanchard, were passing through Tampa and were staying on the premises of the Florida Bible Institute. One of them, the brother of the Wheaton College president, was impressed with Billy's preaching at the Tampa Gospel Tabernacle, but felt that he needed more academic broadening. He should go to Wheaton, the man suggested.

Billy said that his mother would approve of this idea, but that the family did not have sufficient money for it. The next day, while Billy Graham was caddying for the man and a partner also connected with Wheaton, they offered to pay his tuition for the first year there, and to search for funds for the remainder of his time in the college. Graham had no doubt at all that this was an answer to prayer.[38] He enrolled in Wheaton, on the outskirts of Chicago, in the fall of 1940. He was tall and lanky, outgoing and friendly, and yet a deeply earnest young man. He wanted to do graduate work in theology, so for his undergraduate major, he selected anthropology.

Billy Graham didn't want his studies to interrupt his preaching. The first summer's vacation from Wheaton he was back in Florida, fulfilling a variety of preaching invitations. In 1941, his second year at Wheaton, he took on a part-time pastorate, the United Gospel Tabernacle of Wheaton and Glen Ellyn, an independent church previously served by student pastors. There he continued to develop his preaching style, filling his sermons with details of the catastrophes now engulfing Europe and relating them, invariably, to the dispensationalist theology of the imminent return of Christ. Once the U.S. was at war after the Japanese attack on Pearl Harbor in December 1941, he volunteered for service in the army as a chaplain. The military authorities told him that he needed to graduate first, then spend a year in a pastorate acquiring the basic pastoral skills essential for a chaplain.

DR. NELSON BELL'S DAUGHTER

Billy was a popular figure on campus. He took part in student government and spent a lot of time with a professor, Mortimer Lane, who had worked in government, was well traveled, and fascinated the students with his knowledge and insights about contemporary public affairs. However, after the fall of 1940, Graham had one far greater preoccupation in his life than any extracurricular interests or even, at times, his preaching. He had discovered a brown-haired twenty-year-old second-year student named Ruth Bell. The daughter of a distinguished China missionary from North Carolina, Dr. L. Nelson Bell, Ruth had actually been born in China in the province of Northern Jiangsu, where her father operated as a surgeon in the Tsingkiangpu General Hospital, founded in 1887 by the novelist Pearl Buck's father. Unlike Billy, whose early teenage years had been lived without any special sense of purpose in life, Ruth from the age of twelve had wanted to be a missionary. Her chosen destination was Tibet, where she felt sure she would follow in the footsteps of other dedicated women missionaries to China who had remained unmarried throughout their lives of service to the Lord.

Ruth's Wheaton housemother wrote of her that she was "very attractive, beautiful to look at, and [had] excellent taste in dress. The most beautiful Christian character of any young person I have ever known."[39] She was clearly one of the most desirable young women available to any of the earnest young men, including Billy Graham, who were preparing themselves at Wheaton for Christian service in the world at large. Ruth and Billy's first date was to a performance of Handel's *Messiah*. Billy wrote to his mother afterward that he had met the girl he wanted to marry. Ruth herself was not yet in love with Billy, but she had heard him pray aloud at a student prayer meeting in a room next to the one she and others were praying in. "I had never heard anyone pray like it before," she recalled later. "I knew that someone was talking to God. I sensed that here was a man that knew God in a very unusual way."[40] After their first date, she said later, she had silently told God that if she could spend the rest of her life serving God with Billy, she would "consider it the greatest privilege imaginable."[41]

Their courtship was a hesitant, clumsy process, rendered so partly by Graham's personal insecurity, and partly by his fierce determination, despite his affections, not to displease God. He had, after all, earlier been deeply disappointed in love. A second rejection might have seemed calamitous. Ruth later said that Billy "wanted to please God more than any man I'd ever met."[42]

He told her early on that he wasn't sure he wanted to be a missionary, which was an unsubtle way of saying he didn't think they could ever be married, because Ruth had already revealed her sense of calling to Billy. He was authoritarian, albeit with tender intentions, ordering her to take vitamins and do calisthenics to improve her health, always insisting that he was concerned because he loved her so much. Finally, in the late spring of 1941, he proposed. She did not reply until a few weeks later, and then by mail, while he was back in Florida filling in at the Tampa Gospel Tabernacle. She accepted him.

Ruth is a woman of great charm and kindness, but she also possesses a very strong will. I remember seeing her for the first time when she stood next to Billy at an outdoor meeting in Hong Kong in 1975. She exuded the quality often described as "breeding," a combination of natural elegance, strong opinions, skillful and refined manners, and enormous self-confidence. In her home, Ruth was informal and hospitable, but not in a way that encouraged you to be casual around her. Her views on several topics were sometimes more perceptive than her husband's, but often sharper-edged as well.

His courtship of Ruth was not smooth sailing for Billy. Late that summer, Ruth became seriously ill and was sent to a sanatorium in New Mexico to recover. While there, doubts about their mutual compatibility seemed to trouble her. Among other things, she was still wondering whether she ought to proceed with her plans to train for missionary work in Tibet. For the second time in his life, Billy Graham received a "Dear John" letter. At least this time, his fiancée's second thoughts had nothing to do with any other man.

In January 1942, they met back at Wheaton and Billy offered to take his ring back from her. Now she was the hesitant one. At least in part, Ruth Bell was deeply attached not just to Billy Graham but to the growing sense that God's evident and powerful calling on his life might include her. For Billy, the door seemed still to be open.

Hadn't God brought them both together? he asked, his hopes soaring. She thought that was probably true.

Didn't the Bible say that the husband was the head of the wife? he continued. He added, with the subtlety of discharging an elephant gun, "Then I'll do the leading and you do the following." They were married some eighteen months later on August 13, 1943, in Montreat, North Carolina. Montreat was a Presbyterian conference center where Ruth's parents had settled once the war in the Pacific had made it impossible for them to return to China.[43]

Just seven days after the marriage and a brief honeymoon, they returned to Illinois, where Billy had accepted a pastorate at a Baptist church in the Chicago suburb of Western Springs. This was the first required step in the procedure to become an army chaplain. En route, Ruth caught a chill. Graham could have stayed at her bedside and made an excuse to the organizers of a preaching engagement he was committed to. But instead, he checked her into a hospital, sent her a get-well telegram and some chocolates—and kept the speaking engagement. This was one of many occasions when Graham was clearly thoughtless. Yet he was guileless about it, and his weakness derived from his conviction that the very highest occupation in life, for him, was the salvation of the lost. It says something about his ultimate teachability and Ruth Graham's formidable strength of character that such faux pas never led to serious marital rifts.

Graham spent eighteen months at Western Springs Baptist Church, from 1943 until 1945. It was his one and only experience as a pastor, as opposed to an evangelist, and he learned much from it. He organized meetings of Christian business professionals, got to know storekeepers, conducted the usual pastoral house calls for the sick and shut-ins, and came to grips with the fundamentals of what pastors do all over the world. He amused his audience with his garish socks and ties, his rapid and loud speaking style, and his habit of bringing his thoughts on the great dangers and gloomy news of the world at large into his sermons. But his real love was preaching the gospel for the purpose of bringing people to Christ.

Other doors were opening. In October 1943, he was unexpectedly invited to take over a weekly preaching and singing program on a local Chicago radio station. The broadcast, *Songs in the Night,* hosted by Torrey Johnson, was to be beamed each Sunday night at 10:30 for forty-five minutes from station WCFL. Graham not only agreed, he boldly approached a well-known Canadian-born bass baritone soloist, George Beverly Shea, and asked if he would sing on the weekly broadcast. After thinking the idea over carefully, Shea agreed to come aboard in January 1944. The business relationship, and later friendship with Shea, was to become a signature mark of Billy Graham's long career as an evangelist.

Through the broadcasts, as well as through an ever growing number of invitations to preach evangelistic sermons outside of Chicago, Billy Graham was beginning to become well known, at least in the Midwest. His earnestness, sincerity, dramatic delivery, and flashy clothes were a novelty, especially outside the South. If his church had become disappointed that a man they had hired as a pastor seemed to be spending increasing amounts of time away from a normal pastor's functions, they didn't express it.

Just two weeks before the Allied invasion of Normandy on D-Day, 1944, Graham had his first real taste of mass evangelism. Many American cities on weekends teemed with bored, restless, and cynical soldiers on leave from bases all across the country. Even young people not in the armed services had been uprooted as a result of the mobilization of industry and the creation of thousands of jobs in some way related to the war effort. The Great Depression had created a deep disillusionment with life among many people, and now the uncertainties of war had cut them loose from many traditional spiritual moorings. The result was an American youth impatient for peace, yet spiritually uncertain about its future. In Minne-apolis, a young businessman, George W. Wilson, had organized a "Youth for Christ Rally" in an effort to present these young people with the classi-cal evangelical message in a context of entertainment and patriotism.

Torrey Johnson decided to try to replicate Wilson's Minneapolis idea in Chicago with his own organization, "Chicago-land's Youth for Christ." In 1944, he booked the three-thousand-seat Chicago Orchestra Hall, next to the USO Center, for twenty-one consecutive Saturday nights. As the open-ing night at the end of May 1944 approached, he asked Billy Graham to be the speaker. Despite great nervousness about the size of the crowd and the presence of so many soldiers, Graham's rapid-fire and impassioned preach-ing caused forty-two of the twenty-eight hundred present to come forward at the end of the service. By the standards of the day, it was a huge response.

The Youth for Christ meetings in the city went on through the sum-mer. Graham, meanwhile, had other obligations approaching. In October 1944, after accepting a commission from the U.S. Army as a second lieu-tenant, he was scheduled to depart for a chaplains' training course at the Harvard Divinity School. He also needed to resign his pastorate at West-ern Springs. Before he could even make travel arrangements to go east, however, a fierce illness struck. He suddenly contracted a serious case of the mumps and became bedridden. For six weeks he steadily lost weight, became delirious at times, and gave doctors the impression that the illness might reach a critical stage. His condition was regularly reported to listen-ers by the staff of *Songs in the Night,* and letters of sympathy began to flow into the station. One of them was especially welcome: the gift of enough money, once Graham was well enough, for him and Ruth to retreat to the Florida sun for a few days of convalescence.

Technically, Graham was still obliged to fulfill his military training once he was fully well. But Torrey Johnson was convinced that it was evange-lism, not a pastoral position, not even that of a patriotic American chaplain, that beckoned the twenty-six-year-old young man. On a fishing trip Johnson organized for the still-weak Graham in Florida, Johnson put a tantalizing idea before him. What if Billy and a handful of other dynamic young evangelists could come together and form a whole new international or-ganization to preach the gospel? Johnson would be able to pull it together organizationally, he thought, and the name should be Youth for Christ International. The salary was attractive too: $75 a week.

After returning to Chicago, Graham learned that his weight loss and the assessment of his illness now limited his military service to a desk job Stateside. This information must have convinced him that the whole idea of joining the military had not been an inspired one to begin with. Indeed, he had initially made the decision without Ruth's input, and she had never been comfortable with it. When he requested a release from his commission, the army did not object. He was now free to take up Torrey Johnson's proposal. In early January 1945, he accepted it.

GARISH SOCKS AND HAND-PAINTED TIES

Youth for Christ International was officially formed in July 1945. It gave Graham what was to turn out to be the national platform on which his national and international fame were ultimately based. Throughout 1945 and 1946, he traveled incessantly across the country, holding Saturday night rallies in city after city and presenting audiences with a distinctly updated version of the old "revival" meeting. The music was loud and contemporary, the clothes flashy. Various forms of entertainment were provided, including the testimonies of famous athletes who had made Christian commitments. Emcees donned garish socks and sported bow ties that lit up on command. Graham himself continued to preach in his loud, rapid-fire manner, so much so that journalists began dubbing him "God's machine gun." If it all seemed a bit brash, even gauche to a few jaded observers, some people in high places took favorable notice. President Truman was quoted in *Time* early in 1946 as saying, "This is what I hoped would happen in America."[44]

Despite his constant travels, Graham spent at least enough time with Ruth to start a family. But in his eagerness to preach the gospel, as he himself admits, he failed to listen to Ruth's pleading for him not to set off on a preaching tour of Canada in September 1945. Their first baby was due any day, and she wanted him to be at home when it happened. He rashly guessed that there were still two to three weeks of pregnancy to go. He left for Canada September 21, 1945, and the baby was born that night.[45]

From the birth of their first child, Gigi, in 1945, Ruth bore the brunt of raising the Grahams' five children. Often she did so single-handedly for months at a time. Today, Gigi, Anne (born 1948), Bunny (born 1950), Franklin (born 1952) and Ned (born 1958), owe her an enormous debt for striving relentlessly to protect them from egotism to which the offspring of the famous are invariably prone. The children generally seem to have had good marriages, though Bunny went through a painful divorce from her first husband, Ted Dienert, after several years of anguish. She is now happily remarried.

Ruth's life as, in effect, wife of Mr. Protestantism, has at times been extremely stressful, a point she has often alluded to with the quip that, though she has never been tempted to divorce Billy, at times the notion of murder didn't seem so far-fetched. (The joke works in Anglo-Saxon communities, but has turned out to be a disaster when translated, for example, into Korean.) When British Evangelical leader John Stott, something of a liberal on social and economic issues, asked Evangelicals to pledge themselves to "a simple life-style" in the 1974 Lausanne Covenant he helped craft, Ruth refused to sign it. "You have no children," she told Stott, who has never even been married, "I have five. You say your life is simple and mine isn't." She said she would have agreed with the word *simpler*, which was less dogmatic.[46]

There was, in fact, nothing simple about Billy Graham's mode of life in 1946. He was still only twenty-eight and the glamour of constant travel, exciting places, and intriguing people might well have gone to his head. In 1946 Graham, long before the days of "frequent flier" awards, became the most traveled civilian in the United States aboard United Airlines. It was characteristic of him that he seemed to be kept humble by his awareness of his lack of education. Nowhere was this more apparent than during visits to England and the continent of Europe in 1946.

Graham first arrived in the spring of the year with a four-man team, and spent seven weeks traveling and speaking. Britain was still bleak and drab following the ordeal of World War II, subjected to periodic power blackouts and the rationing of many basic food items. Its population was dispirited. The brash clothes of the young Americans put a lot of the British off, as did their "simplistic" evangelical approach to the Bible and salvation. But Graham was described by one observer as "a man of much courtesy and Christian gentlemanliness." His eagerness to learn was appealing in its very innocence. "Learning was an insatiable desire with me," Graham said of this period. "I burned to learn, and I felt my limitations of schooling and background so terribly that I determined to do all I could through conversations, picking up everything I could from everybody."[47]

This eagerness to learn from even the reserved, sometimes cold and cynical British in the early postwar period received a harsh test later in 1946. After returning to the U.S. to raise money, Graham came back to Britain in the fall of 1946 for a six-month tour, accompanied by the new musical team of Cliff Barrows and his wife, Billie. Between October 1946 and March 1947, a period that included the harshest British winter in a century, with severe gas and coal rationing enforced, Graham spoke in twenty-seven cities and towns throughout the British Isles.

In Birmingham he encountered raw opposition from a clergy that was convinced that Youth for Christ represented just another example of American shallow showmanship. After the clergy persuaded the mayor to cancel usage of the civic auditorium, Billy meekly began phoning the clergyman critics who had lined up against him. "He wasn't bitter, he didn't chide me," Baptist pastor Stanley Baker wrote shortly afterward. "He hadn't one word of lecture; he merely wondered" why so many were opposed to what he was trying to do. The pastor was completely won over. "Within an hour I sat in Billy's hotel room," he went on. "His was the nearest spirit to my Lord's I have ever met."[48] Baker went on to convince other skeptical clergy in the Birmingham area that Graham's message should be heard.

Another British clergyman had a very similar impression of a teachability and meekness in Graham. Graham spent two days in a miner's home in Wales poring over Scripture and trying to learn from the man, evangelist Stephen Olford, what it meant to experience at a deep level the work of the Holy Spirit in his life. Olford had told Graham that his own life had been turned inside out a few months earlier by "an experience of the Holy Spirit in his fullness and anointing." "That's what I need in my life," Graham replied with great emotion. Olford's account goes on:

> I can still hear Billy pouring out his heart in a prayer of total dedica-
> tion to the Lord. Finally, he said, "My heart is so flooded with the
> Holy Spirit," and we went from praying to praising. We were laugh-
> ing and praising God, and he was walking back and forth across the
> room, crying out, "I have it. I'm filled. This is the turning point in
> my life." And he was a new man.[49]

The "newness" may have given Graham more power as an evangelist, but it didn't change his perceptions of the world as a truly dangerous place in the first few years of the Cold War. The anti-Communist rhetoric of those years infected Graham's preaching. "You should see Europe. It's terrible. There are Communists everywhere. Here, too, for that matter," he told a rally in Charlotte in 1947.[50] He described Communism as "a fanatic religion supernaturally empowered by the devil to counteract Christianity,"[51] and at least until the mid-1950's he railed against it as though it were indeed the human personification of something demonic. Graham used the often gloomy news of the international scene as a backdrop against which to portray the victorious hope offered by Jesus Christ. But there was more than a little Fundamentalist xenophobia, not to mention bigotry, when he told audiences on another occasion that he would explain to them "how sleek Russian bombers are poised to drop death upon American cities; how Communism and Catholicism are taking over in Europe; how Mohammedanism is sweeping across Africa and into Southern Europe."[52]

Over the years, Graham significantly toned down his apocalyptic, sometimes gauche comments on the international scene in his sermons. But the denunciations of Communism continued to pop up into the 1950's.

Another urgent issue was clamoring for attention in Graham's ministry: the problem, to be blunt, of its success. Youth for Christ rallies had evoked warm responses almost everywhere, and Graham was now increasingly well known throughout the U.S. and Canada. Graham knew that far too many successful evangelists had succumbed to the manifold temptations that went with high visibility, the lonely life of constant travel to new cities, and a system of remuneration that was often ludicrously haphazard. Some churches would provide huge "love offerings" to visiting evangelists; others might be miserly. Often, there was precious little accounting of who earned how much, where the money came from, and where it went.

Though Graham was on a salary with YFC, in the case of independent revivals where he preached, the "love offering" system prevailed. Though nothing of what Graham had received independently was in any way the means to becoming wealthy, both he and his team felt uncomfortable at the inconsistency of the system.

Then there was the matter of sexual loneliness. Graham had been away from his wife for six months while in England in 1946–47. There was never the slightest suspicion about his moral purity during this period, but other men of God had fallen to sexual temptation (and did so in abundance, it seemed, during the 1980's) in far less extreme situations, so it wasn't an issue that would go away by itself. During a break in a campaign in Modesto, California, in 1948, Graham called around him his teammates George Beverly Shea, Grady Wilson, and Cliff Barrows, and together they tried to think through how to deal with these challenges. What came out of it was a system that has protected Graham and his ministry to an extraordinary degree ever since.

First, on the question of finances, they decided that the local sponsoring committee should be responsible for paying all local bills and fees to the preaching team. On the sexual issue, they hit upon a cumbersome, but essentially foolproof way not only of keeping temptation at bay but of basically eliminating any suspicion of it. While on the road, they agreed to occupy hotel rooms close to one another, next door, if necessary. More drastically, and no doubt at considerable inconvenience on some occasions, each agreed that he would never be alone with any woman who was not his wife, whether in a car, at a luncheon, or even in his office. A modest exception was made in 1983 when Hillary Clinton, wife of then Arkansas governor Bill Clinton, wanted to meet privately with Graham. He agreed to have lunch with her at a table in the center of a public restaurant in Arkansas.[53]

At Modesto, the team also agreed on a system to avoid another of the great pitfalls of modern evangelism, gross exaggeration of the numbers involved. Graham and his colleagues decided that, wherever possible, they would accept the crowd size estimates of local police or other officials, even if the estimates seemed too low.

As to how many people had "come forward" to commit their lives to Christ at a crusade, they were at first uncertain whether to avoid estimates at all, or to be meticulous in counting the "inquirers," the preferred name for such people. There has been no escaping criticism on this matter. Some have complained that at Graham's crusades, an inflated visual impression of the number of inquirers is created by the fact that the counselors waiting in the stadium stands walk down into the center of the arena along with them. Graham and his team also agreed that while he was willing to meet with anyone who had issues to raise with him, he would not publicly criticize any local pastor or anyone else in Christian ministry.

The Modesto Manifesto, as this plan came to be called, set standards for public evangelism that have not been exceeded by any other major Christian organization since Billy Graham became nationally prominent half a century ago. For Graham himself, it turned out to be close to a bullet-proof vest against the darts of the proverbial "three g's" that have wrecked so many promising careers in Christian ministry: gold, girls, and glory.

Another more subjective issue gnawed inside Graham at this time: the question of how much education was "enough" for his particular kind of evangelism. Graham has often quite openly complained in his mature years that he has never felt well educated. But he does so in the knowledge that the combination of his achievement, intelligence, experience, and general knowledge far exceeds that of all but a handful of people in global Christian work.

But in 1948, he could not claim the singular "education" provided by the rich life experience he has gained over the decades. And when fellow YFC evangelist Charles Templeton resigned from the organization in order to attend Princeton Theological Seminary, his grounds were not unreasonable. He was worried that the "decisions" his and Graham's gifted preaching was garnering were being acquired too simplistically. Perhaps, he suggested to Graham, it was the personal charisma of the speaker rather than the substance of the message itself that was producing the results. He wanted a much deeper knowledge of Scripture and its background.

Templeton suggested that Graham go with him to Princeton. Billy declined because of increasing responsibilities. In 1947, in fact, he had reluctantly accepted the presidency of the Minneapolis-based Northwestern Schools, a combination of Bible college, seminary, and liberal arts college with a strong Fundamentalist coloration. He was not a good administrator, often making decisions impulsively and on the basis of quick likes and dislikes. To make matters worse, a great deal of the time he was nowhere near the school. This school position was yet another task he had to fulfill, in addition to his evangelism and efforts to see Ruth and the children whenever he could. He remained president until resigning in 1952.

Meanwhile, Templeton's sincere desire to be more learned in Christianity challenged something in Graham. He made a point of trying to meet with his former YFC colleague during the 1948–49 academic year whenever he was in the New York area. The discussions were deep, for Templeton had adapted swiftly to the Bible-criticism climate of Princeton. Slowly but inexorably, he was moving away from orthodox Christian belief in the inerrancy of the Bible because of doubts seeded in his mind by the courses he was taking.

Graham was uneasy. He recognized the power of Templeton's academic objections to traditional, evangelical belief in the authority of the Bible, but he also was certain that when he preached with the conviction that the Bible was God's great authority, people made decisions for Christ. "The finest minds in the world have looked and come down on both sides of these questions," he said. "I don't have the time, the inclination, or the set of mind to pursue them. I have found that if I say, 'The Bible says,' and 'God says,' I get results. I have decided I am not going to wrestle with these questions any longer."[54]

"PUFF GRAHAM"

But he did wrestle, and with increasing discomfort. Templeton had accused him of "intellectual suicide" by refusing to engage in the critical approach to the Bible that he himself was acquiring, and Graham was obviously hurt by this charge. The following year, while attending a student conference at Forest Home in the San Bernardino Mountains near Los Angeles, he met with Templeton again. They were serving as temporary faculty at the gathering, and several problematic issues of the reliability of Scripture had come up in conversations with both Templeton and the students. Graham was in turmoil. He knew that if he tried to deal piecemeal with the sorts of criticisms of the Bible that Templeton raised, the authority and the power would simply go out of his preaching. On the other hand, he recognized that he could not personally respond to the growing number of doubts that Templeton was putting before him.

The crisis came to a head after dinner one evening. Graham wandered up the mountainside in the moonlight with a Bible under his arm. He knew he must either plunge forward with faith that the Bible really was God's Word, even if he was unequipped to cope with the academic attacks on it, or he must hover in uncertainty for the rest of his preaching life. In the second case, he would probably never be a good enough scholar to answer questions raised by people like Templeton, but he would not be an effective evangelist, either.

He found a place to sit down, he recalls, "and I got to a stump and put the Bible on the stump, and I knelt down, and I said, 'Oh God, I cannot prove certain things, I cannot answer some of the questions Chuck is raising and some of the other people are raising, but I accept this Book by faith as the Word of God.'"[55] Once the decision was made, Graham never reconsidered it. As for Templeton, his talents and gifts stayed with him, but his evangelical faith didn't. After graduating from Princeton, and serving for a while as an evangelist for the National Council of Churches, he returned to Toronto and a career in journalism, writing, radio, and television. But he was no longer an orthodox believing Christian.[56]

Graham, of course, went on to become the most famous evangelist in the world. And he continued to quote the Bible. At the Greater Twin Cities crusade in Minneapolis in June 1996, broadcast on TV, I actually counted as Graham quoted from the Bible, either citing chapter and verse, or simply prefacing the quote with the words, "The Bible says . . . ," approximately twelve to fourteen times every fifteen minutes. Then, at the end of his sermon, he repeated the now familiar, famous words of invitation, "I'm going to ask you all to get up out of your seats and come up in front of the platform." Hundreds did so.

It was six weeks after the crisis of choice at Forest Home in 1949 that Graham leaped suddenly into national prominence. The precipitating event was the Los Angeles Campaign, an extraordinary crusade in a Ringling Brothers circus tent erected in downtown Los Angeles at the corner of Washington and Hill Streets. The venue was called the "Canvas Cathedral," and for days before the crusade began, posters, billboards, and radio ads had made it difficult for anyone not to know that Graham was in town. He was billed as "America's sensational young evangelist," a description he apparently didn't object to.

The crusade had originally been scheduled for three weeks, and Graham worked hard in his sermons during that time, denouncing "the Fifth Columnists, the Communists," who, he said, were "more rampant in Los Angeles than any other city in America." He said he saw God's judgment hanging over Los Angeles, "about to fall."[57] Although the crusade had not been an overwhelming success up to this point, the team decided to extend the three weeks on a week-to-week basis. But after extensive radio publicity and the conversion of a popular and well-known radio host named Stuart Hamblen, who spoke of his conversion on the air, curiosity about the crusade began to spread. It finally lasted eight weeks, so long that Graham ran out of sermon topics and was reduced to begging ideas and sermon outlines from his friends.

For Ruth Graham, her husband's inability to get by without seeking help from others and from the Bible itself was a good thing. "I remember his desperate straits in Los Angeles, probably the best thing that ever happened to him—this suddenly having to get down and study, especially the Bible. He was thrown back on simple, straight Biblical preaching."[58]

Meanwhile, the media was finally catching up with Graham. A celebrated telegram was sent by newspaper magnate William Randolph Hearst to his editors in Los Angeles: "Puff Graham." It was newspaper jargon for "Give plenty of space to reporting on Graham." The wire services, then *Time*, *Newsweek*, and *Life*, picked up on the story of the crusade. *Life* said that the meetings had been "the biggest revival in Los Angeles since the death of Aimee Semple McPherson," a reference to the popular Pentecostal evangelist of a few decades earlier.[59]

Graham himself seemed stunned by the newfound fame and genuinely humbled by the unexpected success of the crusade. "I feel so undeserving of all the Spirit has done," he wrote, "because the work has been God's and not man's. I want no credit or glory. I want the Lord Jesus to have it all."[60] It was a commendable sentiment, but from now on, there was to be no turning back to obscurity. Barely thirty years old, the North Carolina country boy preacher, Billy Graham, now stood at the threshold of a lifelong career in the national and global spotlight.

Graham's sudden national fame now made it easier to organize publicity for crusades wherever they were scheduled. In January 1950 he was in New England, conducting a crusade throughout the region that suddenly seemed to be gathering a momentum of its own. Newspaper reporters took down his every word, so he found himself for the first time forced to think through his answers on often complex national and international issues. The same year, the Billy Graham Evangelistic Association, now based in Minneapolis, was founded. One of its most important and significant annual functions has been setting, and paying, Graham's salary. Though he could have become exceedingly wealthy from the proceeds of his many books, he has for some four decades turned all of his royalties and other earnings over to the BGEA. They, in turn, paid him in 1997 an annual salary of $101,250 and further living allowances of $33,750.

Besides the crusades, probably the most decisive factor in keeping Graham's name before Americans on a regular basis at the national level was the *Hour of Decision* weekly radio broadcast. Within a few months of its beginning, the half-hour program was being aired on hundreds of stations across the country. Graham also started a movie production company in 1950 called World Wide Pictures, headquartered in Burbank, California. As an indication of the phenomenal name recognition Graham was now acquiring, during the year 1951 no less than 178,000 letters cascaded into the BGEA offices in Minneapolis.

By 1950 Graham's style incorporated its now familiar characteristics. He paced back and forth, gestured fiercely with huge hands, beamed laserlike blue eyes on his audience, and changed his pace and style of delivery whenever he sensed the remotest shifting of the audience. He liked to introduce his sermons with chilling pieces of recent news on the national or international scene and used this as the bedrock for showing that, left to its own devices, the world was pretty well doomed. It could only be brought back from the brink, he would say—and has said ever since—by the personal change of heart brought about by a personal commitment to Jesus Christ. No place on earth, he told New Yorkers in 1951, was "more ripe for judgment, or closer to catastrophe, than this city."[61] And so it went on.

Between 1950 and late 1997, he had preached 206 crusades in U.S. cities and 182 cities around the world. Some cities in the U.S. he visited not just twice or three times, but as many as four times (New York, Charlotte, London, Berlin) or even five times (Seattle). As he and the organization gained experience, his visits to both states in the U.S. and foreign countries would almost assume the proportions of a visiting head of state. There would be dinners, official meetings with governors or prime ministers and presidents, hugely attended press conferences, tours of areas his hosts wanted him to see (either to impress him or to arouse his Christian sympathy), and introductions to a huge array of important personages who wanted to be sure that they were not passed by when the evangelist came to town. Advance teams would check out every forthcoming detail of the crusade as though a presidential visit were being planned.

As Graham matured and accumulated experience, he was growing away from the cut-and-dried Fundamentalism that, through Mordecai Ham, had been his introduction to Christianity. The world was changing, and in particular the United States. Perhaps the most important change in the American scene was in the arena of race relations.

Graham was never a racist, but he had grown up in North Carolina, a southern state where attitudes on racial issues were sharply polarized. By temperament, he liked people instinctively, and he wanted people to like him. For this reason, he did not feel comfortable saying things that might grievously upset any group of people, especially if he thought he could preach the gospel successfully to them. Thus, when antisegregation protests among African-Americans began to gather momentum in the South in the 1950's, Graham was put in a quandary. If he appeared to be siding with those demanding full racial integration throughout the country, he might alienate the white audiences he was eager to preach to. If he appeared to acquiesce in continuing racial segregation, however, he would undercut any assertion that he himself was not a racist.

The dilemma surfaced painfully when reporters asked him why he had been willing to preach in 1950 at a crusade in Columbia, South Carolina, when blacks were forced to sit in a "colored section." And the following year, during crusades in several southern cities, he did not demand an end to all artificial segregation of seating arrangements in the audiences.

On the theoretical aspect of racist thinking and behavior, Graham was forthright, even courageous. He told audiences in Portland in 1950, "All men are created equal under God. Any denial of that is a contradiction of holy law."[62] In Jackson, Mississippi, in 1952, he said, "It touches my heart when I see whites stand shoulder to shoulder with blacks at the cross."[63] The same year, he told an audience at the Southern Baptist Convention that Baptist colleges were duty-bound as Christian institutions to accept academically qualified black students. It was startling to hear this sort of proposal from a southern Evangelical. In 1953, in Detroit, he explicitly repudiated as unbiblical the contention used by some to justify racism from the Bible (citing Genesis 9:22–27, where Noah cursed his son Ham and his descendants).[64]

Graham, though, may have disliked controversy and hostility among potential audiences more than he disliked racist practice as such. He insisted, after being attacked by white segregationists, that his crusades tried to "follow the existing social customs in whatever part of the country in which we minister," and until 1954 and the Supreme Court decision banning all segregation in schools, he allowed segregated seating areas to be partitioned off, as required at the time by both custom and law. (He personally removed the ropes separating the black and white sections at the Chattanooga crusade in 1953, to indicate how uncomfortable he was with the system.) Biographer William Martin has summed up Graham's position more suggestively than most:

> Consistent with his pacific and conciliatory nature, Billy would al-
> ways prefer decorum to bold example, and he would never be
> comfortable with violent protest or even with nonviolent socially
> disruptive measures aimed at changing the standing order. Neither,
> however, would he retreat from the higher ground he had seized.[65]

"THE BIG LOVE APPROACH"

Graham's caution explains his attitude toward American civil rights leader Martin Luther King Jr. He had been worried that the African-American civil rights movement was being influenced by, if not controlled by, Communists. He had said virtually nothing in public about King during the early 1950's, when the fight against segregation in the South was gathering momentum. Then, at his nine-week crusade in Madison Square Garden, New York, in 1957, Graham emphatically cut all his ties to Christians in the South who still favored segregation. He invited King to brief his own crusade team on developments in the civil rights struggle, as well as on how white Evangelicals could be more sensitive to blacks.

After King explained that the avoidance of violence during the Montgomery, Alabama, bus boycott had been accomplished by "prayer and the Holy Spirit," Graham warmed deeply to him. He invited King to lead the whole congregation in prayer, introducing him with the words, "A great social revolution is going on in the United States today. Dr. King is one of its leaders, and we appreciate his taking time out of his busy schedule to come and share this service with us tonight."[66]

With the advantage of hindsight, and the fact that King is now celebrated as an authentic American hero by Americans of all colors, that endorsement might today seem tepid. But at the time, it enraged many southern Fundamentalists, exposing Graham to some of the most hate-filled abuse he had ever experienced during his career. Now he was being called a "Communist" by many of them.

In fact, the Fundamentalists were already upset by Graham's mere presence in New York. The invitation to hold a major crusade in the city had come from the Protestant Council of the City of New York, representing some seventeen hundred churches and thirty-one denominations. Since the Council was affiliated with the National Council of Churches, the *bête noire* of the Fundamentalists, the association to them seemed to tar Graham with the brush of theological liberalism. Leaders of the Fundamentalist movement such as Carl McIntyre and Bob Jones Sr.—from whose college Graham had fled when just eighteen   had attacked the alleged liberalism of the Revised Standard Translation of the Bible that had appeared in 1952, while Graham had warmly endorsed the new translation.[67] Years later, Fundamentalists were to continue their attack upon Graham for endorsing the *Living Bible*, the best-selling, easy-to-read paraphrase of the Bible by Dr. Kenneth Taylor.

It was in some ways not difficult publicly to repudiate Fundamentalism in 1957. Graham had already endorsed many aspects of the ecumenical movement among Protestant churches, saying that he was willing to "recognize now that God has his people in all churches."[68] At a meeting of the National Association of Evangelicals in 1957, he said flatly: "I would like to make myself clear. I intend to go anywhere, sponsored by anybody, to preach the Gospel of Christ if there are no strings attached to my message." Elsewhere, he had said, "The only badge of Christian discipleship is not orthodoxy but love. . . . Christians are not limited to any church. The only question is: Are you committed to Christ?"[69] At the Madison Square Garden crusade, Graham went farther than he had ever gone in the past in making this viewpoint explicit when the question came up of how to deal with inquirers who came forward at the end of the service if they said they were of Catholic—or even Jewish—background. "We'll send them to their own churches—Roman Catholic, Protestant, or Jewish. . . . The rest will be up to God."[70]

Almost certainly, Graham was more hurt by the attacks on his integrity as a Christian from the right than from the accusations of Elmer Gantry hucksterism that usually came from the left, indeed, from people actively skeptical about Christianity in general. When he founded the magazine *Christianity Today* in 1956, he made it clear that it would be theologically conservative in outlook, in contrast to the prevailing liberalism of ecumenical bodies like the National Council of Churches. At the same time, he emphasized, the magazine had set as its goal "to lead and love rather than vilify, criticize, and beat. Fundamentalism has failed miserably with the big stick approach; now it is time to take the big love approach."[71]

Nowhere had that attitude been more profoundly tested—though not in the face of Fundamentalist criticism this time—than in England in 1954, during the twelve-week Harringay Arena crusade. This particular gathering has gone down as perhaps the most dramatically attended and nationally significant visit by the BGEA team in the entire five-decade history of Graham's evangelism.

Thousands upon thousands descended daily upon the dingy stadium that was normally used as a dog-racing track, complete with the full apparatus of gambling during the often wet and drizzly weeks of late winter and early spring in England. Traffic in side streets was clogged, suburban trains filled up, and the London underground (subway system) was populated by people either talking about the crusade or on their way to or from it. Newspaper reporters were stunned by the response to the crusade of ordinary people, office workers, housewives, and blue-collar workers as they turned into "inquirers" night after night and very often demonstrated a marked change in personality after their experience in the stadium. Anglican seminarians before Harringay who described themselves as Evangelicals amounted to just 7 percent of the total. By 1956, the number had increased to 70 percent, and it was almost as high the following year.[72]

The Harringay crusade almost didn't happen at all. As Graham's large delegation steamed toward Britain aboard the SS *United States*, British Labour Party members of Parliament questioned whether Graham should even be permitted into Britain. They were incensed at a quote taken from a brochure printed for American donors before the crusade, which had read: "What Hitler's bombs could not do, socialism with its accompanying evils shortly accomplished." This statement had infuriated left-wing parliamentarians.

Meanwhile Fleet Street's journalists, in the heartland of the British press, gleefully competed to denigrate Graham's supposedly "hot gospel" evangelistic style. The *London Evening News* wrote that Graham was "like a Biblical Baedeker, [who] takes his listeners strolling down Pavements of Gold, introduces them to rippling-muscled Christ, who resembles Charles Atlas with a halo, then drops them abruptly into the Lake of Fire for a sample scalding." Another newspaper columnist, the acerbic William Conner, who wrote for the *London Daily Mirror,* a pro-Labour paper, under the pen name Cassandra, took several sneering swipes at Graham.

Graham apologized profusely, first by cable, then in person, to Labour members of Parliament, insisting that his crusade had nothing to do with politics. He also went out of his way to meet with his staunchest media critic, *Daily Express* columnist William Hickey. Hickey admitted that he had wanted to be rude to Graham when they met, but found himself overwhelmed by something quite different when the interview took place. "I think he is a good man," he wrote, "I am not sure that he isn't a saintly man. I just don't know." Admitting that Graham was "a remarkable man," Hickey said that he might even be "what Britain needs," which, he said, was "a bitter pill to swallow."

Graham wrote a pleasant note to his other fierce critic, Cassandra—William Conner—suggesting they meet. They did so, at Conner's witty suggestion, at a London pub appropriately called "The Baptist's Head." Something about Graham struck Conner quickly. He described it this way: "I never thought that friendliness had such a sharp cutting edge. I never thought that simplicity could cudgel a sinner so damned hard. We live and learn. . . . The bloke means everything he says."[73]

To the U.S.-based monthly *Christian Century*, often critical of Graham because of his conservative politics and theology (and because *Christianity Today* was now its major competitor), something about Graham's demeanor under the initial British cudgeling reflected the nature of the man. The magazine said that he was "revealing himself as extraordinarily teachable and humble, considering that he is surrounded with the fevered adulation of crowds so much of the time."[74]

Nowhere, perhaps, did that "teachable and humble" spirit evoke a more vivid response in Britain than in 10 Downing Street, the official residence of Britain's prime minister. In 1954 it was the grand old lion of British politics, Sir Winston Churchill himself. "I tell you, I have no hope," Churchill confided to Graham in his rumbling diction at a meeting to which the evangelist had been summoned. "I see no hope for the world. Do you have any real hope?"

Was that a personal question? Graham asked. It was, the old man replied. Graham then took out his New Testament and explained the Christian doctrine of salvation to Churchill, who at one point grumpily waved off an aide who interrupted with the announcement of the Duke of Windsor's arrival for lunch. Then, with Churchill's eager consent, Graham prayed for the man who more than anyone else had saved Europe from Hitler.[75]

Graham's sensitive and intelligent response to Churchill had been learned from hard experience in his encounters with American presidents. His first presidential encounter was a disaster. After he had met with President Truman for a few minutes in the White House in 1950, and prayed for the feisty man for a few seconds, he and his team reported the scene to waiting photographers and reporters—a strict no-no in White House protocol. Then, still on the White House grounds, the four men knelt on one knee and posed for the cameras with bowed heads. Truman was furious, later describing Graham "as one of those counterfeits" whose claim to be friends with the presidents was false.[76] In his final years, he evidently softened somewhat toward Graham, but the two men were never close.

Truman's accusations aside, Graham's claims to be close to the presidents were not false. Since that incident, Graham has been extremely careful in public when describing his friendship with the eight presidents he has known well. In his autobiography, *Just As I Am*, he admits that the book provides readers with no "juicy tidbits," about any of them, though Graham surely recalls an armful of "tidbits." He told me in 1990 that he had once kept a detailed journal of almost all of his meetings with Nixon, and it had been locked in a safe. He said he wasn't sure what had become of the document. If it still exists, it could one day be of immense interest to historians.

If Graham bungled his first encounter with Truman, he had a warm, close, and mutually respectful friendship with Eisenhower. He played a role in persuading the beloved war hero, for example, to run for the presidency on the Republican ticket in 1952. Graham wrote to him personally with this suggestion, then met with him for a face-to-face discussion in Paris where Ike was the supreme commander of the Allied forces in Europe. He personally baptized Eisenhower in the White House after the inauguration in 1953 and remained in close touch with him throughout the two-term presidency. He strongly encouraged Eisenhower to send troops into Little Rock, Arkansas, in 1957, after Governor Orville Faubus had at first refused to permit the racial integration of Central High School.

During the 1960 Nixon-Kennedy race for the presidency, Graham's close friendship with the vice president nearly led him to endorse Nixon publicly when Henry Luce, the founder of both *Time* and *Life*, asked him to write a warm description of Nixon for *Life* magazine. At the last minute, despite his deep admiration for Nixon, Graham felt that he could not do so and retain any semblance of political nonpartisanship. The piece, which he had written and even shown to Nixon, was pulled from the magazine.

After Kennedy's narrow defeat of Nixon in 1960, the young president-elect sought out Graham for a lunch in Florida. It was a prudent thing to do. Some American Protestant leaders had spoken out harshly against Kennedy during the campaign, suggesting that, once in the Oval Office, he might as a Catholic be subject to political pressures from the Vatican. A public and friendly meeting with Graham, it was thought, would help heal some of the wounds, as well as reassure people that, Catholic or not, Kennedy was not going to dissociate himself from America's most famous and popular Protestant evangelist.

At a press conference orchestrated by Kennedy after their luncheon, Graham politely commended Kennedy for his tactful handling during his election campaign of the controversial issue of religious loyalty. Kennedy, in effect, got what he wanted. But so did Graham, and not just in the sense of keeping his lines open to the White House during a Democratic administration. (Graham has often reminded reporters that he is a registered Democratic voter, no doubt in an effort to tone down his close identification with Republican administrations and his obvious social conservatism.)

Graham met with Kennedy from time to time in the brief thirty-four months of the JFK presidency, but he never became really close to him. Ten days before Kennedy's inauguration in 1961, the president-elect was driving Graham around the Seminole Gulf Club in Palm Beach in his Lincoln convertible when he stopped the car and asked Graham, "Do you believe in the Second Coming of Jesus Christ?" Graham said that he did and explained in detail his reasons for doing so, based on what he thought the Bible said about it. Kennedy listened intently and then said they should have another conversation on the subject some other time.[77]

But there wasn't another time. In mid-November 1963, Graham says, he felt an unaccountable sense of foreboding about Kennedy's forthcoming trip to Dallas. He tried to contact Kennedy through Senator Smathers, and he mentioned his misgivings to two other men he names in his autobiography. But he never got through. Less than two weeks later, the thirty-fifth president of the U.S., John F. Kennedy, was felled by an assassin's bullet in Dallas.[78]

It may well have been the trauma of the assassination and Lyndon Johnson's deep sense of vulnerability at the time that caused Graham practically to become a member of the Johnson household, and an intimate of Johnson himself. Like Graham, Johnson was a southerner, a country boy, and indeed he was the great-grandson of a preacher. Within a few days of Johnson's taking office, LBJ invited Graham and Grady Wilson to the White House for a pastoral meeting. The meeting ended up lasting five hours as Johnson unwound with Graham and Wilson, including inviting them both to swim in the White House pool. It was certainly a friendly gathering, for in Johnson's customary manner, all three swimmers were stark-naked.

But Graham came to know Johnson in something of the manner of a personal chaplain to the nation's leader. "I suppose I knew Johnson the best," he has said to many people.[79] Graham was to spend the night several times in the White House during Johnson's presidency, sometimes praying with LBJ as Johnson knelt on the floor in the presidential bedroom. The two men greatly admired each other, and were not shy about saying so in public. Johnson said that Graham was "the greatest religious leader in the world," and Graham responded—understandably—that Johnson was "the greatest political leader."[80] For all of his brashness and occasional gaucheness, Johnson was a deeply sentimental, often highly vulnerable man. He at different times expressed to Graham anguish over whether he was "born again" or serving God as he should, for his mother had wanted the future president to be a preacher. "He thought a great deal about death," Graham has said, "and he talked to me about it several times." Shortly before Johnson died, Graham prayed with him in Johnson's Lincoln convertible after the former president had been chasing deer in the car over his fields.[81]

THE NIXON HE DIDN'T KNOW

Nixon's friendship with Graham was much more complex, and despite the many years the two men knew and saw each other, curiously less intimate than the Graham-Johnson relationship. Graham today seems visibly to stiffen when discussing Nixon with reporters or on television, deeply conscious of how unfavorably his closeness with Nixon was perceived by many at the time of Watergate. Yet in Nixon's own, sometimes clumsy, even impulsive way, he admired Graham deeply, and he trusted him, something he did with exceedingly few other men. The compliment was returned. "Dick, I have thousands of friends, but very few close, intimate friends," he wrote Nixon after the former vice president appeared to be bowing out of politics altogether in 1962.

> There are few men I have loved as I love you. My friendship for you was never because you were Vice-president or an international figure. It was far deeper than that, and I hope we can continue our friendship on a warmer basis than ever before.[82]

Graham had disappointed, not to say hurt, Nixon, by not endorsing his presidential bid in 1960. It was a decision he took after agonizing over whether it would render him too overtly partisan in the political arena, perhaps endangering the credibility of the gospel itself among those who were not Republican or politically conservative. But a few years later, after he had already demonstrated in his friendship with Johnson that he saw himself in a pastoral role, there was no such holding back. He flew down to Key Biscayne in 1967 to help Nixon decide whether or not to run again the following year. Johnson was still president, and he had not yet publicly declared that he would not run for reelection, so Graham had to balance his current, rather close relationship with a sitting president with his longtime friendship with Nixon.

He never said to Nixon, "I want you to run," but he left no doubt in the vice president's mind that he would strongly support a Nixon run for the nomination and the White House. Nixon's version of the encounter is even more specific. Graham told him, he said, "You are the best prepared man in the United States to be president. I think it is your destiny to be president."[83] Graham gave the closing prayer after Nixon's acceptance speech at the Republican Convention in Miami in August 1968, was let in on the decision-making process that led to Spiro Agnew's becoming vice president, prayed with Nixon and his family on the night his election success was sealed, and led the first White House church service in Nixon's presidency the week after the inauguration.

In a way, Graham's problems regarding the Nixon presidency began long before Watergate. He strongly supported the U.S. military efforts in South Vietnam throughout most of the Vietnam conflict, and he fully backed Nixon's efforts to end the war through a process of Vietnamization designed to compensate in military assistance to the South Vietnamese for the U.S. pullout. When Nixon complained about opposition to the war from a growing number of U.S. clergy, Graham tried to downplay the importance of these clerical dissidents in conversations with the president. He continued to praise Nixon in personal notes, phone conversations, and face-to-face meetings well into Nixon's second term, by which time the roiling seas of the Watergate scandal were beginning to lap at the very gates of the White House.

Throughout 1973, Graham supported Nixon in both public and private, despite the growing suspicions that Nixon himself might be involved in the Watergate cover-up. In one of his less inspired predictions, Graham assured Nixon in late December 1973 that the coming year would be "far better than 1973." Yet he had meanwhile given an interview to *Christianity Today* (published in January 1974) in which he said flatly that there were "no excuses for Watergate. I condemn it and deplore it. It has hurt America." In the interview Graham expressed continued belief in Nixon's integrity of character, but it wasn't enough for many of Nixon's strongest supporters. The speaker and writer Norman Vincent Peale (author of *The Power of Positive Thinking* and other popular motivational books) wrote to Graham that he was "saddened" by the evangelist's posture of less than total support for Nixon.[84]

But Graham was actually in a deep dilemma. Even if Nixon, by some miracle, had not personally been involved in the wrongdoing, his responsibility for an administration in which it was taking place could no longer be overlooked. Graham's friendship with Nixon had lasted for more than two decades. Could he in decency now desert the man who had so often relied upon him for council and advice? In fact, Graham had very little contact with Nixon at all in 1974 during the tense months between January, when both Nixon and Graham attended the National Prayer Breakfast, and August, when Nixon resigned the presidency. Graham has maintained that Nixon deliberately told his aides to keep Billy at arm's length in order to protect him from guilt by association.

But it was not even the squalid White House plotting, revealed after the release of the Watergate White House tapes, that upset Graham. What angered him more than anything was the profane and vulgar quality of Nixon's language. "I was terribly disappointed in those tapes," he said. "Not only disappointed, but overwhelmingly sickened by them. Oh, the language. I'd never heard him use those words. I didn't even know he knew them."[85] "And when all that stuff came out," he said elsewhere, "I just felt it was a Nixon I didn't know."[86] Nixon told Graham, somewhat implausibly, that he "never knew" the ugly words that popped up in the tapes before he actually said them. But he nevertheless apologized privately to Graham when the evangelist visited him in San Clemente after Nixon was out of office.

"He was a very emotional man," Graham said of Nixon while Nixon was still alive. "People do not realize how easily he was touched by things. And he is, I think, a true believer."[87] When Nixon died in April 1994, Graham preached the sermon at his funeral. He said, "We've heard that the world has lost a great citizen and America has lost a great statesman, and those of us that knew him have lost a personal friend." Yet the hesitant, defensive way Graham speaks of Nixon in his own autobiography suggests something more deeply discomforting to Graham than Nixon's bad language.

Graham seems troubled above all by his own misjudgment of Nixon. His respect for Nixon as a statesman and his fondness of Nixon as a person for the decades he knew him before Watergate knew few limits. "The essential bond between us," he insists, "was not political or intellectual; rather, it was personal and spiritual."[88] But there were obviously things about Nixon that even the usually perceptive Graham simply never fathomed. As he states in his autobiography: "Looking back these forty-five years later, considering all that has intervened, I wonder whether I might have exaggerated his own spirituality in my mind."[89]

Did Graham's friendship with Nixon compromise him in a national role he could have played—perhaps should have played—during America's anguished turmoil of the Vietnam War and Watergate? Graham obviously could have spoken out more forcefully. Yet if he had done so, as many liberal Christians urged him to, he might then have been fulfilling the biblical role of a prophet rather than that of an evangelist, much less that of a pastor. "I am convinced that God has called me to be a New Testament evangelist, not an Old Testament prophet!" he said at one point in 1973, explaining why he was not saying more about his views on the war in Southeast Asia.[90] A prominent Evangelical of liberal political opinions, James Wall, editor of *Christian Century*, has expressed a similar view. Graham, he said "was much more of a national pastor than a national prophet." In retrospect, he thought, Graham "handled himself rather well" in his relationship with Nixon.[91]

After Nixon resigned, Graham came to know his successor, Gerald Ford, well, though never as warmly as he knew Nixon or LBJ. Ford, a plainspoken, decent man with few apparent complexes, liked Graham, and the affection was reciprocated. He said of Graham, "Whenever you were with Billy, you had a special feeling that he was there to give you help and guidance in meeting your problems."[92] Graham played a major role, for example, in persuading Ford to make the controversial decision to pardon President Nixon for any Watergate crimes for which he might subsequently have been indicted. Some have speculated that this controversial decision cost Ford the election to his successor, Georgia peanut farmer Jimmy Carter.

Carter, a fellow southerner, Southern Baptist, and firm believer in the evangelical's duty to share the Christian faith with others, might in theory have established a closer friendship with Graham than any previous president had. But he simply didn't. It is interesting to speculate why not.

Each respected and admired the other and they certainly agreed deeply on spiritual issues. But Carter's own personality was sometimes chilly and remote, in striking contrast to Graham's warmth. Perhaps Carter was intimidated by the degree of intimacy that Graham had established with other presidents at a time when Carter was not even a prominent figure in his own state, much less the nation's elected leader. Carter, probably more than any president in the twentieth century, was a man determined to be deeply knowledgeable on any matter he considered important—if possible, as knowledgeable as his expert advisers. Yet Graham was one of the few people whose knowledge of the presidency would always surpass his own. It was based, after all, on personal experience of how various presidents had actually operated in the White House.

There is no evidence that Carter ever asked Graham for his insight into an issue involving presidential policy, though that may have been due more to Carter's own leadership style of carefully limiting those with whom he held close council. Carter may also have been uncomfortable with the closeness that Graham had established with many Republicans, including, of course, Nixon. But in the end, there just may never have developed that spontaneous chemistry that endeared Graham to so many other presidents. The chapter dealing with Carter in Graham's autobiography is titled rather neutrally, "Sunday School Teacher from Georgia."

The one on his successor, Ronald Reagan, has a distinctly warmer feel: "Leading with Wit and Conviction."

Graham seems to have loved and admired the Reagans greatly. In 1975 in Hong Kong, he had told me, "I would hate to see a pacifist president," perhaps unconsciously reflecting a concern that the Democratic Party in its post-Watergate angst over "imperial" presidencies might produce just that. Carter was certainly no pacifist, but his expression of surprise at the Soviet invasion of Afghanistan in 1979 revealed a real naïveté about Soviet behavior. By contrast, when Reagan came to power, his determination to catch up with the Soviets militarily must surely have pleased lifelong anti-Communist Graham. But the Graham-Reagan warmth was genuinely personal and not just political. When Reagan was shot in an assassination attempt early in 1981, Graham boarded a private plane almost immediately to be in Washington with his wife, Nancy.

In his autobiography, Graham even defends Nancy Reagan stoutly in the face of revelations, shocking to American Evangelicals at the time, that she consulted astrologers in an attempt to influence the timing of some important presidential events. He quotes Nancy Reagan in his autobiography as saying that the stories contained "possibly 10 percent truth." Some might view this estimate as distinctly on the low side. The fact is, Graham has always been intensely loyal to people he has liked and respected. Reagan, he says, "taught me a lot, not so much through words as by example. His optimistic spirit was contagious," he adds. "I have often been a worrier (if biting my fingernails was any sign), even though I know underneath it all that God is in charge."[93] Reagan was the first president to have been divorced, was not a regular churchgoer, and certainly wasn't a Southern Baptist. Something about him, though, seems to have touched a deep chord in Graham.

Graham was even closer to the Bushes, who frequently invited him to the White House and to Kennebunkport, sometimes just to teach Bible studies to the Bush's Mediterranean-size extended family, on other occasions to be present at crucial political events. Bush was younger than Graham, as Carter had been, but unlike Carter he seemed to take to Graham naturally as both a sort of institutional chaplain to the White House and a personal spiritual counselor to the entire Bush family. Graham was more than ready to reciprocate such warmth in his own public comments about the Bushes. "He says straight out that he has received Christ as his Savior," he informed me during an interview in 1990, "that he is a born-again believer and that he reads the Bible daily. He has the highest moral standards of almost anybody whom I have known," he went on to say with great enthusiasm.

> He and his wife have such a relationship, it is just unbelievable. If you are with them in private, you know, they are just like lovers. When I would go and spend the night, as I did many times when he was Vice President, the room that I stayed in was right across the hall from theirs, and they always kept the door open. And there they were, you know, in bed, holding hands, or reading a newspaper or reading a book.[94]

But Graham's time in the Bush White House was not all simple good fellowship. He was present on January 16, 1991, at the very beginning of Operation Desert Storm in the Persian Gulf. Summoned at very short notice to Washington from North Carolina, Graham at first was surprised to find himself invited by Barbara Bush to watch TV with her. Then, as CNN from Baghdad reported live the massive aerial onslaught by Coalition forces, it was plain why the president wanted him on hand. Bush wanted him to pray. Three times that night, including at the meal table, Graham prayed aloud for the Bushes, for his country, and for the volatile situation in the Gulf overall. The third time of prayer was just before the president went on television to address the American people on what was happening.

Most recently, there has been Clinton. With the two-term Democratic president, Graham has been his usual cordial, unjudgmental self. Clinton, like Graham (and Carter before him), a Southern Baptist, made the requisite public profession of faith in Christ at the age of ten, and was baptized through immersion in water. He says that he later asked his Sunday school teacher to drive him fifty miles into Little Rock so that he could hear Billy Graham speak, and at the age of twelve began sending part of his allowance to support Graham's ministry.

As has become a Washington tradition, Graham gave the invocation at Clinton's presidential inauguration. Graham has made his own view of opposition to abortion—hardly a secret—known privately to the Clintons, but he has been careful not to adopt an adversary position to a president who has been held in deep suspicion by many American Evangelicals. When Graham was awarded the Congressional Gold Medal at a ceremony

in Washington in May 1996, he said of Clinton that he had been "a friend
and a brother for years." This characterization took some courage, for
many evangelicals otherwise admiring of Graham seemed to question
whether Clinton was a Christian at all. Those doubts appear to derive not
from anything Clinton professes, or fails to profess, but from his style of
life over an extended period of time.

TO RUSSIA WITH LOVE

One of the most frequently quoted Scriptures in the Bible is Christ's words
from the Sermon on the Mount, "Blessed are the peacemakers" (Matt. 5:9
NIV). The desire to be a peacemaker has inspired Christian leaders throughout history, ranging from Pope Gregory the Great (540–604), through St.
Francis of Assisi, to Pope John Paul II in the twentieth century. To an unusual degree, Graham in the last decades of his life has tried to respond to
this Scripture verse. The results, though, have not been universally applauded.

Graham's domestic American popularity and international acclaim
were a natural magnet for presidential job offers, often of a diplomatic
nature. Nixon, Graham said, offered him virtually any position he wanted,
including a possible cabinet secretaryship. Eisenhower once said that Graham was "the greatest ambassador that America had."[95] Lyndon Johnson
literally offered him the ambassadorship to Israel. When Graham later sat
beside then Israeli prime minister Golda Meir at a White House dinner
and told her the story, she seemed to have been greatly relieved. As Graham relates the incident, he explained how he had told Johnson, "'I am
not the man. God called me to preach.' And Golda Meir reached and
grabbed my hand. She was so thrilled. I told Johnson, 'The Middle East
would blow up if I went over there.'"[96]

But it has not been just at state dinners at the White House that Graham has had the opportunity to meet foreign leaders. He has met with
dozens of foreign heads of state and government throughout his career as
an evangelist. Once he began conducting regular overseas crusades in the
1950's and onward, there were few countries in which he was not at least
introduced to the heads of government or state. Several times during his
travels in some eighty-five countries over five decades, Graham has acted
as an unofficial ambassador for the U.S. On some occasions, he has actually carried private letters to foreign leaders from the American president

of the day. He has had strongly spiritual conversations with Soviet leader Mikhail Gorbachev and Russia's anti-Communist president Boris Yeltsin, both at state dinners in the White House and on his visits to Moscow.

Starting in the 1980's, however, Graham took a new and highly controversial tack in his foreign trips. In the 1950's and 1960's, a scorching anti-Communist rhetoric had been a trademark of his preaching. There seemed to be no Cold War strategic objective of the U.S. that he did not wholeheartedly support. But in the 1970's, with visits to Hungary and other Eastern European countries, Graham subtly began to adopt a new approach. He had certainly not become a pacifist. But he had become convinced that he could reach out with the gospel to regimes that not only were openly atheistic, but that had a dismal track record of mistreatment of their own Christian communities.

He did so, he said, because of his calling as an evangelist. He was willing to preach the gospel anywhere he was allowed to do so, he insisted several times, as long as there were no strings attached. But in hanging up his old anti-Communist rhetorical shotgun in favor of a lyre of peace among nations, Graham ran into a hailstorm of criticism, much of it as bitter and resentful as that from the Fundamentalists in earlier years. This time, it was not from liberal or Fundamentalist theologians, but from conservative foreign policy specialists.

The first highly controversial decision he made was to attend a patently Soviet-sponsored propagandistic religious event in Moscow in May 1982 at the invitation of Patriarch Pimen of the Russian Orthodox Church. The gathering was portentously and self-servingly called the "World Conference of Religious Workers for Saving the Sacred Gift of Life from Nuclear Catastrophe." It was yet another Soviet government effort to transform quite genuine support for peace in the West into crudely anti-U.S., pro-Soviet "peace" propaganda. Graham was certainly aware of the political risks in accepting the invitation. But he had been assured that he could preach freely in Baptist churches, bring "greetings" (i.e., a mini-sermon) in Orthodox churches, and would also be able to meet with a broad variety of Soviet Christians. Moreover, neither President Reagan nor former President Nixon attempted to dissuade him from going, a sign to Graham that he was on the right track.

Problems arose almost from the start of the visit. The Soviet hosts rescheduled events to limit as much as possible Graham's opportunities to preach directly to the Russian Christian community. At one of the conference sessions, the anti-U.S. diatribe by a Syrian delegate was so intense that Graham removed his translation headphones for most of the speech. American ambassador to Moscow Hartman barely concealed his annoyance that an extremely prominent American seemed to be lending his prestige to a "peace conference" that he—and most observers—judged to be a typical Soviet propaganda show at one of the touchiest periods of the Cold War.

To make matters worse, the U.S. Embassy for several months had been the reluctant host to seven Siberian Pentecostals who had stormed past Soviet policeman guarding the compound in a last-ditch effort to gain freedom from the Soviet Union. Graham could scarcely visit the U.S. Embassy in Moscow without at least meeting them, yet he was reluctant to offend his official hosts by appearing to champion opponents of the regime. After some awkward moments when the Moscow-based Western press corps aggressively demanded to photograph Graham meeting with the Siberian Seven, as the group came to be called, he did in fact have a private conversation with them. At first, they were surly and unfriendly toward him, believing that he and other Western Christian leaders were lending moral support to a regime that persecuted them. It was not a happy moment for the Pentecostals, the Soviets, the journalists, the U.S. Embassy, or for Graham.

The worst was yet to come. Graham unwittingly aggravated the already rising chorus of criticism of the visit in the U.S. by his naive-sounding comments on life in the Soviet Union. He praised the wonderful food he had been eating, adding, "In the United States you have to be a millionaire to have caviar, but I've had caviar with almost every meal I've eaten."[97] It didn't seem to occur to him that, as a celebrity guest of the regime, he was being exposed to luxuries most ordinary Soviets wouldn't see in a lifetime. Though he was also misquoted on the subject of religious freedom, the remarks that were accurately quoted illustrate well the problems his words caused. He said he had visited three Orthodox churches and they had all been jammed with worshipers on a Saturday night. "You'd never get that in Charlotte, North Carolina."[98]

He was right, and not simply because Charlotte's Christians for the most part don't attend churches on Saturday nights. Neither Charlotte nor any other city in America had experienced the government destruction of thousands of churches in Moscow and elsewhere for decades, leaving an overcrowded handful of churches available to the thousands of Russian believers in the city. After his meeting with the Siberian Seven, he was asked by a journalist whether he had witnessed any religious persecution while in Moscow. He replied: "I have seen no religious persecution during my stay in Russia."[99] It was technically true: He had not seen people arrested for attending church or the KGB actually closing down churches. But he had obviously seen the consequences of religious persecution in the Soviet Union: seven Pentecostals forced to take refuge in a foreign embassy because they were permitted neither to practice their religion freely in their own country nor to travel abroad to do so.

The Moscow trip in 1982 was a source of grief both to Graham himself and his Billy Graham Evangelistic Association for years afterward. To illustrate one rather procedural, but nonetheless significant faux pas, Graham's Moscow preaching schedule had been made public by his aides even before the Russians themselves had put it on the record. This guaranteed that, once Graham actually arrived, the schedule would be turned around. It was, to the considerable inconvenience of many people involved in the visit.

Despite the controversy and misunderstanding brought on by the 1982 Moscow trip, the long-term consequences of it for his ministry turned out in the end to be helpful on two levels. The trip opened virtually the entire Communist world to future visits by him, and in the views of some observers was a contributing factor to the actual collapse of Communism in Eastern Europe. Nixon himself, at the end of the 1980's, said he believed that Graham "helped bring about the . . . peaceful liberation of Eastern Europe."[100]

From the Soviet Union, Graham was able to visit, in the same year, both the German Democratic Republic and Czechoslovakia, two of the hardest-line Communist countries within the Soviet bloc. In 1984, he returned to the Soviet Union, this time preaching freely to huge audiences in four Soviet cities. In Leningrad, he preached to six hundred Orthodox seminarians, telling them how to preach, and in a cathedral in that city, he was invited, against all Orthodox protocol, to interrupt a formal service and preach the gospel to six thousand worshipers present. Altogether, he spoke fifty times there on this visit. When he finally was able to preach in Moscow in the manner of a classic Graham crusade, in 1992, approximately one quarter of the nightly crowds of some forty-five thousand in Moscow's indoor Olympic stadium came forward as inquirers. The seeds that had been planted in pain and embarrassment in 1982 bore rich fruit a decade later.

In 1987, Graham turned his attention to China, a nation of particularly strong significance for Ruth Graham, who had been born there and whose father had been a missionary surgeon in Tsingkiangpu, in Jiangsu province. The visit did not actually take place until 1988 but, in contrast to the Soviet experience, was a major success and warmly praised. One reason was that in 1988, before the Tiananmen Square Massacre the following year, China was riding more highly in overall American esteem than at probably any time since the founding of the People's Republic in 1949.

As part of his official program, Graham preached during three weeks in five cities and spoke openly about the gospel to Chinese academic institutions as well as in churches officially permitted to function by China's government-approved Protestant umbrella organization, the Three-Self Patriotic Movement. Graham spent a highly unusual fifty minutes in a personal meeting with the then recently installed premier, Li Peng. Li told Graham that he read the Bible regularly, a fact that he has never revealed publicly on any other occasion. How much he derived from his biblical studies is open to question; Li has sometimes been described in recent years as "the most hated man in China" because of his role in orchestrating Teng Hsiao-p'ing's crackdown on student protest in 1989. But in 1988, Sino-U.S. relations were warm and official approval of many aspects of American life was at a very high level.

On the China trip in 1988 Graham took pains not to appear to cold-shoulder Christians who happened to be out of favor with the government, possibly with some of the controversies of the Soviet trip in mind. While visiting Shanghai, for example, he and Ruth met privately with the renowned Christian leader Wang Mingdao, a man who had spent two decades in Chinese prisons for refusing to recognize the same Three-Self Patriotic Movement that had been hosting Graham. He also organized a private reception in his Beijing hotel for other leaders of China's "house churches," the unofficial, sometimes clandestine, often severely persecuted forms of fellowship to which the majority of China's estimated thirty to fifty million Christians by preference belong. I had met

Wang Mingdao myself in 1985 in Shanghai. Almost blind, but unfailingly faithful to the gospel, he remembered the Grahams fondly. At the end of our meeting, he stood up on his frail legs and sang, in loud English, the hymn "Onward Christian Soldiers." He was ninety-two at the time.

But the China visit led to an opportunity for Graham to visit a far more bizarre and alien regime. In 1992, he was invited to one of the most isolated, xenophobic, and certainly most ferociously anti-American regimes in the world, North Korea. He went accompanied by his youngest son, Ned Graham, with the full foreknowledge, and indeed approval, of the Bush administration, and privately conveyed to North Korea's all-powerful, idolized leader, Kim Il Sung, a message of greeting from both Bush and Pope John Paul II. The content of those greetings has never been made public. Graham managed to avoid, once more, making any naive-sounding generalizations about the status of religious freedom in the country, arguably the most terrifyingly regimented regime in the history of the human race. Of Kim Il Sung, an unpredictable, vain, militarily dangerous man who started the Korean War in 1950, Graham said that he was "a vigorous and magnetic leader." It was not necessarily an endorsement. The same might have been said, after all, of Adolf Hitler, who similarly constructed a political system with himself at the apex of national worship.

Graham went back to Pyongyang in 1994, and this time had a three-hour meeting with Kim Il Sung. Once again, he brought a goodwill greeting from the American president, who was now Bill Clinton. What was said? We may never know. By making any visit at all to North Korea, which of course used his presence for propaganda purposes, Graham upset a lot of Americans and South Koreans, whose memories of North Korean atrocities during the 1950–53 Korean War are still fresh. But if North Korea ever abandons for good its long-cherished plan of uniting the entire peninsula by force, by invading the South, it could be that Graham's uniquely humble and appealing personality played some role in defusing the anti-American extremism of the North Korean regime. At the end of 1997, the jury was still out.

Why this preoccupation with peace? Graham's globe-trotting during his decades of worldwide evangelism, his rich experience of different world leaders, his encounter with hugely varied theologies, ideologies, and politics, had made him a very different man in his sixties and seventies from what he had been three or four decades earlier. He was still preeminently an evangelist, convinced that evangelism alone was his true calling in life. But there was now a depth, a richness, a subtlety, indeed a generosity to his judgments that, whatever his early virtues, had not been present in Graham the zealous young man. (Even Ruth came around to acknowledging that his trips to the Communist bloc, which she had fiercely opposed at first, had been the right thing to do.)

He felt strongly that nations, as nations, should repent of the harm they have done in the world. No nation was guilt-free. "No nation, large or small," he said, "is exempt from blame for the present state of international affairs."[101] In this vein, his thinking strikingly paralleled that of another Great Soul, Aleksandr Solzhenitsyn. And like Mother Teresa, Graham had become convinced that the world's poor did not exist simply for the convenience of left-wing or right-wing theorists of economic growth. "As a Christian," he said, "I believe that God has a special concern for the poor of the world, and a public policy should in some way reflect this concern."[102]

"Public policy." Even the term was more philosophically neutral than his 1950's-era concern for American domestic and foreign policy. It should reflect, he felt, God's "special concern for things like peace, racism, the responsible use of Earth's resources, economic and social justice, the use of power and the sacredness of human life." Graham's universe of evangelism had certainly changed. It had grown larger, more generous. It was not theologically more liberal, but it was inclusive of a larger universe than Graham had set out to evangelize in the 1940's. Curiously, too, Graham is walking a very similar pathway to that of our fifth Great Soul, Pope John Paul II, a man who also had myriad reasons for detesting Communism, but for whom that animosity was no longer the sum of his global concerns.

Depth of pastoral concern—Graham's friendship with U.S. presidents. Breadth of global interest—the entire world, regardless of politics or philosophy, was now his evangelistic parish. Perhaps for this reason, Graham showed no inclination to walk in lockstep with America's conservative Evangelicals—or "Christian Right" to use a less attractive term—in the 1980's and 1990's. While he clearly agreed with them on some, perhaps most, issues—opposition to abortion and the homosexual lifestyle, for example—he was not comfortable with the intense political partisanship that sometimes accompanied conservative Christian campaigning for certain causes in the public marketplace.

Characteristically, he found a graceful way of explaining why he would not join forces publicly with those some might assume to be his natural political allies. His relationships with both Democratic and Republican presidents, he said, made him determined to be politically neutral. He no doubt had the painful memories of Watergate in mind. "I also remember," he added, "Jerry Falwell flew down here to Montreat to see me about the Moral Majority. He said, 'Billy, I want to tell you, you stay out of Moral Majority. You have too big a ministry to be bogged down in politics.'"[103] It was as though Nixon in the ebbing days of his presidency, and Falwell in the ascendant days of his own prominence, both felt there was something about Graham simply too inherently decent to be sullied by association with the grungy squabbles of politics and power.

As he approached eighty, Billy Graham continued to preach at crusades in the U.S., but his struggle with Parkinson's disease had made foreign crusades more problematic. Ruth's own physical ailments also limited his mobility and his work schedule. In 1995 she was hospitalized in critical condition. In November of 1995, the board of the BGEA officially designated eldest son, Franklin Graham, then forty-three and a minister in his own right, to be first vice-chairman of the organization and designated successor to Graham as chairman and CEO.

Not everyone was happy with this decision. Billy himself was delighted that his eldest son, once a prodigal who had drunk fiercely, smoked dope, and lived a wild life, should want to be a preacher of the gospel. Yet he for a long time postponed making any decision on the issue. Other men might have been only too pleased to hand over a gigantic, highly respected, internationally known organization to one of their children, to carry on the work after their death. But Graham was not like other men. He had told several people during the later years of his ministry that he was entirely ambivalent about the organization's continuing once he was no longer around to be associated with it. It was not a question of mistrusting his son—far from it—but of being aware that his own ministry had been so unique, and from his perspective, so phenomenally touched by God's grace, that it could not be replicated through mere human effort, no matter how worthy the goal.

Graham's character, his decisions, and his almost obsessive fear of stumbling morally were derived from a total preoccupation during a lifetime with the calling he had become convinced God had given him, the calling of an evangelist to bring people out of the torpor of sin to salvation from it. He resisted almost in an eye-blink monetary and prestige temptations that would have felled most men. In 1952 the Texas oil billionaire H. L. Hunt offered him $6 million in cash, to his own bank account, if he ran for president. He turned down the offer point-blank. When he once got carried away speculating publicly about the possibility of his running for the nation's highest office if actually drafted to run, Ruth phoned him immediately with the tart point that, if he wanted to leave evangelism for politics, he would have a divorce on his hands.[104] Graham never again spoke of filling any political role in the U.S.

In the late 1960's, another, more subtle, potential distraction came up. Graham had spoken out with increasing frequency on the need for Evangelicals to develop intellectual skills sufficient to handle challenges of a largely secular society. The idea had been close to his heart for several years. He had even shared with trusted friends his dream of a graduate university whose academic achievements might eventually rival those of Harvard or Yale. When the insurance financier John D. MacArthur became intrigued and offered one thousand acres of superb Florida property, along with millions of additional dollars to support the project, the idea suddenly seemed extremely attractive. Once it became known that Graham was thinking about the concept, other pledges of money poured in as well.

But in the end, he backed out, deeply worried that he might be stepping out of God's will for his life. "It would be a diversion of my ministry from evangelism," he wrote later. "I knew that God had called me essentially and basically to be an evangelist."[105] MacArthur was deeply disappointed by this about-face by the evangelist and even years later reminded Graham of the opportunity he thought had been missed.

Of all the Great Souls in this book, Graham was especially favored by the circumstances of his life. He had a warm childhood and adolescence, and he grew up in a free, tranquil America at one of its greatest moments of power in the world arena. There were no occupations of his homeland by foreign invaders or domestic totalitarians, no wrenching confrontations with poverty and degradation, no soul-crushing personal hardships in his formative years.

The test of Graham's soul, indeed, lay not in adversity, but in how he coped with success. Perhaps no other individual in the history of the Western world in modern times has been more tempted by the rewards thrust in front of him by a success-worshiping culture. It is little short of astonishing, especially considering the scandals affecting some evangelists of the 1980's, how entirely Graham avoided any major moral or ethical lapse throughout his career.

Graham's achievement lay in his consistent faithfulness to his original sense of God's calling on his life, despite nearly overwhelming temptations at times to do something more lucrative, more glamorous, and less exhausting. He would have committed no sin by agreeing to be a U.S. cabinet officer or an ambassador, or even a Christian millionaire. But he always seemed to know that if he had yielded to these inducements, he would cease to be the Billy Graham that God wanted him to be. He chose instead to continue to preach the Christian message of salvation, a view of life still winning millions of adherents throughout the globe, but less and less fashionable in many parts of his own country. He preached salvation to kings, princes, presidents, prime ministers, television anchors, to some great sinners, and to a handful of honorable folk who just really didn't want to hear it.

He made mistakes of judgment at different points of his career, some personal, some professional, none of them disastrous, but some of them painful. He may have been a worrier and a hypochondriac at different times, impulsive and occasionally impatient. But he has been extraordinarily generous in his opinions of people, faithful to friends under extreme pressure not to be, fiercely protective of both his family and his subordinates. Of the millions who have attended Graham's crusades and "come forward" as "inquirers," many have doubtless fallen away from faith, or backslidden into old ways, or simply not changed visibly at all. Yet thousands upon thousands more have truly become different. A huge number of clergy currently in the Church of England base their original Christian commitment on attendance at a Graham crusade in Britain in the 1950's. Nor was Graham's influence confined to clergy. When he accepted an invitation by Queen Elizabeth II to dine aboard the royal yacht *Britannia* during the queen's visit to San Francisco in 1983, a high-ranking British naval officer saluted and whispered to Graham as he boarded the ship, "Wembley, '55."

For more than half a century Billy Graham has been dedicated to the message of salvation. He has never stopped proclaiming the gospel and never stopped admitting his own faults and weaknesses while doing so. To remain humble, teachable, and gracious amid success and in the face of sometimes bitter opposition and criticism is the mark of true virtue in any person. And to remain relentlessly loyal to God's call while exposed as consistently as Graham has been to all the world's power and glory, well, 'tis the mark of a Great Soul.

CHAPTER 2

NELSON MANDELA: FORGIVENESS

"Forgiveness is not an occasional act. It is a permanent attitude."
—MARTIN LUTHER KING JR.

"From the moment the results were in and it was apparent that the ANC was to form the government, I saw my mission as one of preaching reconciliation, of binding the wounds of the country, of engendering trust and confidence."
—NELSON MANDELA, 1994[1]

ROBBEN ISLAND IS A low-lying, windswept patch of land more than a dozen miles into the South Atlantic from Table Bay Harbor. From there, Cape Town's physical presence at the southern tip of Africa never fails to beguile. Table Bay Mountain, a ridge of improbable natural flatness, rises majestically behind slopes and valleys on which the city itself sits. For centuries sailors have longed for this sight, knowing that it meant rest, food, water, and friendly faces after months on the forbidding seaway between Europe and Asia.

From the shores of Cape Town, Robben Island offers few reciprocal charms. An angular fragment of land, some three miles by a mile and a half in dimensions and sometimes known crudely as "South Africa's Alcatraz," it sits low in the water. Since its first usage by Europeans in the mid-seventeenth century, it has served as a prison, leper colony, lunatic asylum, naval base, and finally, modern high-security prison. In the Afrikaans language, it is simply known as *Die Eiland* (the Island).

Only recently has Robben Island been opened to tourists, since the South African government made a decision to end its usage as a prison. But until government-authorized tours through the prison began in 1997, the closest you could get to Robben Island was offshore in a harbor cruise-boat. This little craft transported you across the rolling Atlantic swells for the fifty-minute crossing, then loitered within shouting distance to give you a chance to take a look.

From your vantage point offshore, you can see quite a lot. The light-house rises up on the shorefront, along with the prison governor's red-roofed residence and a nineteenth-century Anglican church. Dark-look-ing gun emplacements peer out at beach level. As for me, bobbing gently offshore in the piercing Southern Hemisphere January sun, I wanted to see what a structure called Cell Block B looked like.

Cell Block B, for some eighteen years, had housed Nelson Mandela. In 1994, in an astonishingly peaceful election characterizing a total change of regime, Mandela became the state president of South Africa, the most economically and technologically advanced country on the whole Afri-can continent. For a very long time, until his release four years before that, he had been the world's most famous political prisoner.

As I stared at the island, I wanted the setting of Mandela's incarcera-tion to seep into me. I wanted to see the stunning physical panorama of Cape Town as it would have appeared to him a dozen miles away. For six and a half thousand days of his life, Nelson Mandela glimpsed the vibrant urban life of a country sliced down the middle by its government into two halves. One half was for the whites, the other for everyone else.

The cell block was a gray building with a pale-colored roof and square stone guard towers. In the middle was a central courtyard, a space not much larger than a tennis court. Mandela must have glanced up at those towers thousands of times, wondering if the men in them, all of them white, had any notion of the thoughts, the lives, and the visions of the prisoners they were guarding. There were plenty of common-law crimi-nals in the prison, many of them mean and dangerous, and they were kept separate from the politicals, or *Poqo*, as the Afrikaans jailers referred to them, using the name of the political wing of the Pan-Africanist Con-gress. Mandela and most of his fellow prisoners in Cell Block B were actually members of the ANC—the African National Congress. It was an organization that by then had itself embarked on sabotage and ter-rorist activities, but whose ultimate objective was a multiracial, democratic society. Mandela was as opposed to *Poqo* concepts ("one set-tler, one bullet") as to the white racial superiority theories of most of the warders guarding him. What made Mandela famous in Robben Island was not so much what he had done—powerful ANC leader though he had been. Nelson Mandela was famous because of the ideals that he represented, and because of who, in the innermost core of his being, he was. As is so often the case in great moves of history, it had been enormous adversity, in his case the imprisonment on Robben Island, which inadvertently helped form him into that person.

At first, I did not think of including Mandela among the Great Souls. It wasn't a case of sour grapes, although in my journalistic wanderings I had never been to South Africa. I had spent very little time in Africa at all. I did, however, as a *Time* state department correspondent, accompany then Secretary of State George Shultz on a rapid-fire visit to Senegal, Kenya, Cameroon, and the Ivory Coast in 1987.

But I never met Mandela. In fact, I wasn't even sure that I especially wanted to. He had seemed to pick up over the years some international admirers for whom I had very little admiration or respect: Mu'ammar Gadhafi of Libya, for example, Fidel Castro, and Yassir Arafat. Worse, Mandela's African National Congress Party included in its midst dedicated Communists who presumably would have rejoiced had the Soviet Union won the Cold War. Perhaps it is unfair to judge a man by those who are eager to appear his friends, but if Mandela thought well of Gadhafi, financier and armorer of terrorist groups from Northern Ireland to the Southern Philippines, what could he have in common with greatness?

Slowly, and incrementally, I discovered I was wrong. First, he only came to know Gadhafi and Arafat personally after his release from prison in 1990. When Mandela was first imprisoned, moreover, Gadhafi was not even ruler of Libya, but merely a very junior, twenty-two-year-old army officer. Arafat had not yet taken over the PLO, either. All three men, and various leftist thugs in power around the world, had supported Mandela because he represented opposition to the white South African regime, which was a tacit Cold War ally of the United States. All three presumably hoped that if the South African government fell at the right time, and Mandela came to power, he would be a powerful ally with them in the global war against the West.

While I was slowly dissociating in my mind some of Mandela's admirers from the man himself, bits and pieces of his character began to surface in my research. There was something about him that seemed to command not just respect, but profound admiration, even among those who had been his ardent foes and his jailers. Hardheaded news magazines like Britain's *Economist* spoke unabashedly of the "aura of sainthood" that seemed to surround Mandela. American journalists and writers constantly mentioned his "lack of bitterness," the "sense of serenity in him, of confidence and courtesy" (Anthony Lewis in the *New York Times*); his "rather majestic poise, unmarred by rancor" (playwright Arthur Miller) that had disarmed even strongly conservative Americans when he addressed both chambers of the United States Congress.[2]

More than anything else, in the months and then years after his release from prison in 1990, Mandela seemed to embody, to a degree that utterly overcame people's opposition to him, the quality of forgiveness. The former Anglican archbishop of Cape Town, Desmond Tutu, himself a fierce critic of apartheid, put it quite simply. "Had Nelson Mandela and all these others not been willing to forgive," he said, "we would not have even reached first base."[3]

What did he mean by "first base"? Tutu was referring to the complete transformation of South Africa—one of the most radical and instant changes of government and institutions of any country in history. This happened virtually overnight, by the peaceful exercise of voters at the ballot box, without a civil war, without a hideous wreaking of revenge by the newly empowered upon those just ousted from power, and with at least a reasonable chance of political and economic success in the future. It is true that there was appalling bloodshed among different black South African groups, notably the Zulu adherents of the Inkatha Freedom Movement and the ANC, as it became clear that the ANC would eventually be running South Africa. But there was little trace of the much-predicted vengefulness against whites in general by blacks as the day of changeover approached.

Until February 1990, the month Mandela was released from prison, South Africa had been ruled since its independence from Britain in 1931 under a system that was later to become known as *apartheid,* meaning "apartness" in Afrikaans. It was a system designed to perpetuate the rule and privileges of the white minority on the grounds that black South Africans, for cultural reasons, were not capable of the same degree of self-rule or political maturity as whites. In practice, this ensured that the 14 percent minority of whites (today 6 million in a total population of 45 million) had total political and social control over the 33 million (75 percent) blacks, the 4 million "Colored" (mixed black and white race) citizens, and the 1.5 million Asians (predominantly of Indian origin).

The doctrine of apartheid, which was to become fully formed only after the Nationalists came to power in 1948, was based on the belief that races should develop separately from one another. This belief in turn was often founded on blatantly racist assumptions about the nature of different ethnic and racial groups. The whites of South Africa had come originally in the mid-seventeenth century from Holland and France, speaking a Dutch-based language called Afrikaans and acquiring the name Afrikaner, or African. They were predominantly farmers who had originally immigrated to the area around Cape Town, and who in the nineteenth century pioneered settlement farther and farther inland and to the north. They came to be known over the years to the world at large as *Boers,* the Dutch word for "farmer."

Clashes increased in the second half of the nineteenth century between the fiercely independent-minded Afrikaners, or Boers, and the new interlopers, the British, who had first occupied South Africa in 1806. The British had different and sometimes disturbing ideas about race relations, i.e., that blacks and whites should be treated equally. The worst of the conflicts was the Boer War (1899–1901). Although the British military won the war, they essentially lost control of South Africa.

By 1948, a wave of Nationalist pride among the Afrikaners, who comprised the majority of the white population, ensured that a racist-inclined Nationalist Party held power for the next four and a half decades. From 1948 until the early 1990's, black South Africans were kept in complete subjugation by whites. Racial origin was classified—often quite arbitrarily on the basis of the width of a nose or the shade of a skin—under the Population Registration Act. The Group Areas Act prohibited blacks from living in white areas or from attending white government schools. Various land acts required blacks to live in *Bantustans,* or "homelands," comprising just 13 percent of the total land area. Whites controlled the rest.

Under apartheid, blacks were not simply prohibited from any role in politics. They also had to endure humiliating daily reminders of the racist belief that they should live separately from whites. They could not travel on "whites only" buses, or picnic on "whites only" beaches, or take their sick children to "whites only" hospitals. In one of the most absurd laws of "petty apartheid"—the apartheid dealing with social customs rather than with politics—it was illegal in South Africa for a person of one race—any race—to marry someone of a different race, and if married outside of South Africa, to cohabit with them. Sexual relations of any kind were prohibited between races.

Protests against apartheid crescendoed during the 1950's and 1960's, and led to ever increasing repression from the South African government. Most sober analysts of South Africa, inside and outside the country, anticipated nothing but a bloodbath of some sort or other in the process of implementing political change. The fact that this tragedy ultimately didn't happen, as we shall see later, was universally described as a "miracle." The "miracle" occurred after South Africans of all races turned out to vote for their new government in April 1994.

Many South Africans of all races played a role in ensuring the peaceful transfer of power. But without the extraordinary moral authority of the emerging South African black leader, Nelson Mandela, there would have been no central point or person around which such heroic efforts could coalesce. Mandela's moral authority was based on one simple virtue more than anything else: his willingness and capacity to forgive.

Mandela hates to be considered a sort of "demigod," and he has certainly not worn "an aura of sainthood" all his life. His first marriage broke down in large measure because of his single-minded determination to put his political work ahead of his family obligations. His second marriage collapsed, too, though in this case it was as much the character weakness of his second wife, Winnie Mandela, as his own confinement that brought this about.

And Mandela hasn't solved every problem faced by South Africans. There are still today great inequities of economic power. Whites, who are only 14 percent of the population, still on average enjoy living standards multiple times higher than those of the 33 million blacks (75 percent of the population). A drive through Constantia, a delightful rural suburb of Cape Town, reveals homes and properties and views that would arouse admiration, if not envy, from a resident of Malibu, California. Just a few miles away, thousands of blacks live in grime and unspeakable squalor, several to a room, without indoor running water or proper sanitation, and with community unemployment rates close to 50 percent.

Yet South Africa is a constitutional democracy with a free press, a racially integrated, independent, and incorrupt judiciary, and armed services that are loyal to the government even though still predominantly officered by whites. Could any of this have happened without Mandela's moral stature? The vast majority of whites and blacks alike think not.

"Mandela is such an icon in the eyes of all of South Africa," says Henri Viljoen, a successful Afrikaans Cape Town lawyer. "He is so big and so admirable, that he has dragged along even the most conservative Afrikaner. There is nobody else in the world like him."[4] Streets, squares, parks, and apartment blocks around the world have been named after Mandela. A song, "Free Nelson Mandela," and a musical, *Sarafina,* have brought his name before millions. Rock concerts have been performed in his honor.

All of this adulation could easily provoke cynicism about Mandela. Yet virtually all who have met Mandela say that he is, if anything, more impressive close-up than when seen from afar. People describe an old-world quality to his elegant manners and deferential treatment of everyone he meets. "He has the punctilious manners of a Victorian gentleman," writes Richard Stengel, the *Time* writer who helped Mandela put together his memoirs. "His aides sometimes chastise him for rising from his chair to greet everyone who approaches him."[5]

Arthur Miller writes of "his staid, almost Victorian structure of speech and demeanor," a natural authority that he seems to exude. "Mandela, to put it simply, is a chief."[6] *Newsweek* columnist Meg Greenfield was struck by his "elemental dignity," above all when the ugly details of his wife's behavior toward him became apparent in the divorce hearings in 1996. "Nelson Mandela is about many things," she has written, "but to my mind he is above all about dignity."[7]

Cyril Ramaphosa, who took over the day-to-day leadership of the African National Congress as secretary-general in 1991, says: "He is a person of magnetic presence. If you are in a room with him you immediately sense that you are with a person of unique greatness."[8]

Some of these qualities are clearly a product of Nelson Mandela's childhood and upbringing. He is a direct descendant of Xhosa royalty, and he spent important parts of his childhood witnessing the dignified handling of tribal meetings by his guardian, himself a tribal chief. This

much at least, along with his genetic inheritance, should account for the
"aristocratic" or "Victorian" aspects of his behavior.

But what seems to have elevated Mandela well beyond mere inherited
or environmental influences has been a private spiritual journey intimately
connected to the humiliating ordeal of his long imprisonment. Archbishop
Tutu has said of Mandela that "he is incredibly humble,"[9] an observation
many others have echoed.

American politician Jesse Jackson, himself an ordained clergyman, went
well beyond politics in describing his initial impression on meeting Mandela
in his first weeks out of jail in the spring of 1990. Mandela, he said, told
him that he "began to feel the power of prayer" while in prison, and drew
strength from it. It was that spiritual journey, in Jackson's view, that caused
him to emerge from prison "unbroken, unbowed, and unbitter. He radiated hope."[10] The magazine *Christian Century*, summing up Mandela's
conduct during six years of freedom early in 1996, noted: "What Mandela
is practicing can only be described as a politics of grace—grace in the full-
blown, unadulterated sense of forgiveness and restoration that is
undeserved, unmerited, and unearned."[11]

Certainly Mandela himself would accept that principle, for he has privately been unequivocal about his own Christian faith. In 1984 he insisted
to editors of the *Washington Times*, who were permitted to visit him at
Pollsmoor Prison, that he was a Christian and always had been, despite
assertions of some that he was a Communist.[12] He told Rev. Michael
Cassidy, an Anglican clergyman deeply involved in reconciliation work in
South Africa, that he had been quite impressed by Billy Graham's sermons, which he saw on television while in prison.[13] Indeed, in the 1970's I
remember hearing that Mandela had made a specific Christian commitment after watching a televised Graham crusade, and had then written to
the Billy Graham Evangelistic Association to let them know about his
decision. Very wisely, as the president of a multiethnic, multireligious
nation where he cannot afford to appear partisan even in personal spiritual matters, Mandela has not worn that personal faith on his sleeve. Yet
through it, he became a changed man.

When he entered prison in 1963 for what became twenty-seven years of
incarceration under sometimes harsh conditions, he was an impressive, admired leader, exhibiting some of the same dignity and nobility we recognize
today. But he was also an impatient, impulsive, slightly arrogant forty-six-

year-old firmly set upon overthrowing the white government of South Africa by force, if necessary through a guerrilla war.

The Nelson Mandela who emerged from prison in 1990 was a different person. He was restrained, profoundly thoughtful of others, deeply humble, and eager to detect good qualities even in his political adversaries. He had not deviated an iota from his ultimate goal of a multiracial regime in which black voters had rights identical to those of whites. But he sought it now in a very different spirit. Above all else, he radiated forgiveness.

Nothing inherent in the prison experience would have guaranteed this change. Prison can embitter and envenom men (Hitler, Lenin) as easily as it can ennoble them. Yet how imprisonment shaped a zealous revolutionary into a great statesman over twenty-seven years, endowing him with a moral stature that was recognized even by his political adversaries, is one of the great stories of grace in the twentieth century. It is Mandela's story.

THE GREAT PLACE IN TRANSKEI

Mandela was born July 18, 1918, in the last few months of World War I, in the tiny village of Mwezo in the Umtata district, capital of the Transkei. The lovely rolling-hill countryside of the region lies between the Drakensberg Mountains to the north, and the Indian Ocean on the east. Traditionally, the area had been home to the Thembu people, one of the tribal groups constituting the Xhosa nation of South Africa. Both of Mandela's parents were Thembus.

His father, Gadla Henry Mphakanyiswa, was of Thembu royal blood and was an adviser to the Thembu kings, or chiefs. Gadla Henry was illiterate, but he was obviously intelligent, for he valued education highly when he found it in others. Characteristically for minor chiefs, Gadla Henry had four wives, and Nelson was born to the third of these, Nosekeni Fanny. As it happened, she had become a Christian, and so Nelson was baptized not long after his birth at the local Methodist church. His English name, Nelson, was not bestowed on him until his first day at primary school, so until then he answered to an entirely African name: Rolihlahla Dahlibunga Mandela. Rolihlahla was the name selected for him at birth by his father, and its meaning was unconsciously pregnant with the significance of Mandela's future: "one who causes trouble for himself."

Not long after Mandela's birth, the family moved to the slightly larger village of Qunu, still in the Umtata district, where Mandela lived with his mother in one of three rounded huts, or *rondavels,* as they are called, in a quiet valley crisscrossed by streams. The huts had a *kraal,* or cattle enclosure nearby, and most of the work was performed by women and children. From the age of five, like all children, Mandela was shown how to hold a stick and drive the cattle out of the kraal in the morning and then bring them home at night. From almost as early an age, too, the young boys spent more time together playing or fighting with sticks in the open countryside than they did in their family hearth. Mandela loved this uninhibited, free-range life in the broad veld. He has never forgotten its impact on him.

Mandela was sent off to school by his mother, who was herself illiterate. She had been persuaded to take this unusual step by two brothers who were both Christian and educated. The schoolhouse was not far from Nosekeni Fanny's rondavel and was a one-room building presided over by a woman teacher, Miss Mdingane. On the first day of classes, the teacher conferred on each of the students an English name to add to their African one. Educated Africans of the day had all been taught to consider English and white civilization in general as something inherently superior to anything African. Mandela wrote later: "The education I received was a British education, in which British ideas, British culture, British institutions, were automatically assumed to be superior. There was no such thing as African culture."[14] Nelson was probably named after the famous British admiral who defeated the French at the Battle of Trafalgar in 1805. And he apparently wasn't the least bit embarrassed by his totally un-African new first name.

Gadla Henry died when Mandela was only nine, and the boy was taken under the wing of a guardian who was to leave a deep influence on him. The guardian's name was Chief Jongintaba Dalindyebo. In addition to being Gadla Henry's nephew, he was the acting regent of the Thembu people. He lived in a large home called simply the Great Place, in a village called Mqhekezweni, which was a day's walk from Qunu. There was a church there, as well as a school, two large buildings belonging to the chief, and several whitewashed rondavels.

Mqhekezweni was actually a Methodist mission station as well as a chief's headquarters, and in the new primary school he attended, Mandela was introduced to English, the written Xhosa language, history, and geography. Characteristically, for Africans who had become Christians, both men and women wore Western-style clothes. In fact, church life was an extremely important part of the family, for the chief himself was a Christian. Every Sunday, Mandela would attend along with his guardian's family, listening to fire-and-brimstone sermons from the Reverend Matyolo.

At Mqhekezweni, Mandela later wrote, "religion was part of the fabric of life," and he noticed that "virtually all of the achievements of the Africans seemed to have come about through the missionary work of the church."[15] When the young boy stole some corn (referred to as "mealies" in South Africa) from the clergyman's garden and was spotted doing so, he received a stern berating from the chief's wife during family prayer time at night.

But it wasn't all religious seriousness. Mandela learned to romp outside and ride horses with Justice, Jongintaba's eldest son, who was four years older than Nelson. He had general chores to perform, too, including pressing the pants of his guardian into a knife-sharp crease. When the chief invited guests to the Great Place for a meal or for consultations on important tribal matters, Mandela waited on them.

As various activities took place, young Nelson listened. He observed during the meetings. He noted that there was never a vote on a matter or a determination of what a majority consensus might be. Either there was unanimity or decisions were simply postponed. Speakers of all ages and experience were invited to speak their minds openly, often criticizing sharply Jongintaba himself. "Majority rule was a foreign notion," Mandela reflected later on this period of his life. "A minority was not to be crushed by a majority." The chief himself would not speak until the very end of the meeting, after everyone else had had his say, and then he would try to guide the group to a unanimous decision or a decision to discuss the issue later. "As a leader," Mandela wrote, "I have always followed the principles I first saw demonstrated by the regent at the Great Place."[16]

Mandela stayed at the Great Place until he was sixteen, studying at night by oil lamps, enjoying the privileged ways of someone who lived as the son of the chief, and learning about the relationships of the different

tribal groups to one another through the tales and explanations of respected tribal elders. At this important age he underwent the key Xhosa
manhood ritual of tribal circumcision. For several days, the young boys
of the tribe would leave their homes and live together in a lodge beside a nearby river, enjoying the time together and being instructed on
how to behave in the ceremony by older men. On the day of the ceremony, the ritual itself was performed by a skilled visiting circumcision
expert, using his *assegai* (spear) without any form of anesthetic.
"Ndiyindoda!" ("I am a man!") the young men were told to cry out
after the agonizing cut had been made. The slightest sign of pain was
considered an indication of weakness. Mandela didn't flinch, but later
said that he seemed to take longer than the other boys to call out the
requisite word.

Very soon after this, he was sent off to the Clarkebury Boarding Institute, still in the Umtata district, but about sixty miles from Mqhekezweni.
It was one of the oldest Wesleyan Methodist institutions in the Transkei,
presided over sternly by an English headmaster, Reverend C. Harris.
Mandela had seen several white people at the Great Place, and he noticed
that they treated Jongintaba as an equal, sometimes even with deference.
Amazingly, Nelson, in his formative years, did not seem to run into any of
the crude, racist attitudes toward blacks that were often exhibited by the
Afrikaners in South Africa's major cities.

The young man admired and respected Harris, who demonstrated "an
iron hand" in running the school, yet also seemed to demonstrate "an
abiding sense of fairness," according to Mandela. He encountered for the
first time educated African teachers who did not kowtow either to Harris
or to the other white teachers. As for Harris himself, Mandela says now
that he was deeply impressed by the Englishman's dedication to the education of young Africans and by the gentleness concealed behind his severe
exterior. Harris, he says, was "a model" for him at the time.[17]

After three years in this austere but decent environment, the regent decided that Mandela needed yet more education. He sent him to another
Wesleyan institution, the College of Healdtown, in Fort Beaufort, some 175
miles southwest of Umtata. The college was the largest African school south
of the equator, with around a thousand male and female students. The principal—or headmaster, as he would have been known—was a much more
pompous man than Reverend Harris, "a stout and stuffy Englishman," to

use Mandela's words, who went by the name of Dr. Arthur Wellington. "I am the descendant of the great Duke of Wellington," he would intone, "aristocrat, statesman, and general, who crushed the Frenchman Napoleon at Waterloo and thereby saved civilization for Europe—and for you, the natives." Mandela says that at this point he believed "that the best ideas were English ideas, the best government was English government, and the best men were Englishmen."[18]

Yet Mandela had an African teacher, the housemaster Reverend Mokitimi, who taught Mandela one of his most important lessons at Healdtown. When Dr. Wellington one evening demanded to know the details of an argument between two school prefects that Mokitimi was endeavoring to pacify, Mokitimi flatly refused to explain the story to him. He was polite, but firm, refusing to back down in front of the principal. "I realized then that Dr. Wellington was less than a god and Reverend Mokitimi more than a lackey," says Mandela, "and that a black man did not have to defer automatically to a white, however senior he was."[19]

In 1939, Mandela took another step in an educational process that made him increasingly part of an elite within an elite in South Africa, an African who had attended not simply a college but a university. The regent sent him to the University College of Fort Hare, some twenty miles east of Healdtown, a truly exclusive institution, since it was the only residential higher education campus open to blacks in South Africa. For young black South Africans like himself, Mandela noted, Fort Hare was "Oxford and Cambridge, Harvard and Yale, all rolled into one."[20] Just twenty-one, he was provided with his first suit by his guardian, who seemed proud that Mandela would be the first member of the clan with a university degree.

In addition to his college courses in anthropology, politics, Roman Dutch law, English, and native administration at Fort Hare, Mandela was active in sports, particularly soccer and cross-country running. Running in particular, he said, taught him "valuable lessons" about the way his own diligence and discipline could compensate for what he thought was his lack of natural ability. He continued his Christian studies, too, joining the Students Christian Association and teaching the Bible on Sunday in nearby villages. Here he became a good friend with Oliver Tambo, a man who was to be a lifelong fellow combatant in the struggle against apartheid. Tambo was president of the African National Congress for many years in exile before his death in South Africa on April 24, 1993.

A confrontation with authority at Fort Hare changed the course of Mandela's life. It all began with his nomination for election as one of six members of the Student Representative Council. He and the other nominees believed that the student council should have more power. There were grievances with the college administration, they thought, that needed addressing before any election took place.

They organized a boycott of the election, and when elected nonetheless, promptly resigned. Irritated, the principal rescheduled the election for suppertime the following day. The results were identical with the first election, but all the newly elected council members except Mandela thought that by now they had made their point. They thought the time had come to cooperate with the administration. Mandela disagreed.

The principal was courteous but firm. He said that if Mandela did not reconsider this decision, he would have to expel him from the college. It was an excruciating dilemma. "I had taken a stand," he said, "and I did not want to appear to be a fraud in the eyes of my fellow students. At the same time, I did not want to throw away my career at Fort Hare."[21] Nonetheless, he refused to back down. He was allowed to finish out the year, but was told that he could not return to the college unless he was willing to serve on the committee to which he had been elected.

Gloom descended on the Great Place at Mqhekezweni when Mandela explained to Jongintaba what had happened. The chief was furious. Mandela must obey the principal, he insisted. Mandela said nothing. But other events now intervened. The regent, sensing mortality creeping up on him, was diverted by different priorities. He abruptly arranged marriages for Justice, now twenty-seven, and Mandela, twenty-three. The brides had been selected, he told the astonished pair, and the *lobola*, or bride price, was already paid. Justice and Mandela looked at each other in despair. Appalled at the prospect of a loveless union imposed on them from above, they impetuously decided to run away to Johannesburg. They stole two of the regent's oxen and sold them to a local trader in order to pay the cab fare to the railroad station.

They were almost instantly caught. Disembarking the Johannesburg train at Queenstown to obtain the necessary travel documents and permits for the city, the two fugitives just happened to bump into the regent's brother, Chief Mpondombini. He, in turn, asked the local magistrate, a friend, to issue the necessary paperwork. When a checkup call was made back to Umtata, Jongintaba happened to be sitting in the Umtata magistrate's office. Overhearing the conversation, Jongintaba demanded Mandela's arrest on the spot, but the Queenstown magistrate reluctantly had to let them go. He apparently knew nothing about the stolen oxen, and the displeasure of a chief, however important he was, was insufficient grounds for an arrest.

Chastened by this brush with the long arm of the chief, the brothers hitched a ride to Johannesburg with an elderly white lady who was traveling to the city to visit her daughter. As custom required, they sat in the back of the car while the woman drove with an empty front passenger seat. That night, they slept on the floor of the servants' quarters of a large Johannesburg home. Mandela was angry at everything, but he was also remorseful. He'd made a shaky start of what he had hoped would be an entirely new life.

JOHANNESBURG LAW CLERK

Johannesburg was a bustling commercial city that had sprung up almost overnight in the 1860's after the discovery of gold in the area. Now it was 1941, and the war in Europe had created a demand for South Africa's rich commercial resources. In the gold mines, thousands of Africans toiled away in conditions of barrackslike regimentation and privation. Justice had a job waiting for him in the Crown Mines, but the regent's long reach blocked this opening. When the mine headman, an African who knew the regent, learned about the flight from Umtata, he swiftly fired both Justice and Nelson.

At first, Mandela lodged with a cousin, then moved in with an Anglican clergyman, the Reverend J. Mabutho, a pious man who was also a Thembu and knew Mandela's family. Once again, like an albatross of bad news, Mandela's cheating of the regent hung around his presence in Johannesburg. Another Crown Mines headman who knew of Justice's and Nelson's earlier deceptions happened to drop by when the Mabutho family was having tea. The clergyman said nothing directly at the time, but the next day asked Mandela to find somewhere else to live. In fact, Mabutho himself arranged for him to stay with a neighbor. "I had become so used to my deceptions that I lied even when I did not have to," Mandela recalled sadly. "In my brief stay in Johannesburg, I had left a trail of mistruths, and in each case, the falsehood had come back to haunt me."[22] It wasn't exactly a stunning debut for a young man in his encounter with Johannesburg.

But then Mandela got a break. By chance, he met a real estate manager, Walter Sisulu, who was the son of a white father and an African mother. It was the beginning of a lifelong friendship for Mandela, a friendship that was rooted in African politics. More practically, it opened the door for Mandela to find a job and to set about completing his studies.

Through Sisulu, Nelson was introduced to a Jewish lawyer, Lazar Sidelsky, who was a member of one of the largest law firms in Johannesburg, one that happened, moreover, to do business with blacks as well as whites. The job was humble enough, but it enabled Mandela to continue studies for his bachelor's degree by correspondence, as well as to acquire experience in law itself. Sidelsky was only the first of many Jews who, more than any other group among white South Africans, encouraged Mandela to make it clear that justice should apply to the whole human race, not just to one group within it.

The Sidelsky clerkship opened Mandela's eyes both to the pettiness of race relations in a major city and to the serious political currents churning at subterranean level beneath the surface of South African life. Mandela was treated courteously by his white supervisors and other employees, but the firm's whites were sometimes embarrassed to be seen acting graciously toward him when other whites were around. At one point, when Mandela was dictating something to a white secretary and a white client entered the office, the secretary quickly gave him some money and told him to go off and buy some shampoo at the pharmacy. She didn't want a white to see her taking dictation from an African. Mandela graciously went on the errand, not wanting to embarrass her by making a fuss over the incident.

But for Mandela during 1941 and 1942, life was grim and at times he was almost destitute. He was a clerk living in the densely overcrowded black township of Alexandra, with a total monthly income of eight pounds (approximately $120 U.S. by 1997 standards), much of which he had to spend buying candles to study by. He frequently went hungry. Meanwhile, the apartheid system required him at all times not merely to use separate facilities of transportation, entertainment, sanitation, and accommodation, but to display a shuffling subservience when in the presence of whites. Only at his office was he treated respectfully by the whites.

That office was turning out to be crucial in Mandela's life. Two of Sidelsky's youngest employees, one black and one white, impressed him deeply. Gaur Radebe, the black South African, was an articulate, well-educated young man who was a member of both the African National Congress and of the South African Communist Party. Gaur was a true radical, often speaking quite impertinently to his employer, Sidelsky, who somehow tolerated it.

The white man, Nat Bregman, was Mandela's age, apparently totally lacking in any racial prejudice, and also a dedicated Communist. Through both of them, Mandela came to know several of the leading South African Communists. In those days, Communists were the only politically minded South Africans willing to support without reservation black demands for an end to apartheid. Mandela says that, because he was "quite religious" (meaning Christian) at the time, he was "put off" by the Communist philosophy of materialism. But he had a sympathetic view of Communists because, for all of their other faults, in South Africa they seemed to be antiracist.

By the end of 1942, Mandela had completed his bachelor's degree, and he was even able to return to Fort Hare the following year for the graduation ceremony. His friendship with Gaur was slowly drawing him into politics, for in addition to his Communist Party affiliation, Gaur was active in the ANC. The following year, the black township of Alexandra, outside Johannesburg, boycotted the local bus company after fares were suddenly raised 25 percent. The nine-day boycott radicalized Mandela. "I had departed from my role as an observer," he says, "and had become a participant."[23] Through Gaur and Walter Sisulu, who still worked in his real estate office, Mandela was mixing now with blacks from many different tribal and linguistic origins. At the same time, by attending social functions organized by the Communists, his discontent with apartheid was being honed into a political conviction that demanded his direct struggle against it.

Nelson Mandela badly needed legal skills. So in 1943, he enrolled as the only black student in the law department of the University of the Witwatersrand. His objective, an LL.B. degree, was the essential requirement for a fully qualified lawyer. It was at "Wits," as the university has always been nicknamed, that Mandela first met Joe Slovo, the lifelong white South African Communist who was to be for many years the exiled leader of the military wing of the ANC. Also through Wits, Mandela met for the first time many of the antiapartheid activists of Indian background. They were overwhelmingly young, earnest, and diligent, but they attracted Mandela for another reason too: They organized lively parties.

It was a new, assertive Mandela who by the end of 1943 had completed two years as an articled law clerk at Sidelsky's. At Fort Hare, two years earlier, he had thought his ambition in life was to be an interpreter or clerk in South Africa's Native Affairs Department. Now he wanted to be a lawyer, but not just any lawyer. He was beginning to realize that his life was becoming more and more directed toward political struggle against apartheid. "I cannot pinpoint a moment when I became politicized," he wrote,

> when I knew that I would spend my life in the liberation struggle. I felt no epiphany, no singular revelation, no moment of truth, but a steady accumulation of a thousand slights, a thousand indignities, a thousand unremembered moments, produced in me an anger, a rebelliousness, a desire to fight the system that imprisoned my people. There was no particular day on which I said, From henceforth I will devote myself to the liberation of my people; instead, I simply found myself doing so, and could not do otherwise.[24]

Other convictions were undergoing change too. After intense discussions with Walter Sisulu, Oliver Tambo, the Communist William Nkomo, and others, he was shedding his earlier veneration for the British way of life as supreme to all others. The humiliating daily pinpricks of apartheid had punctured whatever remained of his belief in the superior virtues of European civilization.

He was in fact moving toward an even more radical position than that of opposition to apartheid as a system. He was becoming greatly influenced by a powerful spokesman of a new, militantly antiwhite Africanism: Anton Lembede, one of the handful of full-fledged African lawyers in South Africa. Lembede was a militant African Nationalist who touched a chord of shame in Mandela. Had Mandela not come close to being co-opted by the white rulers of the country into one of "their" preferred educated blacks? Before the term "black consciousness" had assumed a powerful role in the thinking of both African-Americans and South African blacks, Lembede wanted blacks to shake off their traditional feeling of inferiority to whites. He pointed to powerful African-American thinkers and writers like Marcus Garvey and W. E. B. Du Bois as examples of what Africans were capable of becoming. This growing sense of discontent soon erupted into a mini-revolt within the ANC itself. Together with Lembede, Sisulu, Tambo, and others, Mandela was part of a delegation late in 1943 that called on Dr. A. B. Xuma, head of the organization.

The ANC had originally been founded in 1912, and was thus the oldest anticolonial organization in all of sub-Saharan Africa. But it had fallen on hard times. The membership had declined in numbers and the leadership couldn't quite articulate any vision for political activism in the face of apartheid. Mandela's group proposed to Xuma that the formation of a militant youth league would intensify the antiapartheid struggle by several degrees. Xuma, a physician who was proud of the friendships he had developed with the white political establishment, shifted uncomfortably when confronted with this idea. He did not want the ANC to develop into an organization that could jeopardize his own social standing.

Undaunted, the young men went ahead anyway. They took their proposal to the ANC conference at the end of the year, where it was accepted. In the early spring of 1944, the Youth League was formally constituted, with about one hundred people present. The manifesto stated that "the national liberation of Africans" must be achieved by Africans themselves, with no outside assistance. At the time, this meant that there should be no cooperation with Communists, precisely because South African Communists were predominantly white and might prove an obstacle to militant black Nationalism. Mandela himself, though not in any way a black racist at the time, also felt that whites should not be permitted to have any role in the ANC. This, he thought, might simply reinforce the black sense of inferiority and inhibit Africans from developing their own consciousness. The first congress of the Youth League was held in September 1944.

Other emotions were stirring in the energetic twenty-five-year-old too. The dreary, impoverished loneliness of his early years as a legal clerk, struggling to make ends meet each month, nurtured in him a deep yearning for female companionship. He had one or two unrequited infatuations with the daughters of families with whom he'd stayed. Then in 1944, at the home of Walter Sisulu, he met a nurse, Evelyn Ntoko Mase. Evelyn was a quiet, attractive young woman. After a few months of courtship, they were married in the Native Commissioner's Court in Johannesburg. They were so poor they couldn't even afford a wedding reception.

Evelyn's job as a nurse helped pay Mandela's way through law school at Wits, even though they were unable to find private housing for themselves until 1946. They then moved into a two-room house in the Orlando East section of Soweto, made available by the government, before settling into what became Mandela's only long-term housing apart from prison, 8115 Orlando West. By then their first child—a son—was born. He was named Madiba Thembekile, who became known simply as Thembi. The name Madiba was Mandela's Thembu clan name. Over the years, with his growing reputation in South African politics, it became a salutation of honor to him on the part of his ANC supporters.

By 1947, Mandela had completed the required three years as an articled clerk with Sidelsky's firm. He now wanted to study full-time for his LL.B., for he could not otherwise become a lawyer. But within a year, tragedy struck his family. A daughter who was born in 1948 and named Makaziwe never recovered from a puzzling illness that physicians couldn't identify. She died at the age of nine months. Evelyn was devastated. Mandela did his best to comfort her, but he was frequently away at nights and on weekends attending ANC activities. He was already an elected member of the Executive Committee of the Transvaal ANC. Evelyn moped and felt neglected. The life of the marriage seemed to be ebbing away, and nothing looked likely to revive it. Thinking about this as he rushed from one meeting to another, Mandela must certainly have begun to understand the high price that full-time political work inevitably imposes on private lives.

He meanwhile was becoming steadily more militant, more "Africanist" in his politics, and had been so since the formation of the Youth League. Part of this was no doubt due to the influence of men like Anton Lembede, who died suddenly in 1947 at the age of thirty-three. Mandela had also been influenced by the energy and heroism of the Indian community in its struggles against new government laws restricting movement and residence. The intensifying pressures on all of the nonwhite communities by the government must also have been a factor. When this pressure culminated in the winning of the South African elections of 1948 by the Nationalist Party for the first time, politically active Africans like Mandela all realized that the days of polite political remonstrance against the regime were now over for good.

THE POWER OF MY PUNCHES

Overwhelmingly Afrikaans in composition, the Nationalists surged to power in 1948 on a crest of bitter anti-British resentment. Many of those who voted for them had cheered on the Nazis during World War II, and some had been imprisoned for pro-Nazi activity. Now they had an opportunity to get back at the British through the ballot box. They recalled British humiliation and mistreatment of them before and after the Boer War.

These Afrikaners also felt that the emergence of an educated black African community would threaten their way of life, built as it was on cheap labor and an ideological need to define black-white relations permanently in terms of superiority and inferiority. For this reason, the 1948 election campaign was openly and at times savagely racist. Two of its slogans were *"Die kaffer op sy plek"* ("The nigger in his place") and *"Die koelies uit die land"* ("The coolies [i.e., Indians] out of the country"). The Nationalist platform for the first time introduced officially the word *apartheid,* meaning "apartness," and within two years of coming to power the new government had firmly set in place the ugly legal structure that sustained official apartheid.

Between 1948 and 1950 a series of parliamentary laws were passed that all but ensured there could be no further evolution of a positive black-white relationship for the foreseeable future. The laws included the Population Registration Act, which permitted the government to classify every citizen according to race; the Group Areas Act, which forced all nonwhite citizens—Africans, Colored, and Indian—to live within specially designated areas; the Prohibition of Mixed Marriages Act and the Immorality Act, which cut off any racial intermarriage and made even intimate relations across the racial line a crime. In 1950, the politically more sinister Suppression of Communism Act came into play. This set limits not only on the legality of black South African political dissent, but on white oppositionist activity as well.

Mandela seethed during these years. He had started the struggle as an idealist, but he now no longer wanted cooperation even with the Indians or with sympathetic whites, including the Communists, for whom racial liberation was only part of their agenda. "I was angry at the white man, not at racism," Mandela recalled. "While I was not pre-pared to hurl the white man into the sea, I would have been perfectly happy if he climbed aboard his steamships and left the continent of his own volition."[25] But by the early 1950's it was clear that this was not going to happen.

The African National Congress, meanwhile, under pressure from its Youth League, gradually changed clearly from a sort of communal pro-test organization to a highly organized vehicle of oppositionist political activism. In 1950, it finally became more active. After eighteen demonstra-tors were killed by police during a May 1 protest rally organized by the Communists, the ANC declared June 26 as a National Day of Protest. Mandela, recently brought onto the Executive Committee, pushed strongly for the move. Many Africans stayed away from work or refused to do busi-ness. The organization was beginning to see militant protest and organization as a permanent feature of its activities.

As the ANC became more and more radicalized, so did Mandela. His attitude toward the Communists was changing too. He plunged into the Communist classics, finding Marx's *Communist Manifesto* exciting, but *Das Capital* deadly boring. He read widely on Lenin, Stalin, and Mao. For a long time he even had a painting of Stalin, along with a picture of the Bolsheviks storming the Winter Palace in Petrograd in 1917, on the wall of his Soweto home. (Portraits of other admired figures included Winston Churchill, FDR, and Mahatma Gandhi.) "I found myself strongly drawn to the idea of a classless society," he has admitted, "which, to my mind, was similar to traditional African culture, where life was shared and communal."[26]

Of course, looked at across the perspective of Communism's hideous pathway during the twentieth century, this view of Communism was naive. Mandela now says simply that there was more that united the Communists with African Nationalists in the 1950's than divided them. "The cynical have always suggested that the Communists were using us," he adds. "But who is to say that we were not using them?"[27] Who indeed, especially now that Communism is globally a spent force? Fortunately for all South Africans, the ANC never had to struggle for survival, once in power, against a global ideological movement backed up by Muscovite imperialism.

For its own part, the ANC was put in a dilemma by the increasing militancy of the South African Communist Party in the early 1950's. The party, rather than the ANC, at times seemed to set the pace of antigovernment protest. In June 1952, the ANC organized what turned into a several-month "Defiance Campaign" against the new laws. The intention was to mobilize large numbers of blacks to break the law on some technicality of the new Nationalist apartheid legislation and deliberately court arrest. It was hoped that this would so overwhelm the police and judicial authorities that the laws would be unworkable.

Mandela, because of his dynamic personality, organizational gifts, and disciplined work methods, was selected as "volunteer-in-chief" of the campaign. The job required him to travel constantly, subjecting his family to even more pressure than usual. By July 1952 his face was already well known to the police, and he was formally arrested while at work in his new law office. The law invoked was the Suppression of Communism Act. He and other ANC members were found guilty of "statutory Communism"—as opposed to actually being members of the party—and given a nine-month suspended sentence.

The Defiance Campaign eventually petered out, but it had put the ANC firmly on the protest map and led to an enlargement of the total membership to close to 100,000. For Mandela, the militancy was a liberating political experience. He no longer felt "overwhelmed by the power and seeming invincibility of the white man and his institutions. . . . But now the white man had felt the power of my punches and I could walk upright like a man" he said, "and look everyone in the eye with the dignity that comes from not having succumbed to oppression and fear. I had come of age as a freedom fighter."[28]

At the end of 1952 the ANC elected a new president, Chief Albert Luthuli. Unlike most of the ANC leaders, he was a Zulu, not a Xhosa. He was also a very committed Christian. When he was dismissed from his post by the government as a paid tribal chief for refusing to abandon the Defiance Campaign earlier in the year, he wrote a declaration of principles entitled "The Road to Freedom Is Via the Cross," in which he reaffirmed his own personal commitment to passive nonviolence as a means of bringing about social justice. At the same ANC meeting, Mandela was elected one of four deputy presidents.

Nonviolence wasn't the direction in which the ANC was moving. There was a rising level of militancy within its ranks that was clearly heading toward outright armed struggle with the Nationalist government as a means of bringing apartheid to an end. Mandela, in fact, was unable to attend a crucial ANC conference because he had been served his second "banning" order, one of six months, just a few days before it began. "Banning" was the government's way of cutting an individual off from all social and political contacts under threat of arrest. A "banned" person couldn't meet with more than two other people at any one time. Mandela, for example, couldn't even attend his son Thembi's ninth birthday party in 1953. "Banning," he wrote later, "not only confines one physically, it imprisons one's spirit. It induces a kind of psychological claustrophobia that makes one yearn not only for freedom of movement but spiritual escape."[29]

The writing was now on the wall. Sooner or later the government would declare outright that the ANC was no longer a legal organization, just as it had outlawed the Communist Party two years earlier. With ANC approval, Mandela now developed a clandestine program, called the M-Plan, designed to organizationally break the ANC into units as small as cells, which would consist of just a few households in a given area. For the grassroots ANC organs, there would be some freedom of action up to a point, but the main strategy would be planned at the top.

As all this was taking place in 1953, Mandela's personal life was complicated too. He had repeatedly failed his LL.B. exams at Wits for reasons he doesn't explain, but that presumably were related to his frenetic political life. He now found legal work at different white-owned law firms around Johannesburg. By the spring, however, he decided that he wanted both the freedom of operation and the political base that could only come from running his own independent law practice. He succeeded in passing the qualifying exam for legal practice, rather than receiving the LL.B. degree itself, and in August he and Oliver Tambo proudly set up the first African-owned law firm in the nation. With a brass plaque on the door, the offices of "Mandela and Tambo" were located in an Indian-owned building close to the Magistrate's Court in the middle of Johannesburg.

The workload was enormous. Africans of every walk of life needed help coping with the tangled web of government restrictions on their daily activities. Mandela seemed willing to take on almost anything. He had already developed a highly disciplined lifestyle, usually arising in the morning as early as 4:00 A.M., exercising vigorously for half an hour or more, and then methodically getting on with the day's business. Four nights a week, he panted and sweated through ninety minutes of training and sparring as an amateur boxer in the Soweto gymnasium. At 245 pounds and six feet two inches, almost as fit as a professional, he must have been a formidable sparring partner. But outside the gym, he was no jock. He enjoyed donning stylish suits and driving around town in an Oldsmobile, a style of life he could now afford because of the bustling legal practice he owned.

The early morning workouts, the intense legal work, the political organization, the boxing nights: All of these elements were put together at the expense of something, and that something was his marriage to Evelyn. In his memoirs, Mandela speaks kindly and respectfully of her. She had given him Thembi in 1945 and then, after the death of the infant Makaziwe, two more children: a girl, also named Makaziwe, and another boy, Makgatho. The youngest child had warm memories of his father, despite the fact that he was so often away. Nelson liked to wash in the bedroom together with the boys, or take them into town for ice cream. He would also sometimes ask them to accompany him on legal jobs. On Saturdays, if possible, he would drive the three children in his Oldsmobile to a movie theater, though he seldom watched the movie with them. He was stern with his children, especially if he found them being dishonest to him. But he never physically laid a hand on them.

Relations with Evelyn chilled progressively, and politics was an important element in this process. Evelyn was not opposed to her husband's activities, but she had first married Mandela back in 1944 when even he probably had little idea of how consuming the political struggle would become. According to Mandela, Evelyn just couldn't accept that politics had become Mandela's lifework, rather than being a mere hobby. In the early 1950's she became deeply involved with the Jehovah's Witnesses, distributing copies of the *Watchtower* and seeking to draw Mandela himself into the church. Mandela speculates that the new religious activity might have been a form of escape, for he says he felt it contained "an obsessional element."

Evidence that the marriage was on the rocks was clear to many people by 1954–55, and Walter Sisulu, who with his wife, Albertina, was close to

Evelyn, tried one last effort at keeping the couple together. Mandela snapped at him, saying his marriage was none of Sisulu's business, an action that in his memoirs he says he regretted later. Sisulu had never been anything but a close and caring friend. In 1955, Evelyn gave Mandela a sobering ultimatum: He must choose between her and the ANC.

Violence was becoming more and more a plausible eventuality for the ANC. When Walter Sisulu, the ANC secretary-general, said that he had been invited to attend as guest of honor the 1953 World Festival of Youth and Students for Peace and Friendship, a Communist-front gathering in Bucharest, Romania, Mandela urged him to go. And from there, he suggested, Sisulu could go to China to negotiate supplies of weapons from there to the ANC for an armed struggle. Violence was still not the official ANC policy, but Mandela himself was beginning to think that, sooner or later, the organization would have to start using it. "For me," he said, "nonviolence was not a moral principle but a strategy: there is no moral goodness in using an ineffective weapon. . . . in my heart, I knew that non-violence was not the answer."[30]

By June 1953, the militance within Mandela had finally broken the surface. In a speech he was planning to read to the 1953 conference of the Transvaal ANC, of which he was president, Mandela gave a clear signal. "The feelings of the oppressed people have never been more bitter," he said. "The grave plight of the people compels them to resist to the death the stinking policies of the gangsters that rule our country. . . . To overthrow oppression has been sanctioned by humanity and is the highest aspiration of every free man."[31]

The speech later became known as the "No Easy Walk to Freedom" speech, because it quoted a line from the Indian Nationalist and later prime minister Jawaharlal Nehru. "You can see that there is no easy walk to freedom anywhere," he said in the concluding words of his speech, "and many of us will have to pass through the valley of the shadow of death again and again before we reach the mountain tops of our desires."[32] Ironically, Mandela himself never delivered the speech. The banning order made this impossible.

Mandela was not only now militant, he was becoming arrogant. In April 1954, the Transvaal Legal Society was so outraged by his cocky and militant posture that they tried to strike him from the rolls of accredited attorneys. In a way that foreshadowed the support Mandela was later to receive throughout his life from small but important segments of the white community, several white lawyers immediately rallied against the action. It heartened him greatly to see this. Professional solidarity with him by whites, he says, showed that "even in racist South Africa professional solidarity can sometimes transcend color," and that some attorneys and judges "refused to be the rubber stamps of an immoral regime." The able white lawyers who defended Mandela did so without charge. But the white judge, Ramsbottom, was fair-minded too. He held that Mandela had every right to argue for his political beliefs even if these happened to annoy the government. The disbarment was rejected by the court.[33]

But the struggle against apartheid was intensifying. The following year, in 1955 at Kliptown, a village not far from Johannesburg, a landmark convention of African Nationalists took place. It was called the Congress of the People and included, along with liberal whites, Indians and Coloreds. An important document that became known as the Freedom Charter was read aloud during the two-day camp and received rousing support from the three thousand or so delegates. One reason for the charter's evocative impact may have been its echo of the sentiments, and at times the actual phrasing, of the U.S. Declaration of Independence. The preamble read:

> We, the people of South Africa, declare for all our country and the world to know:
>
> That South Africa belongs to all who live in it, black and white, and that no government can justly claim authority unless it is based on the will of the people;
>
> That our people have been robbed of their birthright to land, liberty and peace by a form of government founded on injustice and inequality;
>
> That our country will never be prosperous or free until all our people live in brotherhood, enjoying equal rights and opportunities. . . .[34]

But a few paragraphs down came the hitch. There were phrases that struck many Africans and whites as ardently socialist, if not Communist. The charter called for "the national wealth of our country" to be "restored to the people," and "mineral wealth beneath the soil, the banks and monopoly industry" to be "transferred to the ownership of the people as a whole." "All other industries and trade," the charter read, "shall be controlled to assist the well-being of the people."[35]

Mandela argued at the time, perhaps not very convincingly, that it was a misinterpretation to view the Freedom Charter as calling for state socialism, since it said nothing about class struggle or the elimination of private property, two slogans that would have virtually proved the ANC was Communist in orientation. Phrases such as "ownership of the people as a whole" obviously conjured up confiscatory socialist policies always implemented by Communist regimes once in power. Did Mandela grasp just how brutally Communists in other parts of the world had acted toward dissidents or private property once a revolution was successful? Probably not. His reading at the time was selective and politically tendentious. And, of course, the Communist allies of the ANC were certainly not ready to admit to any serious weaknesses in their theory and practice of politics.

Mandela was hardly alone in his naïveté. In the autumn of 1955, on a visit to several ANC activists in different parts of South Africa, he asked senior ANC officials of the Cape Town region, both of whom were also Communists, what program they had arranged for the Sunday he was with them. None, they replied: Sunday had been reserved for churchgoing. Both men, members of the party, were also ardent and leading Methodists and didn't seem to understand that Marxism was totally atheistic. "Communism and Christianity, at least in Africa," Mandela wryly observed, "were not mutually exclusive."[36]

In March 1956, the government crackdown on the ANC became even harsher. Mandela found himself banned for the third time now, on this occasion for five years. Yet the banning was a mere dress rehearsal for what was in store for virtually the entire ANC leadership late in the year. Early in the morning of December 5, 1956, police swooped down on known ANC leaders throughout South Africa. They found Mandela at home, with Evelyn still there, and the children cowering in terror at the nighttime intrusion. Over the next few days, Mandela was locked up with 155 other ANC activists in a Johannesburg prison for one of the most celebrated South African trials of the century, the so-called Treason Trial. Incredibly, the preparatory hearings, judicial maneuvering (much of it by the skilled legal work of the defense attorneys), and actual proceedings, dragged on for nearly five years.

The basic charge against the accused, who consisted of 105 Africans, 21 Indians, 23 whites, and 7 Coloreds, was high treason, and the penalty, if found guilty, was death. Nonetheless, spirits were high and the able defense counsel, consisting mostly of idealistic Afrikaans and Jewish lawyers, constantly undermined the government's case over the next few years. Still, the toll of the trial on the personal lives of the accused was brutal.

When Mandela returned home late in December after being granted bail (£250 for whites, £100 for Indians, £25 for Africans and Coloreds), he discovered that Evelyn had moved out of the house permanently, with the children, even taking the curtains with her. She had evidently gone to live with her brother, who seemed to think that the separation would enhance conditions for a reconciliation. But the brother was wrong. Mandela had long since opted out of the marriage emotionally.

The children, as Mandela himself admits, were devastated by the breakup of their parents. Thembi, the oldest, and ten at the time, became withdrawn and apathetic about his schoolwork. He even took to wearing Mandela's outsize clothes for a while, as though this would bring him closer to his father. The younger son, Makgatho, started sleeping in Mandela's bed. As for the little girl, Makaziwe, who had always been very affectionate, when Mandela paid a surprise visit to her nursery school one day and she saw him, she froze in fear, uncertain whether to be affectionate or to hide herself. The collapse of his first marriage caused Mandela deep pain, not the least because of his early and deep commitment to Christian principles. Of his first wife today, he speaks generously. "She was a very good woman," he says, "charming, strong, and faithful, and a fine mother. I never lost my respect and admiration for her, but in the end, we could not make our marriage work."[37]

The words are those of a man with a hindsight made generous by his own long years of prison suffering. But the Mandela of the mid-1950's was much younger and more brittle in his personal as well as his professional relations. In court, where he often represented Africans being tried for petty as well as major crimes, and at ANC meetings, he could be both hotheaded and arrogant. "I did not act as though I were a black man in a white man's court," he says, ". . . but as if everyone else—white and black— were a guest in my court. When trying a case, I often made sweeping gestures and used high-flown language. I was punctilious about all court regulations, but I sometimes used unorthodox tactics with witnesses. I enjoyed cross-examinations, and I often played on racial tension."[38]

When he appeared before ANC crowds, he admits, he was "something of a rabble-rousing speaker," and "liked to incite an audience."[39] Even at ANC executive meetings, Mandela was sometimes too impulsive for his own good. He once accused the ANC president, Chief Luthuli, of being frightened of whites because he had attended a meeting with white liberals who intended to form a new political party, the Liberal Party. Luthuli was so offended by this charge that he threatened to resign from the ANC. Frightened, and realizing that he had spoken rashly, Mandela immediately withdrew his charge and apologized. "I was a young man who attempted to make up for his ignorance with militancy," he now says.[40]

He was also impulsive in his personal life. Nothing illustrated this more vividly than an incident a few months after the December 1956 arrests. The trial was still in its tedious preliminary hearings stage, and Mandela was driving a friend to a black hospital in Johannesburg. As his car passed a bus stop, his eye caught a stunningly pretty black woman waiting for a bus. Not long afterward, by coincidence, the woman turned up with her brother in the law offices of Mandela and Tambo. She turned out to be Nomzamo Winnie Madikisela, or "Winnie" as the world came to know her. She was a young social worker from the Transkei. She was just twenty-two. Nelson Mandela was thirty-eight.

He was dazzled by her, as many others had been. Despite the heavy load of the trial preparations and his efforts to keep the law practice going, he invited her out to lunch the day after she had been in his office. Their first date was over spicy food in an Indian restaurant. Afterward, they went for a walk on the open veld and he opened his heart to her on his political and personal hopes and fears. "I knew right there that I wanted to marry her," he wrote, "and I told her so. Her spirit, her passion, her youth, her courage, her willfulness—I felt all of these things the moment I first saw her."[41] His estranged wife, Evelyn, first heard about the romance with Winnie from a newspaper article, and it caused abiding bitterness within her.

The courtship certainly wasn't conventional. Winnie was introduced early on to the other leading Treason Trial defendants almost as if they were part of Mandela's family. Mandela never actually proposed. It was just assumed between them that they would eventually be married. As soon as his divorce was final, he simply made arrangements for her to look for a wedding dress. The wedding ceremony took place at her parents' village in Bizana, in the Transkei, in June 1958 and was an elaborate affair. Mandela needed a special dispensation from the authorities for a six-day leave of absence from his banning order. "Winnie gave me a chance for hope," he says today. "I felt as though I had a new and second chance at life. My love for her gave me added strength for the struggles that lay ahead."[42]

Those struggles quickly involved Winnie too. The two had an intensely passionate physical relationship, as all who knew them at the time testified, and as some of Mandela's letters to Winnie from prison have also confirmed. Winnie had a volatile temper from the beginning, and would lash out at people, including Mandela, when something upset her. But whereas Mandela's absences from home during the final years of his marriage to Evelyn were probably at times prompted by the hostility between them, he hated to be away from Winnie. She had to become used to the raids on their home over the years by South African police and to the almost routine life of political meetings, arrests, jail, separations, and eventually, interminable imprisonments. Four months after their marriage, and when she was in the beginning stages of her first pregnancy, she herself was arrested for being part of a demonstration by the ANC Women's League against "pass laws" now being targeted at women by the government. She nearly miscarried in prison, and when she was released after two weeks, she had lost her job at the Baragwanath Hospital in Johannesburg.

Mandela, meanwhile, was developing a new maturity as a man and as a politician. He was practicing law and working actively for the ANC even while the elaborate and endless legal proceedings of the trial ground forward. A curious kind of mutual respect had developed between some of the white judges and prosecutors on one side and the militant African defendants on the other. Even a few of the police demonstrated indications of human decency that deeply touched Mandela.

One of the relationships that most revealed this decency was between the prosecutor, Oswald Pirow, and the defendants. Pirow was a formidable Afrikaans Nationalist and anti-Communist who had made a convincing case that the defendants were indeed potentially dangerous to the state. On the other hand, he was a man of great personal courtesy who always referred politely to Mandela and the other defendants as "Africans," (rather than the condescending "natives" that defense lawyers even occasionally let slip). When he died suddenly of a stroke just before the trial proceedings opened one morning, none of the defendants, according to Mandela, rejoiced at his passing. He was, Mandela said, both "humane" and lacking in the "virulent personal racism of the government he was acting for."[43] It is hard to estimate the impact upon Mandela, already a man who esteemed "gentlemanly" qualities so highly, of a political adversary who was such a decent human being. It surely confirmed his own intuitive sense of the inherent dignity of all God's creatures.

Unfortunately, the mood of mutual respect between antigovernment activists and some of the government representatives was not to last long. In March 1960, a brutal massacre by South African police of unarmed demonstrators suddenly introduced into the global vocabulary of police violence a new term for brutal repression: "Sharpeville."

The clash was triggered indirectly by the formation in 1959 of a rival black organization to the ANC, the Pan-Africanist Congress, or PAC, as it quickly became known. Founded by embittered or disillusioned former ANC members, it aimed not at a multiracial society for all South Africans on the basis of equality—the ANC objective—but at "a government of the Africans by the Africans and for the Africans." Because it was both anti-ANC and anti-Communist, some observers outside South Africa thought that the PAC might prove a convenient ally against the leftist-oriented ANC. Even some within the Nationalist Party believed the PAC might help split the antiapartheid forces. The PAC embraced many of the militantly antiwhite ideas that had at first appealed to Mandela in the 1940's. It was demagogic and inflammatory in its rhetoric. Mandela, once supportive of it, was now no longer comfortable with it.

When the ANC in December 1959 called for a massive campaign, to begin March 31, 1960, against the "pass laws," the PAC defiantly organized its own pass campaign to begin ten days earlier. For Mandela, this was simply "a blatant case of opportunism."[44] The PAC effort, indeed, might have fizzled out altogether, for it had far fewer organizational resources than its rival. But zealous organizing in some of the townships outside Johannesburg conjured up a massive demonstration of several thousand Africans on March 21 against the seventy-five-man police station in the town of Sharpeville, thirty-five miles south of Johannesburg.

The Sharpeville crowd was noisy and angry, and the police inside the station simply panicked, firing volley after volley directly into the crowd, a total of nearly seven hundred rifle rounds. When the stampede to escape was over, sixty-nine Africans lay dead on the open ground and hundreds more lay wounded. Suddenly, *apartheid* was no longer an unfamiliar word used in some faraway country. Emblazoned on headlines around the world, Sharpeville became the ugly emblem of the real oppression the South African system had created.

The ANC reacted swiftly. The date March 28, 1960, it announced, would be a National Stay-at-Home and a Day of Mourning for those who had died. To underscore their rage at what had happened, several ANC leaders, including Mandela, also publicly made a bonfire that day of their government-issued passes.

The Pretoria government struck back, too, declaring a state of emergency and martial law. Mandela first learned the draconian scope of this new rule at 1:30 in the morning of March 30. He and many other ANC leaders were once more rounded up from their homes in the middle of the night. One who got away was Tambo, whom the ANC, suspecting that the entire organization might eventually be outlawed, decided to send under cover out of the country altogether. Tambo's departure sounded the death knell for the Mandela-Tambo law partnership, for Mandela was under arrest under the emergency regulations and there was nobody else to run the law firm.

Now came yet another of the strange duets of courtesy that the South African government repeatedly played out with Nelson Mandela, by now its foremost political adversary. As the Treason Trial in Pretoria continued to lumber along month after month, he was given permission once a week to travel back to Johannesburg to try to clear out his law office. A tall and imposing Afrikaans sergeant, Kruger by name, was detailed to drive him the thirty-five miles each Friday afternoon. Considering Mandela's supposed danger to the state as a political activist, the South African authorities were amazingly lax.

Kruger would often stop the car, leave his unhandcuffed "prisoner" in it, then go into a store to buy oranges and chocolate for the two of them. Mandela could have escaped easily, melding into the swarming Friday afternoon crowds. Kruger also looked the other way when Winnie showed up—against regulations—to visit Mandela while he was clearing up the office. Characteristically, Mandela repaid the regime's—and Kruger's—leniency with honor. "We had a kind of gentleman's code between us," he said. "I would not escape and thereby get him into trouble, while he permitted me a degree of freedom."[45]

The "gentleman's code." The phrase is revealing, for in many ways it is the key to Mandela's character. In his memoirs, Mandela pays tribute to the white judges in the Freedom Trial as men who "rose above their prejudices, their education, and their background. There is a streak of goodness in men," he adds, "that can be buried or hidden and then emerge unexpectedly." Mandela notes how one judge's wife collected food for the prisoners when a state of emergency declared by the government in 1960 made it hard for some of the defendants even to get food for their families. Another judge, flying once from Durban to Johannesburg with an African lawyer for the defendants, refused to get on a "whites only" airline bus into town after the African lawyer was prohibited from boarding it.

Mandela had already become friends with a handful of whites—liberals and indeed Communists—who unselfishly sacrificed their own careers and even their liberty for the cause of African freedom. He also bumped into representatives of the regime who treated him with uncommon human kindness as well. For Mandela, that decency never excused the hatefulness of the regime, but it convinced him that there was always a difference between a cold and heartless system and the flesh-and-blood human beings who were caught up in trying to run it. Subtly, despite himself, Mandela had already moved far away from his earlier, antiwhite militancy toward a philosophy of human behavior that refused to pigeonhole people by race, class, profession, or any other category.

In August 1960 the state of emergency was lifted. The defendants in the trial were now permitted to live at home with their families. Winnie Mandela had given birth to their first daughter, Zeni, in 1959, the year after their marriage. The following year, just before Christmas, their second daughter, Zindzi, was born. Far more than the children from his first marriage, Zeni and Zindzi were to pay a heavy price for the political career of their father. Essentially, they were to grow up from infancy without a father at all, or worse, with a father whom they could see, but not touch, just a few times each year for half an hour at a time.

Winnie, by now as well adapted as anyone could be to the truncated family life of an opposition political activist in a police state, held up well. She provided Mandela with the emotional and physical support he needed to endure the relentless legal pressures. But over the years apart she became increasingly independent of him emotionally. She grew assertive and impulsive in politics, characteristics that led to her own infidelity and to the eventual collapse of their marriage.

As the year 1961 rolled on, the Treason Trial was still no closer to a verdict. What would happen in the end when it was over? the ANC wondered. It seemed almost certain now that the organization itself would be totally outlawed. The organization decided it was now time to dust off the Mandela-designed M-Plan for clandestine operations. On March 25, 1961, the ANC organized what was to be the last peaceful ANC gathering aimed at inducing the government to discuss political change, the so-called All-in Conference. It was held at Pietermaritzburg near Durban. Mandela warned the government directly, in a letter to Prime Minister Verwoerd, that if he did not respond to the ANC's call for a nationwide convention of political delegates, there would be another massive worker stay-at-home. In Parliament, Verwoerd described the letter as "arrogant."

Four days later, on March 29, 1961, the three-judge panel returned with their verdict at the end of the exhausting five years of the Treason Trial: not guilty. In the courtroom, there was a pandemonium of hugging and cheering when the announcement came. Outside the building the acquitted defendants and their supporters broke into "Nkosi Sielel' iAfrica" ("God Bless Africa"), the ANC's national song.

For the South African government, the legal approach to handling opposition had backfired. There seemed now only one way to contain the growing agitation by the opposition—namely tough, at times brutal, police action. For the first time, South African police began to obtain information by beating and torturing prisoners in detention. Such things became "commonplace" after the trial, Mandela said.[46]

"THE BLACK PIMPERNEL"

As for Mandela, he didn't go home after the trial. He went completely underground, moving from safe house to safe house, never staying more than a few days in one spot at a time. He grew his hair and his beard long, learned how to walk in an inconspicuous, stooping shuffle, like millions of uneducated black laborers. He often donned worker's overalls or a chauffeur's uniform if he wanted to drive somewhere. Once Winnie Mandela nearly gave him away when she pulled up beside him at a traffic light and was astonished to recognize him. Mandela never even blinked.

Surprisingly, he found that he enjoyed his solitude. It gave him time to think, plan, and read. He would infuriate the authorities by calling up white newspaper reporters from phone boxes and letting them know of the ANC's latest decisions or of his own actions. He became known in much of South Africa as the "Black Pimpernel," a reference to the famous novel about the French Revolution by Baroness Orczy, *The Scarlet Pimpernel*.

In this clandestine role, Nelson Mandela was not just avoiding the authorities for the sake of intrigue. In 1961, the ANC appointed him chief of the organization's brand-new military wing, to be called *Umkhonto we Sizwe* (the Spear of the Nation), later simply abbreviated to MK. One of his first moves was to recruit into its leadership a veteran white Communist ANC member, Joe Slovo, and Mandela's earliest Johannesburg friend, Walter Sisulu.

Mandela knew nothing about military affairs and had to try to learn about them on the run. He would hole up by day in hiding places devouring Che Guevara, Mao Tse-tung, Castro, and von Clausewitz, as well as works by such diverse guerrilla activists as Menachem Begin (author of *The Revolt*, and later prime minister of Israel) and the Afrikaans historian of the Boer War's unconventional tactics against the British, Deneys Reitz. In some ways the enforced isolation and the exposure to some of the greatest military tactical minds of the modern era helped prepare Mandela for his eventual prison isolation. Even during his surreptitious wanderings around the country, he did not change some of his own long-established personal habits. He rose regularly at 5:00 A.M. and worked out by running on the spot for half an hour or more.

The MK was actually hesitant about embarking on guerrilla warfare. "We did not want to start a blood feud between white and black," Mandela now says.[47] However, homemade bombs were exploded for the first time December 16, 1961, outside power stations and government offices in Johannesburg, Durban, and Port Elizabeth, and the MK operative who had placed the devices was himself killed.

The explosions were a major jolt to the suppositions of white South Africans. They had thought of the ANC as a misguided, militant, but basically harmless organization that had made a point of avoiding violence ever since it was founded in 1912. Indeed, the year before the MK violence, ANC president Chief Albert Luthuli, a devout exponent of nonviolence, had himself received the Nobel Peace Prize. Now the rules of the game had changed overnight, and perhaps forever.

After a while on the move, Mandela settled during October into a semi-permanent safe house, Liliesleaf Farm, in a pleasant, white rural suburb outside of Johannesburg called Rivonia. While there, he was also able to arrange secret meetings with Winnie. The farm belonged to Arthur Goldreich, a Jewish artist and designer who had been recruited by MK through a liberal white political group. Goldreich had fought with the Palmach, the Palestine Jewish resistance organization, during the 1940's. He was another Jew who risked almost everything for his support of the black South African cause.

Early in 1962, Mandela, who was still operating underground, took his biggest risk to date. With the backing of the ANC, he decided to leave the country to see if the newly independent African nations to the north would either finance or help support the training and operations of MK. His seven-month odyssey took him to several African countries, to Europe, and to the Middle East. In the first hotel he stayed at in Tanganyika, he was astonished to see blacks and whites amiably socializing over drinks on a veranda. In Addis Ababa, at a meeting of the organization later to become the Organization of African Unity, Mandela for the first time watched an entirely black military parade, with soldiers, officers, reviewing officials, and guests who were all African.

In Senegal, the Francophile president and poet Léopold Senghor provided him with a diplomatic passport that enabled him to travel to London. But the trip was double-edged for Mandela. Though he had always been an unabashed Anglophile in the cultural sense—"In so many ways," he says, "the very model of the gentleman for me was an Englishman"[48]— the South African security services kept a close watch on all opposition activity in London. The Conservative British government of Harold Macmillan, while critical of the South African government, was not ready to team up with a guerrilla opposition movement. Mandela met with prominent British opposition politicians, including then Labour Party leader Hugh Gaitskell and Jo Grimond, head of the Liberal Party, and scoured the bookstores for literature on guerrilla warfare.

After a few weeks in London, Mandela returned to Ethiopia, which he deemed the most suitable place for his own hands-on military training. The Ethiopian government assigned him a police officer to oversee a sort of combination course of military basic training and advanced staff college. For eight weeks in the stark countryside outside Addis Ababa, Mandela went through "fatigue marches" and weapons drills, with other African revolutionaries. It was oddly touching, in a way. He was a gentlemanly lawyer at forty-four, trying his hardest to make up for the lack of any previous knowledge of the military life. He was physically fit from years of early morning workouts and training as a boxer, but the use and deployment of automatic rifles, explosives, and land mines were all terra incognita to him.

Whether Mandela would ever have made a successful military commander is dubious. He was single-minded and ambitious, but not ruthless. He was analytical, but also argumentative. Even in his clandestine months planning the MK, he had never ordered the death of another person. Nor, in fact, does it seem that he ever did later on. Could he have undertaken his role as South Africa's Great Reconciliator if his hands had been bloodied by the deaths of innocents? It seems unlikely. If Providence was protecting him, it was also perhaps in the long run protecting South Africa itself.

He had planned on staying six months in Ethiopia, but the ANC suddenly recalled him. The struggle was becoming more intense inside South Africa. After crossing back into South Africa from neighboring (and British-ruled) Bechuanaland, he was driven directly back to the safe house in Rivonia. It was a rushed trip. Mandela was still wearing the combat fatigues he had been using in Ethiopia, but he was also packing something infinitely more lethal: a pistol and hundreds of rounds of ammunition given him by his Ethiopian military trainer.

He slept just one night at Rivonia before the ANC sent him off to an important meeting with MK comrades and supporters in Durban. Overconfident after his months as a world traveler, Mandela not only visited Durban but even attended a party there in his honor. Then, dressed once more as a chauffeur for a white theater director and MK member, Cecil Williams, he drove back serenely the following day from Durban to Johannesburg.

It was August 5, 1962, and the empty countryside looked inviting and comforting in the late winter afternoon. Suddenly a Ford filled with serious-looking white men roared past Williams and Mandela's car, then screeched to a halt in the road, creating a roadblock. Two more cars filled with white men came up behind the Ford. They had chosen the spot well, for on each side of the road was a steep incline that would have made escape impossible. Suddenly, Mandela remembered the pistol and a vital ANC notebook. He hastily stuffed both of them into a gap in the front seat's upholstery. It was in the nick of time. A face appeared at the driver's side window, Sergeant Vorster of the Pietermaritzburg police. Would the driver please identify himself?

"David Motsamayi," Mandela said, using his standard alias. Vorster was not impressed. "Ag, you're Nelson Mandela," he said almost in disgust, "and this is Cecil Williams, and you are under arrest!"[49] As he sat in the car, his heart pounding, Mandela had no idea that it would be the last time he would sit behind the steering wheel of any car, or for that matter sit as a free man in any car at all, for the next twenty-seven years.

"THIS IS THE ISLAND WHERE YOU WILL DIE!"

What had gone wrong? Mandela had almost certainly been betrayed by someone high up within the ANC, though to this day he discounts endless speculation on this subject. He also discredits persistent rumors that it was the CIA that had infiltrated the ANC, turning over to the South African security services the information about Mandela's whereabouts. Some of these reports resurfaced in 1990 after Mandela was released from his imprisonment.[50] Characteristically, Mandela blames only himself for his arrest. He had simply been careless, he says.

The police held Mandela overnight in Pietermaritzburg, then did what by today's police standards would seem an inconceivably rash thing to do. Without even bothering to handcuff their captive, who had for months been at the top of South Africa's most-wanted list, they placed him in the back of a sedan and drove him to Johannesburg. Along the way they stopped for gasoline and refreshments and permitted him to "stretch his legs" outside of the car. Once again, he could simply have bolted. But once again, Mandela's rigid sense of honor would not permit him to attempt it. Why not? The police, he says in his memoirs, had been kind to him. "I did not want to take advantage of the trust they placed in me," he explains.[51]

There were other small acts of kindness once his captivity began. When Winnie was able to visit him in the formidable Johannesburg prison known as The Fort, the warder turned a blind eye when husband and wife embraced passionately. Each sensed that this might be the last opportunity they would have to feel each other's physical presence for a long time. How long it would be, they had not yet dreamed. Other men of honor came forward too.

In one extraordinary incident just before Mandela's trial got under way, the prosecutor himself walked in, asked Mandela's counsel to leave, then confessed, "I did not want to come to court today. For the first time in my career, I despise what I am doing. It hurts me that I should be asking the court to send you to prison." Then he warmly shook Mandela's hand and said he hoped that things would turn out well for Mandela.[52]

The trial was a relatively short one, and Mandela's sentence, for inciting people to strike and for leaving the country without a passport, was relatively mild: five years. But this was just the beginning of the ordeal. After a few months in Pretoria, Mandela and other important political prisoners were suddenly told they were being transferred. They were shackled together in a windowless van and driven through the night, arriving at the docks of Cape Town Harbor in the afternoon. It could only mean one thing: Robben Island, or as the Afrikaans prison guards said simply, *Die Eiland*.

The prisoners were shuffled out of the van, which by now reeked with the stench of sweat and human waste. They moved, still in chains, into the hold of a wooden ferry for the fifty-minute trip into the South Atlantic swell. A single porthole provided some light for the prisoners as well as entertainment for the white warders escorting their new prisoners: Standing on the deck, some of them urinated on their charges through its planks.

As the ferry rose and fell through the long waves close to the island, the green patch of land looked inviting. But the thuggish white warders who met them on the jetty quickly shattered this impression. *"Dis die Eiland! Her julle gaan vrek!"* they shouted at the new arrivals ("This is the island! Here you will die!"). If a prisoner tried to reply in English to the warders, who always spoke Afrikaans at this stage, a warder would be likely to respond,

"Ek verstaan nie daardie kaffirboetie se taal nie" ("I don't understand that kaffir-lover's language").

Mandela and his fellow convicts were marched from the shore to a prison building where they were then forced to undress. It was a water-logged room, and the warders goaded and bullied them even before they entered it. The tension was powerful: The guards were obviously trying to establish an initial dominance over the new arrivals. One warder started picking on a younger prisoner for having hair that was too long. Mandela interrupted him, saying that hair should be as long as the regulations required. The man reddened in fury, turned, then began to move menacingly toward Mandela. He seemed on the point of striking him, but Mandela stood his ground. Then, rising to his full height and speaking in a voice that sounded much calmer than he felt, the prisoner declared, "If you so much as lay a hand on me, I will take you to the highest court in the land and when I finish with you, you will be as poor as a church mouse."

The man stopped in his tracks, dumbfounded. The threat had unnerved him, possibly because the prisoner's demeanor and educated manner of speech indicated that he wasn't just some hooligan from the townships. He asked to see Mandela's "ticket," the official document that indicated the prisoner's name, offense, and length of term in prison. He muttered something about "five years," then retreated. After that, none of the warders ever tried to manhandle Mandela. "I had been afraid," Mandela says now, "and spoke not from courage, but out of bravado. At such times, one must put up a bold front despite what one feels inside."[53]

That "bold front" would be needed again and again throughout the eighteen years that Mandela was to spend on Robben Island. In fact, after just a few weeks, he and other prisoners were returned to the mainland once more and brought to a prison in Durban. It soon became clear why. The government had now uncovered the ANC safe house at Liliesleaf Farm, Rivonia. They had raided it and come across a treasure trove of ANC and MK documents detailing methods and objectives of the sabotage movement already in operation along with plans for a future guerrilla war in South Africa. To the South African government Mandela was no longer just a bothersome strike agitator or daredevil evader of passport regulations. He was a serious danger to the security of the South African state.

A new trial, known in South Africa as the Rivonia Trial, began. From

October 1963 until the verdict and sentences were returned the following July, it was seldom off the front pages of both the South African and the world's press. What made it especially gripping was that the nine defendants, who included ANC President and old Mandela friend Walter Sisulu, could face the death penalty if found guilty. The government had amassed a huge quantity of evidence in its raid on Rivonia, including documents in Mandela's own handwriting, making clear his leadership role in MK.

For the government, the Rivonia Trial was an opportunity to frighten South Africans with the gravity of the MK and ANC conspiracy against the security and stability of the state. For Mandela, it was a sudden opportunity to speak from his heart in a public setting. It was a risky gambit that his own Afrikaans lawyers discouraged him from taking. To speak from the dock would protect him from cross-examination in the court, but his words would carry no legal weight on the question of guilt or innocence. Despite this, Mandela insisted on pushing ahead with it. After two weeks' work, he showed it to Bram Fisher, his defense counsel. Fisher and another lawyer who saw it were aghast. Not only was it a full admission of guilt, they both argued, but it virtually challenged the state to execute him.

But Mandela was adamant. When he got up to begin his address from the dock, Winnie and his own mother were in the courtroom among the spectators. He spoke uninterruptedly for four hours, explaining the political origins of the ANC, its philosophy and motivation, its relationship to the Communist Party, and the slow buildup of argument in favor of military action against the government. It was only desperation by black South Africans that had brought them to this point, he argued; the ANC had certainly never wanted a civil war, but the government was pushing South Africa's black population in that direction through its own repression. The ANC felt that it had a right, he said, to prepare measures in response.

As the minutes of Mandela's address turned into hours, government officials were by turns irritated and fascinated by what they were hearing. Mandela, for example, addressed the issue of the ANC's relationship to the Communist Party. The only reason for ANC sympathy for the Communists, he argued, was that the Communists supported the ANC's goals of treating both black and white South Africans as equals. "Because of this," he added, "there are many South Africans who, today, tend to equate freedom with communism."[54] Mandela admitted that he had been influenced by Marxism, making the point that many leaders of independent African countries in that era had also been. Those leaders, Mandela said, believed that some form of socialism was needed to enable their countries to catch up with the West. (Mandela today almost certainly no longer believes this.) Still, Mandela insisted, he certainly wasn't a Communist, nor was the ANC a Communist organization. He explained, "The Communist Party sought to emphasize class distinctions whilst the ANC seeks to harmonize them." He went on:

> From my reading of Marxist literature and from conversations with Marxists, I have gained the impression that Communists regard the parliamentary system of the West as undemocratic and reactionary. But, on the contrary, I am an admirer of such a system.
>
> The Magna Carta, the Petition of Rights and the Bill of Rights, are documents which are held in veneration by democrats throughout the world. I have great respect for British political institutions, and for the country's system of justice. I regard the British Parliament as the most democratic institution in the world, and the independence and impartiality of its judiciary never fail to arouse my admiration. The American Congress, the country's doctrine of separation of powers, as well as the independence of its judiciary, arouse in me similar sentiments. [55]

What Africans wanted, Mandela insisted, was "a just share in the whole of South Africa; they want security and a stake in society." Above all, they wanted "political rights," he said, because without them the subordinate status of Africans would be "permanent." The struggle, he said, was a struggle for "the right to live."[56] Indeed, to live in dignity, he might have added.

But as Mandela clearly grasped, that was what this trial itself was about. Up to the last few paragraphs of his speech, Mandela had read the text from the manuscript he had put together over a two-week period late at night in his cell. But he had carefully memorized the final paragraph, the one that had most shocked Bram Fisher. Turning toward the judge and putting down his text, he said:

> During my lifetime I have dedicated myself to this struggle of the African people. I have fought against white domination, and I have fought against black domination. I have cherished the ideal of a

democratic and free society in which all persons live together in harmony and with equal opportunities. It is an ideal which I hope to live for and to achieve. But if needs be, it is an ideal for which I am prepared to die.[57]

As his voice fell silent, there was a complete hush in the courtroom. Mandela had indeed mentally prepared himself for the death penalty. He could hardly have confronted his accusers with such an uncompromising, unrepentant admission of de facto guilt unless he had. He was playing for the highest stakes a man can play for—his own life—because he ultimately considered it of less importance than the cause he championed. Yet in staking everything, Mandela had also unleashed forces on his behalf that rained down furiously on the embattled South African government throughout the trial, and especially when it became clear that a verdict would soon be forthcoming.

In London, candlelit vigils were held in St. Paul's Cathedral, and members of Parliament marched in street demonstrations against the trial. In New York, a UN Security Council resolution was passed urging the South African government to offer amnesty to the defendants. Even Leonid Brezhnev, later to be Communist Party chief of the Soviet Union, but at the time the titular head of state as chairman of the Presidium of the Supreme Soviet, got in on the act. He sent a letter to South African president Hendrik F. Verwoerd appealing for clemency for Mandela and all of the accused.

It is unlikely that Brezhnev's particular letter had any effect on Judge Quartus de Wet, the dour president of the court that tried the Rivonia defendants. But the breadth and intensity of the global campaign, especially from the democratic countries, surely did. Eight of the nine defendants were found guilty, and the following day, as expected, the court reassembled to hear the sentence. As de Wet began to explain the argument behind the decision he was going to announce, there was a tense silence in the entire courtroom. "The crime of which the accused have been convicted, that is the main crime, the crime of conspiracy, is in essence one of high treason," he said.

The state has decided not to charge the crime in this form. Bearing this in mind and giving the matter very serious consideration I have decided not to impose the supreme penalty which in a case like this would usually be the proper penalty for the crime, but consistent with my duty that is the only leniency which I can show. The sentence in the case of all the accused will be one of life imprisonment.[58]

"THE PRISONER IS QUITE RIGHT"

A great collective gasp erupted in the courtroom when the verdict of life imprisonment, as opposed to death, was announced.[59] The defendants smiled at each other openly. But the joy was short-lived. Around midnight, the prisoners were roused from their cells and driven to a military airfield outside Johannesburg. From there, they were flown in a DC-3 to the place that was to be Mandela's enforced home for the next eighteen years. His first sojourn on Robben Island had been mercifully brief: two weeks. Now, as far as he knew, he might be there for decades.

For the first few years, Mandela's life was especially harsh. His personal cell was a six-feet by six-feet concrete structure with thick walls off a corridor in the B section building of the prison. It had a small window that looked out on the prison courtyard formed by the one-story, corrugated iron roofed buildings constructed in a seamless rectangle. For furniture there was a desk, a chair, a sisal mattress, three blankets, a rusted iron sanitary bucket, called a ballie, with a porcelain lid that contained water for washing and shaving. The bucket was placed in one corner of the room. The cell, in effect, was open to the corridor through a second, barred window.

Routine was, as in all prisons, infallibly predictable and rigid. Prisoners were awakened at 5:30 A.M. (though Mandela himself had always been up before this), given an hour and a quarter to tidy their cells, wash, and empty their ballies. Then they had to go out into the courtyard to wait for breakfast, a sloplike soup called mealie pap, consisting of a porridge of corn scraped from the cob, accompanied by "coffee" made from roasted corn mixed with water. After breakfast, the prisoners worked until noon— for the first few weeks crushing rocks into gravel in the courtyard—then had "lunch." This would consist of boiled mealies (i.e., corn still on the cob) and a drink called *phusamandla* (drink of strength), consisting of water, powdered mealies, and some yeast.

Mandela and the other prisoners were served their food in the courtyard and then went back to their cells to eat it. At 2:00 P.M. the prisoners were brought out to the courtyard to work until 4:00 P.M. Then they were sent back to their cell blocks for thirty minutes of cleanup in cold water (there was never any hot water) beneath seawater showers or in bathtubs made from galvanized metal buckets. Supper would be delivered at 4:30 P.M. Occasionally there would be a piece of vegetable amid the same mealie pap. At 5:00 P.M., the prisoners were locked in their individual cells. At 8:00 P.M. they were required to go to sleep. Neither the wire mesh–enclosed cell lights nor the corridor lights were ever turned off. The duty warder would himself be locked inside the prison corridor each night with the prisoners.

Humiliation piled on humiliation for Mandela and the other prisoners. The Asian and Colored convicts in the prison population would be given a chunk of bread with margarine; Africans were assumed not to like bread. They were required to wear short pants, because they were, well, "boys." From the very first week, Mandela protested vigorously against this particular deliberate humiliation. To his surprise, the warders provided him with long pants shortly afterward, but when he discovered that the other prisoners had not been similarly outfitted, he refused to wear them. It was not until three years later that long pants were provided for all of the prisoners, African, Colored, and Asians.

Letters and visits were the lifeblood of emotional sanity for all of the prisoners, and no less for Mandela. But these privileges were hedged about with restrictions. As a high-security political prisoner, Mandela was in the D category, the lowest. He was permitted just one brief letter and one visit from a "first degree" relative every six months. Letters were delivered to the prisoners in monthly mail calls after being read and, if necessary, censored. Though he yearned for news of his family as eagerly as anyone, Mandela would walk slowly forward to receive his letter, then wander back to his cell to read it there as though it were a matter of little importance to him. "I would not give the authorities the satisfaction of seeing my eagerness," he explains.[60]

Visits were cherished, yet were excruciatingly frustrating. Prisoners were not permitted to touch visitors in any way, even if they were wives, and had to conduct the stilted, thirty-minute meeting through a glass partition in a cubicle with an identical cubicle for the visitor on the other side of the glass. Conversations had to be in English or Afrikaans, and the warders might interrupt the conversation and inquire if an unfamiliar name came up in the conversation. When Winnie showed up for the first permitted visit in August 1964, she had already been banned for the second time, and as a result fired from her social worker position. Because of various pressures, Winnie was unable to see Mandela after that first visit for another two years.

Within months of Mandela's arrival at Robben Island after the Rivonia Trial, the warders moved the prison work out of the prison courtyard to a lime quarry at another part of the island twenty minutes' march from the prison. Though Mandela preferred the hearty, open-air work to chipping rocks in a courtyard, the glare from the reflection of the sun off the lime permanently damaged the tear ducts of his eyes, eventually requiring an operation. Things improved for all the prisoners in the 1970's when they were moved to the seashore to collect seaweed for export to Japan. Here the pleasures of the open air, of wheeling seabirds and passing freighters, helped punctuate the otherwise grim ordinariness of prison life.

At Robben Island it was strictly illegal to read any kind of newspaper, much less to possess one. But Mandela and his comrades sometimes found ways to bribe the guards to deliver them. The penalty for being caught was harsh: days in the isolation cell. Very early in Mandela's prison time on Robben Island, he was sent into the isolation cell for being found reading a newspaper that he had picked up from a guard. In isolation, there was no food for three days, no release from the cell at all, no exercise, and no company with any other prisoner.

Despite such intimidation, the prisoners, even when they couldn't obtain newspapers, found ingenious ways from day to day to stay informed not just about the outside world, but about the often byzantine world of the prison community itself. The wives of warders sometimes had affairs or got divorced. Information about such things was frequently picked up by the ordinary prisoners if they were on a work detail around the guards' quarters. As for Mandela, he never lost his professional instincts as a lawyer. When the Transvaal Legal Society yet again tried to disbar him, he successfully fought back with a barrage of legal complaints and demands, all of which had to be logged by the prison staff and dealt with by the legal staff of the Supreme Court. Transvaal eventually gave up.

In all of these experiences, courtesy turned out to be one of Mandela's most powerful weapons. Together with his inherent dignity as the former ward of a chief, he deployed courtesy in all situations, invariably either winning over the actual loyalty of his adversaries in the prison system, or at the very least earning their respect. One particularly brutal prison commander, Piet Badenhorst, had been sent to Robben Island in 1970 with the clear mission of demoralizing the prisoners and cracking down on what the authorities believed was a laxity that had developed in the institution. Badenhorst liked to insult prisoners face-to-face with coarse and obscene language. The very first day he arrived, he picked on Mandela.

Under Badenhorst's rule, warders began beating some of the common criminal prisoners. The politicals would be subjected to midnight searches of their cells in freezing weather, the guards often drunk and usually crude in their behavior. When a team of three state judges arrived for an inspection tour of the prison a few weeks later, Mandela immediately reported a beating to them, with Badenhorst fuming at his side and then threatening him with "trouble" afterward.

"Gentlemen, you can see for yourselves the type of man we are dealing with as commanding officer," Mandela told the judges calmly, not even glancing at Badenhorst. "If he can threaten me here, in your presence, you can imagine what he does when you are not here."

One judge turned to the others and commented, "The prisoner is quite right." Soon afterward, Badenhorst was transferred. But before he left, he showed an unexpected warmth toward Mandela, wishing him luck in his future. Mandela was struck by the change. "All men," he reflected later, "have a core of decency, and . . . if their heart is touched, they are capable of changing."[61] Once again, Mandela's own decency, his unassailable core of dignity, had broken through the savagery and brutality.

He became particularly close to one jailer, James Gregory, a white warder who guarded Mandela from 1966, when Gregory first arrived at Robben Island, until 1990, when, now back on the mainland in relative comfort, Mandela was released. At first a typical skeptic of ANC goals, Gregory was quickly won over by Mandela's courtesy, dignity, and extraordinary lack of bitterness. He astonished his jailer, on Gregory's first day at Robben Island, by looking at him levelly, and then saying, "Good morning, welcome to Robben Island."[62] The irony of a prisoner welcoming a jailer to his prison was immediate to both men. It was Gregory who broke the news of the death of Mandela's mother in 1968, and then, the following year, of his eldest son, Thembi, in a car wreck in the Transkei.

Thembi, at the time, was just twenty-three. Mandela was not permitted to attend the funeral of either his mother or his son.

Over the next two decades, Gregory spent more time with Mandela than any other white man did, and the two of them developed a relationship in which, to all intents and purposes, Gregory became Mandela's devoted follower, protector, and friend within the South African prison system. Gregory's son Brent also joined the prison service, inevitably coming to know Mandela well. The two of them would discuss Bible passages in prison together, for Brent was a devout Christian. Then, when tragedy struck Gregory's family, it was Mandela's turn to provide comfort.

Brent Gregory died in a car wreck at twenty-three also, exactly the same age as Thembi had been at his death. It was less than a year before Mandela's release, in 1989. Mandela, now at a comfortable prison farm outside Cape Town, took Gregory into the rose garden and held his hand for a long time. "Let's remember the good times we both had with Brent," Mandela said. "He was a wonderful child and I have a picture of him sitting here reading his Bible, discussing passages with me. He cared, and in a situation like this, that is a quality that is so rare." Then he said, "If there can be any consolation from this terrible thing, it is that you know where he is now."[63] When Mandela was finally released the following year, he wrote Gregory a short, but eloquent note recalling "the wonderful hours that we spent together during the last two decades."

Conditions at Robben Island gradually improved, at least in part because of Mandela's relentless, patient picketing of the authorities to change them. By 1977, compulsory manual labor for the prisoners was ended, and the political prisoners were confined to their own section of the prison. A tennis court was even created in the courtyard where Mandela had previously chipped at rocks, and he was one of the first prisoners to play there regularly. He continued his early morning exercise of running on the spot in his cell and performed a formidable daily routine of calisthenics: 100 fingertip push-ups, 200 sit-ups, 50 deep knee-bends, and even other exercises. He also began to plant vegetables in a small plot of dirt that had been wrested, after years of repeated requests to the authorities, from a portion of the courtyard near a wall. He read widely: Tolstoy, Steinbeck, Daphne du Maurier, the South African novelist (and later Nobel laureate) Nadine Gordimer.

But this more benign atmosphere was not to last for long. In June

1976 a major uprising broke out in Soweto, the gigantic black township outside Johannesburg. The spark that lit the conflagration was a new law requiring schools to use the Afrikaans language for half of the secondary school instruction. As rioting and shooting swept over Soweto and other cities, Robben Island began to fill up with a new brand of political prisoner: angry, confrontational, and often utterly fearless. Many of them belonged to the Black Consciousness Movement (BCM), a militant antiwhite grouping that had sprung up after the ANC had been banned. There were tensions between some of the younger arrivals and the older ANC prisoners, as well as among the ANC, the PAC, and the BCM.

Mandela wrestled with the question of how to deal with this new, chip-on-the-shoulder defiance. Should he angrily rebuke these upstarts, so disrespectful of the older African political prisoners? Should he side with them? Instinctively, Mandela chose to be a mediator. "I regarded my role in prison not just as the leader of the ANC but as a promoter of unity, an honest broker, a peacemaker," he said, "and I was reluctant to take a side in this dispute."[64] Though this move angered some of the ANC members who had been beaten up by the new arrivals, it resulted in a great influx into the ANC of many of the new militants.

HALFWAY HOUSE WITH WINE

In 1982, Mandela and four other top ANC colleagues, including Walter Sisulu, were moved without warning to Pollsmoor Prison not far from Cape Town, in the beautiful wine country of the Cape. No reason was given for the change, but it was very welcome to all of them. The cell sizes were much larger, there was a separate cell with a table, chairs, and a bookshelf for study, and the food was enormously improved. The prisoners for the first time were permitted a broad array of news sources, including *Time* magazine and the *Guardian* from London, whose consistent antiapartheid perspective must have been a constant irritant to the South African government. Mandela was even permitted to work in a makeshift "garden" on the rooftop terrace for two hours each day, carefully tending plants and vegetables grown in soil-filled metal drums.

But the real reason for the government's prison switch became clear before long. The authorities had become increasingly convinced that Mandela was the only representative of the ANC, and indeed of the entire antiapartheid movement in South Africa, whom they could trust and to whom they could talk. In 1976 they had offered to release him from prison if he agreed to renounce all violence and then go to live in the Transkei. He refused, for it would not only have been a form of betrayal of his fellow prisoners but also an expression of approval of the government policy of African-only Bantustans. There were other conditional offers made after that, but he turned them all down.

In January 1985, in the South African Parliament, President Minister P. W. Botha reiterated the offer of freedom to Mandela and all political prisoners if they repudiated political violence. There were no restrictions placed on where Mandela might live. The proposal was as much a propaganda ploy as a serious offer, for Mandela could not have accepted this offer without tacitly accepting the government's right to control all political activity.

In response, Mandela, with the help of Winnie and his lawyer, dictated a reply to Botha that Mandela's daughter Zindzi agreed to read at a rally of the legal South African opposition group, the United Democratic Front. The reply cleverly turned the tables on Botha by challenging him and the Nationalists to make the major political changes essential to a new political peace in South Africa. In words that curiously foreshadowed President Reagan's 1988 challenge to Gorbachev in a speech in West Berlin, during which he faced Berlin Wall, Mandela said:

> Let him [Botha] renounce violence. Let him say that he will dismantle apartheid. Let him unban the people's organization, the African National Congress. Let him free all who have been imprisoned, banished or exiled for their opposition to apartheid. Let him guarantee free political activity so that people may decide who will govern them. . . .
>
> Only free men can negotiate. Prisoners cannot enter into contracts. . . . I cannot and will not give any undertaking at a time when I and you, the people, are not free. Your freedom and mine cannot be separated. I will return.[65]

Botha, of course, did not accept Mandela's challenge. That was left for his successor, F. W. de Klerk, to do. But the words carried such weight to them that they set in motion a process of conversation between Mandela and the ANC on the one side, and the Nationalists on the other, which once initiated, never came entirely to an end.

The first sign of something in the air was when Mandela was hospitalized for prostate surgery early in 1985, after the Botha offer. He had written to the minister of justice, Koebie Coetsee, suggesting an ANC-government meeting. There had been no reply, but an unexpected visitor to the Volks Hospital in Cape Town before the operation was Coetsee himself. He brought with him a case of Cape white wine. The conversation was genial and friendly, almost as if Coetsee and Mandela were old school friends, a bizarre form of communication for prisoner and jailer. But for Mandela, it was very definitely an "olive branch" from the government. Yet again, it was Mandela's unique character that enabled him to accept the gesture as one of good faith, rather than dismiss it cynically and bitterly, as others might have, as too little and too late.

The case of wine, in fact, was not just an olive branch, it was a whole olive tree. After surgery and a few days of recuperation, Mandela was not brought back to the cell area he had shared with Sisulu and the others, but was taken this time to a completely private cell. It was an intelligent move by the authorities, and Mandela immediately picked up on it. Essentially, it enabled Mandela to negotiate one-on-one with the government, something the Nationalists had always wanted to do. It was a situation that his ANC prison comrades, not to mention the ANC leadership in exile in Zambia, would certainly not have tolerated.

Mandela's decision, in fact, was possibly the bravest and most far-reaching of his political career. He had always bent over backward to pronounce himself a loyal member of the ANC, taking pains neither to say nor to do anything that might arouse the suspicion he was not under ANC "discipline." At the same time, the ANC and government positions were so locked in place in opposition to each other that no political breakthrough might ever have occurred in South Africa if Mandela had not single-handedly broken free and been willing to talk privately to his oppressors.

He told no one what he had in mind, sensing that if he did so his ANC colleagues in the same prison would have put word out to forestall any serious talks before they could happen. "There are times when a leader must move out ahead of the flock," he wrote later, "go off in a new direction, confident that he is leading his people the right way."[66] The decision led to cordial talks in Cape Town itself with Coetsee, who instantly grasped the delicate course Mandela was trying to carve out between the ANC and the government. The meeting encouraged Mandela enormously, for it convinced him that the government had finally decided that it simply could no longer govern the country along the old apartheid lines. Already, in 1986, more violent riots had broken out in South Africa's townships, forcing the government to impose emergency regulations once again, and compelling it to understand the urgency of the need for a political breakthrough.

Now the pace quickened. In a further strange initiative, Mandela was taken on the first of several private automobile rides, unguarded, around Cape Town. It was as though the authorities wanted him to become reacquainted with the real world outside prison. His first driver was Pollsmoor's deputy governor. Just as had happened on many earlier occasions, Mandela found himself alone in a car and unguarded when his affable tour guide had disappeared to buy two cokes in a cafe. Escape tempted him horribly. But he stayed put: "Such an action would be unwise and irresponsible," he concluded, "not to mention dangerous."[67] It was as if the Nationalists almost clung to the character and personality of Mandela as the one hope they had for a peaceful transition into a new South Africa.

During 1987 Mandela had more meetings with Coetsee. Now he wanted to embark on a systematic series of talks with him and other government officials. It was time, he now felt, to let his four ANC fellow prisoners in on the business. They were at first highly dubious. So were ANC members outside South Africa. From Zambian exile, ANC leader Oliver Tambo smuggled into the prison a message that he was worried about Mandela's actions. In fact, Mandela was not negotiating directly. He was trying to lay the groundwork not for an actual agreement with the government, but for conditions under which it and the ANC could talk. The next year, he held several secret meetings with a small committee organized by Coetsee, but directly in contact with Prime Minister Botha. It was now obvious that Mandela was no longer just a celebrated political prisoner, but a recognized player in the politics of South Africa. On his seventieth birthday in July 1988, he received birthday greetings from, among others, Pope John Paul II and Elie Wiesel.

The Botha regime had taken the plunge. It now seemed irrevocably committed to change through talks with Mandela. At the end of 1988, he was moved to what would be his final place of detention before freedom, the Victor Verster Prison Farm thirty-five miles northeast of Cape Town. Located amid the beautiful wineries of Cape Province, Mandela's new home was actually the residence of the deputy governor. This was a one-story cottage with a private swimming pool, a flower garden, and a comfortable bedroom, kitchen, bathroom, and living room. To cater to all of Mandela's culinary needs (he was on a low-sodium diet because of high blood pressure problems), the prison authorities provided him with his personal cook, Warrant Officer Swart, whose efforts were so good that outsiders began to comment on Mandela's supposedly "luxurious" new prison lifestyle. The following day, Koebie Coetsee showed up to say hello, once more bringing with him a case of Cape wine.

But though a halfway house to freedom, as the authorities made clear, the cottage at Victor Verster had another purpose: in privacy and security Mandela was able to meet not only with government officials, but increasingly as the year drew on, with ANC leaders, including his former comrades from Robben Island and Pollsmoor. He sent a memorandum to President Botha in March, asking for discussions that would lead to a framework of negotiations between blacks and whites. Botha, temporarily disabled with a stroke, didn't reply. But in July, out of the blue, he suddenly invited Mandela for a face-to-face meeting with him at the Tuynhuys, Cape Town's elegant official residence of the president. Though burdened with a reputation as an explosive, overpowering personality, Botha turned out, as Mandela described him during the brief, half-hour teatime meeting, to be "unfailingly courteous, deferential, and friendly."[68] The mere fact that the meeting took place, in Mandela's eyes, meant that Botha in his own way had now crossed the Rubicon of political change. He could not now step back from his effort to untangle the nation's agonized knot of racial tension.

Events accelerated in August 1989. President P. W. Botha resigned and was succeeded by F. W. de Klerk, a seemingly staunch supporter of apartheid throughout his life as a Nationalist Party politician. Archbishop Desmond Tutu, vigorous and longtime opponent of apartheid, sniffed at first that the change in presidents was "just a change of initials from P. W. to F. W."[69] But Tutu's assessment was later proved wrong. De Klerk was very different from any previous South African prime minister. He began to speak increasingly of the need for "dialogue and negotiations."

He initiated a whole series of changes in the style of apartheid rule that hinted at even more serious movement beyond them.

In October 1989 he announced the immediate release of Walter Sisulu and seven of Mandela's other former Robben Island ANC colleagues. The freeing of political prisoners had been the one demand that Mandela had made of Botha in their historic first meeting. De Klerk had presumably taken notice of this. He also began dismantling the last of the restrictions on racial equality in public places, the "petty apartheid" regulations requiring the segregation of parks, transportation, beaches, libraries, and so forth. He told the South African Parliament in his inaugural speech that he wanted "a totally changed South Africa." This approach was to put him on a collision course with the most conservative of the white South Africans, who had already begun forming groups dedicated to resisting, if necessary by force, any dismantling of apartheid.

Mandela, meanwhile, was being granted access while in Victor Verster to key ANC colleagues, to Winnie, and to his children. The enormous favor Mandela had won seemed to have irritated some of the newer ANC leaders. Cyril Ramaphosa, then the thirty-seven-year-old general secretary of the National Union of Mineworkers, puckishly observed that Mandela's status "was no different from the status of any other member."[70] It seemed that the ANC resented both Mandela's star-status and his role as the ANC's de facto top negotiator.

The entire year of 1989 riveted television viewers and newspaper readers around the world as Communist regimes collapsed one by one in Eastern Europe and as the Chinese ruthlessly clamped down on their own incipient democratic movement in Tiananmen Square. Within South Africa, though, the crucial discussions that would lead to the emergence of black South African political power were still shrouded in secrecy. Early in December 1989, Mandela was invited to the Tuynhuys in Cape Town for his first meeting with de Klerk. On this occasion, both men had carefully prepared themselves beforehand—Mandela by consulting with ANC colleagues, de Klerk by meeting with Coetsee and others who had been parties to the secret talks initiated in 1988.

The two men hit it off well. Mandela later said he thought de Klerk was echoing British prime minister Margaret Thatcher's description of Mikhail Gorbachev in 1985, "a man you can do business with." As for de Klerk, he told South African government colleagues that he considered Mandela "a man of integrity, a man you can trust."[71] During the next months and years, that initially warm mutual impression was to be qualified on both sides. Yet it served as a good augury for the extraordinary process of peaceful change the ANC had always originally sought and which the Nationalist government was now willing to try to implement.

In early February 1990, de Klerk informed a stunned South African Parliament that "the time for negotiation" with South Africa's black opposition had arrived. He announced that all legal restrictions on the ANC, the South African Communist Party, the PAC, and thirty-one other banned organizations would be lifted. Capital punishment would be suspended and political prisoners not convicted of any violent activity would be released. The event occurred for which black South Africans had prayed and campaigned for decades. On February 11 at 4:15 P.M., Mandela, accompanied by an almost unruly crowd of family members and supporters, walked out of Victor Verster Prison to freedom, just twenty-seven years, six months, and five days after first being arrested along a deserted road outside Durban. It wasn't an entirely smooth operation. His release was complicated by the late arrival of several of the delegation who wanted to accompany him on his walk to freedom, and in Cape Town there was rioting as crowds grew impatient for his scheduled arrival to make a speech. But when he finally arrived, he spoke graciously again, even describing de Klerk this time as "a man of integrity."

FREEDOM

When Mandela was picked up on a desolate stretch of road by the Pietermaritzburg police, he had been, in many ways, a cocky and pugnacious man. Oliver Tambo described the young Mandela as "passionate, emotional, sensitive, quickly stung to bitterness and retaliation by insult and patronage." The Mandela who came out of prison, says Richard Stengel, the *Time* writer who came to know Mandela well when helping him edit his memoirs, was obviously quite different. He prized above other qualities "rationality, logic, compromise." He actually distrusted "sentiment," the mainspring of his initial leap into the political opposition movement. "I came out mature," Mandela simply says of his prison years.[72]

In the first few days of freedom he found himself astonished by the press attention from all over the world. His home in Orlando West, Johannesburg, was virtually under siege the first night he was there, with ANC supporters outside singing celebration songs until the early morning hours. He was struck by how friendly many whites were toward him, both when he was being driven to Cape Town in triumph and in many encounters afterward.

If anything, the mood among blacks was more troublesome. During his twenty-seven years in prison much of the population in the black townships had functioned in conditions of near anarchy, boycotting school classes and sometimes enforcing vigilante justice on other blacks. At a massive rally in the Soweto stadium two days after his Cape Town release, Mandela openly criticized "those who use violence against our people"— meaning black activists—and urged an end to the education boycott that had been in effect, on and off, for several years. He also told his audience that though "the fears of whites" about their future in South Africa were an obstacle to progress toward democracy, blacks must "understand" those fears. His words were not especially appreciated by the restless young audience earlier so eager to celebrate his freedom.

On February 27, 1990, he flew to Lusaka, Zambia, for his first official discussions with the ANC leadership in exile. The ANC was eager to ensure that Mandela would not become a negotiating lone ranger, hoping to profit from his national and international prestige and popularity. For the next several months Mandela traveled to more than twenty countries around the world, being feted wherever he went and exhibiting the same combination of courtesy, personal modesty, and human warmth that had won him admirers again and again during his prison years. In Europe he was effusively greeted in Paris by French president François Mitterand. He was honored at an outdoor rock concert in London. On his first trip through the city, Prime Minister Margaret Thatcher scolded him by phone with friendly severity for agreeing wherever he went to too heavy a schedule of meetings.

Once in the United States, that schedule nearly exhausted Nelson Mandela. In New York, African-American Mayor David Dinkins gave him a triumphant ticker-tape parade down Wall Street. In Washington, he was invited in a rare honor to address a joint session of the U.S. Congress. At the White House he was treated by President Bush almost as though he were a visiting head of state. "No notes!" said Bush in gushing admiration

of Mandela's flawless speaking habits. "That's wonderful!"[73] Despite liking Bush personally (the president was the first foreign leader to
congratulate him by phone after Mandela's release from prison), Mandela
would not budge on one key issue of foreign concern over ANC policies.
He would not agree to renounce the use of force as a political tool until
the South African government permitted exiles to return to South Africa
and freed political prisoners (including those who had committed violent
acts). He also annoyed many Jewish leaders by continuing to praise Libyan
leader Mu'ammar Gadhafi and PLO chairman Yassir Arafat, and he irritated most conservatives by complimenting Cuba's Fidel Castro.

However gratifying the foreign plaudits were for Mandela, he knew
better than the ANC leadership how much distance there was to travel
down the road to real political change in South Africa. The first direct
ANC-government talks took place in May 1990, and Mandela was merely
one member of the delegation. These were the first of "talks about talks"
to establish the conditions for an actual negotiation over political change
in the country. It was not until some nineteen months later, after months
of bloodshed between the predominantly Xhosa ANC supporters and Zulu
activists from the Inkatha Freedom Party, that substantial talks to change
South Africa's political structure began in December 1991. These talks were
called the Convention for a Democratic South Africa (CODESA), and they
brought together for the first time representatives of virtually every serious political group in the country, not just the ANC and the Nationalists.

A second round of CODESA talks began in May 1992, but the negotiations foundered in an acrimonious debate over the nature of the framework
of South Africa's future political structure. It was not until June 1993 that the
multiparty CODESA convention agreed on universal-ballot elections in April
1994 to elect four hundred representatives to a constituent assembly.

For Mandela, freedom did not bring about unalloyed happiness. A deep
personal wound opened up in Mandela's life: separation, and finally divorce, from his once beloved wife, Winnie. The passionate relationship
had seemingly survived the almost impossible twenty-year period between
1962 and 1982 when the two could not even touch each other, much less
embrace. Winnie had defiantly resisted apartheid as vigorously during
Mandela's imprisonment as her husband had while still free. For this she
had been "banned" cruelly by the regime for several years, held in prison—
including stays in solitary confinement—twice, sent into internal exile

more than two hundred miles from her Johannesburg home, and finally had her Orlando West house mysteriously firebombed.

However, in contrast to Mandela, who acquired the grace to astound his jailers with his character and moral authority, Winnie became increasingly bitter, imperious in her dealings, and even vengeful. By 1986, for example, political violence against suspected government collaborators or police informants in the African townships had become truly ugly; by 1987 nearly four hundred black South Africans had been murdered by "necklacing," the practice of forcing a rubber tire over the head and shoulders of a victim, filling the tire with gasoline, and then igniting it. In April 1986, Winnie made the now infamous comment: "Together, hand in hand, with our boxes of matches and our necklaces we shall liberate this country."[74] These remarks were to come back again and again to haunt Winnie Mandela, even before her husband was released from jail.

A far more serious problem was her conviction in 1992 on charges of being involved in the kidnapping in 1988 of four Soweto black youths, one of whom, only fourteen, was later found murdered. The evidence against her was so clear that even the ANC began to consider her a liability. Despite this, Mandela loyally stood by his wife, at least in public, until 1992, when the two legally separated, and 1996, when he filed for divorce.

There were obviously deep political differences. But by now they had also come to differ profoundly on issues of faith and human decency. Simply put, Mandela wanted to forgive his erstwhile apartheid foes, while Winnie, representing the still-angry youth of the black townships, did not. Most sadly of all, Winnie had apparently avoided all physical intimacy with Mandela since 1990. "Ever since I came back from prison," he testified in the Johannesburg courtroom in March 1996, "not once has the defendant [Winnie] ever entered our bedroom while I was awake." At the divorce hearings, Mandela told the court that a newspaper editor had shown him a love letter written to Winnie by a much younger personal assistant. Winnie had committed adultery against him.

Despite this deep personal anguish, played out during the two years leading up to the 1994 election, Mandela did not let up in his pursuit of majority rule. He deployed the full force of his immense moral stature, his emotional self-discipline, and his stubborn persistence in continuing negotiations, even when the talks looked as though they had become deadlocked.

Two matters were of grave concern to both Mandela and the ANC. One was the often brutal clashes between ANC supporters and the Zulu members of the Inkatha Freedom Party. The other was the white fear that a new black majority would dominate them as unfairly as the whites had dominated the blacks. Only a Memorandum of Understanding signed by Mandela and de Klerk in 1992 assured the ANC that illegal police action, believed by some to be encouraging violent acts against the ANC by Inkatha, would not be tolerated. White concerns about an intolerant black majority were allayed by constitutional provisions for a five-year government of transition in the new South Africa.

With the deadlock broken, in June 1993 the CODESA met again, this time agreeing on an actual date for elections, April 1994. That move may have influenced the Nobel Peace Prize Committee in Oslo to award the 1993 prize to both de Klerk and Mandela. The two men traveled in separate delegations to the Norwegian capital to receive their prizes and make their respective speeches. It was obvious that there was tension between them. De Klerk felt that he was being upstaged by Mandela, who was still suspicious of the de Klerk government's role in the ongoing ANC-Inkatha tensions. Mandela nevertheless praised de Klerk in his speech as a man who "had the courage to admit that terrible wrong had been done to our country and people through the imposition of the system of apartheid."[75]

Only one obstacle appeared to remain to a peaceful transition to black majority rule in South Africa, and it was a very serious one. This was the refusal of Chief Buthelezi and Inkatha to participate in the process. Two weeks before the scheduled elections of April 1994, the Zulus were demanding a sovereign state in Natal province and were threatening a total boycott of the voting process. An international mediation team led by Dr. Henry Kissinger, former U.S. secretary of state, and Lord Carrington, former British foreign secretary and later secretary-general of NATO, had tried to bridge the gulf between the position of the ANC and that of Inkatha. By mid-April, the two gave up, with Kissinger dispiritedly telling a visiting Kenyan diplomat, Washington Okumu, that disaster was at hand. "I have never been on such a catastrophic mission and its failure now has cataclysmic consequences for South Africa," he said.[76]

But Kissinger had seriously underestimated Okumu, a deeply committed Christian who had made many close friends and contacts among the South Africans working respectively for de Klerk, Buthelezi, and

Mandela. All three men considered their Christian faith vital elements in their private lives and their public philosophies. With just days to go before the April 27 scheduled polling, Okumu came up with a formula that satisfied both Buthelezi's insistence on preservation of the Zulu monarchy and the ANC's demand that South Africa be a unitary, rather than a federal state.

When on April 19 de Klerk, Mandela, and Buthelezi all spoke on South African television, affirming that Inkatha would not boycott the elections after all, the relief was as huge as the amazement at it all. Faith had clearly played a role in the solution. "History has thrown up an authentic miracle," said *Time.* "Faith had role in Apartheid's end," read the headline in the Sunday *Boston Globe.* "How God stepped in to save South Africa," proclaimed the *Daily News* of Durban.[77]

As moving scenes of millions of black South Africans waiting for hours to cast their vote were beamed by satellite around the world, it became clear what Mandela had accomplished. As the results, overwhelmingly favoring the ANC, were becoming clearer, Mandela instinctively sought out his former adversaries to reassure them. His mission now, he said later, was "one of preaching reconciliation, of binding the wounds of the country, of engendering trust and confidence."[78] He said he wanted to congratulate de Klerk "for the many days, weeks, and months and the four years that we have worked together, quarreled, addressed sensitive problems and at the end of our heated exchanges were able to shake hands and to drink coffee."[79]

A few days later, on May 14, 1994, Mandela made his inaugural speech to an audience that included royalty, revolutionaries, and presidents from nations around the world, all assembled as witnesses to the "miracle" of apartheid's end without the nightmare of a civil war that almost all "sensible" observers had predicted would accompany it. Mandela, in his slow, almost pedantically ornate speech, declared:

> We, the people of South Africa, feel fulfilled that humanity has taken us back into its bosom, that we, who were outlaws not so long ago, have today been given the rare privilege to be host to the nations of the world on our own soil. . . .
>
> We have triumphed in the effort to implant hope in the breasts of the millions of our people. We enter into a covenant that we shall

build the society in which all South Africans, both black and white,
will be able to walk tall, without any fear in their hearts, assured of
their inalienable right to human dignity—a rainbow nation at peace
with itself and the world.[80]

Mandela's desire to work for racial reconciliation was startlingly illustrated in his phrase "we, who were outlaws." It was the white South African
government that had experienced global outlaw status, after all, not the
nonwhite people of South Africa. By identifying his own government, just
elected, with the "outlawed" white regime of the past, Mandela was essentially identifying himself with the full history of his country, not just
with part of it. It is hard to come up with a more magnanimous political
act in twentieth-century history—a triumphant new regime willing to
own up to the wrongs caused by its predecessor. That, of course, was
Mandela's doing.

And it was not his last act of reconciliation. With a crushing electoral
victory of 62.6 percent, the ANC had triumphed decisively over the Nationalists, who gained 20.4 percent, and Inkatha, which gained 10.4 percent.
It would have been a simple matter for Mandela to have initiated a judicial
witch-hunt for some of the worst agents of apartheid. Hunting down police
officers or jailers who had conducted tortures of ANC prisoners, or elite
South African military units who had operated raids on ANC hideouts
within South Africa or abroad, would have been hugely popular. Instead,
in June 1994, Mandela announced the establishment of a Truth and Reconciliation Commission charged with investigating the circumstances of
all apartheid-era crimes (including terrorist actions by ANC members
against suspected ANC dissidents) by whites and blacks. This was done
with the promise of amnesty for all those who came forward within a
year of the commission's coming into existence.

The amnesty initially applied to all crimes committed before December 10, 1993 (the date of formal completion of negotiations for transition
to multiracial rule). By mid-December 1996, more than three thousand
applications for amnesty had been received and more and more people
were demanding that the December 10 cutoff date be extended. After painful reflection, Mandela decided to extend it to May 10, the date of the first
constitutional elections in the country's history.

He extended the deadline, he told the South African Parliament, "because on balance I am persuaded that it will further consolidate nation-building and reconciliation in a manner that is all-inclusive."[81] The extension ensured that one of the most die-hard opponents of the incoming new regime, retired Afrikaans general Constand Viljoen, would be forgiven for an actual coup he had planned to coincide with the elections.

In light of his remarkable history, how can one best sum up Mandela? His weakness in balancing his personal and professional personas has resulted in two broken homes. His family life has been marred by sin and pain, some of which has been of his own making. As for his strengths, there are a multitude of adjectives to describe him. Words like *statesmanlike, magnanimous, dignified, honorable, patient,* and *gentlemanly* spring to mind.

Above all else, as we contemplate the story of Mandela, we see the virtue of forgiveness emerging again and again. Forgiveness always requires a conscious choice rather than a feeling, and there must have been times when Mandela consciously chose to forgive people for whom he had anything but natural empathy. There had to be incidents of injustice, brutality, and deprival to which forgiveness seemed a weak and unsatisfying response. It cannot always have come easily to him. Yet, decade after decade, Mandela chose to forgive.

For this reason, we see in his life a dimension of generosity and magnanimity in both political defeat and political victory that is rare in all of history. Mandela could have, after all, made his willingness to sit down with the enforcers of apartheid subject to a great wall of conditions. Those enforcers had oppressed his own people for centuries. But forgiveness is supremely a Christian virtue. Unless it is conferred on others without demanding anything in return, it is not genuine.

Mandela forgave unconditionally. And he chose to believe that by displaying dignity and by consciously withholding animosity, he could accomplish far more than he could possibly achieve armed with a fistful of ultimatums and threats. Although his beliefs ran against the grain of the post-Christian logic of the twentieth century, Mandela was right. For that alone—for the reintroduction of the virtue of forgiveness into the ravaged countryside of twentieth-century politics—Nelson Mandela is reckoned among the Great Souls.

CHAPTER 3

ALEKSANDR SOLZHENITSYN: TRUTH

"One word of truth shall outweigh the whole world."

—ALEKSANDR SOLZHENITSYN
Nobel Prize Speech, Oslo, 1974

IT WAS MAY 1989, and the lovely early spring of Vermont was spreading through the buds of birch trees and maples. At the general store of Cavendish, a hamlet of barely one thousand souls in the central portion of the state, a prominent sign on the wall sternly warned: "No restrooms, no bare feet, no directions to the Solzhenitsyns!"

With my assigned photographer, Steve Liss, I waited by arrangement at the village post office, opposite the general store. Around 9:00 A.M., a blue Mercury pulled up, driven by Leonard Dilisio, Solzhenitsyn's American secretary. Steve and I followed in a rental car as Dilisio guided us to the one-hundred-acre Solzhenitsyn compound, set in the hills behind the town. The winding county road was unpaved in parts. Nothing indicated who might live behind the wire fencing and the thick cluster of trees of the Solzhenitsyn estate; no mailboxes or nameplates, certainly no signs. Perhaps, years from now, a Vermont state historical marker will finally reveal that the greatest Russian writer of the twentieth century, and perhaps one of the greatest writers of any language, lived for eighteen years in this rustic corner of a modest, sometimes quirky part of New England.

When I met him face-to-face, the writer belied the almost forbidding figure I had unconsciously imagined from dozens of articles about him. Aleksandr Isayevich, his traditional Russian first name and patronymic, almost bounded out of the house to greet us, accompanied by his wife, Natalya. The patriarchal beard framed the bottom half of his face, but what was most striking about him were his piercing blue eyes.

I had anticipated, perhaps from the knowledge of his strong convictions, a certain sternness of expression. Instead, I found myself facing a broad, utterly charming smile and a sense of comforting informality. Solzhenitsyn wore a loose, khaki-colored Royal Robbins shirt outside brown pants and stood at ease in well-worn brown shoes. The skin on his face was fresh-looking, the almost red-tinged hair thinning and a little unruly. Just to the right of the middle of his forehead was a scar from a fall he had experienced during his youth. He was ready for the interview, eager to get started without further ado or small talk, but neither defensive nor suspicious in his manner. I took it to be a good omen.

I had followed the career of Aleksandr Isayevich Solzhenitsyn at different times throughout my adult life. As a student of Russian at Oxford in the early 1960's, I struggled through the first few pages of *One Day in the Life of Ivan Denisovich* in the original Russian, stunned by the vigor of the language and frustrated by the rich thieves' jargon of the camps that brings the tale so vividly to life. In those days, the best Russian-English dictionaries, all composed and printed in the Soviet Union, failed to acknowledge with a single entry the underworld of Stalin's Gulag network of prison labor camps.

Later, in graduate school and beyond, I watched from afar as this extraordinary writer took on the entire apparatus of Soviet power and somehow emerged triumphant from the struggle. I had certainly dreamed, perhaps like hundreds of others, of one day interviewing him. But I had dismissed the thought as a Walter Mitty fantasy, which any journalist, from time to time, does no harm by modestly nurturing.

But then serendipity—or Providence—struck, as it occasionally does in the lives of journalists. In the early spring of 1989, I happened to be the only fluent Russian speaker in *Time*'s Washington Bureau, other than bureau chief Strobe Talbott. It was then that Solzhenitsyn's U.S. publisher, Farrar, Strauss, persuaded the writer to give his first major interview in years to an American news organization. Talbott, later the deputy secretary of state in both Clinton administrations, could have done an excellent interview himself, but was kind enough to ask me to take on the job.

Farrar, Strauss was just coming out with the new and greatly enlarged version of Solzhenitsyn's novel *August 1914*. Would the writer be open to an interview?

Unspoken in this request was the publisher's awareness that Solzhenitsyn's name had lost some of its luster in the U.S., especially among ardent liberals, ever since his outspoken Harvard commencement speech of 1978. There he had harshly criticized some of the crassness of popular American culture and had blamed the U.S. media for actively contributing to it. He had also cited a decline in courage and values in the nation. American journalists, by and large, do not like being held up to negative scrutiny as a group by anyone, least of all by a foreigner who openly rejects some of the values they embrace.

What would the media reaction be to the new *August 1914*? Farrar, Strauss may well have wondered. They suggested the *New York Times*, or *Time,* as an avenue to express his ideas. Which would he prefer? *Time,* said the Nobel laureate, without excessive hesitation. Talbott asked me to deal directly with both the publishers and the Solzhenitsyn family to make arrangements for the interview.

But just arranging the first interview was no ordinary journalistic procedure. At the outset Solzhenitsyn ruled out any discussion of the momentous changes in the Soviet Union that had been touched off by the reforms of Mikhail Gorbachev. Yet it was precisely those views that would probably be the most interesting to our magazine's readers. Second, as far as possible, Solzhenitsyn wanted the topics raised to refer to literature, and indeed to his latest novel itself. Third, the Solzhenitsyn family— understandably, in light of some unpleasant experiences at the hands of certain journalists—wanted to be sure that what was printed as interview text was in fact what he had said. Essentially, he would have close to a veto over the material to be published.

I swallowed hard and went to work preparing for this extraordinary opportunity. I didn't realize at the time that the initial encounter with Solzhenitsyn would be the first of three meetings with him over a six-year period, ranging in location from Cavendish, Vermont, to Khabarovsk, in the Russian Far East, after the writer's return to his homeland five years later, and then to Moscow itself more than a year after he had settled back into the life of a Russian writer on Russian soil. In the course of that time, I became friendly with members of his family: his wife, Natalya, first, and later his son Yermolai, a remarkably talented linguist at home in three cultures: American, Russian, and Chinese.

But if the cliché that familiarity breeds contempt often applies to acquaintances with the famous or powerful, in the case of the writer Aleksandr Solzhenitsyn, the opposite was true. I never became "familiar" with him or his family, but I certainly came to know them more closely than most reporters. In doing so, my sense of awe about Solzhenitsyn's character and his gifts grew rather than diminished. Aleksandr Solzhenitsyn is not perfect, and he cannot readily be described as saintly. But in every other respect he comported with my own understanding of a truly great man, a person who had single-handedly, in many ways, changed the world in which we live.

The initial *Time* interview subsequently ran to four pages in the magazine and was well received, perhaps helping in a small way to untangle some of the confusing impressions about Solzhenitsyn that had coalesced in the decade and a half he had already spent in exile from his motherland. He had not taken comfortably to American culture and his stern criticism of some of its crasser characteristics had aroused much hostility against him. Partly because of his refusal while in the U.S. to embrace the culture and values of his adoptive land of refuge, partly because of his Harvard speech in 1978, some of the hostile impressions of Solzhenitsyn approached the absurd. He was referred to as a monarchist, or an anti-Semite, or an advocate of theocratic authoritarianism as an antidote to Communism. The 1989 *Time* interview gave him an opportunity to dispel some of those misconceptions.

But no amount of interviews, even by writers sympathetic to his views, will ever really do justice to Solzhenitsyn's achievements as a writer and a person. The majority of his literary work—more than five thousand pages of the Russian version of his *Red Wheel* cycle of novels—has still not been translated into English. It will probably take another thirty years before the literary measure can be taken of this particular epic in the context of the twentieth century's overall literary output. Nevertheless, Solzhenitsyn's stature as a Great Soul is already clear. Through the passion of his preoccupation with the truth about the effects of Communism on Russia, his brilliance as a novelist and a documenter of that truth, and his stubborn resistance to totalitarian dictatorship as a person, Solzhenitsyn demolished whatever was still left of the moral pretensions of the Soviet Union as a system of government and a global superpower. "It is you and your writing that started it all," an angry Russian almost shouted at him in an auditorium in Ula Ude in Siberia during Solzhenitsyn's long train journey across his homeland to Moscow in 1994, referring to the collapse of Communism and the end of global superpower status for both the Soviet Union and its successor state, Russia.[1]

The encomiums for Solzhenitsyn offer some indication of the writer's greatness. The Russian poet Yevgeny Yevtushenko, one of the first Russian writers to decry Stalinism in public in the Soviet Union in the 1950's, has referred to Solzhenitsyn as "our only living classic."[2]

Vadim Borisov, a Russian writer who has represented Solzhenitsyn's literary interests in Russia, has said: "When his epic historical cycle is read in its entirety, it will have the same significance for Russian literature as Dante's *Divine Comedy* has for European literature."[3]

David Remnick, a former *Washington Post* Moscow correspondent and author, and one of the most astute journalistic observers of the Russian scene today, has put it simply. "In terms of the effect he has had on history, Solzhenitsyn is the dominant writer of the century," he wrote in a seminal article on the writer shortly before Solzhenitsyn's return to Russia in 1994.[4]

The British journalist Bernard Levin, speaking of Solzhenitsyn's appearance on a British television interview in 1976, said that he could not recall any time in recent history when "a single man with no power—he wasn't a king, a dictator, a general—but with the power of the moral force of his own will and beliefs and character, has compelled the world to listen to him."[5]

Fellow Englishman Malcolm Muggeridge, commentating on the same television program, put it even more eloquently and simply. "He is the greatest man now alive in the world," he said.[6]

That 1976 judgment would probably not be accepted by many people in the 1990's. The world has moved far from the chilly tensions of the Cold War era and indeed from the great moral issues that to many seemed to underlie the U.S.-Soviet global rivalry. In the second half of the 1970's many commentators felt that, in the wake of the American debacle in Vietnam and Indochina, the survival of the West itself was at stake. Perhaps, they thought, the Soviet Union was actually winning the race for global hegemony. Solzhenitsyn was one of the few global public figures to reject the new U.S. administration policy of detente toward Moscow.

Insisting that the issues separating the Soviet approach to life from that of the West were profoundly moral in origin, Solzhenitsyn seemed to many to be summoning the West back to the taproots of its original moral and philosophical greatness. Others, of course, especially those worn out by the endless struggle of the Cold War, thought Solzhenitsyn at best a religious and philosophical crank, at worst a warmonger. Solzhenitsyn himself later admitted that he had fought the Communist "dragon" with a tone of voice that was uncomfortable to many in the Western world. "In the West," he explained, "one must have a balanced, calm, soft voice: one ought to make sure to doubt oneself, to suggest that one may, of course, be completely wrong. But I didn't have the time to busy myself with this. This was not my main goal."[7]

His main goal, of course, was the destruction of Communism in his homeland, although he did not start out with this intention.

POVERTY, THE YOUNG PIONEERS, AND LITERARY AMBITIONS

Solzhenitsyn was born, in fact, a year after the Bolshevik Revolution, on December 11, 1918. His birthplace, Kislovodsk, was a health resort in the Caucasus popular in prerevolutionary times among the Russian gentry. His mother, Taissia Zakharovna Sheherbak, gave birth to Aleksandr in circumstances of both grief and local political chaos. She was only twenty-three years old, and her husband, Isaaki, had been killed six months before the birth in a tragic hunting accident. At the time Isaaki, a former artillery officer who had served with the czar's armies against the Germans in World War I, was only twenty-seven.

Back and forth over Kislovodsk the armies of the Reds (the Bolsheviks who had seized power in a coup in Petrograd in November 1917) and the Whites (the various armies who rose up in opposition to the new Bolshevik regime) fought bitterly for two years, executing hostages and presumed opponents of their rule on the occasion of each capture and recapture of the town. Finally, by 1920, the Reds had triumphed over most of Russia, and Kislovodsk was firmly under Bolshevik control for the remainder of Communist rule in Russia.

Taissia, Solzhenitsyn's mother, lived with Roman, the brother of her late husband, and with Roman's wife, Irina. The family still occupied what had once been a comfortable home in the town, but were reduced by the pressures of famine in the surrounding countryside to sell off their furniture piece by piece merely to provide food to live on. Solzhenitsyn as an infant was comforted, he said later, by an icon—a devotional portrait of Jesus Christ commonly found in every Russian Orthodox church and in many pious Orthodox homes—that looked down on him in his bedroom, illuminated at night by a flickering candle. He also recalled vividly an incident in 1921 when Soviet troops rudely barged into a service of the Russian Orthodox church of St. Panteleimon, where his mother went regularly to worship. The toddler, insisting on seeing what the disturbance was all about, was lifted high by his mother to observe the scene.[8] He never forgot the incident.

His mother, meanwhile, was running out of money, and decided to move to the busy port of Rostov-on-Don (at the mouth of the River Don and the Sea of Azov, which leads into the Black Sea), where she took a course that qualified her to become a stenographer. Young Aleksandr stayed for two and a half years with Taissia's elder sister, Maria, in Kislovodsk, moving each summer to his aunt Irina's house in a village just outside Kislovodsk. When he was six, he was taken by train to Rostov to rejoin his mother.

The city suited him. Rostov was a lively, attractive town, the largest city in the North Caucasus. Because of her late husband's role as an officer in the czarist army, Taissia had difficulty finding work. She and Solzhenitsyn were reduced to living in a shack at the end of a dead-end street close to the center of the town. With no plumbing or running water, drinking and washing water had to be carried in by bucket from a pipe about 150 yards from the house. In this run-down, impoverished home Solzhenitsyn grew up through his school years, from 1924 until 1936, until he was eighteen. His mother never remarried, although it would have helped her and her son financially if she had.

She doted on Solzhenitsyn but was probably relieved when he began to spend a few weeks each summer with his aunt Irina and her husband, Roman, who had moved to a small fishing town not too far from Rostov. Solzhenitsyn had learned early to fend for himself, the "man" of the two-person family. He liked to be alone, to wander in the countryside during his vacation period, and above all to indulge himself in the rich library of Russian classics that his aunt had somehow saved. At a very early age he became familiar with the great writers of nineteenth-century Russian literature, Gogol, Turgenev, Dostoyevsky, and Tolstoy. He claims to have read Tolstoy's

War and Peace when he was only ten years old, a feat of astonishing precocity. He also read in translation Shakespeare and the American writer Jack London, a perennial twentieth-century favorite of Russian readers.

Irina's influence on Solzhenitsyn was not only literary. She was a woman of deep Russian Orthodox Christian conviction, and she regularly attended the small local church. During the summer vacation months, Solzhenitsyn went with her, absorbing, perhaps unconsciously, the rhythms and rituals of the ancient Russian faith, and hearing from Irina how central Orthodoxy was to the history and identity of Russia itself. Family conversation at his aunt's home was open and invariably critical of the Bolshevik regime; the revolution had been a disaster for both sides of the Solzhenitsyn family. Inevitably, what he was hearing from his own family differed sharply from the revolutionary propaganda being peddled constantly at school and in society at large. He was, Solzhenitsyn admits, "slow in coming to terms with the Soviet world."[9]

But he was not slow in discovering his destiny as an artist. "From the age of nine I knew I was going to be a writer," he told me in 1989 in our first interview, "though I didn't know what I was going to write about." His literary mind was filled with the rich material of classical Russian literature: the following year, it was bowled over by the genius and range of Tolstoy. At school, Solzhenitsyn's quick intelligence and far-reaching curiosity made him popular with the teachers at the Pokrovsky Gymnasium. This joint elementary school and high school in Rostov enjoyed an excellent reputation going back to prerevolutionary times. During this period, he began to fill notebooks with literary efforts, including one tale called "Science Fiction Story," completed in 1929, and a journal called *Twentieth Century*, with a subtitle essentially revealing, decades in advance, the literary preoccupation of Solzhenitsyn's entire life: "On the Meaning of the Twentieth Century."[10]

Unlike many children or adolescents who show literary precocity at an early age, only to abandon such pursuits in adulthood, Solzhenitsyn revealed a sense of identity as a writer essentially as early as he could hold a pen in his hand and put thoughts on paper. For the entirety of his life he never once stopped writing, even when the physical conditions of imprisonment demanded that he compose and memorize only in his head.

Three childhood incidents made indelible impressions upon him. The first was when, at the age of ten, members of the Young Pioneers, the heavily Communism-orientated Soviet version of the Boy Scouts, ripped from his neck the cross he had worn since early childhood. The ridicule he received from Young Pioneers after this, and the intense peer pressure to join their organization eventually had their effect: Solzhenitsyn decided to join at the age of twelve.

The second incident took place about a year later, and literally left a scar on him for the remainder of his life. A schoolyard scuffle over possession of a knife led first to a cut on the hand, and then, when the blood began to flow, a fainting fit. Solzhenitsyn collapsed against a doorpost on his way to having his hand washed, leaving a deep gash on his right forehead that never properly closed and is visible to this day. Evidently, the sight of blood sometimes resulted in Solzhenitsyn's fainting later on in life, creating some embarrassment when he joined the Soviet army as a young man and was required to undergo vaccinations.

But the third event was in some ways more symbolic for the remainder of Solzhenitsyn's years as a witness to the tyranny of Communism. His mother had become friends with a young, highly talented engineer, Vladimir Fedorovsky, whose wife, Zhenia, was the daughter of Taissia's former teacher. Solzhenitsyn himself had spent much time socially in the Fedorovsky household as a precociously intelligent and independent young boy, enjoying what he could grasp of the stimulating adult conversation. Then, in March 1932, at the very height of the Stalinist purges of suspected "wreckers" and "saboteurs" of the new Soviet economy (i.e., anyone remotely suspected of an independent view of life), Solzhenitsyn was about to enter the Fedorovsky household when he witnessed a nightmarish scene. Fedorovsky was being arrested by Stalin's secret police, the OGPU, to use the Russian abbreviation of the organization, and taken away in a large car. It was his first direct experience of the Soviet terror of mass arrests, and it was to embody, in some respects, the theme of his major work, *The Gulag Archipelago*.

Solzhenitsyn and his mother lived in conditions that by today's standards would be considered destitute. Shoes and clothes, however worn or stained, would have to last for two years or more before being replaced. Water had to be fetched from a location outside the home. There was never really enough food or warmth. Yet few of his school friends were much better off in the 1930's, a time when to the privations of Stalin's massive collectivization policies was added the almost total absence of any consumer goods. The only modest luxury that became available to the serious, energetic youth was a bicycle, which he was given by the school in 1936 as a high achievement award. The next summer and the two following, he and two friends bicycled far and wide through the Caucasus, visiting many of the locations made famous by the great nineteenth-century writers of classical Russian literature.

Despite his poverty, the shattering experience of the Fedorovsky arrest, and the huge political tensions of the mid-1930's, Solzhenitsyn seems to have both flourished in school and embraced with zeal everything the still-new Communist regime in Russia stood for. (In 1935, the Soviets had been in power eighteen years—as long, in fact, as the Islamic Republic of Iran had been in existence by the year 1997.)

By 1936 he had formed the basic outline in his mind of what was to become his life's literary achievement, *The Red Wheel*. This cycle sums up, through the medium of fiction, the tragic cycle of revolution and tyranny that was to be Russia's experience throughout most of the twentieth century. The work was to be "a big novel about the Revolution." At this point, he labeled the multivolume project simply *R-17*.

Solzhenitsyn's approach to the Revolution was warm and enthusiastic. His exposure at school and within the Young Pioneers to the Communist view of Russia's history had made a deep impression on him. Yet he also understood that it would be impossible to comprehend how and why the Revolution had taken place in Russia at all without first studying Russia's involvement in World War I. That provided him, thirty-five years ahead of time, with much of the essential material for the first *Red Wheel* novel, *August 1914*, which was published in 1971. Solzhenitsyn in 1937 and 1938 researched intensively the Russian military campaign of 1914 in East Prussia.

By attaining the highest scores possible in high school academic performance, fives in all subjects, Solzhenitsyn was easily accepted into Rostov University. Literature was not a university subject, and it would have been both financially difficult and politically risky in the paranoid 1930's to try to embark on a literary career as a young man. Solzhenitsyn took a much safer option: majoring in physics and mathematics during the three years he spent in college.

The bright and passionate young man had by now been completely won over by Marxist-Leninist thought. Like virtually all other Young Pioneers, he had transitioned at the age of seventeen to the Konsomol, the Young

Communist League. While many, perhaps most, of the Konsomols simply went along with the routine of Communist indoctrination with neither special zeal nor real skepticism, Solzhenitsyn was not one for half-measures. While pursuing his formal academic studies at the university, he read as much as he could of the Marxist-Leninist classics, increasingly convinced of the correctness of their view of life.

Aleksandr and his closest friend, a high school classmate named Vitaly Vitkevich, devoured the works of Lenin as though they were holy Writ; in the Soviet context of the day, of course, they really were. Yet even then, the admiration for Lenin did not at all extend to admiration for Stalin. Privately—and later, with profound consequences for each of them—the two young men despised Stalin, convinced that it was only Stalin's diversions from Leninist doctrine that had brought about the crueler and highly questionable aspects of Soviet life.

They were both entranced by the world of knowledge and scholarship, so they decided to enroll as external students in Moscow's Institute for the Study of Philosophy, Literature, and History (MIFLI according to the abbreviation in Russian of its full name). Vitkevich chose to study philosophy, and Solzhenitsyn chose literature. After traveling to Moscow in the summer of 1939, just before their final year at the University of Rostov, the two spent an idyllic three weeks exploring the Russian countryside, traveling by dugout canoe up the Volga River.

This outing with his closest friend came hard on the heels of a marriage proposal Aleksandr had made to Natalya Reshetovskaya. A young and pretty student of chemistry whom he met at the university in 1936, she was also a gifted pianist. Their "dating" had been eccentric in the extreme, even by the strict standards of Soviet customs in the 1930's. Solzhenitsyn was—as he has remained throughout his life—extremely conscious of the need not to waste time. If his fiancée showed up five minutes ahead of time and he was still studying, he would ask her to wait another few minutes until he was ready. He was brusquely unsubtle in some of his conversations with her. He didn't like the idea of having children, he told her in advance, and he was worried that their marriage might interfere with his literary plans and her professional ones. They told no one in advance about their engagement other than intimate friends. When they went ahead formally with the marriage in April 1940, they were wed in the Rostov city registry office with no family members present.

That summer, the last one before their final university year, Natalya, Vitaly, and other fellow students in chemistry studies took the train to Moscow to study chemistry at a Moscow scientific institute. Solzhenitsyn followed a short time later to take more of his needed exams at MIFLI. It was not until June that he and his bride were both in a position to take a honeymoon away from fellow students and the rest of Moscow. From an uncle of Natalya they borrowed a simple dacha, or country cottage, in a delightful rural area outside of Moscow.

Even then, the zealous student of philosophy and apprentice writer was not content merely to relax in the normal pleasures afforded by the first few weeks of marriage. In the mornings, he was up early reading Karl Marx. He may not have been unique, but he was surely rare as the bridegroom who spent much of his honeymoon devouring *Das Kapital*. Finally, from the bucolic surroundings of Tarusa, outside Moscow, where their modest dacha was located among the often sumptuously well-appointed country homes of the Moscow cultural elite, the young couple took the step of informing their parents of the union.

We do not know how Solzhenitsyn's mother received the news. She was already going downhill physically as the first stages of tuberculosis took their toll on her body. But Aunt Irina, whose childhood influence on Solzhenitsyn had been enormous, was not pleased. She was unwilling to recognize as a valid marriage any union in her family that was not sanctified in an Orthodox church. The suddenness and the secretiveness clearly rankled the family.

For Solzhenitsyn, this expression of disapproval was surely hurtful, but only additional evidence that the new "science" of Marxism-Leninism into which he had thrown himself required decisively parting company with the old ways. During his last year at the university, in 1941, he pursued Marxism feverishly, editing the student newspaper and continuing to reap accolades for his academic achievements. He had been awarded a Stalin scholarship for academic achievement, and this provided a stipend considerably higher than a normal student scholarship. His diligent Konsomol and editorial work would certainly have opened the door to full membership in the Communist Party and probably a brilliant academic or literary career within the bosom of Soviet society. But this was not to be.

Instead, events from far outside his own universe came crashing into it. On June 22, 1941, the Nazi military juggernaut roared across the borders of

Poland into the Soviet Union, marking Hitler's most ambitious, and ultimately disastrous, military gamble of World War II. From henceforth, Solzhenitsyn's life tumbled through unforeseen and often terrifying circumstances that he would never have chosen. The often nightmarish ride might well have killed most men, and it would have cowed the rest into silence and fear. For Solzhenitsyn, it became the providential pathway to indomitable character. It became his course into national leadership in a crusade for truth about his nation's twentieth-century history. And ultimately it became the impetus of his worldwide acclaim as one of the greatest literary and moral figures of the era.

On the afternoon of June 22, Moscow was in near panic. The total surprise of the German invasion was as shattering as its staggering power. Stalin, though warned in advance that a German attack was imminent, had been unable or unwilling to cope with this possibility. At MIFLI, the decision was quickly made to abandon all regular coursework. Many students simply went directly to their local draft stations to sign up. Solzhenitsyn also wanted to volunteer instantly, like thousands of other Soviet youths, but he had left his draft card back in Rostov, and he was not accepted at the Moscow registration points.

Infuriated, he returned to Rostov as quickly as he could, seeking to enroll there. But he was rejected on grounds of marginal physical fitness stemming from a groin condition that had not been properly treated in childhood. Now he had to fall back on the only professional opening available to him as a recent university graduate, an assignment as a village teacher to a rural hamlet called Morozovsk, some 180 miles northeast of Rostov. Natalya, to the relief of both of them, was given a job teaching chemistry in the same village.

Had the war gone differently, Solzhenitsyn and Natalya might have remained in their rural backwater for months or years longer. But the news of the German advance continued to worsen. By mid-October, the Nazi military tide was lapping at the outskirts of Moscow. In a desperate effort to stop it, the Soviet high command ordered the mass mobilization of every able-bodied male who had still not gone off to the front. Along with many of the Cossacks of the region, Solzhenitsyn found himself drafted into a rear-area unit responsible for military transportation using horses. Despised both for his city and educated style and his incompetence with horses, Solzhenitsyn was soon reduced to such basic chores as mucking out the manure in the stables. It was a humiliating occupation, especially since it was far removed from the glamour and excitement of the front.

After repeatedly pestering his superiors, he succeeded in being assigned as the courier of an official packet to the nearest main military headquarters of Stalingrad on the Volga. The desperate fighting that was to make the city's name an emblem of Soviet resistance to the Germans was still many months away. Solzhenitsyn persuaded key officers in the cadre department that his university degree and his mathematics training made him ideal material for the Soviet artillery. After a false start with one artillery unit, which discovered he had not even had basic officer's military training, he was assigned in the spring of 1942 to the Third Leningrad Artillery School's course in Kostroma, north of Moscow.

Aleksandr was instructed in the newly emerging art of artillery instrumentation through acoustics—locating and targeting enemy artillery by measuring sound wave patterns. By October 1942, he graduated from the course as a second lieutenant. He had been outraged by the triviality of the harsh officer training course with its endless punishment drills and constantly inadequate food. But now it seemed to have been worth it all. He was exhilarated to be embarking on a patriotic pathway in artillery, the very segment of the Russian army in which his own father, whom he had never known, had served during World War I.

As the Germans surged deeper into the Caucasus and the Crimea in 1942, Solzhenitsyn's unit tracked and backtracked across central Russia. The only contact for the first two years with Natalya was by letter, and his correspondence shows an astonishing intellectual preoccupation with his writing projects despite the hectic pace and intense life of a Soviet military officer. He also wrote with enthusiasm to his university friend Vitaly Vitkevich, who had become an infantry officer in a different part of the front.

Despite the titanic nature of the ongoing military struggle, he and Vitkevich—fatefully, as it turned out—resumed their discussions of possible future political options for their country. At one point, they even drew up a political manifesto, "Resolution Number One," for an imaginary new political party. Solzhenitsyn was still an ardent Leninist and Marxist, but he knew enough about the incompetence and corruption of Communist Party life in the Soviet era to grasp that life in his country would never significantly improve unless political changes took place. He despised Stalin and made disparaging comments about him.

In July and August 1943 the Germans fought furiously for Orel and Kursk in central Russia, gambling their last available reserves on breaking through the slowly consolidating Russian lines. In August, Solzhenitsyn was awarded the Order of the Patriotic War for gallantry in battle. In May 1944, he succeeded in arranging, through his sympathetic senior officers and various false ID's, to have Natalya live in uniform as an orderly in his own unit.

Despite the intense regimentation and militarization of Soviet society, the breakdown of order caused by the war made such arrangements possible, although they were rare. Nonetheless, the young couple were not moving forward harmoniously. What Solzhenitsyn wanted from his marriage was a literary partnership, without children, with a woman who was also feminine and attractive; what Natalya wanted was a normal life where husband and wife could share a romantic attachment without interference by the world. After a few weeks, to the evident relief of both, Solzhenitsyn's superior officer said that Natalya must return home.

This parting was undoubtedly less traumatic than the news that finally reached him in March that his mother, Taissia, had died two months earlier from tuberculosis. The information was all the more brutal for its delay in reaching him. Like many young men who had been doted upon by their mothers, Solzhenitsyn probably at times took her for granted until, all of a sudden, she was no longer there to be the emotional backstop of his life. Along with the normal burden of grief, he must have borne the added weight of personal remorse, since she had died sick and virtually destitute.

By the end of 1944, the tide of military success had totally run out for the Germans. The Soviet forces were now pushing them back from Poland into Germany itself. Solzhenitsyn had been promoted to captain, and evidently enjoyed the various privileges of position available to a Soviet officer. Long gone was the enforced egalitarianism of officers and men of the early Soviet period. In its place were epaulettes and a shiny leather belt, side arms in a holster and a star on the cap.

Meanwhile, in his correspondence with Vitaly, Aleksandr was eager to explore the political ideas and speculation that had drawn them together in the first place. In one letter he had referred to Stalin not by name—out of a perfunctory worry that military censorship might disapprove—but by the term, "the moustachioed one," a Russian word that also meant, in general, something like "gang leader." It was a terrible error.

"ME? WHAT FOR?"

By January 1945 the Soviet advance had taken Solzhenitsyn's unit into East
Prussia and its handsome capital, Königsberg, the location of Russia's initial
advances against Germany during World War I. Solzhenitsyn had familiar-
ized himself with the area during his youthful library researches into the
nature of World War I back in Rostov. It was exciting to be on the very
ground over which his father had fought in Samsonov's army in 1914, seeing
firsthand the scenes of what he undoubtedly hoped would be the locale of
his future literary work. Rifling through an abandoned German farmhouse,
Solzhenitsyn came across a German book with small photographs of famous Russian figures, including the late Tsar and Stalin's archrival Leon
Trotsky, who had been murdered in exile in Mexico in 1940. He neatly cut
the pictures out of the book and kept them. Another error.

The Soviet forces were amassing troops, vehicles, and equipment for
their final push against Berlin. Solzhenitsyn's unit was busier than ever, so
it was not a surprise to him when he was told on February 9, out of the
blue, to report to the office of the Forty-sixth Army's commanding officer, Brigadier General Zakhar Travkin, who liked and admired him. The
general, to his surprise, asked him to step forward and hand over his re-
volver. Then two officers he had never seen before suddenly stepped out
of a group of men gathered on one side of the room and shouted, "You're
under arrest!"

"Me? What for?" answered Solzhenitsyn, who was genuinely puzzled.

The men didn't reply, but instead ripped the officer's epaulettes from
Solzhenitsyn's shoulders and the star from his cap. They also took away
his belt. Clearly something alien, something political was happening. The
two aggressive officers were not regular army officers at all, but belonged
to the Soviet counterespionage unit, SMERSH, an acronym for the Russian words *Smert shpionam!* (Death to Spies!). And Solzhenitsyn was now
caught in its talons.

Bewildered, shocked, and convinced—as political prisoners during the
1930's in the Soviet Union were almost always convinced—that some terrible mistake had been made, Solzhenitsyn began to move toward the door
with his captors. Travkin, amazingly, told him to wait. "Have you a friend
on the First Ukrainian Front?" he asked Solzhenitsyn carefully, in an act of
almost insane bravery in front of SMERSH agents. Angrily, the two men

ordered the general to be quiet. It was forbidden to speak to prisoners under arrest. But the question had gotten through to Solzhenitsyn. Of course—Vitaly, his friend from Rostov. Despite Solzhenitsyn's almost contemptuous view of the military censorship, they had not only read his letters, they had detected treason in them. "I wish you happiness, Captain," Travkin said gravely, extending his hand for Solzhenitsyn to shake. And so the long nightmare began.[11]

The two SMERSH officers were so inexperienced with real combat situations that at first they drove off in the wrong direction, drawing salvos of German artillery shells down on them. They stopped, then sheepishly asked Solzhenitsyn to help them find the way back to their headquarters. It was night, and they knew nothing about reading maps. Solzhenitsyn obliged. He was convinced that before long everything would be resolved and he would be a free man once again.

But he was desperately wrong. From the makeshift counterespionage headquarters, he was marched for forty-five miles over two days to a railroad station in Poland from where a train could be taken into Belorussia. He found himself among a handful of "liberated" Russian prisoners of war who were being moved from imprisonment in an enemy state to imprisonment in their own country. Stalin believed that any Russian soldier—any among hundreds of thousands—who surrendered to the Germans or who had been captured by them was a traitor and potentially a dangerous source of political discontent within the Soviet Union.

As they trudged along, Solzhenitsyn insisted, as an officer, that they carry his small suitcase. Another grotesque reversal of roles occurred when, after taking the train from Minsk to Moscow, Solzhenitsyn's SMERSH escorts admitted that they did not know the location in Moscow of the Lubyanka Prison, the terrifying destination of all political arrestees in the city. Once again, Solzhenitsyn, familiar with the city from his summer stints at MIFLI, helped them out. It was not the last time he reluctantly found himself compelled to cooperate with the agents of Stalin's political tyranny.

Aleksandr Solzhenitsyn had been sucked into the hideous maw of Soviet totalitarianism. The early stages of arrests of political prisoners in the Soviet Union had been designed to humiliate, shock, and finally subdue even the most recalcitrant prisoner. In the windowless subterranean recesses of the Lubyanka, Solzhenitsyn was repeatedly ordered to strip naked for a thorough body search, for a shower, for a medical examination, even for an obligatory shaving of his entire body hair from the crown of his head to his private parts.

Solzhenitsyn found one of the most distressing of all the regulations to be the one that required all prisoners to keep their arms outside their blankets when they slept at night. A 200-watt bulb burned in each cell day and night, and warders frequently glimpsed into the cells through peep-holes in the door, so the slightest infringement of the rule resulted in an instant and rude awakening by a warder barging into the cell. In his masterpiece about the Soviet prison system, *The Gulag Archipelago*, Solzhenitsyn dwells on this feature of the treatment of inmates with special irritation.[12]

In fact, it was a general rule of thumb for all Soviet prisoners to be deprived of sleep almost round the clock during their period of initial interrogation. Taken to its refined conclusion, deliberate sleep deprivation was the most general form of torture in the Soviet prison system, and was sometimes referred to as "the conveyor." The disorientation, the loss of alertness, and finally the physical agony that resulted from enforced wakefulness was usually enough to subdue the most obstinate prisoner into a willingness to agree to sign anything put in front of him. Sometimes, these "confessions" related to crimes the prisoner could not conceivably have committed because he was physically in a different place. It was generally understood that "the conveyor" would succeed in breaking down a prisoner even if he had somehow resisted "old-fashioned" physical beatings or worse forms of duress. After three days of sleep deprivation the poisoning of the system would be so complete that a prisoner would agree to do almost anything to permit the body to recapture its stability. Some prisoners were deprived of sleep for as long as a week, which resulted invariably in total collapse.[13]

In Solzhenitsyn's case, no such extreme measures were needed during the four days of his interrogation. Still a "Soviet man," to use the jargon of the system, that is, a believer in the fundamental cause of Communism and in the rightness of the Soviet system, Solzhenitsyn eagerly anticipated that once he could explain everything to the authorities, he would be off the hook. He was terribly mistaken. He soon learned that the only purpose of the interrogation was to provide as much tendentious evidence as possible to demonstrate the guilt of the accused and to frighten the prisoner into signing any confession brought in front of him. Dragged from his cell during the night hours, when virtually all interrogations took place, Solzhenitsyn was shocked to discover that his investigator, I. I. Ezepov, had on his desk the intercepted correspondence with Natalya, Vitkevich, his partner in political speculation, and Kirill, another college friend from Rostov.

The MVD (Russian initials for Ministry of Internal Affairs) officers had also extracted the copy of "Resolution Number One," from his map case. The rude comments about Stalin in Solzhenitsyn's letters ("the moustachioed one"), the discussion of how Leninism had become corrupted in recent years, the portentous demand for a new Leninist Party in Resolution Number One—all these were ample proof for the cynical Ezepov that Solzhenitsyn was guilty under Article 58, paragraph 10, of the Soviet criminal code: "propaganda or agitation containing an appeal to overthrow, undermine, or weaken the Soviet regime, or to commit individual counter-revolutionary acts." But what Ezepov wanted to add to Solzhenitsyn's charge sheet was clause 11: "any type of organizational activity directed towards the preparation or commission of crimes dealt with in the present chapter."[14]

Desperate to protect Vitkevich, Natalya, and Kirill from any possible taint in these matters, Solzhenitsyn protested that his letters to them had been almost entirely focused on family and inconsequential experiences relating to his separation from them during the war. But for Ezepov an "organization" was any human aggregation that consisted of more than one person. To Solzhenitsyn's timid protests he offered the unattractive alternative of beginning the interrogations all over again, perhaps under much harsher physical conditions.

In fact, Solzhenitsyn had been transferred in the middle of his investigation to a cell that eventually contained four other inmates, all of them caught up in the lunatic paranoia of Soviet judicial vindictiveness at the end of World War II. One was an "old Bolshevik" who had known Lenin before 1917, traveled to North America, then returned only to be arrested in the great vacuuming up of potential political opponents in the 1930's. One was an Estonian lawyer. One was a Russian who was the cell stool pigeon. The fourth was a peasant-turned-engineer who had benefited from the revolution only to grow arrogant from greed and power in his job in Central Asia. It was from these men that Solzhenitsyn first began to see close-up, as it were, through the microscope of upturned individual lives, just what Soviet power had wrought in his beloved Russia.

While the interrogations and the waiting for sentences wore on, World War II came to an end. On May 9, the Lubyanka inmates heard Moscow erupt in the biggest fireworks display ever as the entire citizenry celebrated the defeat of the Nazis. Not long afterward, his judicial stage of arrest now over, Solzhenitsyn was moved to another Moscow prison, the Butyrki, to await sentencing and transfer to what were to become a series of "islands" in the "archipelago" of prisons, labor camps, and transit stops that comprised the entire "Gulag Archipelago."

The word *gulag* is yet another Russian acronym (*glavnoe upravlenie lagerei*) that in English translation means "Main Administration of the Camps." The Russian title of Solzhenitsyn's most famous work, *Gulag Arkhipelag,* has a mournful, rhyming lilt to it, underlined by the stress of each word falling on the last syllable (i.e., gu-*lag* arkhipe-*lag*).

In the Butyrki, relatively new arrestees for the first time met with seasoned inmates of the camps, some of them being shifted around the archipelago to suit some forgotten purpose or pretext of the system. It was here that, sitting alone in a room with a bored MVD officer, Solzhenitsyn found out that he had been handed down a sentence of eight years of corrective labor, a relatively mild sentence considering the almost routine award of "tenners" (ten years) for indescribably trivial offenses. The entire procedure, issuing a customary slip of paper, was probably not unlike being given a piece of paper scheduling a driving test at the Department of Motor Vehicles.

From Butyrki, Solzhenitsyn was moved in August 1945 to another Moscow prison, Krasnaya Presnya, where for the first time he was to experience the brutal way in which ordinary criminal prisoners preyed on the softer and often naive "politicals." On his first day his belongings were picked clean by ratlike juveniles in his cell. This was done under the smirking eye of a brutal convict who had spent much of his life inside.

For a few more weeks he was at a site ironically named "New Jerusalem," some thirty miles from Moscow, with convicts being ordered to dig clay from a pit for bricks. It was here that he learned more of the brutal ways of prison: the need to act with enormous cunning, to avoid "general duties," the most arduous and physically exhausting camp labor, and to be extremely wary of the hard-core inmate thugs and their gangs.

Yet another move, to a Moscow camp called Kaluga Gate, brought him face-to-face with one of the most insidious pressures ever asserted against denizens of the Gulag: recruitment as an informer. To his regret for the rest of his life, Solzhenitsyn agreed, under threat of serious consequences if he declined, to inform a prison security official if he heard of any plans to escape among fellow prisoners. In fact, he never informed upon anyone, demonstrating in the process perhaps the first hint of determined resistance to the Gulag as he became increasingly familiar with it.

All the while, Solzhenitsyn's philosophical world was slowly crumbling around him. In Butyrki he had engaged in long debates with two Moscow intellectuals, committed Christians who made mincemeat of his Soviet textbook atheism. They shared his disdain for Stalin, but went far beyond that. To his astonishment, young men the same age as he was, in their mid-twenties, had total contempt for the entire Soviet revolutionary experiment itself.

It amazed him that someone who had grown up entirely within the matrix of Soviet education could reject out of hand the core principles, teachings, and comforting promises of a bright new future, that he, despite his intellectual brilliance, had taken for granted as he grew up. It amazed him, yet it prepared him early on for the great sea change in his outlook. That sea change would not only ensure his survival throughout eight years in the Gulag, but would set within him the steel core of character and conviction that, in the end, was to contribute to the collapse of the Soviet system itself.

If Solzhenitsyn had been dispatched to Siberian camps from the Moscow region in the 1940's, he might well have died. He was neither psychologically nor physically prepared for the appalling privations of the labor camp system. In particular, he was still a half-apologist for the Soviet system, well aware of its cruelties and deficiencies, but not yet committed to an alternative worldview that could have protected his soul amid the suffering of corrective labor.

Providentially, however, he had raced through a recent Russian-language book on the U.S. military nuclear testing while at Kaluga Gate. In a fit of both chutzpah and cunning, he designated himself on a camp registration form as an "atomic physicist." He was nothing of the sort, of course, but he at least had some solid mathematical and scientific training from undergraduate days. What prompted the braggadocio were persistent rumors that the regime had constructed special scientific institutes to take advantage of the often brilliant scientific minds who wound up among the multitudes of political prisoners.

These unique scientific penal institutes, many of which contained talented German prisoners of war picked up in the great sweep of Soviet armies to Berlin, were called *sharashkas*, a name whose origins seem obscure. Prisoners transferred to them were permitted privileges unheard of in the Gulag as a whole: proper mattresses, sheets and blankets to sleep on, access to well-stocked libraries, exercise time—including games like volleyball—in the prison yard, unlimited receipt of letters and books (subject to censorship, of course), and a meal regime positively luxurious in comparison with the watery soup or porridge dished out in the prisons or camps.

In July 1946, Solzhenitsyn was transferred out of Kaluga Gate to two temporary locations, including one where the work was on jet engine development. This became, for his future intellectual and moral development, the most decisive prison experience of his entire eight years. The sharashka at Marfino was a former theological seminary in Moscow next to Ostankino Park, very close to what was to become the Soviet broadcasting center of Ostankino. Known bureaucratically as "Special Prison No. 16," Marfino in reality was the Mavrino of Solzhenitsyn's Nobel Prize–winning novel *The First Circle*. Indeed, the novel is in many ways a thinly disguised autobiographical account of his own sharashka experience.

The good treatment at the sharashka was evident enough in the food available to the prisoners. For breakfast there was a generous helping of bread and margarine, and at lunch not only meat, but actually dessert. Movies were sometimes shown on Sundays and instead of the glaring, 200-watt light burning all night, the sleeping cell had merely a much dimmer, blue-painted bulb. Lights out was at 10:00 P.M., and wake-up was at 7:00 A.M. Even more gratifying than the good treatment at the sharashka, however, was the companionship of truly outstandingly talented and moral fellow prisoners. The nearly three years Solzhenitsyn spent at Marfino could hardly have been better designed to sharpen his mind, test his philosophical loyalties, and harden his emerging convictions.

In this respect, two men deserve particular attention, at least partly because they feature fictionally with such prominence in *The First Circle*. One was a brilliant, charming, and indefatigably generous Jew, Lev Kopelev. He was six years older than Solzhenitsyn, a literary historian, who had been arrested on the same front as Solzhenitsyn—as a major in the Soviet army designing and broadcasting German-language, anti-Nazi propaganda. Kopelev's offense: He had been "soft on the Germans."[15] Again, like

Solzhenitsyn, Kopelev was a convinced Marxist-Leninist and believed his arrest had been simply some horrible bureaucratic mistake.

The second man, Dimitri Panin, was almost his antithesis, at least on paper. A civil engineer who had witnessed the horrors of Bolshevik atrocities during the 1918–21 civil war in Russia, Panin was resolutely anti-Soviet and a devout Russian Orthodox Christian. He had first been sentenced in 1940 after denunciations by a fellow engineer.

In *The First Circle*, Panin's character is Sologdin, Kopelev's is Rubin, and Solzhenitsyn is Nerzhin. The details of the sharashka as described in the novel are very close to the actual conditions at Marfino. Even more important, though, is the portrayal of what is almost a dialogue between two friendly philosophical adversaries with the unstated prize, in effect, of Nerzhin's (and Solzhenitsyn's) own soul—or at least his future orientation of life.

In actuality, Kopelev, intimately familiar with the evolution of socialist thought in Russia, still believed in the rightness of the cause of the Communist Party, as long as Stalin was not in charge. So, at this point, did Solzhenitsyn. But Panin was implacably hostile to Stalin, to the Party, and to Leninism in any form. He was convinced that Communism in Russia had been literally a satanic importation from abroad, and that only God's supernatural intervention would free Russia from it.

The three men would debate one another furiously, but as fast and even devoted friends, conscious of one another's intellectual brilliance and strength of character. All three were aware of how extraordinarily privileged they were. Not only were they serving their prison terms in remarkable comfort, they could endlessly debate the deepest philosophical and political questions of their own time and eternity without fear of being sent to prison—after all, they were already in prison. In fact, at this moment of Russian history, Solzhenitsyn's sharashka at Marfino was perhaps the freest location in the entire Soviet Union. The Gulag system of Soviet labor camps was certainly the equivalent of Dante's *Inferno*, or hell, but the sharashka was only the *"The First Circle"* of it, as Panin drily noted.[16]

Solzhenitsyn found that he couldn't sustain in debate any support for Marxism as a system when confronted by the superiority of arguments against it offered by Panin and others. For a time, he didn't seem to believe in anything, having come to a midway point between ardent Leninism and whatever might have replaced it. He had resumed reading Dostoyevsky in the sharashka library and it influenced him greatly. "I began to move ever so slowly," he told biographer Scammell later, "towards a position that was in the first place idealist, as they call it, that is, of supporting the primacy of the spiritual over the material, and secondly patriotic and religious. In other words, I began to return slowly and gradually to all my former [i.e., childhood] views."[17]

Amid the highly charged intellectual atmosphere of the sharashka, two other emotional components of Solzhenitsyn's life surfaced. One was the sudden appearance at Marfino of Vitkevich, Solzhenitsyn's accomplice in youthful political dissidence. Vitkevich had also been arrested early in 1945 and had at first been sentenced to the Urals. The reunion was exciting and rewarding for both men, but each had changed since their last meeting. Vitkevich had lost his passion for politics almost completely. Solzhenitsyn, by contrast, was just catching the intellectual stride of mature adulthood, plunging into the rich library of literature and philosophy of the sharashka—including books by Russian authors who were absolutely taboo in the Soviet Union as a whole—and becoming increasingly passionate about what he considered the most important elements of life itself. Particularly because Solzhenitsyn had already established warm and close relations with Kopelev and Panin, he and Vitkevich began to drift apart.

The second emotional element for Solzhenitsyn was the state of his marriage to Natalya. Through hard work and guile she had secured a research assistant's job in a laboratory in Moscow in order to be near her husband. The two were actually permitted to meet each other in 1947 and then twice in 1948, each time under conditions of enormous constraint in a completely separate prison. Officially, there was no such thing as a sharashka anywhere in the Soviet Union, so elaborate systems of disguising a prisoner's location had to be undertaken before any meetings with outsiders was permitted. Solzhenitsyn and Natalya nevertheless relished the brief minutes in each other's presence. Their correspondence was tender and affectionate. Solzhenitsyn now regretted the abrupt tone he had adopted toward his wife early in their marriage. For her part, Natalya responded with equal warmth to her husband's romantic sentiments.

But late in 1948, during their second meeting together that year, a new shadow came over the relationship. Natalya's workplace had suddenly declared all work being done there was classified. Stringent new security checks had to be carried out into the backgrounds of all the employees. Hitherto, Natalya had managed to conceal the fact that she was married to a man who had been declared a counterrevolutionary and was a political prisoner. Now, if she were not to be summarily fired, she would have to secure a legal divorce as quickly as possible and write "unmarried" against her name to impede any further investigation into her past.

Solzhenitsyn accepted the news calmly, but it hurt him deeply when she first discussed it. Yet there were still many tender moments between them. In April 1949, he heard his wife play the piano in a concert that was broadcast from the Red Army Theater over the radio. It was the day before their ninth wedding anniversary. "I listened and my heart was pounding," he wrote her later. "How I wanted to catch a glimpse of you at that moment."[18]

The divorce petition went ahead anyway. Natalya meanwhile was fired from her Moscow laboratory job on flimsy security grounds and managed to secure a position in Ryazan as a chemistry lecturer. The city was not far from Moscow, but too small for her to send food parcels to Solzhenitsyn and at the same time preserve the fiction that she was unmarried. In March 1950, they met for what neither realized would be the last time until October 19, 1956.

The work in the sharashka on which Solzhenitsyn was busy was a top secret effort by Soviet scientists to develop a scrambler telephone for secure conversations. Solzhenitsyn's contribution was not merely in the area of mathematical probability theory, but in analysis of the actual phonological structure of the Russian language. But in his spare moments he had cautiously resumed the project of writing a great historical novel about the October Revolution that he had first conceived a decade earlier.

His view of the original Bolshevik goals was still idealistic; he thought it was merely under Stalin that the excesses and the brutality had reached full flower. Thus his newest title for the work, *Love of the Revolution,* reflected without irony what he considered the central theme of the great historical event that fascinated him. Of necessity, he could only compose in total confidentiality, inscribing his thoughts in tiny handwriting on sheets of paper carefully kept away from the eyes of others. He was reading more, too, especially from classic Russian literature.

He now found Dostoyevsky a more interesting writer than Tolstoy. But he was attracted to many other literary personalities, including a favorite, the Chinese Lao-tsu (ca. 604–531 B.C.), a near contemporary of

Confucius who advocated a spontaneous, unstructured approach to daily life that emphasizes a harmonious relationship with one's environment. Panin, the devout Christian, disapproved of this interest, perhaps because the way of life of Daoism, the philosophy associated with Lao-tsu, stresses magic and even occultic practices.

Panin was also becoming less and less comfortable with his own role as a coerced agent of Stalin's totalitarianism. During 1949, a more urgent task was assigned to the acoustic section to which he and Solzhenitsyn belonged: identification of the recorded voice of an unknown Soviet diplomat who had warned the British and Americans that a spy in the U.S. had betrayed American atomic secrets to Moscow. Kopelev worked eagerly on this, but Panin was disgusted with the project. When a tighter disciplinary regime was imposed on the sharashka in 1949, the added sense of repression caused something in Panin to revolt altogether. He now refused to work on Sundays, going out to chop firewood instead, and revealing an almost brazen attitude of passive resistance to the authorities.

Solzhenitsyn began to follow suit. He had already developed a habit of rapid-fire verbal delivery of complaints during the one time each day when the prisoners were permitted to address the authorities with such points. In effect, Solzhenitsyn was turning increasingly against the regime that had nourished and educated him, and in whose legitimacy he had at least entered prison believing. Kopelev was witty, erudite, and encyclopedic in his knowledge of the history of the world and the Russian socialist tradition. But Panin was rocklike, even quirky in his flat denial of the entire premise of Soviet life: the idea that a new universe could be constructed in any country by means of conscious social engineering. Solzhenitsyn was not yet entirely in Panin's camp, but he was skirting its outer borders.

"ON ROTTING PRISON STRAW"

In May 1950, Panin's and Solzhenitsyn's sullen noncooperation caught up with them both. They were transferred out of Marfino into the deepest and most unforgiving recesses of the Gulag. This involved a several-week train journey—punctuated by transit stops in Omsk and Kuibyshev—in prison transportation wagons, fifteen men confined in a windowless, stifling compartment originally designed for eight, far out of Moscow, through Siberia, to a remote labor camp in the northern reaches of Kazakhstan.

The place was called Ekibastuz. It was located in the middle of the arid Kazakh plain, dusty and stifling hot in summer, in winter buffeted by snow, ice, and winds of shocking force for weeks at a time. The camp, with its double rows of barbed wire fencing, perimeter ploughed strip, machine gun coverage of every conceivable area, its use of floodlights the entire night, was emblematic of the Gulag as it has come to be known to us. It is the model for the camp depicted in Solzhenitsyn's most widely read work, *One Day in the Life of Ivan Denisovich*.

In Ekibastuz, more than anywhere, Solzhenitsyn learned firsthand the horrors of living in a "special prison" from which it was not expected that a prisoner would normally be released: the commandant of Ekibastuz even boasted that only three men had gone free under his rule. The daily, brutal labor, the marches to the worksites in rain, or slush, or cold so intense it was like a knife against the skin, the endless searches before you left the camp in the morning, the searches on your return, the waiting in line morning and night for the thin gruel, the absence of books, the conscienceless brutality of the criminal prisoners. All of this for 330 days a year (there were three days of rest each month), killed thousands upon thousands of prisoners, or turned the survivors into cowed, zombielike men.

Determined not to repeat his early mistakes of the presharashka camps, Solzhenitsyn volunteered for nothing and avoided any possibility of being manipulated into a stool pigeon. Much of the time at Ekibastuz, he was a bricklayer, occasionally even experiencing the exhilaration of hard physical labor performed with comrades he had come to trust and indeed at times to rely on for survival. In *One Day in the Life of Ivan Denisovich*, Solzhenitsyn relates just how vital such friendships could be.

Prisoners were permitted to write or receive just two letters a year, and there was no assurance at all that a letter actually handed in for censorship and mailing would ever reach its destination. The "special" category of prison also required that all prisoners be known to the authorities in the camp not by their names, but by numbers sewn onto their uniforms on their chests, caps, and trouser-legs. Solzhenitsyn's number was Shch-262, the *Shch* (pronounced "sh-cha" in Russian) being the second-last letter in the Russian alphabet. So outraged was he by this humiliating procedure that, when he was eventually released from prison, he smuggled out his numbers and had himself photographed wearing them while he was still in exile.

Amid the thugs, the toadies, and the weasels with whom he found himself, however, there were also some utterly remarkable characters. One of them emerges in *One Day* as the character Alyosha the Baptist. In fact Alyosha was based, as almost every Solzhenitsyn fictional character is, on a real individual whom Solzhenitsyn came to know well in Ekibastuz. He was Anatoly Silin, a talented Baptist poet who could memorize vast pages of verse and who had thought long and hard about the question of suffering and its relation to the sovereignty of God. More than forty years old when Solzhenitsyn met him at Ekibastuz, Silin must have been in many ways a saintly person. "Day in and day out he was meek and gentle with everyone, but reserved," Solzhenitsyn wrote later, acknowledging that it was only when the poet opened up to him that he discovered how extraordinary he was.[19] Solzhenitsyn even recalled some of Silin's verse:

> Does God, who is Perfect Love, allow
> This imperfection in our lives?
> The soul must suffer first, to know
> The perfect bliss of paradise.[20]

Silin's distillation of poetic beauty from suffering etched itself deeply in Solzhenitsyn's soul, and further agonies made it more meaningful than ever. In January 1952, he was troubled by a large, painful lump in his right groin. It was diagnosed in the camp hospital as cancerous, and he underwent an operation after a few days with a local anesthetic. But the camp was in a tumult after a near mutiny by rebellious Ukrainian inmates, and some of the suspected or real camp informers had taken refuge in the camp hospital or prison.

Recovering from the painful operation on the straw mattress of his hospital bed, Solzhenitsyn was visited by a Jewish physician, Dr. Boris Nikolayevich Kornfeld, who spent the evening hours fervently describing how he had just recently become a Christian believer. The following morning there was an uproar in the nearby corridors. Solzhenitsyn learned that Kornfeld's body was being carried out. He had been bludgeoned to death in his sleep, suspected of having been a stool pigeon.

The discovery of cancer, the almost weekly murders of suspected stoolies in the camp, the trauma of the operation, and finally the brutal death of a man who had spoken fervently and with kindness to Solzhenitsyn just hours earlier: All these coalesced in Solzhenitsyn's mind. There was no Damascus

Road experience, no blinding revelation of a new truth about life. Instead, he experienced a slow, inexorable process of plumbing life's greatest depths and bringing up a truth for which he had never consciously been searching. In some of the most powerful words of the entire *Gulag Archipelago*, Solzhenitsyn slowly, almost painfully describes his spiritual awakening.

> Once upon a time you were sharply intolerant. You were constantly in a rush. And you were constantly short of time. And now you have time with interest. . . .
>
> Formerly you never forgave anyone. You judged people without mercy. And you praised people with equal lack of moderation. And now an understanding mildness has become the basis of your uncategorical judgments. You have come to realize your own weakness—and you can therefore understand the weakness of others. And be astonished at another's strength. And wish to possess it yourself.
>
> . . . In the intoxication of youthful successes I had felt myself to be infallible, and I was therefore cruel. In the surfeit of power I was a murderer, and an oppressor. In my most evil moments I was convinced that I was doing good, and I was well supplied with systematic arguments. And it was only when I lay there on rotting prison straw that I sensed within myself the first stirrings of good. Gradually it was disclosed to me that the line separating good and evil passes not through states, not between classes, nor between political parties either—but right through every human heart—and through all human hearts. This line shifts. Inside us, it oscillates with the years. And even within hearts overwhelmed by evil, one small bridgehead of good is retained. And even in the best of hearts, there remains . . . an unuprooted small corner of evil.
>
> Since then I have come to understand the truth of all the religions of the world: They struggle with the evil inside a human being (inside every human being). It is impossible to expel evil from the world in its entirety, but it is possible to constrict it within each person.[21]

Solzhenitsyn's insights were the consequence of reality's humiliations relentlessly smashing against the bastions of pride and self-reliance he had long constructed around himself. He was certainly not perfected by the suffering. He retained his share of personal failings that sometimes hurt others terribly and indeed created more difficulties for himself than might have been necessary. But he was exposed in prison to the ultimate folly of a life based on the self, a philosophy based on a series of materialistic accidents. His former Marxist-Leninist worldview was in shambles.

At Ekibastuz, the question was, How could he write, create literature from all of these insights in an environment where it was a crime to commit anything at all to paper in permanent form? The prisoners were permitted pencils and paper, but they were not permitted to keep anything written. Solzhenitsyn and other poets and indeed novelists in the Gulag, including Silin, therefore composed in their heads in verse or prose as they worked, or lay on the boards of their bunks, or marched to the worksites.

Employing verse made it simpler to memorize the compositions, but even for Solzhenitsyn, a simple lyric poem here and there was not enough. He composed and memorized in his head literally thousands of lines of his own verse compositions, much of it later forming part of *The Way*, an unpublished autobiographical survey of his life that amounted to more than ten thousand lines, every one of which he committed to memory.

To aid himself in this phenomenal feat, he used broken matchsticks to jog his memory, one line of matchsticks representing single digits, another line the tens. Later still, he asked some religious prisoners to fashion for him what they thought was a one-hundred-bead rosary, but which in fact was another mnemonic device, with every tenth bead shaped differently to assist him in recalling what he had already remembered. By the time he left prison, Solzhenitsyn had committed to memory scores of thousands of his own compositions, far more than the accumulated memorization of most people's entire lifetime.

Solzhenitsyn's scheduled date for release was February 9, 1953, exactly eight years to the day after his original arrest in East Prussia. His actual departure from the camp took place four days later. He was an infinitely tougher, wiser, more cunning, bolder, and humbler man than the boisterous young officer whom the MVD officers had whisked out of the Soviet army on the Prussian front. Along with a group of other released inmates, he was taken by train to southern Kazakhstan. Solzhenitsyn was to be kept in what, at the time, looked like permanent exile in Kok Terek, a small settlement in Kazakhstan close to the border with Kirghizia. He was approximately 1,800 miles from Moscow and 1,580 miles from Ryazan, where Natalya lived.

But the divorce had now gone through, and Natalya had filled the lonely hole in her life with the friendship of, and ultimately the common-law marriage to Vsevolod, a Ryazan man ten years older than she, and the father from a previous marriage of a thirteen-year-old boy, Sergei. In theory, she was only following Solzhenitsyn's own cold-blooded advice to her soon after his arrest to cut her ties with him and start a new life. But the news was still bitter for Solzhenitsyn. They were to reconcile and resume their relationship later, but neither mutual need nor memories of real affection could eclipse the sense of a betrayal.

Solzhenitsyn took the only job he could find even remotely suited to his education and talents, teaching mathematics and physics in the local school. At first he lived in a mud hut with an earthen floor, no electricity, and ceilings so low he could not stand up properly. Later, he was able to move to a slightly larger, whitewashed hut with a thatched roof. Here, night after night, in the long hours between the end of teaching and his sleep, he wrote out, secretly, passionately, the stored up fruits of his gargantuan memory. Terrified that he might be discovered, he composed in a tiny, spidery handwriting on little pieces of paper that he meticulously hid around the hut, even outside it, before retiring for the night. This initiated a habit of composition that he maintained almost throughout his remaining two decades in the Soviet Union. Only later did he acquire a typewriter, and with it the habit of using up the entire width of the page and leaving no space between the lines.

He loved the teaching job, which he was very good at, but more important, he relished the exhilaration of having no one barking at him morning, noon, and night, and the freedom to be entirely by himself. He was still under close surveillance by the local MVD and had to be exceptionally careful how he behaved in public. He was certainly lonely, and he was tempted at different times to take up with local Russian women to whom he was introduced. But more important to him than any physical or emotional need was the sense of responsibility he felt to his manuscripts and to the men he had left behind in the camps, whose experience with tyranny he would psychically share as long as he lived. He made two fast friends, Nikolai and Elena Zubov, themselves "permanent" political exiles who had survived the camps and ended up in this remote corner of the Soviet imperium. They became, Solzhenitsyn said later, "like father and mother to me."[22]

Then, in December 1953, when he was just beginning to come into his own in this strange, almost monklike existence as teacher by day and clandestine writer by night, catastrophe engulfed his health. He started to experience severe abdominal pains. A diagnosis by local physicians among the exile community confirmed it: His cancer had returned. He was, they told him, rapidly going downhill with the disease. At the worst, he might have barely three weeks left to live. His only hope, they said, would be to seek radiation treatment in a hospital in Tashkent. He had to get MVD permission to leave his place of exile for medical reasons and could not plan the trip until the very first day of 1954.

Frantic with worry about his still-uncompleted work, Solzhenitsyn stayed up night after night, despite the pain, copying out whatever he could on tiny pieces of paper, squeezing them into tiny metal cylinders, then pushing these into a champagne bottle that he buried in the yard of his mud hut. Only the Zubovs would know where he had buried his literary treasure. He never expected that a single line of his verse would be published in his lifetime. But he believed that, at some distant point after his death, men and women would read with awe and fascination what he had put down on paper. Barely able to walk, Solzhenitsyn expended all his remaining strength to board a train and, as he recalled later, "set off for Tashkent to meet the New Year and to die."

THE THIRD ATOM BOMB

Astonishingly, he didn't die. Slowly but decisively, and with massive doses of radiation, his health began to return. By the spring of 1954, he was well enough to be released from the hospital. The radiation treatment evidently had killed off whatever remained of his cancerous growth. But for Solzhenitsyn, what had taken place was nothing less than the supernatural hand of God at work in his life.

"With a hopelessly neglected and acutely malignant tumor," he wrote in his autobiography, The Oak and the Calf, "this was a divine miracle; I could see no other explanation. Since then, all the life that has been given back to me has not been mine in the full sense: it is built around a purpose."[23] On leaving the hospital, he happened upon a Tashkent church that, surprisingly, was still open, went in, and gave a solemn prayer of thanks.

From 1954 until 1956, he worked away quietly as a teacher in Kazakhstan, austerely dividing his time into precise portions between schoolteaching and writing. Suddenly, a great stirring in the entire Communist world was unleashed in February of 1956. Soviet leader Nikita Khrushchev's famous "Secret Speech" was a riveting denunciation of the crimes of Stalin to the Twentieth Congress of the Soviet Communist Party. By April, an amnesty was announced for millions of former political prisoners, including Solzhenitsyn. He was now a completely free man, permitted to live wherever he wanted in the country.

Even more changes were in store: A chance meeting with Natalya in his old sharashka friend Panin's home reopened a relationship that she had thought completely dead. Though she and Vsevolod had not officially married, they lived together in Ryazan as man and wife, and she had not foreseen ever resuming any kind of relationship with Solzhenitsyn. His reappearance in person, however, and his warmth toward her, soon changed all this.

By December 1956, he had returned to Ryazan and in February re-registered his marriage to Natalya. In the fall of 1957, after an interval teaching at an industrial settlement some one hundred miles east of Moscow, where he was inspired to write one of his best-known novellas, "Matryona's House," Solzhenitsyn secured a regular job teaching physics and astronomy at the High School Number Two in Ryazan.

He and Natalya were now reunited, but their lives in Ryazan followed no typical pattern of professional husband and wife. Though they attended concerts, the ballet, and the theater occasionally, most of Solzhenitsyn's spare time from teaching or grading his students' work was spent writing. The few major social contacts he permitted himself were with his old sharashka friends Lev Kopelev and Dimitri Panin. Once a year, in February, on the anniversary of his arrest in East Prussia in 1945, he would observe his own private "convict's day": 23 ounces of bread, water with two lumps of sugar in it, and reflection on his experience—and that of millions of others—in Stalin's Gulag.

Meanwhile, he wrote and wrote, in complete secrecy. Only Natalya, who faithfully copied and helped conceal the drafts of his compositions, and later a very small circle of trusted friends, were completely aware of what he was creating. Between 1957 and 1961, he succeeded in completing *The First Circle*, his story of life in the sharashka, the first drafts of what became *The Gulag Archipelago*, and three plays.

It was the year 1959 that produced the work that was to change

Solzhenitsyn's life, the Soviet Union, and ultimately the whole world. It was a simple, yet searing and surprisingly short semiautobiographical narrative of one man's day in the Ekibastuz labor camp of Kazakhstan. It was called *Shch-854*—the letter and number sewn onto the prisoner's clothes to identify him, just as Solzhenitsyn himself had been forced to wear the number Shch-262. The only person to whom Solzhenitsyn showed the text, apart from his wife, Natalya, was Veniamin Teush, a Jewish mathematician and political exile who had lived with his wife, Susanna, in Ryazan since Stalin's bitter anti-Jewish campaign of the 1940's. Solzhenitsyn had become warm friends with the Teushes and had, with his typical and impulsive intuitiveness, decided in 1960 to confide the secret of his writing to the couple.

Without Solzhenitsyn's permission, Teush showed the manuscript to another friend, also Jewish. The story astounded the two men, who praised it lavishly. Bestowing an almost messianic blessing on the novel, Veniamin, according to Solzhenitsyn, "solemnly intoned Simeon's *Nunc Dimitis*: 'Lord, now lettest thou thy servant depart in peace [Luke 2:29 KJV].'"[24] Teush also added, according to another observer, "There are three atom bombs in the world: Kennedy has one, Khrushchev has another, and you have the third."[25] Natalya, Solzhenitsyn says, found the work "boring and monotonous," though she had been highly complimentary of the still-unpublished *The First Circle*.[26]

The story *Shch-854* might have slowly decomposed in the hidden archives of an obscure Ryazan physics teacher—Aleksandr Solzhenitsyn—had not the entire Soviet Union been experiencing serious ferment, both internal and external, catalyzed by Khrushchev's famous "Secret Speech." Most important, the speech galvanized the Soviet cultural and intellectual elite out of its fearful passivity. Young poets like Yevgeny Yevtushenko, just twenty-three in 1956, had sprung into prominence with public readings of daring new verse that attracted thousands upon thousands of listeners. The brilliant Christian poet, Boris Pasternak, had been awarded the Nobel Prize in 1958 for his novel *Dr. Zhivago*, then forced under official pressure to relinquish it. This heavy-handed official clubbing of a deeply admired literary figure only deepened the distaste among Soviet creative artists for the brutality, stupidity, and arbitrariness of Soviet officialdom's control over the nation's cultural life.

By 1961, well aware of the discontent among the intelligentsia,

Khrushchev sensed that the time might be right for another assault upon the bastions of Stalinist rigidity within the Communist Party. The Twenty-second Congress of the Soviet Communist Party in October of that year provided the forum for this new effort to loosen the tight restraints upon society. In Ryazan, Solzhenitsyn and other intellectuals devoured the official reports of the speeches at the conference carried by the government newspaper *Izvestiya*. Here and in Moscow, intellectuals wondered whether it was not now time for Soviet writers to tell the unvarnished truth about what had happened to an entire nation during the long, nightmarish decades of Stalinist rule.

For several weeks in 1961, Solzhenitsyn had left a copy of *Shch-854* in Moscow in the hands of his old friend Lev Kopelev. Kopelev had judged that, by autumn of that year, the time might be right to submit it to a major literary journal. He and Solzhenitsyn agreed that the relatively liberal (by Soviet standards) monthly *Novy Mir (New World)* might be the best avenue to pursue, since its editor, Aleksandr Trifonovich Tvardovsky, had made a moving speech at the Party Congress fervently supporting Khrushchev and appealing for writers in general to tell the healing truth about the horrors of the "cult of personality," as Stalin's era was euphemistically termed.

Kopelev's wife, Raisa Orlova, physically took the manuscript into the editorial offices of *Novy Mir*, where an intelligent and clever copy editor, Anna Berzer, as dazzled by the story as a handful of others had been, ensured that the great Tvardovsky personally took possession of the piece. The manuscript was still in the physical form that Solzhenitsyn had arranged for all of his precious materials: copy-typed by Natalya on ultrathin paper with no margins and with inadequate line spacing. It was signed by the obviously pseudonymous "A. Ryazansky," a transparent reference to Solzhenitsyn's town of residence.

Tvardovsky, an expansive, hard-drinking, but generous-spirited man of peasant background, took the manuscript back to his dacha outside Moscow to read over the weekend. In fact, he read it twice from beginning to end that night, not going to bed at all because he was overwhelmed by the truthfulness and power of what he was reading. The story totally engulfed him; he immediately announced to everyone he knew that he had discovered a great new writer. On December 11, 1961, in Ryazan, Solzhenitsyn received a cable from Tvardovsky enthusiastically inviting him to Moscow to discuss the work. It was the writer's forty-third birthday.

In a sense, it was the birthday of an entirely new existence for him. No longer the cautious, secretive, provincial schoolteacher, he was thrust quite unwittingly into the glare of Soviet and eventually global publicity that did not let up for the next fifteen years. During that time, Solzhenitsyn's extraordinary character slowly revealed itself. His convictions never changed; he detested tyranny throughout the period. But his approach to the authorities changed. He began nervously, hesitantly, unsure of how far he could go in expressing himself. He ended up a roaring lion, a man who appeared to have lost all fear in his toe-to-toe challenge to a corrupt, dictatorial, and morally bankrupt political system.

Tvardovsky's ebullient approval of *Shch-854* was only the first stage of a tension-filled year between November 1961 and November 1962, when the novel finally appeared in *Novy Mir*. In the course of that time it underwent a name change. Everyone at the periodical felt that *One Day in the Life of Ivan Denisovich* would be a far better title, and Solzhenitsyn acquiesced. There were other, much tenser moments of confrontation between Solzhenitsyn and Tvardovsky and his fellow editors regarding various details, partly reflecting the varying degrees of Communist orthodoxy among different *Novy Mir* staffers.

The biggest issue for everyone, though, was whether the highest authorities of the Communist Party of the Soviet Union, up to and including Khrushchev, would finally approve publication. For *One Day* was not merely a harrowing tale of a former political prisoner—a *zek*, to use the Russian acronym for "imprisoned person." It was a devastating revelation of just how brutal and arbitrary the entire Soviet labor camp system had been from the very beginning. In September 1962, Tvardovsky even had twenty-three copies of the story formally printed and bound by *Novy Mir*—photocopies were all but unheard of in Moscow at this time—so that key party leadership figures could express their views on publication or nonpublication.

So tense was the issue posed by *One Day*'s publication that Khrushchev's private secretary, Vladimir Lebedev, became personally involved, requesting certain minute editorial changes in the text to soften the blow of the story as a whole. In October, just days before 100,000 copies of *Novy Mir* carrying *One Day* were to be printed, the Cuban Missile Crisis broke.

The Soviet Union and the U.S. edged closer than they ever had before to the brink of a nuclear confrontation after Washington ordered missiles brought into Cuba by the Soviet navy removed. But the crisis miraculously eased, and the missiles were removed. From one end of the Soviet Union to the other, *One Day in the Life of Ivan Denisovich* hit newsstands or arrived in subscribers' mailboxes in mid-November 1962.

The acclaim throughout the Soviet Union on publication of the story was instantaneous and unanimous. Since the work could never even have been published without approval by the Communist Party's leadership itself—meaning Khrushchev, of course—the Soviet official press fell over itself to praise Solzhenitsyn. *Pravda*, the Communist Party newspaper, compared Solzhenitsyn to Tolstoy, though explaining that the writer was merely advancing the party's own cause of doing away with Stalin's personality cult. "The possibility of telling the truth has been affirmed by the Party and the people," it said.[27] The government paper *Izvestiya* echoed this theme, with no less unintended irony, proclaiming that Solzhenitsyn had "shown himself a true helper of the Party in a sacred and vital cause—the struggle against the personality cult and its consequences."[28] Most Soviet readers, though, saw the story in a very different light. For them it appeared to mark a new era of literary and historical truthfulness after years of official obfuscation and mendacity.

The rest of the world was no less dazzled by *One Day* than the Russians were. In 1963, within months of the original publication, there were foreign-language editions being prepared throughout Western Europe. I remember as an undergraduate at Oxford how one of our professors, Ronald Hingley, was delightedly pointing out the thick array of prison camp argot of the novel in the Russian edition. Back in Moscow, meanwhile, so totally oversold had the November 1962 issue of *Novy Mir* been that a new, separate edition of the book was published with an astonishing print run of 750,000 copies. Solzhenitsyn's literary star was in full ascendancy. What could he do for an encore?

From the beginning, there were demands by Tvardovsky and others to follow up *One Day* with additional works by Solzhenitsyn. In January 1963, *Novy Mir* published two short stories by Solzhenitsyn, "Matryona's Place" and "An Incident at Krechetovka Station," both based heavily on Solzhenitsyn's own experiences. As in *One Day*, Solzhenitsyn showed a masterful grasp of detail, pithy observations, and economy of expression in evoking, at times, lyrically interesting personalities. What made "Matryona's Place" so powerful was Solzhenitsyn's portrayal of an old peasant woman who stubbornly returned good acts for evil ones. She did so in a community rendered soulless and corrupt by Stalin's harsh economic policies in the countryside. At the end of "Matryona's House," Solzhenitsyn concluded with the words,

> We all lived beside her, and never understood that she was that righteous one without whom, according to the proverb, no village can stand.
>   Nor any city.
>   Nor our whole land.[29]

It was a bold moral generalization with which to end a story in a Soviet periodical. Tvardovsky's initial complaint when Solzhenitsyn first showed it to him was that it was "a bit too Christian."[30] Others who did not share Tvardovsky's warm affection and admiration for Solzhenitsyn no doubt had more serious doubts.

In fact, within a year of the initial *Novy Mir* success, Solzhenitsyn's star began to fall in the Soviet literary firmament. Khrushchev's brave effort in 1961 to resume the process of de-Stalinization in society was itself under attack within the party. Few elements of that process were easier to criticize than the literary attacks on the "cult of personality" by writers who could be interpreted as harboring a more radical agenda altogether. Solzhenitsyn's works were so starkly at variance with the conventional uplifting, pro-party literature most readers had grown up with that it was simple enough to begin the process of counterattack against Khrushchev through the medium of his literary protégé. Solzhenitsyn, to put it simply, was the most obvious target at hand for resurgent Stalinists.

The writer himself was not initially aware of these developments. On the strength of *One Day in the Life of Ivan Denisovich* royalties and formal admission to the Soviet Writers Union (which permitted a writer to write full-time without being charged with "parasytism," that is, not having a state-ordered job), he was now earning enough royalties to quit for good his teaching job in Ryazan. He was spending more and more time in Moscow, speaking out at seminars and forums arranged for him by various Soviet professional institutions. With the Soviet literary reading public, he was an unqualified success. He was even beginning to receive hundreds of letters from former Gulag inmates detailing aspects of the Gulag experience of which even Solzhenitsyn had hitherto been ignorant.

But marital strains developed because of this sudden fame. As he spent more and more time in Moscow or doing research in Leningrad for his further writing, relations with Natalya became tense. She disliked the lime-light and was uncomfortable with the amount of attention Solzhenitsyn's prominence was bringing her as well as him. He, meanwhile, did not need to live a life of hermetic secretiveness now that he was formally recognized by the authorities as a major literary figure. A new, unbridgeable gap was now opening in the marriage.

In 1964, the first major official rebuff came to Solzhenitsyn's official literary career when the Soviet establishment decided not to award him the Lenin Prize. The writing was already on the wall for him, and indeed for Khrushchev, who was later deposed in a Kremlin coup in October of that year. But for Solzhenitsyn, the major blow was the refusal of Khrushchev's secretary, Lebedev, to permit the publication of *The First Circle*.

"HOW THESE PEOPLE MUST HAVE YEARNED FOR THE TRUTH!"

With his characteristic careful planning, Solzhenitsyn had partly prepared for the possibility that the doors of literary access might slam shut upon him once again. He had continued his meticulous early habits of copying his works and secreting them in hiding places around his home or among carefully selected friends. He had graduated to the use of a camera and microfilm to make the copies, greatly facilitating the reduction of their bulk. The most complete collection of everything he had written had been entrusted to Veniamin Teush, who was now living on Mytnaya Street in Moscow.

Perhaps gripped by a sense of urgency that the window of opportunity was again closing on him, Solzhenitsyn, during 1964 and 1965, was working furiously on *The Gulag Archipelago*, though not even Tvardovsky was aware of the project. With royalties from *Ivan Denisovich*, he bought a plot of land and a simple rural cabin in the village of Rozhdestvo, near Obninsk, about one hundred miles east of Moscow. A stream ran nearby and overflowed annually with the runoff of melted snow, partly flooding Solzhenitsyn's property. Working and living by himself, he was able to avoid the social and other pressures of Moscow, where, in any case, the political mood had toughened greatly in just a year.

But while he was relatively secure writing in his hideaway in the countryside, his very prominence, and the private outspokenness of his views, had now attracted the attention of the authorities. By a catastrophic coincidence in September of that year, an intensifying crackdown on Moscow literary dissidents and their suspected supporters led to a police raid on the Ryazan apartment of Veniamin Teush. There the KGB not only seized three of the only four copies of the novel *The First Circle*, but all of Solzhenitsyn's earlier, and still-unpublished works, including two stridently anti-Soviet plays, *The Feast of the Victors* and *The Republic of Labor*.

Solzhenitsyn had still not authorized the official publication of either of these works, but a quotation from the first of these plays, made available to the Soviet Politburo in September 1965 by the KGB, amply illustrates the thrust of *The Feast of the Victors*: "The USSR! Its impenetrable forest! [sic in translation] A forest. It has no laws. All it has is power—power to arrest and torture, with or without laws."[31]

The blow to him brought about by the seizure of his manuscripts was utterly devastating. Solzhenitsyn, in his memoir *The Oak and the Calf*, described it forthrightly as "the greatest misfortune in all my forty-seven years." He went on, "For some months I felt as though it were a real, unhealing physical wound—a javelin wound right through the breast, with the tip so firmly dislodged that it could not be pulled out." He even had, he said later, "thoughts of suicide."[32]

Under Leonid Brezhnev, who together with Premier Aleksey Kosygin, had been ruling the Soviet Union since Khrushchev's ouster, what had often been described as "The Thaw" of de-Stalinization, initiated by Khrushchev in 1956, was clearly coming to an abrupt end.

Solzhenitsyn, in fact, had already attracted the unwelcome surveillance attention of the KGB simply through his friendship with Teush, whose anti-Soviet critical essays at the time were thought far more subversive than anything Solzhenitsyn had published. Listening in on Solzhenitsyn's conversations with Teush in the latter's apartment in Ryazan, the sleuths heard words from the writer's mouth that were both bitterly hostile to the Soviet Union and extraordinarily prescient and prophetic, coming as they did a full quarter-century before the collapse of the Communist regime. "I'm amazed that the liberal Russian people don't understand that we have to separate from the republics; they don't understand that we have to face this," he said in private conversation at one point. In effect, Solzhenitsyn understood intuitively that Communism would eventually collapse in his homeland, and that one consequence of this would be the breakup of the Soviet empire Lenin and Stalin had forged from 1917 until 1944.[33]

It was in 1965, indeed, as *The Solzhenitsyn Files* make clear, that the highest organ of Soviet power, the Politburo of the Communist Party, focused specifically on Solzhenitsyn as an internal adversary of extraordinary tenacity and danger to the regime. While the "organs," to use a term employed by Soviet citizens to describe the KGB, knew more about Solzhenitsyn's work and ideas than he realized, they still were flummoxed by his boldness and unexpected moves in what came to be a running cat-and-mouse game with the authorities.

For a while, Solzhenitsyn went into hiding after the Teush raid, convinced he was about to be arrested. But on realizing that this was not actually likely to happen, Solzhenitsyn instead resumed his writing with intensity, staying in the dachas of friends outside Moscow. He completed *Cancer Ward* in 1966, but *Novy Mir* decided not to publish it. To them, Solzhenitsyn was becoming less a literary star than a liability.

In November, invited to read publicly some chapters from the work at the Lazarev Institute of Oriental Studies, Solzhenitsyn launched a public attack on the KGB and the entire censorship apparatus of the country. He denounced them for having "made use of excerpts from my papers, taken out of context, to launch a campaign of defamation against me."[34] Solzhenitsyn was referring to the unauthorized use of excerpts of his confiscated material by the KGB and other Soviet authorities to discredit his reputation among people who might otherwise have been sympathetic to him.

In taking the offensive so dramatically and publicly against the authorities, Solzhenitsyn knew he was crossing some sort of Rubicon in the relations of a Soviet writer with his government. "This was perhaps the first time, the very first time," he wrote, "that I felt myself, saw myself, making history." He was astonished by how explosive the impact on his audience was of open denunciations by him of KGB harassment. "Almost every sally," he wrote, "scorched the air like gunpowder! How these people must have yearned for truth! Oh God, how badly they wanted to hear the truth!"[35]

Solzhenitsyn seemed to be responding to a new sense of calling, not simply to write the truth in defiance of the wishes of the authorities, but to stand up in public against the authorities themselves. For two months during the winter of 1966–67 he disappeared from public view again, forcing himself into one of the most drastic work schedules any writer may ever have sustained. Arising initially at 2:00 A.M. in the dacha of the Chukovsky family where he was staying, he would write for eight hours, rest for one, then resume for another eight hours from 11:00 A.M. until seven at night. His goal was to complete the second draft of the first six parts of *Gulag Archipelago.* In some ten weeks, he revised and retyped fifteen hundred manuscript pages of the work, completing an entire second draft.[36]

Relations with Tvardovsky were meanwhile growing testier as it became increasingly obvious how antagonistic Solzhenitsyn was to everything Soviet. *The First Circle* seemed permanently on ice, largely because a copy of the manuscript had shown up, with other, far more antiregime writings, in the Teush raid. But early in 1967, Tvardovsky made it clear that he would never publish the far less provocative *Cancer Ward,* either, chiefly out of annoyance with Solzhenitsyn's radical views. That left Solzhenitsyn with essentially no choice: The only place where his books would ever be published was the West.

In April 1967, he asked Olga Carlisle, an American woman of Russian background, to go ahead with publication in the West of *The First Circle,* microfilms of which had been carefully smuggled abroad by a close circle of reliable friends. He also began arrangements for moving all of his important writings for publication to the West, reducing them first to microfilm, then operating an elaborate system of contacts with trusted couriers.

There was one major act of defiance he wished to make against the Soviet literary establishment. Carefully planning who the recipients should be, Solzhenitsyn composed and mailed some 250 typed copies (still no accessible photocopy machines) of a thundering letter to participants of the May 1967 Congress of Soviet Writers. He stunned the congress, almost all of whose attendees read the letter in some form or other, with a wholehearted attack on the entire Soviet censorship system. Then he excoriated the Writers Union's leaders for never protecting any of its writers from regime persecution, and for specifically doing nothing to interfere with the numerous petty harassments and acts of persecution to which he himself had been subjected.

To his surprise, the letter was warmly received, at least in private. But the Writers Union and other Soviet officials were annoyed that the text of the letter had already been smuggled abroad and read back in Russian to the Russian people, via the BBC. When he eventually met with top Writers Union leadership, Solzhenitsyn was attacked rather than complimented. And he was blamed for the anti-Soviet tone of earlier, unpublished works like *Feast of the Victors*.

He was now living a life that was at one level almost underground, writing furiously in near isolation at the Chukovsky dacha in Peredelkino, not far from Moscow. He had developed what became a lifelong habit of listening daily to BBC Russian broadcasts, in part to find out which of his views were being rebroadcast back to the Soviet Union and how much ordinary people knew about his circumstances. Many within the intelligentsia, in fact, had already read some of his writings other than *Ivan Denisovich* in samizdat form, that is, in copies that had been surreptitiously made and circulated among a handful of friends.

Very occasionally, he scheduled meetings at this time with foreign journalists. Though he disliked interviews in general, his views were invariably insightful. Regarding the need for artistic balance in subject matter when writing, for example, he told a Slovak journalist, "The writer needs to maintain a balance between the two categories of the present and eternity. If his work is so topical that he loses his view of things sub specie aeternitatis [in the context of eternity], then his work will quickly die." Of course, if it focused too much on the eternal, it would lose "its color, force, and 'air.'"[37]

A letter to three students, later released in samizdat, discussed the idea of justice. He thought that the concept was "inherent in man, since it cannot be traced to any other source. Justice exists, even if there are only a few individuals who recognize it as such." He added, "There is nothing relative about justice just as there is nothing relative about conscience. Indeed, justice is conscience, not a personal conscience but the conscience of all mankind."[38]

In 1968, Solzhenitsyn's life and career moved in a direction from which there could be no turning back. His second two novels, *The First Circle* and *Cancer Ward*, were suddenly published overseas, causing an uproar in the Soviet literary establishment that reverberated all the way to the top of the Communist Party's political hierarchy. He also, for the first time, began to take a direct interest in the activities of the fledgling Democratic Movement, a tiny but vigorous grouping of various dissidents who were challenging Soviet power more and more openly. With the Soviet invasion of Czechoslovakia in 1968, he spoke out publicly on behalf of those who had protested the invasion, alienating still further some of his erstwhile supporters.

Cancer Ward was first published in excerpted form in Britain in the *Times Literary Supplement* in April 1968, an unauthorized development that irritated Solzhenitsyn. When *The First Circle* also appeared in Britain in Russian and English translations in the summer of 1968, there could be no more question of Solzhenitsyn's attitude toward Soviet reality as a whole. A KGB report on the book, made available after the September 1965 seizure of the three copies in the Teush apartment, had already branded it as characterized by "the author's obsessive desire to slander literally everything having to do with Soviet reality."[39]

Cancer Ward, in its haphazard lurch toward publication in the West, received cautious and reserved reviews. It was a different story with *The First Circle*, which appeared in October and was greeted by rave reviews almost instantly. In the *New York Times*, Harrison Salisbury compared Solzhenitsyn's writing to that of Tolstoy, Dostoyevsky, and Chekhov, as well as to nineteenth-century European authors like Dickens and Balzac. In Britain, Ronald Hingley (my own former professor who had so enthusiastically greeted *One Day* five years earlier), said in the *Spectator* that *The First Circle* was "arguably the greatest Russian novel of the twentieth century."[40]

Solzhenitsyn was now no longer an eccentric Soviet critic of Stalinism whose memoirs of a Gulag experience, by some fluke, had made it into official Soviet literature. He was a novelist of international stature who was forcing both the Soviet Union and Western audiences to come to regard him as a person of rising personal authority in his own country.

Solzhenitsyn himself was certainly aware of his growing international fame. But it was the brutal Soviet invasion of Czechoslovakia in August 1968 that further propelled him into the public eye at home and abroad. Solzhenitsyn was outraged by this development, and very much aware that he had done nothing publicly to protest the earlier Soviet invasion of a Communist neighbor, namely Hungary, in 1956. He felt he now had to see what common ground there might be between himself and the sudden new star in the Soviet dissident world, the nuclear physicist Andrey Sakharov.

Sakharov would have been an extraordinary figure in any society: brilliant, exceptionally focused intellectually, but gentle, almost saintly in his disagreements with his government. But in the context of the Soviet Union he was, as Solzhenitsyn observed, "a miracle, an irrational phenomenon" by comparison with "the swarms of corrupt, venal, unprincipled scientists" who flourished within the Communist Party dictatorship.

Sakharov, born in 1921, had risen so high within the Soviet scientific establishment that he was given major responsibility for developing the Soviet nuclear program. Indeed, he has been familiarly described as "the father of the Soviet H-Bomb." But by the 1960's he became increasingly disillusioned with his country's entire nuclear program. He tried at first to limit Soviet nuclear testing only through formal and permitted channels. Because of his immense prestige as a scientist, Sakharov could not be directly punished for his emerging dissent from Soviet orthodoxy. But his access to the nation's top scientific secrets also required him to function within a sort of gilded cage of official scrutiny, constantly protected and under surveillance by bodyguards. He could live comfortably on his stipend, but he could not travel freely even within the Soviet Union.

In May 1968, he had infuriated the Soviet leadership, and intrigued the rest of the world, with a memorandum entitled "Progress, Coexistence, and Intellectual Freedom." The document, available only in samizdat, was nevertheless quickly published overseas. It unveiled the mind of a man deeply disturbed by the possibility of a war between the two superpowers, yet convinced that the best of the two societies could somehow be merged in a process of convergence. At the urging of many in the Democratic Movement, Solzhenitsyn and Sakharov met in late August 1968 to see if they could combine their influence to protest the Czech invasion and to explore points they might have in common. Both were to write about the encounter.

Solzhenitsyn was dazzled by Sakharov's sweet personality, his almost childlike innocence and naïveté. "Merely to see him, to hear his first words, is to be charmed by his tall figure, his look of absolute candor, his warm gentle smile, his bright glance, his pleasant throaty voice, the thick blurring of the r's to which you grow accustomed." Solzhenitsyn respected and admired him instantly.

But he also disagreed with Sakharov's relentlessly beneficent view of human nature. He was, Solzhenitsyn thought, "too pure. He never supposed that here, too, men might be moved by something other than novel impulses and the quest for truth, that they might be selfish and greedy." During their first, four-hour meeting, they discussed a broad series of issues involving Russia's present and past freedom, the responsibility of intellectuals in society, and other topics. Sakharov's account of Solzhenitsyn is less warm, possibly because of the sharp disagreements that came to cloud their relationship in the early 1970's, especially between their wives. But his description of Solzhenitsyn is nevertheless intriguing. "With his lively blue eyes and ruddy beard," Sakharov wrote, "his tongue-twistingly fast speech delivered in an unexpected treble and his deliberate, precise gestures, he seemed an animated concentration of purposeful energy."

Sakharov's often sharp-tongued wife, Elena Bonner, who is Jewish, irritated Solzhenitsyn and later Solzhenitsyn's second wife with her apparent lack of sympathy for Solzhenitsyn's own strong Russian national sentiments.[41]

The writer and the scientist disagreed over many issues. While Sakharov believed that humankind was fundamentally healthy and capable of further progress, Solzhenitsyn did not believe in progress at all. Sakharov thought Solzhenitsyn was too attached to romantic perceptions of old Russian culture, with its culturally powerful Russian Orthodox Church and village-based and localized decision making. Solzhenitsyn considered Sakharov not only naive, but also dangerously unaware of the weakness and decadence of the West. Finally, while Sakharov believed in pursuing human rights questions item by item, devoting huge energy to assisting specific individuals in their quest for emigration or justice from the authorities, Solzhenitsyn wanted to focus on the macrocosmic nature of the struggle between Communism as a whole and the still-healthy portion of the human race.[42]

The dispute was never resolved, even though both men were lambasted by Moscow's official propaganda machine into the early 1970's as though part of a smoothly working conspiracy against socialism. Despite their mutual disagreement, Solzhenitsyn never stopped admiring Sakharov, later warmly inscribing to him a personal copy of the original version of his memoirs, *The Oak and the Calf.* He later was also to advocate Sakharov for the Nobel Peace Prize, and the honor was conferred on the physicist in 1975. What almost certainly influenced Sakharov in the long run to take a cooler view of Solzhenitsyn was the poor relationship between Solzhenitsyn and Elena Bonner; the problem was partly Solzhenitsyn's unwillingness to focus special attention on the suffering of the Jews in the Soviet Union in contrast with Russians and other nationalities, and partly bad chemistry.

DANGEROUS LIAISONS

Chemistry of another kind now transformed Solzhenitsyn's private life. Many of his research assistants and semiconspiratorial helpers were women, for whom Solzhenitsyn was either a slightly impractical-seeming genius who needed a certain mothering, or else a heroic, almost macho-like champion of truth and justice. He was self-confident, energetic, highly disciplined—in sharp contrast to most Russian men—extremely intelligent, and not at all bad-looking.

Scammell, in his biography, alludes to a brief romantic liaison that Solzhenitsyn had in Leningrad in 1964 while researching for his writing.[43] In *Invisible Allies*, published only in 1995 after Solzhenitsyn had returned to Russia, he himself describes the formidably dedicated circle of friends, including some of these women, without whom he could never have taken on the entire Soviet security and political establishment so defiantly. Whatever sentiments the women harbored toward Solzhenitsyn, it seems that he himself behaved with respect and restraint toward them. Again, his marriage had been slowly and painfully crumbling for a number of years. But it was his meeting with Natalya Svetlova that sounded its death knell.

After the appearance of *Ivan Denisovich* in 1962 and its immediate immense success, Solzhenitsyn was able both to quit his Ryazan teaching job and to spend more of his time in Moscow, at Rozhdestvo, at the homes of friends around Moscow, and traveling. Natalya, who had remarried him in 1956, came to see less and less of him. At one level, she was simply uncomfortable with her husband's fame and his life in the limelight. At another level, Solzhenitsyn himself was growing more rather than less focused in his single-minded pursuit of a lifetime's calling to expose the truth about the Soviet Union.

Natalya visited Solzhenitsyn whenever she could and continued to perform some of the functions of his literary production machine, but her heart was not in the project. By the second half of the 1960's, the emotional warmth that had once existed between them gradually turned to an icy civility. They slept when in the same house in separate rooms and shared no more of each other's intimate dreams.

It was in this emotional vacuum that a very attractive, athletic, brilliant, and feisty female mathematician, just twenty-eight, suddenly appeared in August 1968, just two hours before his first meeting with Sakharov. By their second meeting, Solzhenitsyn already trusted her enough to ask her to copy out the ninety-six-chapter version of *The First Circle*. Her name was Natalya Dmitrievna Svetlova. A graduate student at Moscow State University, she had a six-year-old boy from a marriage that had lasted a very brief time and had ended three years earlier.

Solzhenitsyn was instantly dazzled by her, or as he puts it quaintly, by "her fervent social concern—this was my kind of temperament," he adds. "I could not wait to involve her in our work!"[44] Or to share a deep emotional life with her, either, apparently. As lyrically as he has ever permitted himself to write about deeply personal matters of relationships, he describes Svetlova in terms that suggest not simply a detached admiration of professional quality, but someone who truly enraptured him. In his account, she

> worked with an alacrity, meticulousness, and lack of fuss that were the equal of any man. Her grasp of tactics, of how and when to act, was instantaneous—"computerlike," as I called it—and from the outset she matched my own impetuous behavior at the time. Moreover, I had dreamed in vain of finding a male friend whose ideas would be as close to my own as were those that Natasha came out with unprompted. As if this were not enough, she revealed a deep-rooted, innate spiritual affinity with everything quintessentially Russian, as well as an unusual concern and affection for the Russian language.[45]

The fourth or fifth time they met, according to Solzhenitsyn, he put his hands on her shoulders "as one does when expressing gratitude and confidence to a friend"—a stiff description of deep mutual attraction, if ever there was one—and instantly, an intense love affair took root. Within a few months, they were intimate, and though Solzhenitsyn was still officially married to the first Natalya, a son, Yermolai, was born to Natalya Svetlova in 1970. Two more children, Ignat and Stepan, were to be born to Solzhenitsyn and Svetlova in 1972 and 1973. It was only in 1973 that Natalya Reshetovskaya finally agreed to a divorce and Solzhenitsyn was able to marry the love of his life.

By the end of 1968, Solzhenitsyn was almost certainly one of the most popular figures in the Soviet Union. In fact, a 1967 Soviet poll asking who Russians' favorite writer was overwhelmingly placed Solzhenitsyn at the top of the list.[46] When he celebrated his fiftieth birthday back at Rozhdestvo, in December that year, telegrams poured into his little hut from all over the Soviet Union. But Solzhenitsyn was not distracted by this outpouring of support. He only redoubled his efforts to tell the story that had enveloped his imagination since 1936, the epic drama of Russia in a decades-long struggle with the anaconda of revolution. He once again during 1969 drove himself relentlessly to complete *August 1914*, what was to be the first "knot" in his gargantuan *Red Wheel* cycle encapsulating in the form of a multipart novel the origins and development of events leading up to the Revolution of 1917.

His sense of near invulnerability, though, was the cause of a serious miscalculation. When the Soviet Writers Union decided arbitrarily to expel him in November of 1969, he was taken completely by surprise and unable to respond in his usual vigorous manner. He was summoned to a pre-programmed meeting of the Ryazan chapter of the union at which there was no consideration of heading off the decision against him. Solzhenitsyn instantly penned an intemperate response to the Writers Union protesting the expulsion, which was formally announced November 12, 1969. "Dust off the clock face. You are behind the times," he thundered.

> Throw open the sumptuous heavy curtains—you do not even suspect that the day is already dawning outside. . . .At this time of crisis you are incapable of offering our grievously sick society anything constructive and good, anything but your malevolent vigilance, your "hold tight and don't let go!"[47]

But many of those who had supported him for *One Day* did not sympathize with his venomous hostility to the society in which they lived. For one thing, the party authorities were bearing down on *Novy Mir* for having tolerated Solzhenitsyn so long in its midst. Many Soviet intellectuals preferred

Tvardovsky's semiacceptance of the Soviet dream to Solzhenitsyn's out-right rejection of it. Solzhenitsyn wrote a separate letter to Tvardovsky af-ter the uproar had subsided. "I feel that my whole life is a process of rising gradually from my knees," he said, "a gradual transition from enforced dumb-ness to free speech, so that my letter to the congress and this present letter have been moments of high delight, of spiritual emancipation."[48]

Solzhenitsyn now found refuge at his most comfortable semi-exile to date, the personal dacha of internationally famous Soviet cellist and con-ductor Mstislav Rostropovich. The refuge was taken none too soon. The regime was losing patience altogether with pestilential dissident critics like Solzhenitsyn. Had Solzhenitsyn been in a less prestigious location, he might have run into serious problems of harassment and worse.

Increasing numbers of dissidents were being incarcerated in mental institutions (on the Orwellian grounds that no one so opposed to Soviet reality could be "normal") where they were subjected to incapacitating drugs and other humiliations. Solzhenitsyn wrote an essay protesting this practice entitled "The Way We Live Now" in which he described such incarceration methods as "spiritual murder." He was anxious to complete *August 1914*, the first "knot," or "nodal point," of the emergent historical novel, *The Red Wheel*.

Overseas, his novels *The First Circle* and *Cancer Ward* had prompted his name to be raised in discussion of the Nobel Prize for Literature. Nothing had happened in 1969, but in July 1970 the French Nobel laureate François Mauriac, who had already played a decisive role in "discovering" Great Soul Elie Wiesel, formally proposed Solzhenitsyn's name to the Swedish Academy. On October 8 he received a call from a Moscow-based Swedish correspondent informing him that he had indeed won the prize.

There followed a turbulence in his personal life that might have felled a man of lesser determination and resilience. In August, Svetlova, his bril-liant young assistant, had informed Solzhenitsyn that she was pregnant by him. With her pregnancy he could put off no longer confessing every-thing to his wife, Natalya, and he did so in a letter that was honest, contrite, and full of apologies. Unfortunately, this only convinced Natalya that the marriage could still be saved. Natalya came to Moscow to meet with Solzhenitsyn and discuss the matter just at the time the news of the Nobel Prize was exploding around Moscow. There were loud and noisy argu-ments in the dacha, threats of suicide, and then, the night of October 14, a real attempt at suicide by Natalya through an overdose of sleeping pills. Solzhenitsyn fortunately discovered her early enough in the morning to get her to a hospital and save her life.

The rest of the world knew nothing about this at the time. What they did learn was that Solzhenitsyn was unwilling to apply for a travel permit to Stockholm for the Nobel ceremony out of fear that he would never be permitted back into his country. Later, it trickled out that the Swedes, unwilling to offend the Soviets, would not consent to a prize award ceremony in the Swedish Embassy in Moscow. No one outside of Solzhenitsyn's closest circle of friends was aware of the domestic drama and near tragedy unfolding around Solzhenitsyn during what should have been one of the greatest moments of personal triumph in his life.

His wife recovered sufficiently to return to Ryazan in October, but after first agreeing to Solzhenitsyn's request for a divorce, changed her mind and decided she would withhold consent. She evidently still clung to the hope that Solzhenitsyn would return to her. In fact, it was not until late in 1972 that she agreed to the divorce, which finally came through in March 1973. The next month, in April 1973, Solzhenitsyn and Svetlova were finally married, none too soon for the sake of family cohesiveness. Natalya Svetlova's second son, Ignat, had been born in September 1972. Their third boy, Stepan, was born in September 1973.

Solzhenitsyn was continuing to write at the Zhukovka home of Rostropovich, but he also, from time to time, withdrew to his favorite, completely private nook, the cabin at Rozhdestvo. But in August 1971 the KGB made a clumsy raid on it and were caught in the act by a friend of the Solzhenitsyns'. Furious, the writer fired off a letter to Yuri Andropov, chairman of the KGB. "For many years," he wrote with sustained invective,

> I have borne in silence the lawlessness of your employees: the inspection of all my correspondence, the confiscation of half of it, the tracking down of my correspondents, their persecution at work and by state agencies, the spying around my house, the shadowing of visitors, the tapping of telephone conversations, the drilling of holes in ceilings. . . . But after the raid yesterday I will no longer be silent.[49]

What Solzhenitsyn could not have known was that he had become such a public nuisance to the Soviets that the ruling Politburo was frequently debating what to do with him. At a Politburo meeting chaired by Leonid Brezhnev in March 1972, for example, several Politburo members spoke openly of expelling him from the Soviet Union altogether. He was, said one, "a degenerate," "a hostile person," "an anti-Soviet slanderer of the first order."[50]

Yet there was an enormous amount at stake with him too. Thanks to his prestige in the rest of the world and to the Nobel Prize, there was no question of simply incarcerating him in an insane asylum, much less packing him off to the Gulag once more. The Soviet Union was in the delicate process of trying to establish trade, cultural, and armes control agreements with the United States. It could no longer play Stalin's role of neighborhood thug in international affairs. Now the risk of a nuclear war breaking out with almost no provocation had reached a critical point. By the early 1970's Moscow and Washington had intercontinental nuclear missiles, submarine-launched nuclear missiles, and bomber forces capable of destroying each other's country several times over on a few minutes' warning.

It was in September 1973 that the seal was finally set on Solzhenitsyn's fate in the Soviet Union. In September in Leningrad, the KGB arrested one of Solzhenitsyn's faithful copyists, Elizaveta Voronyanksaya and interrogated her so brutally that she broke down and revealed the hiding place of one of the copies of The Gulag Archipelago. When the agents seized the manuscript, they knew they had in their hands one of the most damaging exposés of the reality of Soviet totalitarianism that had ever been written. Solzhenitsyn, of course, had already secreted to Paris a microfilmed copy of the entire manuscript, but he had been unsure when to give permission for the Y.M.C.A. Press, his by now preferred publishing house, to bring it out.

Based on his personal experiences in the Gulag, on extensive research, and on material provided him by 227 other Gulag survivors, the full title of the book was The Gulag Archipelago 1918–1956: An Experiment in Literary Investigation. On learning of the manuscript seizures, and the tragic news of Voronyanksaya's subsequent suicide shortly afterward, Solzhenitsyn gave instructions through his trusted emissaries that the book should be published immediately in Paris.

By December, the first volume was already in print in English in the U.S. and Great Britain, and the impact on the reading public was startling.

Though in 1972 Solzhenitsyn had in fact released in Paris his novel *August 1914*, it had received mediocre reviews in the West. Critics disliked the formal, detailed realism and no longer were comparing Solzhenitsyn to Tolstoy and Dostoyevsky, but to Pearl Buck and James Michener. Some wondered if Solzhenitsyn had been something of an overrated writer at his initial appearance.

Gulag silenced all these voices. Though at first only Volume One appeared, containing the first two of six parts, the impact of the work was profound on all who read it. The precise methods used in arrests of political prisoners, the tortures used during interrogation, the transportation system of prisoners around Moscow (sometimes prisoners were carried in vans marked "Bread" on the outside), and innumerable other details were all introduced with an accompanying commentary by Solzhenitsyn. By turns sardonically funny, anguished, or burning in slow fury, Solzhenitsyn accomplished something truly rare in all literature, the moral impaling of an entire political system with sustained literary power. Prominent U.S. Kremlinologist and diplomat George Kennan termed the work "the greatest and most powerful single indictment of a political regime . . . in modern times."

In the U.S. and Great Britain, where attitudes toward Soviet Communism had been hostile since the Cold War dominated global politics in the late 1940's, Kennan's acclaim for the book was echoed broadly. But in Europe, where leftist, even pro-Stalinist anti-Americanism had been a fashionable stance of many intellectuals, *Gulag* stripped away the last fig leaf of pretense that the Soviet Union was anything other than a monstrous structure of lies and coercion. As David Remnick has commented, "Largely thanks to Solzhenitsyn, the *nouveaux philosophes* [new philosophers]— former Marxist thinkers like André Glucksmann and Bernard-Henri Lévy— took a strong anti-Communist stance and assumed an intellectual authority in France."[51] Norman Podhoretz, editor of *Commentary* magazine, described *Gulag* and Solzhenitsyn's powerful and moving memoirs of his struggle with the Soviet authorities, *The Oak and the Calf*, "among the very greatest books of the age."[52]

"AN ANTI-SOVIET SLANDERER OF THE FIRST ORDER"

These sorts of accolades only enraged the Soviet leadership even more. On January 7, 1974, a lengthy and urgent discussion of what to do with

Solzhenitsyn took place once more in the Politburo. Once again, Brezhnev, as general secretary of the Communist Party, chaired the meeting, and KGB chief Yuri Andropov spoke up prominently. The mood was one of both fury and exasperation. Veteran ideologist Mikhail Suslov, for example, fumed that Solzhenitsyn had become "impudent," and had "encroached upon the holiest of holies, Lenin."[53] (He didn't bother to explain how anything could be "holy" in a regime that officially denied the existence of God or anything transcendent.) *Gulag* was referred to as "a contemptuous anti-Soviet lampoon." When it came to what should be done with Solzhenitsyn, however, a consensus had now clearly formed. First, the full fury of the Soviet propaganda apparatus, for consumption inside the country, was to be unleashed against Solzhenitsyn. Second, as soon as Moscow could find a country willing to accept the writer, he was to be exiled there involuntarily.

Pravda, the official organ of the party, uncoiled the first vituperative whip against Solzhenitsyn. An authoritative, eighteen-hundred-word article on January 14, 1974, entitled "The Path of a Traitor," rehearsed many of the early accusations against Solzhenitsyn—that he was a "counter-revolutionary," for example—but added to them a new gloss: He had been, supposedly, pathologically anti-Soviet from the very beginning of his career. Other Soviet news organizations chimed in with a new list of charges: Solzhenitsyn was a "Vlasovite" (i.e., someone who wanted to betray the Soviet Union to the Germans), a Maoist, a Judas, a blasphemer, an ally of hawks in the Pentagon.[54] That the frenzied insults contradicted one another didn't seem to bother anyone in the Kremlin.

Solzhenitsyn, his new wife, and their young children had now moved out of Rostropovich's dacha back into that of the Chukovskys' at Peredelkino. Solzhenitsyn continued to write six days of the week, still measuring out his life in carefully calculated minutes, but on Mondays he would move into Moscow and stay overnight on Gorky Street not far from Svetlova's apartment. Early in February, in the very eye of the storm raging over his head, he took time off to consider what the regime might do next. "Forecast for February," he wrote. "Apart from attempts to discredit me, they aren't likely to do anything, and there will probably be a breathing space."[55]

He was utterly wrong. After weeks of searching, Moscow had found a country willing to take Solzhenitsyn. On February 2, West German chancellor Willy Brandt had inserted into a speech on a separate topic the comment that Solzhenitsyn would be welcome, if he chose to come, to live and work freely in West Germany. In the afternoon of February 12, the authorities made their move. Solzhenitsyn had come into Moscow the previous day, a Monday, as was his habit, and stayed the night in the apartment. Solzhenitsyn had already been summoned to the prosecutor's office to be confronted with criminal charges, but he had ignored the order. Now, two men from the office showed up at the door supposedly "to clear something up." Grumpily, Solzhenitsyn took the chain off the hook to let them in. Suddenly, there were not just two of them, but six, pouring into the apartment from recesses in the landing outside where they had been hiding.

"Nothing in my heart warned me," Solzhenitsyn recalled later. "I had lost my sense of alertness."[56] Despite his intimate knowledge of how the KGB operated, how arrests were made, how the victims usually succumbed in fear and confusion to the onslaught of state power, Solzhenitsyn was totally unprepared, after years of distant artillery duels with the Soviet regime, for this sudden assault by its infantry soldiers, so to speak.

With the agents waiting impatiently, Solzhenitsyn returned to his study to find a school satchel to use as the repository of the necessities for prison, lovingly kissed his wife good-bye, made the sign of the cross over her, and with no further word went down the stairs with his new guardians. Even in the Soviet Union, handcuffs were not the norm during arrests, so Solzhenitsyn was simply manhandled down the three flights of stairs to the door of the apartment building and into the waiting black Volga limousine that had come for him. The driver had driven the car right onto the sidewalk outside the apartment front door, and the agents had opened the rear car door to make sure Solzhenitsyn would not be able to make a break for it once he was outside. Accompanied by four agents in the first Volga and four in one following, the cars sped off to Lefortovo Prison.

To his surprise, Solzhenitsyn, despite his fame, received no special treatment once in the very place he had first been interrogated almost exactly twenty-nine years earlier. He was stripped, searched, and taken to a cell where there were already two other "normal" criminal prisoners undergoing investigation. He suffered from high blood pressure, and the following morning during a medical examination it appeared to have gone through the roof. He was given some medicine for this, and after break-fast given a white shirt and tie to add to a suit and new shoes that had been given him soon after his arrival the previous day. Now he was taken from his cell once more, ordered to sit down in front of Mikhail P. Malyarov, Soviet deputy prosecutor-general, and read an official decree declaring that he was being deprived of Soviet citizenship and would forthwith be expelled from the Soviet Union itself.

A short time after this, he was taken out to a waiting car and driven at high speed to Sheremetyevo International Airport, Moscow's principal gateway to the outside world. There, with no regular customs or immi-gration procedures whatsoever, he was escorted onto the tarmac and to the steps of the plane, a regular Aeroflot jetliner scheduled to depart for Frankfurt. The flight had been delayed for three hours—officially for rea-sons of "fog"—while final arrangements were made to bundle Solzhenitsyn onto it. The writer had no clue where he was going, but he crossed him-self and bowed to his homeland as he departed.

Following an uneventful flight, shortly after 5:00 P.M. the plane landed and through the windows Solzhenitsyn saw where he had arrived: Frank-furt Airport in the heart of West Germany. He was welcomed by German foreign ministry officials and driven in a Mercedes at high speed to the village home outside Bonn of the German novelist Heinrich Böll, who was his "official" host in the country at the outset of his exile. He was told by Böll to be as open as possible to the media who were now swarm-ing around Böll's house and not to hide from the mass of photographers pursuing him. But what could Solzhenitsyn now say? "All my life I had been tortured by the impossibility of speaking the truth aloud," he re-called later. "Now, at last, I was free, as I had never been before, no ax was poised above my head, and dozens of microphones belonging to the world's most important press agencies were held out toward my lips. Say something!"[57]

But Solzhenitsyn was unnerved by the aggressive behavior of the world's media. He was still worried about Natalya and their children back in Moscow. He had no new pearl of wisdom that he wished to lay before the world. There was, however, one farewell counsel from him to his fellow Soviet citizens that had been circulating in samizdat along with several other dissident documents. It was called "Live Not by Lies," and it was, as many in Russia termed it, "Solzhenitsyn's moral testament." He had been asked how one could resist Soviet tyranny without actively taking up arms against it. People wanted to know how one could improve the moral atmosphere of the entire country. In his essay, Solzhenitsyn came up with one answer: People should never permit falsehood of any kind to invade their conversation, their professional work, their meetings, or their writings. It was a simple choice, he averred: "Either truth or falsehood: towards spiritual independence or towards spiritual servitude."[58]

Late in March 1974, accompanied by huge crates bearing his literary archive, the rest of his family arrived in Zurich, where Solzhenitsyn had moved less than two weeks after his stay in Bonn. He was determined to pursue research on Lenin, who was inevitably a central player in at least part of *The Red Wheel* cycle. But his exile had hardly removed him from the political and philosophical fray of which he had been a central figure in Soviet life since 1962.

In March he approved the official, Russian-language publication of his *Letter to Soviet Leaders*, a fifteen-thousand-word document that he had altered slightly from the original form that had been sent to the Politburo while he was still in Russia. The seven-part document denounced the ideology of Marxism forcefully and warned of the dangers of any war the Soviets might be thinking of conducting against China. It proclaimed Christianity as "the only living spiritual force capable of undertaking the spiritual healing of Russia." And it called for major political changes. But Solzhenitsyn also spoke critically not just of the weaknesses that existed within Western democratic systems, but of the West as a whole. There was no ethical basis for democracy in the West, he wrote, if it was entirely secular in origin.

A WORLD SPLIT APART

The publication of *Letter to Soviet Leaders* did more to split Western opinion over Solzhenitsyn than anything he had written earlier or was to write later. As Edward Ericson Jr. has eloquently pointed out, those most shocked by Solzhenitsyn's prescriptions were political liberals who assumed that anyone who opposed Soviet power must be, well, just like them.

Jeri Laber in *Commentary* described Solzhenitsyn as "reactionary, authoritarian, chauvinistic," and took issue with him for blaming not just

Stalin for Soviet political terror, but Marxism itself. She failed to explain how someone as strongly opposed to Russian imperial control over any neighboring country as Solzhenitsyn was could be a "chauvinist."[59] But Laber's view of Solzhenitsyn, comprised of an almost visceral distaste for his Christian view of life and his strong reservations about the real weaknesses of Western democratic pluralism, was to characterize the attitudes of many Western literary and political observers of Solzhenitsyn not only in the first few months of his freedom, but throughout the rest of his life.

In December 1974, Solzhenitsyn traveled to Sweden for the formal presentation of his Nobel Prize that he had been denied in the Soviet Union. He was now able publicly to deliver his Nobel speech, a moving oration that touched on politics, but only as a footnote to something much closer to his heart, the very notion of artistic creation (not just in terms of the visual arts, but in all expressions of the arts). "Art inflames even a frozen, darkened soul to a high spiritual experience," he wrote.

> Through art we are sometimes visited, dimly, briefly, by revelations such as cannot be produced by rational thinking. . . . And literature conveys irrefutable condensed experience in yet another invaluable direction; namely from generation to generation. Thus it becomes the living memory of the nation.
>
> . . . In the struggle with falsehood art always did win and it always does win! Openly, irrefutably for everyone! Falsehood can hold out against much in this world, but not against art.
>
> . . . Proverbs about truth are well-loved in Russian. They give steady and sometimes striking expression to the not inconsiderable harsh national experience: ONE WORD OF TRUTH SHALL OUT-WEIGH THE WHOLE WORLD.[60]

In Zurich, Solzhenitsyn first publicly indicated that he was certain he would return to his homeland in his own lifetime. He told the British journalist Malcolm Muggeridge (who had earlier written about Mother Teresa), "In a strange way, I not only hope, I am inwardly convinced I shall go back [to Russia]. I live with that conviction. I mean my physical return, not just my books."[61]

No one at the time believed Solzhenitsyn could possibly be realistic.

Not only was the Soviet Union more powerful than ever, but at the time, within weeks of the collapse of all of Indochina to Communist rule, it looked as though the West itself was in retreat.

Furthermore, Solzhenitsyn's comments about the weakness of the West further shocked his audiences in Britain and the U.S. Speeches he made in these two countries during 1975 and 1976 were later published under the title *Warning to the West*. His comments came across to many as strident overestimates of the danger of Communist power in the world. Speaking of the 1975 Helsinki Accords on security and cooperation in Europe, Solzhenitsyn described the proposed agreement as "the funeral of Eastern Europe."[62] He said he thought that the West was "on the verge of a collapse created by its own hands."[63] He also turned on its head a phrase popularized by the British antiwar philosopher Bertrand Russell, "Better read than dead." "All my life and the life of my generation," he responded, "the life of those who share my views, we all have had one viewpoint: Better to be dead than a scoundrel."[64] Years later, he acknowledged that he had spoken too melodramatically during this period of his exile. He commented, "Perhaps I even exaggerated the danger of Communism, perhaps even consciously, to inspire the West to stand more firmly. But remember—countries were falling to Communism one after another."[65]

He was right. The year 1975 was a grim one for those regimes, for example South Vietnam, which had for years tried to resist takeover by its Communist neighbor to the North. But it was also a year in which Solzhenitsyn's message was openly repudiated in the White House. President Gerald Ford refused to invite Solzhenitsyn to the executive mansion during the writer's 1975 visit to the U.S. Dr. Henry Kissinger, secretary of state at the time, regarded Solzhenitsyn's entire personality as an affront to his efforts to cultivate a new relationship with the Soviet Union under the heading of "detente." Solzhenitsyn's views, he said, were "an embarrassment even to his fellow dissidents."[66]

This was palpably untrue for the vast majority of the Soviet dissident community. But an illustration of how totally out of touch even the pragmatic-minded Ford was with the significance of Solzhenitsyn was an aside disclosed by Ford's press secretary, Ron Nessen. Ford reportedly said that Solzhenitsyn's chief reason for wanting to meet with the U.S. president was to drum up more lecture dates. Ford's error of judgment was to come back and haunt him during the 1976 Republican National Convention. Supporters of his chief rival for the presidential nomination, Ronald Reagan, wanted the Republican platform specifically to praise Solzhenitsyn by name and to repudiate "detente."

In July 1976, Solzhenitsyn and his family finally found a refuge from controversy and public debates in the village of Cavendish in central Vermont. It was here that he decided to settle in order to complete, in almost total seclusion, the immense epic of twentieth-century Russia of which he had first dreamed four decades earlier at the age of eighteen. For him and his family, friends found a large, comfortable, though certainly not opulent fifty-acre estate in a part of New England where local people protected their privacy zealously. The locals seemed honored to play a role in protecting that of Solzhenitsyn. The hamlet of some 1,325 people (in 1994) was zealous to the end in performing this function, occasionally reporting to the police and FBI cars that bore out-of-town license plates and might have been driven by Soviet agents.

Once again, Solzhenitsyn set for himself a punishing work schedule. Rising at 6:00 A.M., he worked until noon, took a brief break for lunch, then resumed work in the afternoon. He stopped working around nine at night. He did this virtually every single day—seven days a week—during his entire eighteen-year sojourn in the United States. There were exceptions for his occasional travels and excursions for public events.

In the morning, the family would gather for prayer to God to save Russia from Communism, and in the early years, Solzhenitsyn himself would tutor the young boys in mathematics and the sciences. Occasionally, he would take just fifteen minutes to play tennis on the court that was on the property. From time to time he would venture forth for research at institutions with major Russian research holdings (notably at the Hoover Institute at Stanford University, for example). And in his most controversial foray of all since arriving in the U.S., he gave the commencement speech at Harvard University in 1978. His address, "A World Split Apart," more fully developed the themes critical of the weaknesses of Western and U.S. culture that he had touched on earlier. He spoke out against what he called a loss of civic courage in the Western world,[67] and its overall loss of will. But some of his most controversial references were to the American media. "Hastiness and superficiality—these are the psychic diseases of the twentieth century and more than anywhere else this is manifested in the press," he said. He also denounced "today's mass living habits," characterized by "the revolting invasion of commercial advertising, by TV stupor, and by intolerable music."[68]

Predictably, reaction to the speech was split, with conservatives praising his insights lavishly and liberals denouncing him as an unreconstructed reactionary. In perhaps the most hysterical reaction to his ideas expressed by establishment news organizations in the West, the *Washington Post* opined that Solzhenitsyn was speaking for "boundless cold war," the *New York Times* characterized his worldview as "dangerous," and Kennedy-era White House adviser Arthur Schlesinger Jr. said that what Solzhenitsyn really wanted was "a Christian authoritarianism governed by God-fearing despots."[69]

Ironically, Solzhenitsyn's very point in his speech about the dictates of intellectual fashion in the American media was borne out by the relentless repetition, for years afterward, of entirely unsubstantiated assertions that the writer was a monarchist, an ultranationalist, and an anti-Semite to boot.

The anti-Semite accusation arose from the 1989 version of *August 1914* in which Solzhenitsyn attempted to explore the thought processes of an individual of Jewish background called Bogrov, the real-life assassin of the pre–World War I reformist, Russian prime minister Stolypin. Some critics felt that Solzhenitsyn was repeating stereotypes and revealing prejudice against Jews in his unflattering depiction of Bogrov. Though Lev Kopelev, who was Jewish and had been an intimate friend of Solzhenitsyn in the Moscow sharashka and much later, defended Solzhenitsyn against any such accusation, some were still not mollified.

During my 1989 interview with Solzhenitsyn in Vermont, I specifically raised the subject of the accusations of anti-Semitism against him. Describing anti-Semitism as "a prejudiced and unjust attitude toward the Jewish nation as a whole," he emphatically denied that anything like this colored his attitude toward Bogrov. "It would be impossible," he said, "to have any anti-Semitism in any genuinely artistic work. No real artist could be prejudiced toward any entire nation without destroying the artistic integrity of his entire work."[70]

Solzhenitsyn was indignant. He felt he had been lied about in the West and that his opinions had been misrepresented. He repudiated any desire whatever for Russia to return to a monarchy, much less to a society run by priests. As for the distinctly frosty attitudes toward him by some American intellectuals and journalists, he said, "Maybe democracy likes and wants criticism, but the press certainly does not."[71]

Solzhenitsyn had not wanted to discuss the current situation of the Soviet Union during our 1989 interview, but he made it clear in conversations then and later that day that he was certain he would return to his homeland a free man. His only precondition was that all of the judicial procedures that had been taken against him be annulled and that his books should be freely printed and distributed throughout the country.

Even at that time, there were signs that Gorbachev was willing to go all the way toward meeting Solzhenitsyn's conditions. By September 1991, Soviet prosecutor Nikolai Trubin declared that all of the charges against Solzhenitsyn made in 1974 at the time of the writer's involuntary exile were in fact "baseless." By late that same year, Solzhenitsyn had finally completed the mammoth *Red Wheel*. Of the five-thousand-page opus, only the first "knot," *August 1914*, was already in English. The other three books, *November 1916, March 1917,* and *April 1917,* completed the cycle in Russian.

Back in Solzhenitsyn's homeland political and social events were now accelerating. In December 1991, the hammer and sickle flag of the Soviet Union was pulled down from over the Kremlin for the last time. In its place rose the white, blue, and red striped flag of the Russian Federation. Gorbachev was no longer in power and his place in the Kremlin was taken over by Boris Yeltsin, a former Communist who openly admired Solzhenitsyn. It was clearly time for Russia's greatest living author to return to his homeland.

In May 1994, he did so, though not in the manner any had anticipated. He did not choose to return to a great fanfare at Moscow's Sheremetyevo Airport more than two decades after his unceremonial and forced departure from it. Instead, Solzhenitsyn, accompanied by his wife, his eldest son, Yermolai, and a BBC television crew, flew via Alaska to the city of Khabarovsk, on the Russian Pacific Coast. He had arranged to travel slowly back across the massive breadth of Russia by train, stopping frequently at different cities, meeting with local people and officials, and taking the pulse of the country. Before setting off from Cavendish, he thanked the people of the hamlet both for forgiving him his eccentrically sealed-off lifestyle and for helping to protect it.

I caught up with him once again in Khabarovsk, and accompanied him by train part of the way through Siberia. He was ebullient and brimming with energy, filling notebook after notebook with conversations and impressions of people and situations that he was witnessing. But he also sternly told his audiences that they must now take responsibility for their country at the local level and not simply wait for orders to arrive from Moscow.

Before leaving the United States, he had reassured some observers by making it clear that he had nothing but distaste for the then rising mode of ultranationalism in Russia. He dismissed the dangerous anti-Semite and xenophobe Vladimir Zhirinovsky as "an evil caricature of a Russian patriot."[72] Obviously, whatever his emotional sympathies for the ethnic Russian character, he was totally uninterested in grandiose dreams of the restoration of Russian power. Indeed, in his 1994 book, *The Russian Question at the End of the 20th Century*, he reiterated a theme that had echoed again and again through his writings: Nations, like individuals, have moral responsibilities to other nations. "We must build a moral Russia, or none at all—it would not then matter anyhow," he said. Nations must demonstrate "self-limitation" in their dealings with others, he said, taking up a point he had elaborated in his *Letter to Soviet Leaders*.

Solzhenitsyn nevertheless did not play a major role in Russian life after his return to his homeland. He spoke once to the Russian Parliament, the Duma, to mixed reviews. For a part of a year he presided over a fifteen-minute television talk show aired twice a month, and called "A Meeting with Solzhenitsyn." But though his selected topics and personalities were always interesting, Russian society, impatient with seriousness, and anxious to catch up with the consumerism of the rest of the world, seemed impatient with his reflective, and at times didactic, discourse. The show was pulled in September 1995 without notice, and without Solzhenitsyn being given an opportunity to say good-bye to his audience.

I saw Solzhenitsyn for the third time in October 1995, this time bringing along a camera crew to the Moscow apartment he continues to use for business meetings in the city. He seemed more tired than during previous meetings, a little more impatient with any threats to his time. He spoke of his country's "fatigue of culture, its emaciation," the decline of literature both in mass consumer societies and in dictatorships. He spoke warmly of patriotism ("a whole and deliberate feeling of love towards your country, your nation"), and yet of the need for repentance in his own country for the terrible wrongs committed there under the rule of Communism. With great passion, he took up the theme of freedom and truth with which he had dealt in his Nobel Prize speech two decades earlier. "In the Gospel it says," he reminded me,

> "You shall know the truth and the truth shall make you free." It is fascinating, astounding. What does this mean? It means that the path to freedom lies not in the fact that the parliament made a law of greater freedom today, but [rather] that you have to go through the truth. And if you go through truth just a little, then you will no longer say things such as, "Well, if the people are good, truth doesn't matter."[73]

I wondered aloud to Solzhenitsyn if he believed in the notion of a calling, the idea common to Judaism and Christianity that God actually summons certain people to accomplish—or at least to perform—certain things in their lives. He quickly replied,

> Everybody has a purpose and the main purpose of each of us is how to understand it. Given the everyday preoccupations of ordinary life, people don't spend enough time thinking about this. They have their daily troubles. Only self-deepening, reflection, prayer, only reflection can discover that purpose.[74]

Did Solzhenitsyn believe he had completed his own life's task? I asked. "At the end of my life, I will have fulfilled my debt," he said.

Debt? What debt? And then I remembered: Solzhenitsyn had spoken of his debt to those who had given him their knowledge of the truth of Russia under Communist rule. These were men and women who had died with no certainty at all that what they had told him would reach the light of day, much less help change their country from top to bottom.

I remembered, too, a question I had asked Solzhenitsyn in 1989, of whether his life in the camps was not something that he cherished—as part of his calling, so to speak—rather than regretted. "Yes," he said then, "because in those circumstances human nature becomes very much more visible. I was very lucky to have been in the camps—and especially to have survived."

For that imprisonment, for his survival, and for Aleksandr Solzhenitsyn's unwavering commitment to speaking the truth at all costs, the entire world should be grateful.

CHAPTER 4

MOTHER TERESA: COMPASSION

"The meaning of my life is the love of God.
It is Christ in his distressing disguise whom I love and serve."[1]

"That is what I am. God's pencil.
A tiny bit of pencil with which he writes what he likes."[2]

—MOTHER TERESA

I FIRST MET HER in July 1975. My editors in New York had sent me from my base in Hong Kong, where I was a foreign correspondent, to cover the latest political crisis in India, the imposition of emergency rule by then Prime Minister Indira Gandhi. All normal democratic rights, including freedom of the press, had been suspended. In fact, I had to leave India rather quickly when the government required all visiting or resident foreign reporters to sign a pledge of self-censorship as a condition of continued accreditation in India. I refused to do this and so was confronted with the choice of expulsion or voluntary departure. I selected the second option. But, fortunately, in my short time in Delhi before my departure, I managed to meet and interview Mother Teresa, who was visiting the Indian capital briefly from her base in Calcutta.

The Delhi residence of the Missionaries of Charity was an unpretentious single-story building at the end of a narrow lane between the walls of private gardens and residences. In fact, it appeared to be crumbling apart. As I approached the main entrance with *Time*'s resident Delhi reporter, a pleasant Anglo-Indian named James Shepherd, we could already see Mother Teresa. She was deep in conversation in the front reception room of the house with a fiftyish, well-coiffed American woman named Kitty Brinnand, a benefactor of the Missionaries of Charity in Delhi. Kitty looked ill at ease and even rather worried by something. Mother Teresa, by contrast, conveyed the presence of a quiet, orderly calm.

The aging nun's deeply wrinkled face reflected at the same time deep fatigue and great energy. The vertical lines around her mouth suggested a woman much older than her sixty-five years. Her eyes, an intense blue, were set in remarkably deep sockets. She wore the characteristic white Indian sari with a blue border that represented the Missionaries of Charity, the order that she had founded in 1949, and on her left shoulder hung a simple wooden cross, attached by a safety pin.

My colleague had some bread-and-butter questions to ask about the expansion of Mother Teresa's work in India. I, on the other hand, wanted only to know about the core of her faith and spiritual life. "You need double grace for faith," she said in response to a question from me about what constitutes faith. "First, for the grace itself, and then for the courage to act upon it. Faith is a gift, but it is available to everyone."

"What motivates you," I inquired, "to perform the extraordinary works of charity for which you've become famous?"

She replied, "Ours is not a social work. We work twenty-four hours a day to express God's love. We evangelize by showing God's love. It is only through God's love that the poor can have their needs met."

Then she turned her attention to me and my profession of journalism. "Your work is different," she said briskly. "Your task is to do as good a job writing as you can. This is how you may glorify God, by writing the truth and not expressing a bad influence. We express our adoration of God in our work."[3]

I swallowed hard and tried to maintain an expression of calm detachment from this little sermon. But it wasn't easy. How would any journalist respond when exhorted to glorify God in his work by the woman who was unquestionably regarded as the saintliest exponent of Christian charity in the twentieth century?

Our questions continued and covered a range of matters touching on both Christendom and the world as a whole. She had met Billy Graham, she said, and approved of what he was doing. She thought Malcolm Muggeridge, the erstwhile cranky British journalist who had helped make her famous with the book *Something Beautiful for God*, was "completely dedicated to God." She liked Senator Ted Kennedy and the Shriver family. But on some contemporary issues, she was almost feisty. She was not at all enthralled by the agenda of that summer's gathering in Mexico City in honor of the International Women's Year. "Women are unique," she insisted. "They are made to serve. They are not the same as men and they should not try to be. If they try to be like men and become the same, they lose that quality. Women should first learn to love each other more."

When the formal part of our interview was over, Mother Teresa led us across a child's playground to the home's chapel. En route, she was immediately besieged by a beguiling pack of little Indian children, calling out to her, "Mother, Mother!" Some of them were severely physically handicapped. One boy with a very large head had fingers and toes that were almost web-like in formation. As he clutched her skirt, she caressed him gently, smiling all the time. Once in the chapel, without a word to us in advance, she quickly knelt down and prayed in silence for about a minute, her face immediately becoming serious. Then, just as swiftly, her smile returned.

Ours was not a long interview and in fact the magazine never quite found a way to use it. Nothing Mother Teresa had said was really "news." But I was quite content with having enjoyed the rare privilege of meeting one of the greatest human personalities of this or any age. Was I changed by the encounter? I don't know. But something inside me was illuminated by her presence in an incomparable way.

Malcolm Muggeridge, the British journalistic curmudgeon whom Mother Teresa mentioned to me, had first met her in 1968 on a visit to Calcutta for a BBC television documentary on the Missionaries of Charity. Watching her receding into the distance aboard a train at the Calcutta station, he wrote, "When the train began to move and I walked away, I felt as though I were leaving behind me all the beauty and all the joy of the universe. Something of God's universal love has rubbed off on Mother Teresa, giving her homely features a noticeable luminosity; a shining quality."[4]

Muggeridge, no doubt in some measure because of his encounter with Mother Teresa, converted in 1982 from a lifelong religious skepticism to Christian belief and membership in the Roman Catholic Church. But his reaction to Mother Teresa was not at all unique, any more than was mine. The insights into Mother Teresa's character that various people have expressed over the years have helped build a composite, at times almost holographic portrait of the woman.

She was, wrote Prince Michael of Greece, who met her in 1996, "a tiny figure, bent almost double; her hands, as tiny and wrinkled as her face. She took our hands between hers," he continued, "and electrified us with her smile—the smile of a young girl. An extraordinary warmth seemed to surround her—and immediately enveloped us too. With all the love in the world, without a trace of judgment, she seemed to understand each one of us."[5]

Jim Twoey, a former aide to Oregon's longtime and now retired senator Mark Hatfield, and one of a handful of Americans to know Mother Teresa really well, reflected for several seconds before answering a question about his own impression of Mother Teresa. Finally, he said, "She was such a presence. It's been said that St. Francis of Assisi was the most Christ-like person since Christ. I think Mother Teresa was the most Mary-like person since the Virgin Mary. When you think of the Virgin Mary and Mother [Teresa], you cannot meet her and not be struck by her motherhood."[6]

Generic "motherhood" in a woman who was never married? Qualities that are "Mary-like," that is, close to the presumed qualities of Mary, the mother of Jesus, who for Roman Catholics is the closest any human being apart from Jesus Christ Himself has ever come to human perfection? Even before her death, the attributes mentioned in the same breath as Mother Teresa's name made it difficult to separate admiring, even reverential accounts of her life from scarcely believable narratives of medieval saints.

Certain things are obvious, however. No matter how many of her flaws eventually surface in the biographies that are bound to be written now that she has died, no one can deny that Mother Teresa's unwavering orientation of compassion to the poor, the handicapped, and the dying struck an imaginative chord across the entire human race. Her very name has become synonymous with saintliness and self-sacrificing concern for others. Through her actions and words, perhaps more people than ever before have come to understand the ultimate expression of the word *compassion*. Better yet is to use a more ancient and specific Christian term: "love" when translated from the Greek word *agape*, connoting giving without any thought whatever of return.

Mother Teresa founded a worldwide organization, active in some 126 nations, that has carried her name and that of the Missionaries of Charity to every continent except Antarctica. Yet it is hardly a mammoth multinational enterprise, with a bare four thousand "professed" (that is, having

completed six arduous years of preparation and training before final vows)
nuns. Its physical assets are paltry compared with any normal corporation, even a nonprofit one. It is nevertheless present in cities as diverse as
San Francisco and Zanzibar, Guatemala City and Sydney. It commands no
armies, controls no governments, and exists entirely by the offerings of
ordinary members of the public around the world. It offers charity, but it
is supported by charity. And it is only a part of what made Mother Teresa
the very personification of compassion. The rest of the equation is quite
simple: Mother Teresa was throughout her life revered most of all for her
personal example and the teachings about God's love that she spread
around the globe.

In the half-century after she responded to what she called "the call
within a call" and left a secure, if cloistered existence as a member of the
Sisters of Loreto in Calcutta, India, she reached out to serve "the poorest
of the poor," to use her own words. In so doing, she succeeded in imposing on the consciousness of the entire human race a practical, workable
demonstration of Christ's commandment "Love your neighbor," at the
grassroots level in one of the poorest of all human societies.

Lots of people in the world, of course, don't share the Christian faith.
So how have they responded to Mother Teresa? And how do they define
her work? A secular Indian journalist, Desmond Doig, had struggled with
this when writing an admiring, but certainly not uncritical, account of
Mother Teresa and her work. "The Sisters," he wrote, meaning the Missionaries of Charity,

> . . . have come to symbolize not only the best in Christian charity,
> but also the best in Indian culture and civilization, from Buddha to
> Gandhi, the great saints, the seers, the great lovers of humanity with
> boundless compassion and consideration for the underprivileged;
> what Shakespeare called the quality of mercy.[7]

At the ceremony in Oslo in 1979 in which Mother Teresa was awarded
the Nobel Peace Prize, another nonreligious, or perhaps more precisely,
generically religious effort was made to define Mother Teresa's achievement. It came from the speech of Committee Chairman John Sanness.
He explained the ground rules upon which the Nobel Peace Prize had
traditionally been conferred on people. The Committee in the past, he
said, had "awarded the prize to idealists who explored avenues leading to

a better world, in which war would be meaningless or inconceivable, and where traditional statesmanship would be superfluous."[8]

It had previously honored "champions of equality and fraternity," he said, and "champions of human rights." He said that "brotherhood and peace" were still "our goals." Then he asked:

> Can any political, social, or intellectual feat of engineering, on the international or on the national plane, however effective and rational, however idealistic and principled its protagonists may be, give us anything but a house built on a foundation of sand, unless the spirit of Mother Teresa inspires the builders and takes its dwelling in their building?[9]

The Nobel Committee, Sanness emphasized, while impressed with the size and scope of Mother Teresa's work, didn't want to attach great significance to "statistical information." What it wanted to emphasize, he said, was "the spirit that has permeated this work." He said that this had been Mother Teresa's "fundamental contribution to the Order she has created and run."

What on earth was this spirit, this spirit of Mother Teresa? According to Sanness, it was Mother Teresa's "own fundamental attitude to life and her very special personality," both of which, he acknowledged, were "clearly and firmly rooted in her Christian faith."[10] What her work demonstrated, he said, was that any kind of giving, even the giving of aid on a national scale by wealthy nations to poor countries, must be done in a way that honors the self-respect of the recipient. In short, if giving isn't done with love, it violates the very concept of giving—an interesting point from a Nobel bureaucrat unwilling to get too spiritual in his talk.

Actually, the Nobel Peace Prize has been conferred on recipients without any regard for their personal religious belief or lack of it. Recipients in recent years have included Buddhists (the Dalai Lama, Burmese democratic activist Aung San Suu Kyi), Muslims (Yassir Arafat), Jews (Elie Wiesel, Yitzhak Rabin), Christians (Bishop Desmond Tutu), and even a self-professed atheist (Mikhail Gorbachev). By definition, therefore, the conferring of the award seldom in itself explains how a particular religious commitment has motivated certain kinds of behavior toward peace.

The Templeton Prize for Progress in Religion, by contrast, has no such inhibitions. A recognition of outstanding achievement in the field of religion, the award, backed by the personal fortune of Sir John Templeton, the British financier, was first awarded in 1973, and Mother Teresa was its first honoree. The Templeton citation said that Mother Teresa had been "instrumental in widening and deepening man's knowledge and love of God and thereby furthering the quest for the quality of life that mirrors the divine."[11]

Mother Teresa might well have smiled inwardly at the suggestion that she was seeking an improvement in anyone's "quality of life." She emphatically and repeatedly denied that what she did was "social work." Perhaps it is our secularized and impoverished vocabulary that makes our age so clumsy in its efforts to grasp the core of Mother Teresa's motivation. She was no Albanian mystic who founded a nirvana for charitable efforts on the Indian subcontinent. The definition of Mother Teresa is at once very simple and very complex. She sensed a call of God on her life from a very early age in the form of service and the disciplined life of a Roman Catholic nun.

The notion of charitable giving without thought of consequence is alien to the ethos of the twentieth century, where charitable contributions themselves have sometimes become yet another way of avoiding taxes, or even of influencing governments. It was, of course, Mother Teresa's utter remoteness from all this that focused the attention of the entire world on her life.

THE BOJAXHIUS OF SKOPJE

Mother Teresa was born in that cauldron of ethnic and religious strife within Europe, the Balkans. She came into the world on August 26, 1910, in the town of Skopje, modern-day Macedonia. The baby girl was actually named Agnes Gonxha Bojaxhiu, the second child of a family that was Albanian, part of the 10 percent of the Albanian population who were devoutly Roman Catholic. The majority were Muslim. The day after her birth, Agnes was baptized in the Sacred Heart Catholic Church in Skopje, a parish that was predominantly Albanian.

Mother Teresa's own mother was called Dranafile (almost always shortened to Drana) Bernai. She came from a prosperous, middle-class family in Prizren, nowadays the predominantly Serbian town of Pristina. Mother Teresa's father, Nikola Bojaxhiu, was a successful businessman, a partner in a Skopje-based building construction company and an importer of wholesale foods. He was a world traveler who spoke Serbo-Croatian, Turkish, Italian, and French, in addition to Albanian, and his business took him at times as far afield from Macedonia as Egypt. He would be gone for several weeks at a time, and when he returned would delight his children with gifts from distant cities. But he was also a church-going Roman Catholic and a serious man. He seems to have been an affectionate but demanding parent, expecting high standards from his children, especially Mother Teresa's only male sibling, Lazar, who was born in 1907 and was thus three years older than she. "Never forget whose son you are," Lazar later recalled his father telling him many times.

Both Mother Teresa and Lazar have described their father, Nikola, as a financially generous man who gave away money and clothing to the poor and who actually preached to his children the virtues of charitable generosity. "Papa used to say," Mother Teresa told an Albanian Roman Catholic friend much later, "'My daughter, never accept a mouthful unless it is shared with others.'"[12] The family was as good as the father's word, frequently providing food and money to the local poor. Mother Teresa's oldest sister, Aga, was also closest to their mother. Born in 1904, she was six years older than Agnes.

Nikola Bojaxhiu was active in Skopje's civic affairs. He was a communal council member in the town, a strong believer in the value of education for both women and men, and a passionate Albanian patriot. Under the Ottoman Empire, any display of ethnic nationalism was dangerous, but when Mother Teresa was just two, Serbian and other Balkan allies rose up against the Ottomans and brought an end to Turkish rule in Macedonia. Just a few months after Serb forces entered Skopje in 1912, Albanian patriots themselves declared an Albanian state.

His Albanian Nationalist sentiments may have been, in the end, Nikola's downfall. In 1919, he visited Belgrade for discussions with other Albanian civic leaders. There was a banquet or some other major meal, and something went terribly wrong soon afterward with Nikola. By the time he had returned to Skopje by train toward the middle of the evening, he was seriously ill with internal hemorrhaging. Some doctors at the time speculated that the symptoms of his illness suggested poisoning. He was operated on the following day at the hospital in Skopje, but he did not survive. A vast crowd of citizens from several different ethnic and religious communities attended the funeral, and the city's jewelers closed up for the day in order to be present as well. Nikola was only forty-five years old at the time. Agnes was just nine.[13]

The emotional loss of their father for Aga, Lazar, Agnes, and their mother, must have been devastating, but the financial blow was even greater. Nikola's business partner ran off with the company funds, leaving the entire burden of supporting the family on Drana—or as she was often affectionately called by the children, Nana Loke, or "mother of the spirit." But Drana was resourceful, and was soon earning a living by embroidering bridal gowns and costumes for various festivals.

Later, Lazar—whose name in some biographies is Italianized to Lazzaro—described his mother as "gentle, engaging, generous, and full of compassion towards the poor. She was also very religious," he adds. "I think that Agnes [Mother Teresa] resembles her very much."[14] Lazar was especially struck by Drana's generosity toward the less fortunate. Once, he says, she looked after an alcoholic woman whose sores needed dressing twice a day, along with an impoverished widow with six children to feed. Lazar said he thought his mother "acted as she did because she felt sure she was giving to God what she was giving to her neighbor." To her own children, Lazar remembered, Drana would say: "When you do good, do it as if you were casting a stone into the depth of the sea."[15]

Drana's "religious" nature was not just one of private piety—a quiet, furtive trip to Mass or a room filled with the accoutrements of Catholic devotionalism. The entire Bojaxhiu family, father's side and mother's side, had been Catholic for several generations, and in Skopje both the archbishop and the local parish priest were frequent visitors to their home. After Nikola's death, Nana Loke presided over family prayers every evening, and ensured that the children attended private elementary school and then religious instruction in the Sacred Heart Church. She also helped organize the family visit to the church for the rosary and the benediction each May.

"Sometimes my mother and sisters used to live as much in the church as they did at home," Lazar said. "They were always involved with the choir, religious services, and missionary topics."[16] By far the most important annual religious event Drana carefully helped organize, both for the Bojaxhius and all of the other Albanian Christian families in the region, was the annual pilgrimage retreat to a prominent local shrine,

Our Lady of Cernagore in Letnice, not far from Skopje on the slope of a mountain.

The religious aim of this annual pilgrimage was for Catholics to express their veneration for the Virgin Mary at the shrine, which contained a seated statue of the Madonna and Child. Some of the pilgrims, Drana Bojaxhiu herself, for example, would make the pilgrimage on foot. Others, such as Aga and Agnes, would reach the mountain by a horse-drawn cart about six weeks before their mother and stay in a house that Nikola had helped build for the owner. The nearly two months spent at Letnice each year were more a fun-filled summer vacation than a serious weeks-long religious exercise. Days were spent taking walks around the mountain or playing in the warm sun outside. Evenings were spent in laughter-filled gatherings around the family hearth listening to stories.

Both spiritually and physically, the Letnice pilgrimages were to play an important role in Mother Teresa's life. For one thing, the healthy, dry climate helped cure her of a cough and other respiratory problems, along with what Lazar says was an incipient bout with malaria.[17] At Letnice, the young Mother Teresa was already acquiring a natural affinity for praying by herself, for times of listening in God's presence.

As a child, Mother Teresa was shy and introverted. After fragile health in her early years, the summers at Letnice helped make her more robust. She was a disciplined, thoughtful little girl who didn't seem to mind helping her brother and elder sister whenever they asked her assistance in something. "We thought of her as a rosebud," Lazar said. "When she was a child she was plump, round, and tidy. She was sensible and a little too serious for her age." At times, this meant that Agnes would be the only one of the three children who did not steal from the jam pot. She would, however, help Lazar pull open the cupboard and draw high against the wall to get to the jam, but soberly remembering the requirement to fast before Communion at Mass the next day, she would remind Lazar not to eat after midnight. She somehow managed to be virtuous without a trace of self-righteousness.[18]

She adored her childhood. "We were all very united," she once said, "especially after the death of my father. We lived for each other and we made every effort to make one another happy."[19] Her mother's instinctual charitableness, the daily prayers, the frequent visits to the church, which was almost next door, and the summer pilgrimages to Letnice, meanwhile, must cumulatively have nurtured in young Mother Teresa's mind the seeds of a desire to serve God to the exclusion of everything else. She was about twelve, she said, when she first realized she wanted to do this. She explained later: "I was still young, perhaps 12 years old, when in our family circle I said for the first time that I wanted to belong wholly to God. I thought this over for six years and prayed about it."[20] Her mother seemed to have sensed the ferment taking place in the heart of her youngest daughter, and hinted in remarks to the other children that Agnes would not remain long within the family.

Agnes became deeply involved in the events of her neighborhood Sacred Heart Church. The local archbishop, a popular man who knew the Bojaxhiu family well, had been transferred to another diocese, leaving something of a priestly vacuum in the Skopje district. To help out, the Jesuits agreed to send clergy to the town, and in 1921, the first of these, of Albanian ethnic background, arrived. It was the beginning of a period of broad international influence on the Skopje parish, for the Jesuits had outposts all over the world.

For Mother Teresa, the most influential of the newcomers was Fr. Franjo Jambrenkovic. A Croatian Jesuit, he harnessed her powerful and growing religious yearnings to a Roman Catholic layperson's association—called a "sodality" in the Catholic church—which he had introduced into Skopje. Perhaps more important, Jambrenkovic opened her eyes to the concrete possibility that she might devote her life to God as a missionary.

The Sodality of the Blessed Virgin Mary had originally been established in 1563 among lay students in the newly established Roman college of the Society of Jesus—the Jesuits—and had spread to lay Catholic groups all over the world. It challenged young people to dedicate their lives more seriously than ever before to serving Christ, putting before them a threefold question that the founder of the Jesuits, St. Francis Xavier, himself posed in his Spiritual Exercises. The question was, "What have I done for Christ? What am I doing for Christ? What will I do for Christ?" For Agnes Gonxha Bojaxhiu, whose spirituality had hitherto been nourished within an almost entirely local setting, it was intoxicating to read about the lives of the great, historic saints from such a variety of countries.

It was probably Father Jambrenkovic's keen interest in missions that finally pushed Mother Teresa down the path to India. Agnes devoured accounts of Jesuit missionaries who were serving in the subcontinent. By the time she was thirteen, she made a point of meeting any missionaries who returned to her own area, and she listened raptly to their stories. She helped organize concerts and other gatherings to raise money for the missionaries, took part in prayer meetings for them, and showed a growing sense of direction toward a life wholly dedicated to God.

Her older sister, Aga, although also devout, displayed no such missionary tendencies, and seemed to prefer to stay as close to her mother as she could. She went out to study economics in Yugoslavia, before departing for Albania itself in 1932. She worked briefly as a translator of Serbo-Croation to Albanian and then served as a radio announcer in Tirana. After Agnes's departure for the mission field, Drana joined Aga there in 1934. The two women were never to see Agnes—Mother Teresa—again. Drana died in 1972, and Aga in 1974.

Agnes's carefree and ebullient brother, Lazar, had left home in 1924, first for military school in Graz, Austria, then for secondary education at a high school with other Albanian boys. Though he was at first able to return home during vacation times, in 1925, when he was eighteen, he left Skopje permanently to take up a military career in Tirana, capital of Albania. He was a second lieutenant at twenty-one, in 1928, and a military aide to the country's king, Zog. Lazar remained in Tirana until 1939, the year war broke out in Europe, and then moved to Italy, where he stayed until his death in 1981.

Between 1925 and 1928, Agnes soberly counted the cost paid by all missionaries in their separation from families and beloved friends. By the time she was seventeen, the sense of God's call upon her had reached a certain point of urgency. She now decided to spend an extra two weeks during the family outing to Letnice in the hope of hearing clearly from God. She wanted to be a missionary, but she did not particularly want to become a nun. As a Roman Catholic, however, it would have been impossible for her to go anywhere in the world as a layperson, and the priesthood itself was closed to women. "How can you know when the Lord is calling you into some vocation?" she asked Father Jambrenkovic. "You can know by the happiness you feel," he told her.

If you are glad at the thought that God may be calling you to serve him and your neighbor, this may well be the best proof of your vocation. A deep joy is like the compass which points out the proper direction for your life. One should follow this, even when one is venturing upon a difficult path. [21]

It was wise advice. The turning point in her difficult decision-making process seems to have been August 15, 1928. Her time of prayer at Letnice was probably more anguished than ever before and yet more filled with joy. By the time she returned home, Agnes knew what she had to do. "It was at Letnice that for the first time I heard God's voice," she recalled later.

> My vocation convinced me that I should serve God and be at his disposal. I remember the feast of Mary's Assumption, when before Mary's altar [at Letnice], and with a burning candle in my hand, and singing with my heart about to burst, I had decided: "I want to belong to God!"[22]

Did she literally hear an audible voice? She never said, but probably not, for when she was to have the second major sense of God's direct instruction to her, eighteen years later in India, she was equally convinced that she was hearing directly from God, yet not in a literal, audible manner. In any case, she broke the news to her mother, who had been expecting something like this to happen.

It was still difficult for Drana to digest. According to Mother Teresa herself, Drana went immediately to her room on hearing Agnes's decision and stayed there for twenty-four hours, no doubt pouring out her heart to God in anguish at the price she herself would have to pay. When she finally reemerged, though she had probably wept copiously behind the closed door, her emotions were under control. "Put your hand in His hand—in His hand—and walk all the way with Him," she told Agnes simply. Agnes Gonxha Bojaxhiu, the future Mother Teresa, had only just turned eighteen.

The question was: Where and how would Agnes begin her life as a missionary? She wanted very much to go to the Calcutta area of India, but she needed council on which order to join in order to be sent there. The recommendation of Father Jambrenkovic: the Sisters of the Institute of the Blessed Virgin Mary, or as they were more commonly known, the Sisters of Loreto. Several weeks before her dramatic encounter at Letnice in August 1928, Father Jambrenkovic had personally traveled to Paris to speak with Mother Eugene McAvin, the sister in charge of the Loreto house in France. Mother Eugene agreed that she would interview Agnes, and another Yugoslavian aspirant for membership in the order, if they came to Paris. She would then decide whether to recommend them to Mother M. Raphael Deasy at the Motherhouse in Rathfarnham, just outside Dublin.

The name "Loreto" derived from Loreto, Italy, where the house traditionally believed to have been that of Mary, the mother of Jesus, had been physically brought from Nazareth to the Roman province of Dalmatia, and from thence to Italy. Though the Irish province of the sisters had been founded in 1822, the name Loreto Sisters remained. The Motherhouse of the Loreto order in its efforts toward India was in Rathfarnham, Ireland. It was from here that the first six postulants and two priests had sailed for India in 1841 to try to minister to the soldiers and their offspring who were serving in the British Raj but were of Irish and Roman Catholic origin.

Preparations for her journey began immediately. A concert was organized the day before her departure by the Sodality to bid farewell to the most active and enthusiastic member. All of the young people of the parish gathered to sing and be with one another. A group photo was taken, and Lorenz Antoni wrote in his diary:

> That evening, September 25, 1928, all of us were gathered in Agnes' house to say good-bye. All brought her some gift: one a pencil, another a book, or something of the sort, as a souvenir or a "thank you" token. I gave her a gold fountain pen which she used for a long time.[23]

About a hundred of the same friends, and others, were at the Skopje railroad station the next day to see off Agnes, Drana, and Aga. "Just as St. Peter left his nets behind," reported *Catholic Missions* in its last issue of 1928,

> . . . so did Agnes leave her books behind and departed in God's name. This amazed everybody because she had been the first in her class and was much esteemed by all. She was the soul of the women's Catholic activities, and of the church choir. All felt that with her departure a vacancy would be created.[24]

As the train pulled slowly out of the station and gathered speed into the distance, Agnes waved her handkerchief from the train window to prolong her farewell, saying good-bye to all that was full of love and familiarity to her. She did not return to Skopje until forty-two years later.

Even in the relatively modern era of 1928, the journey from Skopje, Macedonia, at one end of Europe, to Rathfarnham, in Ireland, at the other, was long and arduous. Agnes, Drana, and Aga stayed for a few days at first in Zagreb, Croatia, where, by prearrangement, another aspirant to the Loreto order, the Croatian Betike Kanjc, was to join Mother Teresa on the odyssey to their new way of life. Agnes and Betike boarded the train for Paris on October 13, 1928. Agnes's farewell to her mother and sister was tearful and, ultimately, final.

Their stay in the French capital was brief; it was only necessary as a formality to ensure their suitability for travel onward to Ireland. Finally, after a crossing of the English Channel and then the Irish Sea by boat, the two girls arrived for their very brief novitiate in Rathfarnham. They stayed just six weeks, only long enough to begin to come to grips with the English language, which was entirely unfamiliar to Agnes. By the time of their departure at the beginning of December for India proper, they were both so overwhelmed with homesickness and the unfamiliarity of their surroundings that they paid little attention to Ireland, England, or much of what they encountered en route. The only thing Mother Teresa says she remembers of that time was the dining room at Rathfarnham.

The English ship *Marcha,* with Agnes and Betike aboard, sailed from Liverpool on December 1, 1928, and traversed the familiar route for all Indian-bound vessels in that era: the Irish Sea to the English Channel, across the volatile expanse of the Bay of Biscay before entering the welcome respite of the Straits of Gibraltar and the Mediterranean. Then it was on to Port Said in Egypt and the Suez Canal, the Red Sea, and the Indian Ocean, and next to last, Colombo, leafy capital of the then British-ruled Ceylon (today called Sri Lanka). There was no priest aboard the ship, so it was not until the *Marcha* docked in Port Said that the two aspirants, along with three Franciscan nuns, were able to attend their first Catholic Mass since leaving Dublin. They finally sailed up the Ganges and docked in Calcutta on January 6, 1929.

A long letter from Mother Teresa to the editors of *Catholic Missions,* dated January 6 and describing the first impressions of the country that was to be her homeland for the rest of her life, survives today. She was shocked by the poverty she saw in Madras, where the ship's passengers had disembarked for a few hours. As the *Marcha* slowly steamed into her final destination of Calcutta proper, though, excitement at the new experience overwhelmed her. "On the docks [of Calcutta]," she exulted, "our Indian Sisters were awaiting us, and in their company, with indescribable joy, we set foot on the soil of Bengal."[25]

Even then, the journey was not yet over. Novices of the Sisters of Loreto conducted their training not in Calcutta itself, but in Darjeeling, the pleasantly cool hill station and sometime summer capital of the British Raj. Darjeeling is 450 miles to the north of the city by train, in the foothills of the magnificent Himalayan mountain range. The almost idyllic location must have been a refreshing contrast to the heat and dirt of Calcutta itself, and it was a good place to embark on the first formal stages of religious life. After a few months of preparation, and many hours of private prayer, Agnes Gonxha Bojaxhiu formally became a novice in the Sisters of Loreto, along with her fellow Yugoslav, Betike, on May 23, 1929. Henceforth, she was known to the outside world as well as to her fellow sisters not as Agnes, but as Maria Teresa of the Child Jesus. Betike was Sister Mary Magdalen Kanjc.

Agnes was profoundly happy with the step she had taken. On a copy of the photo that she sent to her aunt in Skopje, she wrote, "I am sending you this photo as a souvenir of the greatest day of my life, in which I became all Christ's. All my love, from your Agnes, little Teresa of the Child Jesus."[26]

CHASTITY, POVERTY, AND OBEDIENCE

The preparation for the first, temporary vows, to be taken after two years of novitiate, was both educational and rigorously spiritual. In addition to continuing to improve her English, Mother Teresa had to adopt the more challenging language of Calcutta itself, Bengali. Later, she was also to take up Hindi. The novices were closely monitored on their spiritual development through weekly sessions with a confessor as well. They rose before dawn to pray and read the lessons prescribed in the breviary—Psalms and other Old Testament passages, selections from the New Testament and the writings of the early church fathers. They had instruction in religious topics and they also had two hours each day teaching in the small one-room school, St. Teresa's, run by the Loreto Sisters in Darjeeling for Indian children from the surrounding hillsides. The novice mistress carefully supervised all of their activities.

At mealtimes the nuns had an opportunity for expanding their minds and knowledge of great forebears of the Catholic church. There were readings from the lives of some of the great saints, often embellished with accounts of miraculous happenings (whether real or legendary, it was not always made clear) that had accompanied them throughout their lives. Mother Teresa was particularly struck by the story of a French Carmelite nun, Thérèse Martin, who had been canonized a saint in 1925 after dying of tuberculosis in Hanoi at the age of twenty-four. Her autobiography, *The Story of a Soul*, had a great impact on millions of readers, not for any great supernatural incidents described in it (there were none), but through the young woman's focus on diligent and humble performance of life's simple tasks. "I prefer the monotony of obscure sacrifice to all ecstasies," she wrote.[27]

On May 25, 1931, just two years after her vows as a beginning novice, Mother Teresa made her second vows in the long eight-year process of becoming a fully professed Loreto Sister. Soon afterward, she was sent down from Darjeeling to a mission hospital in Bengal, where she experienced a sharp contrast in sights, sounds, and smells from the carefully cloistered, calm environment of Darjeeling. She duly mailed a vivid description of that time to *Catholic Missions* in Zagreb, where it appeared in the November 1931 issue of the magazine. She described the desperately poor patients who had showed up in the hospital, their backs "full of bumps and cavities because of their many ulcers."

She was suddenly faced by victims of stabbings, people with broken arms, desperately undernourished children. In a prophetic foretaste of her future work of rescuing cast-off children from the streets of Calcutta, she described an encounter with a poor blind boy who was close to death and was handed over to the sisters in the hospital as a last resort. "With great pity and love I take the baby in my arms," she wrote graphically, "and put him in my apron. The little one has found a second mother. 'Whoever receives one such little child in my name receives me,' said the divine lover of children. This episode of the blind boy was the crowning joy of my weary day's work."[28]

After a few months' work at the hospital, Mother Teresa was asked to continue with her studies toward a teacher's certificate at the large compound of the Loreto convent in Calcutta, colloquially known as Loreto Entally, after the name of the district. It is in the heart of Calcutta, not far from Lower Circular Road, where the Missionaries of Charity Motherhouse is located today, on the eastern side of the Hoogly River. Established originally in the mid-nineteenth century, Loreto Entally enclosed within its grounds a large school with about five hundred female students of high school age, mostly from higher class Indian families. But within the compound there was also a smaller school, St. Mary's, whose two to three hundred students were from a much wider variety of backgrounds. The Loreto Sisters charged no fees for the poorest of the students in this school, where the language of instruction was not English, as in the larger Loreto Entally school, but Bengali.

Mother Teresa loved teaching from the start. During her novitiate she formally studied education, as well as learned about the subject that she subsequently came to teach for some seventeen years, geography. Later, she also taught history.

It was not so easy breaking through to the Indian students she taught. Many of the Bengali-speaking students were nervous in the presence of Europeans, and the nuns themselves were closely cloistered within the compound. If they did ever leave, they had to be accompanied by another nun, and they were not permitted to take public transport. Mother Teresa's outgoing personality nonetheless made her a popular teacher, particularly at St. Mary's, and she had opportunities not available to other nuns to teach outside Loreto Entally itself. Naturally, she observed the squalid living conditions of the families whose children attended St. Mary's.

She loved her students from the first days of her teaching career. "When we got to know each other better," she wrote of her teaching encounters in the early 1930's,

> . . . they could not contain themselves for joy. They began dancing and singing around me until I had placed a hand on each of those dirty little heads. From that day on they called me "Ma," which means mother. How little it takes to make simple souls happy!
>
> Mothers bring me their little ones, to bless them. At first I was

amazed at this request, but in the missions one has to be ready to do anything, even to give blessings.[29]

Inhibitions were quickly broken down. To illustrate this, Mother Teresa told the story of an encounter with one of her younger boy students shortly before her final vows in 1937. The fellow had heard about the forthcoming, solemn ceremony, and had been told that Mother Teresa would become "Mother." For him it meant not a term of affection but of authority and distance. He protested to Mother Teresa.

"What is wrong, my boy?" she asked him. "Don't be afraid. I will come back, and I will always be your 'Ma.'" His face creased into a smile, and he dashed off, satisfied.

That solemn, final vow ceremony took place in Darjeeling on May 24, 1937, in a ceremony presided over by the archbishop of Calcutta. She had been a missionary in India for nine years. She had been happy in her vocation, never once doubting that God had called her to be a nun. She had been challenged in her medical work, her teaching, and in her busy interaction with some of the families of the children under her care. "I was the happiest nun in Loreto," she said later. "I dedicated myself to teaching. That job, carried out for the love of God, was a true apostolate. I liked it very much."[30] She had seen firsthand the poverty of Calcutta, and it grieved her to the quick. But in most respects, in the comfort of the Entally compound, she was more or less isolated from India's urban dirt and disease, from the country to which she felt God had called her.

Content as she was, Mother Teresa was homesick for her family. She had not seen Lazar since his departure for the last time to Tirana in 1925, to pursue a cadet officer's career. He had been stunned by her decision to join the Loreto Sisters, perhaps thinking he knew his sister better than she knew herself. He wrote her with his concerns after a long time of considering her 1928 decision: Was she not throwing away her entire life? Wasn't his own life much more exciting, an officer in the court of a European king? Agnes replied boldly in a letter: "To you it seems something very important to be an officer in the service of a king with two million subjects. Well, I'm an officer too, but I serve the King of the whole world. Which of us is in the better position?"[31]

She also exchanged letters with both Aga and her mother, reporting in detail the different experiences of her life. She loved to express the joy she felt in her vocation as a nun, as a teacher, and as the resident of one of the most physically attractive communities in Calcutta. "Our center is a lovely place," she wrote to her mother. "I teach, and this is the kind of work I like best. I am also in charge of the whole school, and everyone here loves me."[32] But her mother brought her down to earth with a reminder of what had taken her onto the missionary field in the first place. She wrote back perhaps a little too brusquely: "My dearest daughter, do not forget that you went out there to help the poor."[33]

But Mother Teresa hadn't forgotten. Whenever she left the compound at Entally, even if it was simply en route to the railroad station that took her each year to the cool hill station of Darjeeling, she was confronted by the presence of the destitute just outside the solid walls of the convent. Her success as a teacher, meanwhile, kept her busy, and not long after her final vows in 1937, she was appointed principal of St. Mary's School within Loreto Entally. At the same time, she was put in charge of the Bengali High School in Calcutta. The daughters were nuns, but they wore Indian saris in their work, a practice that was to have a profound impact upon Mother Teresa just a few years into the future.

A TRAIN TO DARJEELING

Even in the cloistered calm of their compound in Calcutta, the Sisters of Loreto would have known about the war clouds gathering over Europe during the 1930's. In 1939, perhaps fearful of developments in his own Albania, Lazar himself moved to Italy, where he remained until his death in 1981. For Loreto Entally, though, not even the outbreak of war in Europe in September 1939 or Hitler's near invasion of Britain in 1940 seemed to interrupt the orderly, disciplined flow of life for the nuns and their ever changing student charges. It was only in 1943 that the catastrophic effects of the war launched by Japan at Pearl Harbor in 1941 hit Bengal, in the form of a terrible famine.

The British had sequestered Calcutta's watercraft for their war effort against the Japanese. Rice deliveries from Bengal paddy lands were disastrously held up. Millions flocked around the handful of soup kitchens operating in the perennially overcrowded city, but charitable handouts were insufficient to meet the need. An estimated two million Indians died in the famine.

The British, meanwhile, worried about possible direct attack on Calcutta by the Japanese in nearby Burma, took over many of the Loreto Entally facilities for their own war wounded. The Loreto Entally boarding students were farmed out to institutions as far afield as Darjeeling and Lucknow. As the Japanese danger receded, the British returned Entally entirely to the Sisters of Loreto, and life was able to resume something of its normal course.

But not for long. The sight of the military humiliation of the British by the Japanese in Malaya and Singapore in 1941 and 1942 had given impetus to the forces of Indian nationalism that had been steadily gathering strength during the 1930's. After World War II, the pressure on Britain to grant independence to India created a new crisis of uncertainty on the subcontinent. At issue was the longtime rivalry and tension between India's Muslims and its dominant Hindu majority. In Calcutta the Muslim League declared a Direct Action Day for August 16, 1946, and prepared for a mass rally by Muslims in the Maidan, Calcutta's main park. Hoping to avoid serious Hindu-Muslim clashes, the city administration announced that the day would be an official holiday from all work.

But the gesture of goodwill backfired. After the scheduled mass rally in the Maidan broke up on Direct Action Day, an uncontrolled frenzy of killing broke out between Muslims and Hindus throughout the city. Buses, cars, even rickshas were plundered in the streets by wandering gangs of Hindus or Muslims, their occupants dragged out or hacked to death on the spot if they belonged to the "wrong" side of the conflict. Normal life stopped dead in its tracks in Calcutta. Disemboweled bodies putrified for hours in the streets until the authorities were able to impose martial law and restore order.

At Loreto Entally, the high walls separated the students and nuns from the Brueghelian horror show outside. The sisters even helped, impartially, the occasional Hindu or Muslim who clambered over the wall in frantic flight from the slaughter outside. But there was no food, since all deliveries of supplies had collapsed for several days. Breaking the sisters' own rules, Mother Teresa walked out of the compound alone into the horror visible everywhere on the streets outside. She saw bodies lying beaten and stabbed, sometimes, she recalled later, grotesquely contorted in death. As she cautiously walked out from the front gate, a truck filled with soldiers drove up and stopped. She must get off the streets immediately, they ordered her; it was too dangerous.

"I told them I had to come out and take the risk," she said. "I had three hundred students who had nothing to eat." Miraculously, the soldiers had supplies of rice in the truck with them. They drove back with Mother Teresa to Entally and unloaded it for her and the St. Mary's students.[34] When peace was finally restored to the city, more than five thousand people were found to have perished in the slaughter.

The fratricide and hatred appalled Mother Teresa. But there is no evidence—and she herself denied it—that the experience of August 16, terrible as it was, had anything to do with the decisive turning point in her life that took place less than a month later. It was then, aboard the small-gauge mountain train that wound its way up the Himalayan foothills on the way to Darjeeling, that Mother Teresa clearly heard the call that was to transform her life and ultimately that of thousands upon thousands of the poor throughout India and the rest of the world. Mother Teresa said she heard a divine summons, a "call within a call," as she put it later.

She described the incident on many different occasions. "While I was going by train from Calcutta to Darjeeling to participate in spiritual exercises," goes one account, "I was quietly praying when I clearly felt a call within my calling. The message was very clear. I had to leave the convent and consecrate myself to helping the poor by living among them. It was a command."[35] In another version she said that the divine command was specifically "to follow Him into the slums—to serve Him in the poorest of the poor."[36]

Again, Mother Teresa never suggested that she heard an audible voice, but some sense of God's presence was so apparent to her that she never hesitated to describe it as God's call to her. "I was sure this was the voice of God," she once said. "I was sure he was calling me."[37] She was also convinced of the direction of the call: to the festering, stench-filled, disease-infested slums of Calcutta with their human detritus of the sick and the dying. The constitutions of the Missionaries of Charity refer to this event, on September 10, 1946, as "a special Chrism," meaning the actual communication of God's will, through the Holy Spirit, to Mother Teresa. But a sense of direction isn't a road map. She recalled later that as the train slowly heaved its way up the Himalayan foothills, "I understood what I needed to do, but I did not yet know how to go about it."[38]

Back at Darjeeling for her retreat, she struggled in prayer for clarity on how to proceed. She was confident enough of the divine call to discuss it with the other Loreto Sisters in Darjeeling. But many were shocked, however much they respected Mother Teresa. It would require special permission from the Mother General of the order for a nun to work outside the walls of Loreto in any capacity.

Beyond this initial hurdle was the complex chain of Catholic ecclesiastical command starting at the very top with the Catholic Archdiocese of Calcutta. Unless every link in this complex chain of authority was connected, Mother Teresa's "call within a call" would remain unanswered. God might indeed have spoken to Mother Teresa, but if the hierarchy of the Catholic church itself didn't cooperate, it would be next to impossible for her to obey what He had said.

Who to turn to? The first person she had to convince that God had spoken to her was her spiritual adviser at Loreto Entally, Fr. Celeste Van Exem, a Belgian Jesuit who had been in India for just a few years. Coming down to sweaty Calcutta from the cool of the Darjeeling hills in October 1947, she wrote out for him in great detail the sense of what she believed God was calling her to do. Wisely, Van Exem advised her to make her first appeal to the archbishop of Calcutta, another Belgian.

The archbishop was shocked. How could a Loreto nun immerse herself—alone—in teeming Calcutta's poorest of the poor? She would have to wait a full year, he wrote Van Exem, before anything would be decided. Meanwhile, he quietly sought counsel in both India and Europe concerning what to do about the request. He did not reveal the identity of the one who had made it.

The entire year of 1947 was a turbulent one for all India. Independence from Britain had taken place that August and with it the beginning of the murderous, nightmarish process of the partition of the subcontinent into India and Pakistan. Hundreds of thousands, perhaps millions of Hindus and Muslims died in outbreaks of communal slaughter as populations surged in differing directions across the landscape. The number of refugees fleeing in both directions between India and Pakistan soared into the millions.

As India groaned, Calcutta's archbishop Perier had decided that Mother Teresa's basic idea ought not to be turned down outright, but it should be carried out within the cloistered Loreto community. Perier told her to write to the mother general of her own order in Rathfarnham with the request to be released from the community. But when she duly wrote the letter, which was then typed for her by Father Van Exem, the archbishop was irritated. She had requested "exclaustration" from Loreto, a technical term that meant that she could work in a different setting from that of the Loreto Sisters, but would remain faithful to her vows as a nun. The archbishop insisted that she change the term to "secularization," a far more drastic change of life that would mean relinquishing her vows altogether in order to return to the status of a laywoman.

Secularization was precisely what Mother Teresa didn't want. If she were merely a laywoman, it would be impossible for her to establish her own community of nuns—which she felt God was going to bring together—to help with the kind of work she wanted to do. "She must trust God fully," was Perier's terse reply when Van Exem tried to argue Mother Teresa's position with him.

Early in January 1948, the now revised letter was sent off to Rathfarnham. The response, by the standards of the Catholic bureaucracy, was almost instant. The words of Mother Gertrude, the mother general of the Loreto Sisters in Rathfarnham, all but brimmed with encouragement. "Since this is manifestly the will of God," she replied, "I hereby give you permission to write to the Congregation in Rome. My consent is sufficient." Then came the icing on the cake. As ordered to do so by Archbishop Perier, Mother Teresa had dutifully requested the unwanted status of "secularization." Mother Gertrude ignored this request completely and specifically told her that she was to write to Rome for approval of "exclaustration," precisely what Mother Teresa had been praying for all along.[39]

Once more, through Father Van Exem, the letter went before Archbishop Perier for his approval. Once again, he flatly rejected the idea unless she altered the word *exclaustration* to *secularization*. Once more she obeyed, and the letter began the process of what would normally be a long meandering through the corridors of the Vatican bureaucracy.

But then Providence seemed to intervene in a remarkable way. For some reason, the letter never made it to Rome at all, instead attracting the attention of Luigi Raimondi, the Italian papal nuncio who happened to be in the Delhi nunciature (Vatican representative office) at the time. Raimondi did not even bother forwarding the letter to Rome, personally approving Mother Teresa's request for leave from the Loreto Sisters, but once again altering the term to "exclaustration" from the "secularization" that Perier—for the second time—had insisted upon. Raimondi was perfectly familiar with the squalor of the Calcutta slums. He must have thought it absurd that a nun should be given permission to work there for just one year and at the same time should have to function totally outside the protective missionary apparatus of the church. Between them, the Loreto mother general and the papal nuncio locked in place the vital element Mother Teresa had needed to begin her work.

How long the papal nuncio in Delhi took to make his decision is unclear. But it was not before the end of July 1949 that Perier summoned Van Exem to announce what the result of the application was. Van Exem himself did not waste time getting back to Mother Teresa. He celebrated Mass in the Entally compound August 8, preaching consecutively in both Bengali and Hindi. Then he quietly called Mother Teresa aside for a private talk, informing her that the papal response (meaning the nuncio's decision) had come. She paled visibly. She asked if she could go to the chapel for a few moments of private prayer. When she returned, he broke the good news. She signed three copies of the required permission document, then quietly asked the priest, "Can I go to the slums now?" Not until 1971 did she discover that it was the papal nuncio, not Pope Pius XII, who had made the decision on her behalf.[40]

She was now free to leave the Loreto Sisters, the one thing she had yearned and prayed for daily since the dramatic experience of God's presence on the way to Darjeeling. But she was lonely and almost certainly somewhat apprehensive. She had lived all her adult years at Loreto, half her entire life, following her first arrival in India nineteen years earlier. Now she was to abandon the cloistered security and tranquillity of Loreto Entally and Darjeeling for a way of life that would be unpredictable, dangerous, and profoundly lonely. "To leave Loreto was my greatest sacrifice, the most difficult thing I have ever done," she wrote later. "It was much more difficult than to leave my family and my country to enter religious life. Loreto, my spiritual training, my work, meant everything to me."[41]

She wasted no time before making immediate and important decisions about her work. As the supervisor at Entally of St. Anne's, the entirely Indian order of nuns who dressed in saris, Mother Teresa had realized how important it was, in ministering to the poorest of the poor, to wear that simplest of Indian garments, the graceful sari. She selected a cheap white cotton sari with a blue border—representing the Virgin Mary—as her garment of choice. By August 16, 1949, she was ready for the first step into her new life. After the briefest of farewells from Loreto, she set off on foot for Calcutta's Howrah Station and the train ride to Patna, 240 miles away in Bihar State. Her destination: the Holy Family Hospital at Patna, run by the Medical Mission Sisters, an order dedicated to medical work in the setting of a fully equipped hospital.

The four months at Patna were a vital time to learn some utterly basic skills: how to identify illnesses, for example, and how to perform the simplest of medical procedures. She helped with obstetrics, surgery, and laboratory technical work. She had agreed to be present every time a physician was summoned for an emergency case, and whenever there was surgery. She comforted patients before or after surgical procedures, holding the hands of nervous expectant mothers, or gently caressing children. Above all, she encountered the poor on a daily basis as they brought their boils, abscesses, fevers, and wounds to the hospital for attention.

In her white-and-blue sari, Mother Teresa shocked some of the nurses, who had been Mother Teresa's own students at Loreto Entally. Yet the time at Patna helped sharpen and refine her own vision. One of her ideas, for example, was quickly rejected. She wanted future helpers to live deeply spiritual lives along with her, accompanied by much prayer, fasting, and the eating of the same kind of very basic foods that the poorest of the poor themselves ate. She thought that she and her future coworkers could survive on rice and a little salt. A down-to-earth American sister, an M.D., quickly corrected her on some of these notions. "From our own experience of hard work and poor conditions," she wrote in a later description of meeting with Mother Teresa, "we stressed strict rules of prayer, but no prayers after 9 P.M. We talked of simple meals, but the absolute necessity of plenty of food, with adequate protein, and no exceptions, except for illness."

The superior of the Medical Mission Sisters was even more blunt. "If you make your sisters do that, eat only rice and salt, you will commit a serious sin," she told Mother Teresa. "Within a short time, those young girls will fall prey to tuberculosis and die. How do you expect your sisters to work, if their bodies receive not sustenance?"[42] Mother Teresa got the point. Even today, the Missionaries of Charity do not eat gourmet food of any kind, but there is no shortage of what they eat and there are strict requirements for periods of rest and spiritual retreat away from the extraordinarily demanding work.

The real test for Mother Teresa's calling was now what awaited her on her return to Calcutta from Patna. She arrived by train December 8 with just five rupees of personal money to her name—less than one U.S. dollar at the time. She had begun her journey with no place to stay, but the ever thoughtful Father Van Exem had arranged for at least temporary accommodations with the Little Sisters of the Poor, a French-founded order that operated a home accommodating destitute older people. She was eager to help them in their work as a way of contributing to their community. But much of the time she spent simply in prayer, earnestly asking God to show her what to do next.

After some two weeks, she felt she knew. She sought out the location of one of Calcutta's poorest shantytowns, Moti Jihl, located very close to Loreto Entally, as she was to discover. One day, she simply walked there by herself. To the desperately poor locals scrubbing their clothes on the sidewalk or nursing malnourished infants beneath some tattered awning, she must have been a strange sight: a European woman wearing a sari, her head fully covered, walking alone among the dirty hovels.

Children began to follow her, clutching at her sari, begging for money. She had no money to offer them, but they were nonetheless intrigued by something about the way she moved, the way she responded to their presence. She was in the area of Calcutta where some of her former students had worked among the poor. On the morning of December 21, 1948, she stopped in an open area of Moti Jihl and began writing in the packed dirt beneath her feet in Bengali. Ragamuffin children gathered round, giggling and fascinated. She talked to them. They stayed. She was starting a school.

The open-air lessons continued the following day, and thereafter. She found a cheap hut to rent for the pupils, who were barefooted, suffered from malnutrition, and lacked schoolbooks, paper, or pencils. The "school" itself had no desks, no blackboards, nothing that remotely resembled a place where children could learn. But the children loved this pale-faced European woman who spoke fluent Bengali, dressed like an Indian, and seemed to want to be a mother to all of them. They responded, too, when she brought them milk at lunchtime, paid for from a generous initial contribution she had received from the sisters at Patna. She rewarded attendance or good lesson performance in writing or arithmetic with bars of soap. And before she would give them the soap, she explained how they should wash themselves, and why being clean was a vital component of a healthy life itself.

Not a few fellow Catholics thought she was seriously misguided. One convent where she stopped by to eat her lunch ordered her to eat under the back stairs like a common beggar. A Yugoslav Jesuit, of the very nationality and order that had first inspired her love for India, commented brusquely, "We thought she was cracked."[43] She was lonely, and at times tempted almost to desperation by the thought that it would be only too simple to rejoin the Loreto Sisters and return to the calm and orderliness of her previous, cloistered existence. At the request of Archbishop Perier, she kept a journal of her experiences, thoughts, and prayers. On one occasion she wrote:

> God wants me to be a lonely nun, laden with the poverty of the cross. Today I learned a good lesson. The poverty of the poor is so hard. When I was going and going till my legs and arms were paining, I was thinking of how they have to suffer to get food and shelter. Then the comfort of Loreto came to tempt me, but of my own free choice, my God, and out of love for you, I desire to remain and do whatever is your holy will in my regard. Give me courage now, this moment.[44]

By now it was becoming awkward to live in St. Joseph's and yet to work every day so far away in Moti Jihl. She knew that she could never attract helpers to her work unless they could all live together in a community, which would have to operate under religious rules. Once more, the diligent and thoughtful Father Van Exem came to her aid. Through a Bengali contact, he located a house at 14 Creek Lane where the owner, Michael Gomes, was a lay member of the Legion of Mary and had empty rooms to spare on the second floor. Mother Teresa moved in with a single chair, a packing case as a desk, and extra wooden crates as seats. Working out of the Gomeses' home, she continued her teaching forays into the alleyways of Moti Jihl. The Gomeses' eight-year-old daughter would often accompany Mother Teresa there or on her occasional visits to the city's pharmacies. Already, Mother Teresa realized that she would have to try to provide simple medical treatment to the poor wherever she found them. She had no sources of medicine whatsoever when she started, so she would sometimes walk into a pharmacy with a long list of what she needed, wait until all of the regular customers had been attended to, then present her list with a smile to the manager. Would he be willing "to do something beautiful for God?" she would ask, using a phrase that came to characterize her approach to how people should give to the work. Again and again, the pharmacists would comply; she would be given the medicines for free.

Meanwhile, ordinary people had begun to hear of her work and were contributing cash and food items in kind toward it. The money would instantly buy food or more medicines. As for Mother Teresa and eventually her coworkers, she had already resolved that none of them would ever receive any payment at all for their work. Their sole personal wealth, she insisted, must be two saris, coarse undergarments, personal toiletries, and a prayer book. But there was one issue that gnawed constantly at her: Would anyone else actually want to join her in this new ministry?

An answer finally came with a shy knock on the door of her room at the Gomes house. It was February 1949, and the visitor had been a former student of Mother Teresa's at St. Mary's for nine years. A Bengali girl named Subashini Das, from a prosperous family, she had adored her teacher and had been devastated by Mother Teresa's departure from Loreto Entally. Now she wanted to join Mother Teresa in the work her teacher had started.

Wisely but gently, Mother Teresa told her to go away and pray about it for several more weeks before committing herself. Subashini did so. In March 1949, she was back. She had made up her mind, she said. She would start as an aspirant. Mother Teresa allowed her to take the name that she wanted to adopt in the work, Sister Agnes, the real given name of Mother Teresa before the young Albanian had become a nun at the age of eighteen.

A few weeks later, another St. Mary's student, Magdalena Gomes— not a relation of the Michael Gomes family—also quietly asked to join. She took the name Sister Gertrude. A third and a fourth young woman came, too, becoming Sister Dorothy and Sister Margaret Mary respectively. All wore the same cheap cotton sari Mother Teresa had adopted and lived in the same room at 14 Creek Lane. During the day they went out to teach in Moti Jhil or provide rudimentary medical treatment for the very poor in the area. Before a year was out, some ten girls had joined as aspirants, almost all of them former students of Mother Teresa at St.

Mary's. Since many of them interrupted their formal schooling to join the not yet formalized order, Mother Teresa made sure that they had sufficient time while under her care to fulfill the academic obligations they would have had if they had remained in school.

The sisters were already following a disciplined daily way of life: up very early for prayer and Mass (at first in St. Teresa's, a parish church not far from Creek Lane), then a breakfast of Indian chapati flat bread and tea. They would be out in the slums in the morning, back at noon for a meal and a time of rest and spiritual reflection, then return to work once more until early evening. There would be a short period of spiritual reflection before supper, more prayer, and bed around 10:00 P.M.

There was still no name for the movement. It was not until early in 1950 that, with the help of Father Van Exem, Mother Teresa began drafting a constitution for the new order that would express her goals for the work and the rules that would apply to new sisters.

The document, entitled in English "Constitutions of the Society of the Missionaries of Charity," was submitted to Archbishop Perier, and through him to Rome. Approval was given without any changes, and the official acceptance of the Missionaries of Charity as a new congregation within the diocese of Calcutta was formalized on October 7, 1950. At a Mass held in one of the upper rooms of the Gomes house, the words of the decree of recognition were read out. The Missionaries' purpose, they read, was this:

> To fulfill our mission of compassion and love to the poorest of the poor we go:
>
> —seeking out in towns and villages all over the world even amid squalid surroundings the poorest, the abandoned, the sick, the infirm, the leprosy patients, the dying, the desperate, the lost, the outcasts.
> —taking care of them,
> —rendering help to them,
> —visiting them assiduously,
> —living Christ's love for them, and
> —awakening their response to His great love.[45]

It could all be summed up in this declaration, as the constitution made clear: "Our aim is to quench the infinite thirst of Jesus Christ on the cross for love of souls by the profession of the evangelical counsels and whole-hearted free service to the poorest of the poor."

Today, next to the large crucifix behind the altar of every Missionary of Charity chapel there are the words, "I thirst." These are, of course, the real words of Christ on the cross. But to Mother Teresa they have always expressed Christ's desire, indeed His yearning, for us to love Him. "Jesus is thirsting for our love," she has often said, "and this is the thirst for every-one, poor and rich alike."[46] It is a revolutionary idea: God yearns for His creatures to love Him so much that He thirsts for it. But the radical nature of this is exactly the spiritual muscle power that continued to propel Mother Teresa after her historic train ride to Darjeeling in 1946.

"The distressing disguise of the poorest of the poor." These were also words included in the new constitution of the order. It was very early in her missionary work that Mother Teresa discovered with stomach-churning clarity exactly what this meant. She had started her work by seeking out the chil-dren for a makeshift school. But all around in the slums there were people literally dying on the street. Mangy, covered in oozing abscesses, their fes-tering wounds crawling and stinking with maggots, many of them had been thrown out of whatever hovel-like shelter they had known in the terminal stages of their illnesses by superstitious landlords or family members.

For many Hindus, death itself was considered a pollutant of the place where it occurred. It was these castoffs of the human race, the most physi-cally degraded and rejected, to whom Mother Teresa next turned her attention. They were, she felt, Christ Himself, but "in a most distressing disguise." By physically caring for, cleaning up the wounds, and washing the unclean bodies of these near-death human beings, she explained, "ac-tually we are touching his body. It is the hungry Christ we are feeding, it is the naked Christ that we are clothing, it is the homeless Christ that we are giving shelter."[47]

Very early on, Mother Teresa came across a dying woman whose body, while she was still alive, had been eaten by rats and ants. She picked her up and carried her to the nearest hospital. When the hospital staff initially balked at accepting the case, Mother Teresa simply refused to move until they changed their minds. On subsequent occasions, she hailed taxis to take the people she had scooped up from the gutter from hospital to hos-pital until the person was admitted. Often the taxi would not take the near corpse away if the first hospital rejected the patient. She would then bargain with nearby ricksha men to transport the unfortunates. When all else failed, she herself would trundle the dying around to a hospital in a wheelbarrow. Increasingly the hospitals refused adamantly to accept these desperate cases. In many instances, they were simply too ill to save.

"We cannot let a child of God die like an animal in the gutter," Mother Teresa insisted.[48] A place was needed for the destitute and dying. At first, she tried renting cheap rooms in the slums themselves, but the numbers of people who were close to death continued to rise beyond the capacity of slum huts to accommodate them. Finally, the city authorities of Calcutta turned over to the Missionaries of Charity a pilgrims' rest house next to a temple of the Hindu deity Kali, the goddess of death. The place was known as Kalighat, the syllable *ghat* referring to cremation places for Hindus close to the Kali temple.

Within barely a day, Mother Teresa and her helpers, now numbering in the teens, had cleaned up the hostel and turned it into a place where the very poorest of the poor could die in dignity. It was renamed *Nirmal Hriday*, Bengali for "Pure Heart." At first some Hindu zealots, enraged that a place so close to the temple of their own goddess should have been given to Christian workers, reacted angrily, hurling stones at the building or repeating death threats. Other Hindus were perplexed by the idea of charitable work for the suffering. For many Hindus, suffering is believed to be the result of a person's bad karma, that is, insufficient good deeds performed in a previous life. Reincarnation, of course, is not a Christian concept: "Just as man is destined to die once, and after that to face judgment" (Heb. 9:27 NIV). Furthermore, blaming everything on karma can also easily lead to a fatalism about human degradation, itself the very opposite of Christ's commandment to love our neighbors, regardless of what they have done in life or failed to do.

Mother Teresa responded to the threats calmly. "If you kill us," she told the zealots, "we would only hope to reach God sooner."[49] The Hindu opposition subsided markedly when the Missionaries accepted a Kali priest in the last stages of tuberculosis after he had been turned away from several Calcutta hospitals.

Countless visitors have wandered around Kalighat, amazed to encounter a strange joy and peace in a place where the nuns continuously clean up the bodily waste of patients unable to control their bladders or bowels, where groans and moaning fill the air, where many must be lovingly fed by hand in their last days on earth. In a famous passage from his book *Something Beautiful for God*, Malcolm Muggeridge described Kalighat as "overflowing with love, as one senses immediately on entering it. This love is luminous, like the haloes artists have seen and made visible round the heads of the saints."[50] Sometimes, the sisters have accepted mentally disturbed people who had to be tied down to beds with rags in order to prevent them from harming others. On other occasions, the card in the slot attached to the wall above a patient's bed simply read, "Unknown."

To describe why she, why the sisters, should bother with the socially "irredeemable" detritus of humanity, Mother Teresa always explained with a reference from the New Testament. "It is not enough to say, 'I love God,'" she told a Washington, D.C., audience. She continued,

> But I also have to love my neighbor. St. John says that you are a liar if you say you love God and you don't love your neighbor. How can you love God whom you do not see, if you do not love your neighbor whom you see, whom you touch, with whom you live? . . . Jesus makes himself the hungry one, the naked one, the homeless one, the unwanted one, and he says, "You did it for me." On the last day he will say to those on his right, "whatever you did to the least of these, you did to me," and he will say to those on his left, "whatever you neglected to do for the least of these, you neglected to do it for me."[51]

I was sitting barely twenty feet from Mother Teresa as she said these words, as mesmerized by the power of her presence as everyone else was. Then she spoke of the work of the Missionaries of Charity at Kalighat. "There was the man we picked up from the drain, half-eaten by worms," she said, almost matter-of-factly, as diplomats and dignitaries leaned forward to catch what she was saying and get a better glimpse of her:

> And after we had brought him to the home, he only said, "I have lived like an animal in the street, but am going to die as an angel, loved and cared for." Then, after we had removed all the worms from this body, all he said—with a big smile—was: "Sister, I am going home to God." And he died. It was so wonderful to see the greatness of that man, who could speak like that without blaming

anybody, without comparing anything. Like an angel—this is the greatness of people who are spiritually rich, even when they are materially poor.[52]

In an interview with *Time* magazine in 1989, Mother Teresa said that the Missionaries had picked up around 54,000 people from the streets of Calcutta, and that somewhat more than 23,000 of these had indeed died there. She was asked in the same interview if her work had achieved any lasting change in either Calcutta or the rest of the world. "I think so," she answered. "People are aware of their presence, and also many, many, many Hindu people share with us. Now we never see a person lying there in the street dying. It has created a worldwide awareness of the poor."[53]

When Nirmal Hriday was dedicated in August 1952, there were already thirty women in the Missionaries of Charity. The original twelve who had joined Mother Teresa between 1949 and 1950 were now officially novices, the first stage of the six-year pathway to being a fully professed Missionary of Charity. The rest were all postulants, that is, sisters in the first year of entry into a religious order. They were still "guests" in the second floor of the Michael Gomes home, but the makeshift motherhouse of the new order was bursting at the seams.

Father Van Exem and another priest, Father Henry, began to explore alternatives, bicycling around Calcutta in search of suitable premises. In a truly ironic turn of fortune, the property that materialized belonged to a former Muslim magistrate, appropriately named Mr. Islam. He had built it before the partition of India at its independence in 1947, but was now ready to move to Dacca in East Pakistan (later Bangladesh). He was one of the many Muslim friends of Van Exem, and he agreed to part with the property for little more than the value of the land it stood on, some £7,500. "I got that house from God," the ex-magistrate said sadly as he left it for the last time. "I give it back to him."[54]

So it was that, just as a Hindu hostel had become a Christian home for the destitute dying, so the home of a former Muslim magistrate became the motherhouse of the order that cared for those unfortunates. Archbishop Perier bought the property, at 54A Lower Circular Road, on behalf of the Missionaries of Charity, and the sisters moved in during February 1953. It remains the motherhouse to this day, though the Indianization of

Calcutta's British names transmuted the home country's "Lower Circular" into "A. J. C. Bose," the current name of the road.

The work with the dying had started, like everything else in Mother Teresa's ministry, without forethought. There was a desperate need, and without thinking about it, Mother Teresa and her sisters responded. "In our choice of works," she told the audience that came to hear her receive the Nobel Prize in 1979, "there was neither planning nor preconceived ideas. We started our work as the suffering of the people called us. God showed us what to do."[55] This was true of another major initiative of the work during the early 1950's, work with the lepers of Calcutta.

I do not recall having seen lepers in person. But I can still remember my recoil, my feelings of shock and fright, upon seeing photographs of leprosy victims at an exhibit in London in the 1960's, in the heart of the elegant Whitehall district. How could human beings become so deformed in this way? I wondered. It was easy to understand how leprosy had been considered the scourge of Europe in the Middle Ages. Lepers were out-casts from the rest of society, forced to warn others of their presence by ringing a bell as they moved, and compelled to live—and die—in squalor and isolation from the rest of humanity. With improved hygiene and ad-vances in medicine, leprosy has been all but wiped out in Europe.

In Mother Teresa's India, however, the condition of lepers was horri-fying. The Missionaries of Charity had cared for individual lepers among the poorest of the poor, but had not addressed the overriding problem of the isolated, ostracized community of Calcutta's lepers, perhaps number-ing around thirty thousand at this time. By 1956 they were operating a mobile clinic, a medical van that visited six different neighborhoods of the city. The following year, when five lepers knocked on the door of the motherhouse on Lower Circular Road, it seemed to Mother Teresa that the Missionaries of Charity were being challenged to come up with a major response to the dreaded illness.

At first, Mother Teresa tried to take on the Bengal government, which had decided to close the one hospital in Calcutta specializing in treating lepers. But after the Gobra Hospital, as it was called, was closed down to make room for construction projects the government deemed more im-portant, she took her campaign to the entire city of Calcutta. Eventually, the government of India donated a plot of thirty-five acres some two hun-dred miles from Calcutta. It was called *Shanti Nagar* (City of Peace). From that modest beginning there developed some eighty leprosy medical centers throughout India.

"One Christmas I went to visit them," Mother Teresa said about the leprosy centers,

> . . . and told them that God loved them very specially; that all they had was God's gift; that God was close to them; that their illness was no sin. An old man, hardly able to move, with difficulty came up to me and said: "Please, repeat that once more; I never before heard anything of the kind. All my life I only heard that nobody wanted me. How beautiful it is to know that God loves me!"[56]

Lepers were one very obvious category of outcasts. But tragically, so were tiny, abandoned children. From the beginning of her work, Mother Teresa came across babies and infants literally thrown away onto garbage heaps, dumped in trash cans, or brought to her because their mothers could not or would not take care of them. In many cases the children were physically or mentally handicapped, making it unlikely that they would ever be able to fend for themselves or contribute to a family's livelihood. As more and more of these infant castoffs were left at the door of the Missionaries of Charity, the need became obvious to accommodate them properly. Thus in 1955, the Missionaries of Charity opened the Shishu Bhavan, or Children's Home, just a few hundred feet away from the motherhouse down Lower Circular Road.

Many, perhaps the majority of the babies, had been abandoned almost as soon as they were born, and almost all were suffering from acute malnutrition or tuberculosis. Their eyes were weary and sunken into their skeletal little faces, their limbs often mere sticks, incapable of independent movement. Several were beyond saving even when immediately provided with the proper medicines and nutrition. And, of course, all of them were starving for love.

Since the mid-1950's, both the police of Calcutta and vast numbers of ordinary people have known about the Shishu Bhavan as the refuge of last resort for unwanted babies. "Up to now," Mother Teresa claimed a few years ago, "we have never turned away any person, any child. We always have a place ready, a bed for one more."[57] The Missionaries of Charity seek out families that will adopt the children, no matter what age they are, or what social background. They try to match adoptees with families of the same religious faith. But even without adoption, the Missionaries of Charity have found sponsors who will support these children financially through the Calcutta school system.

It was the dignity of life—or the lack of it she saw around her—that first goaded Mother Teresa into taking care of the poorest of the poor. It was the sanctity of life that continually preoccupied her. In 1979 she told her Nobel Peace Prize audience, "I feel the greatest destroyer of peace today is abortion, because it is a direct war, a direct killing, direct murder by the mother herself."[58] Two years earlier, at a celebration of life in Italy, she explained her views with some precision on the subject. "The life of the unborn child is a gift of God, the greatest gift God can make to the family," she said. "I am not discussing whether there is any need to legalize abortion or not. I simply believe that no human has the right to cut down a life. Every existence is the life of God in us."[59]

The words were acceptable for a friendly audience. But in February 1994 she marched right into a lion's den on the same topic. During her address to the National Prayer Breakfast in the Washington Hilton, to an audience that included President Clinton and Hillary Rodham Clinton, Vice President Al Gore and Tipper Gore, several cabinet officers and senior political figures, she said, "The greatest destroyer of peace today is abortion," using a phrase she had first spoken during her Nobel Prize speech in 1979. "And if we can accept that a mother can kill even her own child," she went on, "how can we tell other people not to kill one another?"[60] Most of her listeners were on her side, but others clearly were not. Some shifted uncomfortably as Mother Teresa warmed to her topic. She went on:

> We are fighting abortion by adoption—by care of the mother and adoption for her baby. We have saved thousands of lives. . . . Please don't kill the child. I want the child. Please give me the child. I am willing to accept any child who would be aborted, and to give that child to a married couple who will love the child, and be loved by the child. From our children's home in Calcutta alone, we have saved over 3,000 children from abortions.[61]

Mother Teresa's stand against abortion has sometimes put her squarely at odds with the established authorities. After the Indo-Pakistan War of

1971, which led to the transformation of East Pakistan into Bangladesh, there was a major crisis in coping with the countless Bangladeshi women who had been raped—and in many cases impregnated—by troops of the retreating Pakistani army. Deep Hindu and Islamic prejudices against rape victims imposed a double burden upon them: the stigma against rape itself, and the humiliation of having a child outside wedlock. With a small group of fellow Missionaries of Charity, Mother Teresa openly criticized the government-supported policy of encouraging abortions for the rape victims. "It was a terrible fight with these people," she said later.

> I told them, "Our girls were misused, they were forced, they didn't want sin, but what you are going to make them do, or help them to do, is to commit murder, and this will be with them for life. They will never forget that as mothers, they have killed their children."[62]

Mother Teresa's deliberate policy of taking in homeless and unwanted children led many Hindu families into doing something previously unthinkable, namely taking in as their own the children of the "untouchable" class. She herself campaigned vigorously on behalf of India's "untouchables," the outcasts of the complex Indian social caste system. In November 1995, she led prayers in New Delhi at a protest meeting of Christian converts from the untouchables. The demonstrators said that the Indian government had failed to provide job quotas for untouchables of Christian faith even though other untouchables were guaranteed such quotas by law. "We must help the government help us to live in peace by not making any differences," she told reporters outside the Sacred Heart Cathedral, New Delhi's largest Catholic church.

REACHING OUT INTO THE WORLD

By 1959, the ten-year probation period required for the Missionaries of Charity by Roman Catholic canon law had passed. The Missionaries had established their first house outside of Calcutta in 1959 in Ranchi, Bihar State. Meanwhile, another symbolic probation period also was at an end. Mother Teresa had applied for Indian citizenship in 1949, and she was now visibly part of the Indian social and political landscape. When she opened a new children's home in Delhi in 1960, to her surprise none other than the famous prime minister of India, Jawaharlal Nehru, decided to attend the inauguration. She wanted to explain to him how her workers operated, but he stopped her. "No, Mother," he said, "you need not tell me about your work. I know about it. That is why I have come."[63] The Missionaries of Charity had expanded their work into more than twenty Indian cities; today, they have more than seven hundred sisters working there.

But it was not just India that suddenly seemed to open up to Mother Teresa in 1960, it was the entire world. In August of that year, she made her first trip outside India since 1929, flying directly to the U.S. In Los Angeles, U.S. Immigration and Naturalization officials politely asked where in the U.S. this diminutive, sari-clad nun was headed. "Las Vegas," she responded brightly. The peals of friendly laughter that this evoked mystified her. In fact, she was headed for a convention of the National Council of Catholic Women that was being held in the city of instant fortunes, marriages, and divorces. She told the women attending the conference that the Missionaries of Charity refused to own property and would not accept any regular financial support from any one source. "I don't beg," she said.

> I have not begged from the time we started the work. But we go to the people—the Hindus, the Mohammedans, and the Christians—and I tell them: "I have come to give you a chance to do something beautiful for God." And the people, they want to do something beautiful for God, and they come forward.[64]

The American women also came forward in droves, stuffing money into a homemade canvas bag carried around by one of Mother Teresa's assistants. As to Las Vegas, Mother Teresa summed up her impression of the glitter and the fantasy with one word: *Dewali,* a reference to the Hindu festival by this name in which Indian towns and villages are lit up by thousands of candles and electric lights. She brought back to India from Las Vegas a souvenir of a great moment—long cactus spines that she collected from the edge of the desert and that could be woven into a crown of thorns for the crucifix in the chapel back in Calcutta.[65]

She flew to Peoria, New York, and Washington, D.C., before going on to Europe. She had her first glimpse of America's "poorest of the poor," winos and hoboes in those days, in New York on the sidewalks of the Lower East Side. She often perplexed her various hosts by maintaining rigorously the rule of her order not to accept food when visiting a person's house, or to eat in public. Several meals were postponed or missed because of this.

She traveled on to Europe, stopping in London and Germany. Their Catholic relief organizations had also given considerable financial support to Calcutta. While in Munich, she took a side-trip to the site of the concentration camp at Dachau. It was her first encounter with Hitler's machinery of death and the vestiges of the Holocaust. Standing in front of the ovens and gas chambers, she observed: "This stands for the Coliseum of our day. But then it was pagans who threw innocent people to their death. It was not idolaters of those pagan gods who threw these lives away—and how many millions of them. We are getting worse, not better."[66]

Rome was Mother Teresa's primary and longed-for destination on this first worldwide odyssey from Calcutta. For the first time, she met a pope, John XXIII, and alone of those present, she stopped to kiss his ring and receive a personal blessing from him. But it was not just a sentimental visit. Roman Catholic prelates worldwide had heard of Mother Teresa's work by now, and some of them were beating a path to her door in Calcutta, begging the Missionaries of Charity to come and establish homes in their own countries. Mother Teresa was eager to do this, but she could not do anything until Rome recognized her order as one "of pontifical right," that is, approved directly by the papacy for work around the world.

The order's prayer books, details of training for the novices and precise way of life, were all subjected to detailed scrutiny during her Rome trip, and she herself went through something approaching an interrogation by Vatican officials about the nature of her work and the ecclesiastical basis of it. Not until 1965 was the long examination process complete and Vatican approval given.

But there was something much more personal for Mother Teresa to do in Rome. She had last seen anyone in her family in 1928. Now, providentially, she could meet with her brother, Lazar, who had moved to Italy from Albania in 1939, but whom she had not set eyes on since 1925. He was a graying fifty-three now, married to an Italian, and living in Palermo.

The long-awaited reunion was bittersweet. Lazar's presence was a reminder that it was now impossible for Mother Teresa to see her mother, Drana—dear "Nana Loke"—or her elder sister, Aga. Both were locked behind the xenophobic walls of Albania, where the country's tyrannical Stalinist leader, Enver Hozha, ensured that the country remained almost hermetically sealed off from the outside world. Mother Teresa even visited the Albanian Embassy, trying out her halting Albanian, unpracticed after three decades, to obtain a visa to Albania. They turned her down flat. It was not until 1989 that she was able to visit a country that had proclaimed itself in the 1960's "the world's first atheistic state." By then, both Drana and Aga had died.

THE FROSTS OF NORWAY

She returned to India several weeks after setting out, totally exhausted, yet invigorated by the growing recognition of her work around the world. In India, it was now ready to expand rapidly beyond the confines of Calcutta and Delhi. Agra, Asansol, and Amhala opened houses in 1961, then Amravat, Bombay, Patna, Old Goa, Darjeeling, and several other cities in the next few years. The poorest of the poor were surely gratified; many Indians who admired Mother Teresa's efforts applauded her success.

But some Indians, especially Calcuttans, were unhappy that, through the Missionaries of Charity, India was gaining the world's attention as a breeding ground of poverty, disease, and squalor. Outspoken as ever, Mother Teresa made her first walking tour of the slums of Bombay in 1962, and commented that the housing conditions there were worse than Calcutta's. Editorials growled and snapped back at her as the commercial capital of India reacted to its public humiliation. Later, there were to be similar moments of embarrassment, self-doubt, and complaint among the prominent citizens of New York, London, Melbourne, Rome, Santiago, and many other advanced world cities when it was learned that the Missionaries of Charity had arrived. Could London contain anything resembling "the poorest of the poor"? Could New York?

In the days before widespread drug abuse, rampant homelessness, and AIDS, perhaps not. There had always been alcoholism and the phenomenon of "bums" in the heart of the Western world. By the late 1960's the combination of widespread youth alienation from mainstream culture, the failure of social services to keep pace with rapid economic change, and the availability of cheap narcotics had transformed the urban landscapes throughout the Northern Hemisphere. A decade later, the AIDS plague struck. The Missionaries of Charity now had a new "third world" to deal with in the heart of the first.

Interestingly, when the final Vatican approval of the "pontifical right" was conveyed to Calcutta in 1965, giving the Missionaries of Charity the right to reach out to the world, it was to Venezuela that they went first. Four Indian sisters arrived in Cocorote, two hundred miles southwest of Caracas, to provide relief for destitute families and orphans. In many ways, this modest missionary outreach was a landmark in the development of Christianity in Asia. For centuries, European priests, clergy, and missionaries had traveled around the Cape of Good Hope or through the Suez Canal with the goal of bringing the message of Christianity into the heart of the Indian subcontinent. Now that same message, transmuted into service to the poorest of the poor, was returning to the legacy of the West in the New World.

By 1965, about three hundred sisters in the Missionaries of Charity were either postulants or fully professed nuns. The vast majority had been born in India, though a growing handful were now joining from Western Europe, the Americas, and even Australia. Traditionally, the Catholic church has been dominated within the hierarchy by bishops of Italian origin. Though all of the orders by the twentieth century were entirely international in composition, Europeans or Americans tended to dominate the leadership. Under Mother Teresa's leadership, the Missionaries of Charity became one of the first international Catholic orders with most of the leadership positions filled by Indians.

Even in Washington, D.C., where the Gift of Peace home for AIDS patients was established in 1986, the superior is Sister Sabita, originally from Madras in South India. The sisters she presides over are from North, Central, and South America, from France (which has provided many sisters), and Poland. English from the beginning has been the official language of the Missionaries of Charity. "We are trying to keep the international character of the order," Sister Sabita explained.

The work was now exploding: Rome, Tabora in Tanzania, Amman in Jordan, Melbourne, London, had all opened their doors to the Missionaries of Charity as the radical nature of their commitment to the poor, their humility, and their willingness to take on social problems that no one else wanted to handle became known. By 1979, the year in which the Nobel Peace Prize was conferred on Mother Teresa, the Missionaries of Charity had opened sixty-one new houses outside of India in some twenty-eight countries, ranging from Brazil to Tanzania, and in cities as diverse as Liverpool and Lima, Peru. Mother Teresa visited every single one of the locations before a home was begun.

Sometimes there was resistance to the Missionaries because of a misunderstanding of their identity. In Gaza at first they were mistaken by some Palestinians for Israeli nurses—and shunned—because the blue border of the Missionaries' white saris was mistaken for the design of the Israeli flag. On other occasions they were made to feel unwelcome for ideological reasons. In Lima, Peru, even after their work was established and was providing welcome assistance to a very poor community, some Catholic priests complained. The Missionaries of Charity should be working to change structures, they said, not putting Band-Aids on the sores of an unjust society. But the sisters ignored this challenge from supporters of liberation theology and continued their work without arguing. Often, there was resistance from neighbors of the houses being used for medical or other services for the poor. Even in Washington, D.C., where the Gift of Peace home for AIDS patients was established in 1986, the local community, including a Baptist pastor, complained for years to the city authorities. It took action by Mother Teresa's supporters in the U.S. Congress to stiffen the backs of the Washington municipal authorities to permit the home to stay open. "We always have a problem [like this] somewhere," said a smiling Sister Sabita, superior of the D.C. home for AIDS patients.

A disciplined, orderly way of life was now well established in Calcutta, and with some inevitably regional modifications, in other houses around the world. At 4:30 A.M., the sisters would be awakened in each motherhouse or house by a bell and the call of "Let us bless the Lord," to which they would call out in response, "Thanks be to God." They would pray over their saris while dressing and over their sandals before walking over to the chapel. "Of my own free will, dear Jesus," a sister would pray, "I shall follow You wherever You shall go in search of souls, at any cost to myself and out of pure love of You."[67] Then, in the Indian custom, leaving their sandals at the entrance to the chapel—whether the chapel was in Delhi or San Francisco, they would kneel or sit on the floor of the chapel. It was always a plain room devoid of pews or chairs, with a large crucifix behind the altar and the distinctive words on the wall next to the crucifix, "I Thirst."

The sisters would often pray aloud from their prayer book the prayer of abandonment of St. Ignatius Loyola, founder of the Jesuit order:

> Take, O Lord, and receive all our liberty, our memory, our understanding and our whole will, whatever we have and possess. You have given us all these; to you, O Lord, we restore them; all are yours, dispose of them in any way according to your Will. Give us your love and your grace for this is enough for us.[68]

Breakfast of tea and, in the Indian houses, of the Indian flat bread chapatis would follow, and a few household chores until 7:30 A.M. Then the sisters would spread out, if in Calcutta, for example, to work either in Nirmal Hriday, (the home for the dying destitute), or with the lepers, or in the orphanages and schools. At 12:30 P.M. they would be back for lunch and some housework, followed by half an hour of rest. To settle into the frame of mind for more work in the afternoon, there would be a time for examining their consciences, for saying the divine office or the stations of the cross (specific Catholic prayers), for hearing a spiritual reading of some kind or other, having some tea, and then setting off again at 3:00 P.M. During this time, the novices and postulants would be in the house attending classes on Scripture, theology, and other matters.

Between 6:15 AND 6:30 P.M., there would be a great bustle once again as the Missionaries came in from the afternoon session of work. Then would follow a spiritual time of adoration of the Blessed Sacrament, a traditional spiritual exercise. Dinner would take place at 7:30, followed by brief preparation for the next day, and then came the one time of day when everyone would relax, from 8:30 to 9:00. Officially, the time was recreation, but whatever activity was taking place, there would be a huge roar of conversation as the sisters released some of the tensions of the day's work in excited descriptions to one another of what had taken place. At 9:00 there would be night prayers and a final examination of consciences (despite the Patna recommendation of no prayers after 9:00 P.M.) and lights out by 9:45 or 10:00 P.M. Lights out, of course, for everyone except Mother Teresa, who would often labor on to the wee hours dealing with correspondence or planning long-range new expansion for the order.

With the expansion of the Missionaries of Charity to all of the continents in the world in the course of the 1970's, and particularly after Malcolm

Muggeridge's book *Something Beautiful for God*, the trickle of awards and indications of international recognition became a flood. Mother Teresa was in Rome in January 1971 to receive the Pope John XXIII Prize for Peace from that pope's successor, Paul VI. Even the secretary-general of the UN, U Thant, sent a telegram of congratulations to the Vatican.

As for Mother Teresa herself, she almost didn't make it to the ceremony. She took a city bus to the Vatican and soon found herself attempting to persuade a security official at the door of the reception hall that she was supposed to be in the hall. He hadn't a clue who she was. The day was saved only by a passing bishop, who recognized Mother Teresa and demanded that she be admitted. She had given away the entire pile of admission tickets to other sisters who were present in Rome at the time.

Later in 1971, Mother Teresa was in Boston for the Good Samaritan award granted by the Joseph P. Kennedy Jr. Foundation. It was no mere formality. The foundation had organized a symposium entitled "Choices on Our Consciences," which dealt in depth with the most profound and troubling moral issues humanity was facing or had recently faced. Mother Teresa spoke of dealing with the discarded people she found each day on the streets of Calcutta.

Another speaker, Elie Wiesel—the sixth of this book's Great Souls— was also present, meeting Mother Teresa for the first time. In his talk, Wiesel warned of how humankind's indifference to crimes like the Holocaust might create a moral environment in which similar events could take place again. Eileen Egan, who was present at the conference, observed: "Wiesel's presence as a witness to man's death-dealing powers, in the same room with Mother Teresa's witness to life's inviolable sacredness and the duty to nurture it, formed the most poignantly dramatic conjunction of the symposium."[69]

Other international awards piled up: the Jawaharlal Nehru Award for International Understanding from the Indian government in 1972; the Templeton Prize for Progress in Religion in 1973; the Mater et Magistra Prize from the Third Order of St. Francis of Assisi in 1974; a medal coined in her honor by the Food and Agriculture Organization of the UN in 1975; the Albert Schweitzer Prize in 1975. For a while, a bewildering array of honorary degrees were also bestowed on her.

What to do with all of this attention? Mother Teresa once said that if getting into heaven were a matter of works—which is certainly not what

she believed—the labor that would earn her admission would be confronting the bombardment of press attention she faced over the years. Journalists
can sometimes be crass—I say this as a journalist—supinely ignorant of
religion, and prone to the strangest of questions. Mother Teresa thus
wrestled with a difficult dilemma from the time her work became truly
famous. Should she have accepted the awards and the honors as a way of
drawing attention to her message of the dignity of the poor and the
pricelessness of all human life—and therefore have risked the accusation
that she was desirous of fame (though not of fortune)? Or should she
have avoided all international attention, stayed in Calcutta except when
traveling to establish new houses abroad or visit existing ones—thus risk-
ing missing opportunities to spread around the world the message and
the mission she believed God had given her?

Either choice had its drawbacks, but after her initial reluctance to receive that first Indian award in 1962, Mother Teresa, with enthusiastic support
from Rome, decided that the pathway of global recognition, however painful and exhausting it might be at times, was the road she should walk.

The conflicts inherent in this decision must have been uppermost in
her mind when she and a few faithful sisters journeyed to Oslo early in
December of 1979 to receive the Nobel Peace Prize. Winter comes briskly
to Scandinavia, with early nightfall and the chill of deep frosts when the
sun is gone. Yet when Mother Teresa flew into Oslo that December, the
city was illuminated by a brilliant burst of winter sunshine. At the airport,
she faced more reporters than she had probably ever seen in one place
before, all eager to size up the diminutive woman who had captured the
world's attention. Why had she come all the way to Oslo for the award,
she was asked, since it was known that she would not accept the money
for herself? "I am myself unworthy of the prize," she answered. "I do not
want it personally. But by this award the Norwegian people have recognized the existence of the poor. It is on their behalf that I have come."[70]

The award ceremony was held the following day in the Aula Magna
(Great Hall) of the University of Oslo, in the presence of the Norwegian
royal family, government officials, diplomats, academics, and prominent
religious figures. Professor John Sanness of the Norwegian Nobel Committee showed great sensitivity and insight in describing exactly what it
was about the "spirit of Mother Teresa" that marked her out. "Better than
anyone else," he said,

she has managed to put into practice the recognized fact that gifts given de haut en bas (from a superior to an inferior), where the recipient has a feeling of one-sided and humiliating dependence on the giver, may prove to be hurtful to the recipient's dignity as a human being, that it may well breed bitterness and animosity instead of harmony and peace. . . .

With her message she is able to reach through to something innate in every human kind—if for no other purpose than to create a potential, a seed for good. If this were not the case, the world would be deprived of hope, and work for peace would have little meaning.[71]

After the applause died down, Mother Teresa, seeming smaller than ever beside the tall Scandinavians, rose to speak. Her words ranged through every major aspect of her life's work and her thoughts, from loving God, to loving the poor, to the problem of human rejection in wealthy countries, to the nature of love itself, and, of course, to abortion. The mention of abortion in her speech prompted the *New York Times* to headline its story: "Mother Teresa, Receiving Nobel, Assails Abortion."

More lucidly, perhaps, than she has ever done elsewhere, Mother Teresa went deep into the motivation of the Missionaries of Charity's work. Denying, as she always did, that theirs was social work, she carefully explained:

We may be doing social work in the eyes of the people. But we are really contemplatives in the heart of the world. For we are touching the body of Christ 24 hours. We have 24 hours in this presence, and so you and I. You too try to bring that presence of God in your family, for the family that prays together stays together.[72]

The idea of "just get together" to solve the world's problems certainly has the ring of naïveté to it. As we shall soon see, Mother Teresa may well have stepped out of her calling when, at the insistence of many earnest political leaders and social idealists, she tried at various times to be an active intermediary for peace in Northern Ireland, to solve the hostage problem in Iran, and even to prevent convicted criminals from receiving the death penalty.

Yet in Oslo, her insights into the very essence of compassion starkly defined her philosophical identity. First, she made clear that the giving of love itself is always of greater importance than the provision of material needs. Second, she did not apologize for her belief that it was only through a daily communication in prayer with Jesus Christ that she acquired the spiritual energy necessary really to love the poor. She explained the first point with a sad tale from one of her American trips:

> I'll never forget an opportunity I had in visiting a home where they had all those old parents of sons and daughters who had just put them in an institution and forgotten maybe. . . .They are hurt because they are forgotten, and see—[this] is where love comes. That poverty comes right there in our own home, even neglect to love. . . .
>
> When I pick up a person from the street, hungry, I give him a plate of rice, a piece of bread, I have satisfied, I have removed that hunger. But a person that is shut out, that feels unwanted, unloved, terrified, the person that has been thrown out from society—that poverty is so hurtable and so much, and I find that very difficult. Our Sisters are working among that kind of people in the West.[73]

As for her spiritual strength, Sanness had already made it clear that Mother Teresa was Christian through and through. But in case anyone present still wasn't sure, at the very beginning of her Oslo talk she asked the distinguished audience to start off by reading the Prayer of St. Francis, that begins with the well-known words, "Lord, make me a channel of Thy peace. . . ."[74]

Some Americans—admittedly a very small, very narrow group—have developed a sort of cottage industry on the Internet trying to prove that Mother Teresa is not a Christian at all, but some sort of syncretistic groupie of every belief system that's out there. Her Nobel speech, it seems to me, rebuts this notion once and for all. Here's a portion on Jesus:

> [Jesus] being God became man in all things like us except sin, and he proclaimed very clearly that he had come to give the good news. . . .
>
> And as if that was not enough—it was not enough to become man—he died on the cross to show that greater love, he died for you and for me and for that leper and for that many dying of hunger and that naked person lying in the street not only of Calcutta, but of Africa, and New York, and London, and Oslo—and insisted that we love one another as he loves each one of us. . . .

To be able to do this, our lives have to be woven with prayer. They have to be woven with Christ to be able to understand, to be able to share. Because today there is so much suffering—and I feel that the passion of Christ is being relived all over again—and we are to share that passion, to share the suffering of people.[75]

Journalists in Oslo were, as they always have been, both awed and baffled by the personality of Mother Teresa. Who was she really? How could she be, just to take the nationality issue, Albanian, Yugoslav, and Indian, all at the same time? She replied to their questions: "By blood and origin, I am all Albanian. My citizenship is Indian. I am a Catholic nun. I belong to the world. As to my heart, I belong entirely to the heart of Jesus."[76]

"WE WILL HAVE A CEASE-FIRE TOMORROW"

After the Nobel award in 1979, Mother Teresa rarely seemed to stop traveling. She visited North America almost annually, but she also went to Haiti, the Sudan, Papua New Guinea, Brazil, and Australia, to name but a few of her far-flung destinations—wherever, in fact, the doors were open to the Missionaries of Charity. She would sometimes show up in countries during moments of immense turmoil, or in the aftermath of man-made or natural catastrophes.

In 1982, she arrived in Beirut after a several-hour, exhausting boat trip from Cyprus at the very height of the Israeli army's bombardment of the PLO-dominated western part of the city. "I'm certain we will have a cease-fire tomorrow," she told the respectful, but kindly skeptical senior U.S. diplomat in place, Ambassador Philip Habib. There was. (I was in Beirut at the time, though I never actually saw Mother Teresa there.) During the lull, she organized a civilian convoy to drive into the western part of the city to retrieve retarded and handicapped children cut off from usual services in a home there. She brought carloads of them back into the safety of a home run by the Missionaries of Charity in the eastern part of the city.

After the Chernobyl nuclear disaster in the Soviet Union in 1986, Mother Teresa asked if she could visit Kiev to provide comfort to the victims of the massive radiation fallout. She finally arrived in Moscow in August 1987 as a guest of the Soviet Peace Committee, an organization usually staffed by slightly overweight KGB officers. The Missionaries had already broken through part of the traditional Communist prejudice against Christian activity by establishing homes in Cuba and East Germany. Within a few years, Mikhail Gorbachev permitted them to open homes in what is now the former USSR.

In 1988, as the Soviet Union under Gorbachev slid toward disintegration, she showed up in Armenia after a devastating earthquake at the end of the year killed thousands of people there. Gorbachev was made Man of the Decade late in 1989 by *Time* magazine. In an accompanying story called "Faces of the Decade," *Time* singled out glamorous personalities whose star had risen (and sometimes fallen) in the previous ten years. They included Madonna, Bruce Springsteen, Michael Jackson, Nancy Reagan . . . and Mother Teresa. "She is the celebrity of the poor," the magazine opined, "the antithesis of the decade's dominant values."[77]

Her fame, she always said, was her peculiar cross. Yet it also enabled her, as Billy Graham's has, to have a deep impact on a curious variety of people, ranging from the queen of England and Princess Diana (who was reportedly buried with a crucifix given to her by Mother Teresa), to big financiers and Communist Party bosses.

She always refused any payment for herself or her nuns, or any property ownership of any kind except where, without it, the work of the Missionaries would not be permitted. When the Knights of Columbus in the U.S., a high-profile Roman Catholic private institution, offered a considerable monthly sum, she replied: "I prefer the insecurity of divine providence."[78] There were several huge sums of money made available to the sisters by both private individuals and institutions, but Mother Teresa repeatedly spoke out against any sort of financial or material security for the Missionaries. "The greatest danger we could encounter would be to get rich,"[79] she often said. She was certainly right. One of the reasons the Franciscans failed to maintain the momentum of service to the poorest of the poor in Europe in the Middle Ages after the death of St. Francis himself was the rapid enrichment of the monastic order as a result of gifts from admiring and wealthy laypeople. "We need poverty if we are to live free, both materially and spiritually," Mother Teresa explained.

> We need such freedom, a freedom like the one we find in those around
> us, so as not to become enslaved by wealth. Nobody can oblige us to

enrich ourselves. We must consecrate ourselves exclusively to poverty. Christ chose liberty. If we truly want to belong to Christ, then we must be poor.[80]

In practice, the Missionaries of Charity do have bank accounts, and they have not turned down some extremely useful, and sometimes quite strange gifts. In 1973, the British corporation Imperial Chemical Industries handed over to the Missionaries of Charity a huge former manufacturing compound in Calcutta, complete with several buildings ready for immediate occupancy. When Pope Paul VI visited India in 1964, he donated to her the white Lincoln sedan used during his visit. Mother Teresa immediately auctioned it off for $100,000 and put the money to good use throughout the ministry.

"Mother," as her close associates within and outside the Missionaries of Charity invariably called her, enjoyed free lifetime flight privileges on Air India and sometimes other airlines. She was also given a permanent free pass aboard the Indian railroad system. But her fame inadvertently created problems whenever she traveled, resulting in a paradox. For many years, she insisted on flying economy class everywhere she went. Once she became instantly recognizable, however, ordinary passengers would be so intrigued by her presence or would so much want to talk to her, even touch her, that the airliner's aisles became totally blocked, preventing movement by other passengers or the normal work of flight attendants. The result: She eventually agreed to travel first-class to avoid the disruption caused by her fame.

Despite these challenges, Mother Teresa from the beginning showed a canny wisdom in mobilizing support for the Missionaries through a network of supporting organizations. The Co-Workers of the Missionaries of Charity, for example, formally recognized by Pope John Paul VI in 1969, have often been present in countries, paving the way for the Missionaries of Charity, so to speak, before the sisters themselves arrived. There is even an order of Missionaries of Charity Brothers, but they are far fewer in number than the sisters, and they work in only a tiny fraction of the countries where the Missionaries of Charity are present.

Mother Teresa seemed to lead a protected life throughout most of her career as head of the Missionaries of Charity. But there were exceptions. She had a near brush with death in 1964 when the car she was traveling in

screeched suddenly to a halt near Darjeeling to avoid an oncoming vehicle. Mother Teresa hurtled forward and struck her head, requiring
nineteen stitches. In 1983 there was a far more serious setback. Already
seventy-two years old, she was in Rome in June when she was hospitalized for a fall that led to broken ribs. After her release several weeks later,
she suffered the preliminary phase of a heart attack while visiting the sisters in New York. She was hospitalized twice during 1988 and 1989, and on
the second occasion fitted with a heart pacemaker in a Calcutta hospital.
In April of the following year, she reluctantly stepped down from the leadership of the Missionaries of Charity, Superior General, as the title had
become. But after the chapter meeting in September 1990, she was asked
to come out of retirement and resume charge. Three years later, the pace
of her work and travel once more took their toll. Back in the U.S. yet
again, she was hospitalized in La Jolla, California, this time after bacterial
pneumonia brought on a brief episode of congestive heart failure.

Her most serious medical setback was undoubtedly the combined heart
failure and collapsed lung that she experienced in Calcutta in August 1996.
For a brief period of time, her heart stopped beating altogether, and she
had to be revived by emergency resuscitation equipment. She was then
kept on a respirator for a few days until her strength slowly came back.
"Our sisters have been storming heaven for her," one sister in Calcutta
told a friend at the time. It was this same heart condition that eventually
took her life in September 1997, at eighty-seven years of age.

"I GET ANGRY SOMETIMES"

Before her death, she was called "a living saint" by wire services nonplussed
to come up with any better description of a person whose moral life has
been utterly exceptional for decades. But in fact, she was far from perfect,
as she herself was the first to acknowledge. She was impatient with in-
terruptions or resistance to what she wanted to do, and as she herself admitted, not only impatient. "Yes, I get angry sometimes. When I see waste,
when the things that are wasted are what people need, things that could
save them from dying. Frustrated? No, never."[81] She had a tendency to
make abrupt and arbitrary decisions about people she had appointed to
positions within the Missionaries of Charity, and then remained reluctant
to correct them when it had long been obvious that a mistake was made.

A few nuns who were close to Mother Teresa left the order in disgruntlement about one aspect or another of its operation.

Her efforts at international problem solving were always sincere, but not often blessed by divine Providence. Under intense pressure from well-meaning people, she tried to help solve the problem of the U.S. hostages held by Iran during 1979–80. The Iranians rebuffed her efforts with the barest effort at politeness. In 1990, she tried to stop the impending Gulf War from breaking out. She wrote letters to President Bush and Iraqi president Saddam Hussein, appealing to them not to let the Iraqi occupation of Kuwait turn into a war. When a journalist asked her if she thought there could be such a thing as a just war, she shook her head. But when the reporter persisted, asking if just-war theory wasn't a part of Catholic doctrine, she retorted sternly: "Do you think I'm not a good Catholic, then?"[82]

She was actively opposed to capital punishment, even petitioning directly for clemency on behalf of condemned criminals. She unsuccessfully appealed to California governor Pete Wilson in 1992 not to execute Bobby Harris, who was convicted of kidnapping and murdering two teenagers. In 1991, she talked from Calcutta by speakerphone to Judge Joseph Augello in Wilkes-Barre, Pennsylvania, requesting that convicted murderer Steven Dunn not be sentenced to death for the murder of his girlfriend's 16-month-old son in 1990. "Killing a child is a terrible thing," she said by phone, but she felt that Dunn should nevertheless be given a chance to make reparation for the crime (Dunn's lawyer had previously met Mother Teresa in Rome). None of these interventions apparently succeeded.

Mother Teresa's openness to the potential for good in all people led her at times—as it was with Billy Graham for the same reason—into associations that later proved embarrassing. In 1981, during a visit to Haiti, she sang the praises of Michele Duvalier, wife of Jean-Claude "Baby Doc" Duvalier, son of the ruthless dictator "Papa Doc" Duvalier. She had "never seen the poor people being so familiar with their head of state as they were with her," she said of Michele Duvalier. But the Duvaliers, though probably far less brutal than the sadistic "Papa Doc," were forced to flee for their lives aboard a U.S. aircraft five years later because of unrest stirred up by the inequities of their rule.

The Missionaries of Charity also received huge financial contributions, reportedly totaling more than one million dollars, from Charles Keating, later convicted on charges of massive fraud in the U.S. Savings and Loan crisis of the 1980's. Keating had personally met Mother Teresa, and as a Roman Catholic, greatly admired her work. During Keating's trial in 1992, Mother Teresa wrote to the judge (who happened to be Lance Ito, later to judge the O. J. Simpson case), appealing for clemency for Keating. "I do not know anything about Mr. Charles Keating's work or his business or the matters you are dealing with," Mother Teresa wrote. "I only know that he has been kind and generous to God's poor, and always ready to help whenever there was a need."[83]

Naïveté can be grating. During the authoritarian Emergency Rule period of Prime Minister Indira Gandhi in India from 1975 to 1977, she declared, "People are happier. There are more jobs. There are no strikes."[84] But while many ordinary people might have agreed with this sentiment, the imposition of political press censorship and the jailing of political opponents by the government were widely condemned both inside and outside the country as arbitrary and dictatorial. More seriously, one of the consequences of Emergency Rule was the coercive sterilization of thousands, perhaps millions of Indians, a practice that Mother Teresa could not and would not possibly have approved of had she known about it.

In South Africa for the first time in 1988, she astonished reporters with the admission that she had been unaware of the existence of apartheid before she came. This, even though she was planning the commendable step of setting up a home in one of the most destitute black townships outside Capetown.

Mother Teresa's ignorance of world affairs, of course, confirmed her total absence of political malice or axes to grind. Although she hobnobbed with dubious political figures on the political right like "Baby Doc" Duvalier and his wife, she also enjoyed the "peace-loving" hospitality of the Soviet Peace Committee, the ultra-Stalinist government of Albania in 1989 before the fall of Communism there, and the nasty East German Communist regime of Erich Honecker before the fall of the Berlin Wall. Her response to criticism for these associations was the same in all cases: "We serve all people, children of God," she said in Moscow in 1987.[85] She enjoyed excellent relations with the Communist administration governing Calcutta, a point that ought to soften some of the criticism of her from the left.

Mother Teresa's obvious saintliness as a servant of the poor—the *New York Times* at one point oddly called her "a secular saint"—did not protect her from some vigorous, and sometimes vicious, public criticism. It has come from both left and right, religious and secular, Hindu and Christian. After she received the Nobel Peace Prize, some militant Hindus objected, saying that "her sole objective is to influence people in favor of Christianity, and, if possible to convert them."[86]

Christopher Hitchens, a left-wing journalist and a vituperative critic of Mother Teresa, has griped, on the basis of reports to him from former Missionaries of Charity workers, that the sisters have sometimes clandestinely "baptized" the very sick on their deathbeds while pretending to wipe their brows with a damp cloth.[87] Why this, of all things, should upset Hitchens, a self-described "convinced atheist," is a mystery. Others, generally strongly anti-Catholic Protestants, have raised the charge, already mentioned, of religious syncretism. To make this case, they have actually distorted quotations from a *Time* interview, citing her as saying, "I love all religions," but omitting the remainder of the sentence.[88] Mother Teresa, in public discourse, bent over backward to avoid offending other religions, but that is not at all the same thing as saying she valued them equally. In the *Time* interview of 1989, which was deliberately misquoted, she made this very clear:

Q. What do you think of Hinduism?

A. I love all religions, but I am in love with my own.

Q. And they should love Jesus too?

A. Naturally, if they want peace, if they want joy, let them find Jesus. If people become better Muslims, better Hindus, better Buddhists by our acts of love, there is something else growing there.[89]

The "something else," of course, implies that once a person encounters God's love through the medium of Christian mercy, he or she may be drawn to find out how to tap into that love.

Roman Catholic liberals have often criticized Mother Teresa from a perspective of what might be called "Roman Catholic Marxism." An article in the *National Catholic Reporter* by Mary Bader Papa at the time of the Nobel Prize complained that Mother Teresa's work was "merely bandaging the wounds of capitalism."[90] It is not known whether the same writer complained after the Missionaries of Charity began working in East Germany a few years later and thus, presumably, were "merely bandaging the wounds of socialism."

Many Indians, too, including Calcuttans, have resented the unpleasant reputation their city has acquired, as a result of worldwide publicity on the work of the Missionaries of Charity, of being one of the most squalid and destitute places on earth. This is an understandable sentiment, but it could be applied to any part of the world where appalling conditions have been made public in the process of attempting to deal with them.

By far the most public and relentless assault upon Mother Teresa's reputation was made by the aforementioned Hitchens. In 1994, the BBC in London aired a Channel Four documentary called "Hell's Angel," in which Hitchens unveiled the core of his assault on Mother Teresa. The associations with Keating and Michele Duvalier were brought up, along with complaints about the nature of the work in the houses of the Missionaries of Charity from disgruntled former volunteers who had helped there. Later, Hitchens wrote an article for *Vanity Fair*, describing with obvious glee how much he had offended people by creating "Hell's Angel," but adding a new vocabulary of vitriol to his attack on Mother Teresa. She was, he said, "the ghoul of Calcutta," "dangerous," and "sinister."

Hitchens's sneering and sexually suggestive book, with its intentionally derisive title, *The Missionary Position*, is a diatribe chiefly against the Christian faith itself, which he describes as "the promulgation of a cult based on death and suffering and subjection."[91] The chief fault of Mother Teresa, whose universally admired persona he mocks, is that her work is "nothing but a fundamentalist religious campaign." Other words in his vocabulary of invective are *fanatical, obscurantist,* and *demagogue.*

There is something not just somewhat sophomoric about all this, but petulant and whining. It is, in a sense, characteristic of the human condition as a whole. How dare Mother Teresa remind us of something we don't want to be reminded of: our vulnerability as human beings, our sinfulness and selfishness, the inability of our technological modernity to solve such age-old problems, not just of poverty, but of the fundamental need of every human being to be loved?

Many have questioned the obsession with poverty on the part of the Missionaries of Charity. Especially in the West, it would be simple for them to operate homes with all of the accoutrements of, say, a well-equipped nursing home. None of the homes anywhere are permitted to own a washing machine, and the very few concessions to climate and convenience are the provision of air-conditioning in a home or two in Washington and New York, and the use of clothes dryers where climate makes it impossible for clothes to dry by exposure to the outside air. There are no computers in any of the homes, and a rudimentary manual typewriter seems to be the way most correspondence is dealt with. Television sets are kept out of the houses, except on special occasions like the Olympic Games.

Arguing that the obsession with poverty of lifestyle is a form of cultural extremism, some critics have said that the Missionaries of Charity are turning themselves into a new version of, say, the Amish or the Mennonites. Yet if anything is clear at all, it is above all that Mother Teresa and her sisters have been able to reach out to the poorest of the poor by identifying with them in lifestyle. Had she not been firmly told at the very beginning of her ministry that the health of the sisters would break down unless they ate properly, she would have chosen to eat as sparingly as the very poorest themselves ate—when they ate, that is. As Jim Twoey has noted: "The majority of the sisters are Indian in the homes all over the world. It's a hard life." He adds: "I think when Mother tells the sisters that their poverty is their dowry, that whole concept is very foreign to the West."[92]

The very idea seems odd, especially in a world of modernity where the word *dowry* has a medieval ring to it. Yet it represents one of the most radical ideas in the whole of Christian thought, the metaphor that the church is the bride of Jesus Christ and that a nun taking her vows is, in a spiritual sense, becoming wedded to Jesus. Mother Teresa herself has spoken of this relationship with such familiarity that it is almost startling. In her Nobel Prize lecture she described a visit by American college professors and their spouses to the motherhouse in Calcutta. One woman visitor asked her, "Are you married?"

Mother Teresa described what she said next. "I said: 'Yes, and I find it sometimes very difficult to smile at Jesus because He can be very demanding sometimes.'"[93]

The intimacy of this closeness that Mother Teresa always expressed toward Jesus, above all when speaking to fellow Christians, explains another characteristic of the Missionaries of Charity. This is the emphasis on the Communion service, or Mass. Partaking of the body and blood of Christ in the form of bread and wine have, since the beginning of Christianity, been central to the community of Christian faith and worship. Mother Teresa put it this way in a letter to her brother, Lazar, in 1975: "Mass is the spiritual food that nourishes me. Without it I could not survive a day or an hour in the life I lead. Jesus comes to us in the Mass under the appearance of bread."[94] It is obvious that the Communion for Mother Teresa and for the other sisters was not some ancient ritual, some out-worn ecclesiastical tradition that they wearily carried out as a daily chore. It was—and continues to be for the sisters—a daily source of real spiri-tual, physical, and emotional strength in their lives. This strength is something Christians have always called "grace."

As Mother Teresa approached the end of her days, skeptics and faith-ful alike were still trying to second-guess the very core of her motivation and inspiration, as well as what inspired thousands of followers in the same direction all around the globe. Her answer to this question was al-ways the same: "Jesus." In the hospital in Rome in June 1983, after her fall and physical near collapse, she reflected more intensely than before on her relationship to her spiritual "husband." She wrote a brief meditation in answer to the question, "Who is Jesus to me?" "Jesus is the Word made Flesh, Jesus is the Bread of Life," she starts off, conventionally enough for any orthodox Catholic—or Protestant or orthodox Christian, for that mat-ter. Then, close to the end, she inserted, in the same script as the original question, the words, "to me." She went on:

> Jesus is my God
> Jesus is my spouse
> Jesus is my Life
> Jesus is my only Love
> Jesus is my All in All
> Jesus is my Everything.

We are said to be living in a postmodern age, an epoch where ancient and long-held beliefs are not only no longer accepted by most people, they are not even considered worth holding up to the challenge of logical skepticism. People of the wretchedly named "Generation X," the chil-dren of the baby boomers, are themselves aging. Will they and those who follow them out into life confirm Friedrich Nietzsche's prediction of a century ago that, with God supposedly banished from men's discourse, human culture will become increasingly "weightless"? It will be up to later generations, of course, to provide a definitive answer to that question.

But in an important way, Mother Teresa herself provided a refutation of Nietzsche's prediction. It is certainly true that the twentieth century has witnessed more horrors of human barbarism in the space of one hundred years than the rest of human history in its entirety. Yet Mother Teresa was born and lived her life through nine of the ten decades of that same century, achieving the highest possible human recognition of attainment, the Nobel Peace Prize, becoming one of the most easily recognized and most instantly admired human beings on the entire planet.

Was she not impossibly old-fashioned? Of course. Wedded unquestioningly to Roman Catholic tradition? For sure. Unapologetically opposed to such designer conveniences of modern life as abortion on demand, narcotics of choice, and the inane self-delusion of sexual gratification as an end in itself? Until her last breath. Against the weightlessness of so much of modernity, Mother Teresa laid out a plumb line—God's plumb line, to be precise—of what the human virtue of compassion really means. More precisely, she lived out the total significance of the New Testament Greek word *agape*—its deepest meaning has to do not with feeling, but with the giving up of one's life.

One person's life, of course, is never a sufficient source of light to disperse the darkness threatening to engulf entire cultures. But in our twentieth century, with its frequent inability to distinguish true light from mere glitter, Mother Teresa not only demonstrated what true light is. To her dying day, she pointed the way for millions and millions of others to find it too.

CHAPTER 5

POPE JOHN PAUL II: HUMAN DIGNITY

"Be not afraid! Open up, no, swing wide the gates to Christ. Open up to his saving power the confines of the state, open up economic and political systems, the vast empires of culture, civilization and development. . . . Be not afraid!"

—POPE JOHN PAUL II
In his inaugural sermon as pope,
St. Peter's Square, Rome, October 22, 1978

I HAVE ALWAYS LIKED the Poles. As a correspondent covering Eastern Europe from West Berlin at the height of the Cold War, I came across many wonderful, indeed heroic, people in all of the countries I was able to visit. But of them all, the Poles were the most refreshingly transparent. They said what they thought without beating about the bush. They collectively seemed to identify with that part of the Western tradition that has always valued truth as much as freedom; their contempt for Communism seemed to be almost a part of their genes. Of course, there were plenty of committed Polish Communists—they just never quite gave the impression of being entirely Polish.

The late 1970's were an exciting time to report on Poland, for much of the intelligentsia was girding itself up for what became eventually a wholesale attack on Communist rule through the initially illegal labor organization known as Solidarity. There were "flying universities," illegal seminars conducted in preselected locations by dissident scholars on such taboo topics as the Katyn Forest Massacre of forty-five hundred Polish officers by Soviet troops in 1940. There were underground printing presses that reproduced essays and books the regime would not permit into the country at all, much less to appear officially in print in Poland. And there were the brave Catholic intellectuals who pushed the envelope of permissible political discussion in periodicals that were legal but constantly sniped at by the Communist authorities.

One of my favorite such intellectuals was Turowicz. He was the impressive editor in chief of the Catholic weekly *Tygodnik Powszechny*, a Krakow-based publication that sought, year after year, to bring before its small but highly influential readership the public issues, personalities, and talents with which the regime, as a whole, was not comfortable. It was during a visit to Krakow in 1977 or early in 1978 that Turowicz first indicated to me, in an oblique way, how impressive the archbishop of Krakow was, how energetic he was in the diocese, and how deeply spiritual he was.

As journalists sometimes do, I was so preoccupied with his views on the larger political issues of Poland that I completely failed to grasp what he was telling me. He was trying to alert me to the formidable character of a local bishop named Karol Wojtyla, within a matter of months to become the first-ever Polish pope, better known around the world as John Paul II.

I did not meet Wojtyla while he was still archbishop of Krakow, and once he became pope, my reporting responsibilities never made it possible for me to cover his papacy directly. But having a sense of how formidable Polish intellectuals could be, and how totally uncompromising they were in what they believed, I had little doubt that this pope from Poland would make an impact that would overshadow by far that of most of his predecessors in modern times.

When leaders and dignitaries from scores of countries, hundreds of thousands of citizens of Rome, and hundreds of millions of television viewers around the world witnessed Karol Wojtyla in Rome on the international stage in the fall of 1978, they may have had the same intuition that I had. Certainly the scene was unprecedented in modern times. Here was the newly elected pontiff of the Roman Catholic Church, formerly Cardinal Karol Jozef Wojtyla, archbishop of Krakow, Poland, celebrating his first Mass. As pope, he was participating in an ancient ritual acted out on a huge raised platform in St. Peter's Square.

The solemn proceedings of an ancient ritual were being performed: the clouds of incense spread around the altar by altar boys swinging censers, the choristers singing out the great liturgical choruses of the Roman

Catholic Church, and the cardinal deacon of the Vatican, Pericle Felici, placing on the pope's shoulders the white stole of papal office. One by one, the III cardinals who had gathered to elect John Paul II in the Sistine Chapel just six days earlier then rose from their seats to pledge their loyalty to the new leader. They were joined by seven others too old, at eighty, to have participated in the conclave. High prelates of the Roman Catholic Church, they approached the pope's throne by the altar one by one, knelt down, and kissed the pontiff's ring.

Then came John Paul II's sermon and the ringing words cited at the beginning of this chapter. "Brothers and sisters," he proclaimed, "don't be afraid to welcome Christ and to accept his power. Help the pope and all those who wish to serve Christ and, with the power of Christ, to serve man and the whole human race." As a recent biography (one of whose authors is a secular Jew) put it in describing this scene: "There was only one leitmotif in Wojtyla's sermon: Christ."[1]

The pageantry of a papal enthronement had been witnessed several times before by the citizens of Rome and, since the age of television began, by observers around the world. The pope, after all, was the Vicar of Christ and spiritual overseer to some 950 million Catholics. The installation of a new pontiff was a matchless event in the life of the Catholic church.

But there was something clearly different about this scene. Before John Paul II, all of the seven new popes elected in Rome since 1900 had been Italian. All of them were old at the time of their installation, perhaps elevated to the papacy as the crowning achievement of a long life of clerical service. But here was someone who was emphatically young at fifty-eight, the youngest pope since Pius IX in 1846. Other popes had seemed to shuffle, hobble, or at least tread tenderly through St. Peter's Cathedral and the corridors and audience halls of the 109 acres of Vatican City, the world's smallest sovereign state.

Here, too, was a pope who was not even Italian, and was the first foreigner on the throne of St. Peter since the Dutchman Adrian VI, elected in 1522, 456 years earlier. "This Pole, this Slav," as John Paul II was sometimes later to describe himself, was unmistakably healthy-looking and self-confident. Amid the magnificent pageantry of the installation, he strode around St. Peter's Square. Wielding his crosier over the crowds in the sign of blessing as though it were a two-edged sword, he kissed babies, embraced worshipers in wheelchairs, and acted as though he had prepared all his life for a starring role in one of the greatest historical dramas of the twentieth century.

Today, the energetic stride is gone, replaced by a stooping, cane-assisted walk. The white hair is thinner than it was nineteen years ago, and John Paul's right eye is often wider and more piercing in its stare than the left one, the mark of a man whose body has taken its revenge on the will and energy of its occupant. There are frequent signs of physical pain in the hesitant gait, the slowed-down movements, and the absence of that earlier, winning smile.

John Paul's left hand now trembles, too, from what Vatican officials privately concede is a form of Parkinson's disease.[2] He has had four major abdominal surgeries, two after an assassination attempt against him in 1981, the removal of an orange-sized tumor from his colon in 1992, and an appendectomy in October 1996. He broke his right arm and dislocated a shoulder in 1993 in, of all things, a skiing accident, and he had hip replacement surgery after falling and breaking his leg in 1994. Sometimes, awkwardly leaning on the cane in his left hand, he winces unwittingly as his body protests his movement. At other times, his eyes seem to be glazed, as though he is daydreaming of a faraway place.

Yet some things are hardly different, despite the physical aging, from what they were nineteen years ago. As he continues what seems at times a relentless, determined global pilgrimage to every country on earth where there are Catholic communities (by the end of 1995 he had visited 112), he is still met by huge, expectant, sometimes roaring crowds as fascinated as those Romans were in the late 1970's. In August 1997, his appearance on the Longchamps horse-racing track outside Paris was greeted by an incredible one million people, some three times the number church officials had predicted for France. It is as if there is something about his presence that reminds believers and skeptics alike of the transcendent element in human life.

"People who see him—and countless millions have—do not forget him," wrote *Time* magazine, declaring him Man of the Year for 1994. "His appearances generate an electricity unmatched by anyone else on earth."[3] Many concur. Writing in *The New Republic*, Jennifer Bradley, author of the "Baltimore Diarist" feature, who terms herself a Catholic with views on some doctrinal issues that leave her "unexcited about the pope and the papacy," described the impact on her of attending a Mass celebrated by the pope in Camden Yards, Baltimore, in October 1995. "I was moved in a way I never expected," she wrote.

> But I'm not sure how to explain this without lapsing into the senti-
> mentality that horrified me in the hours before the pope appeared.
> But John Paul II complicated me. . . . It was like every Mass I have
> ever attended—the same cadences, intonations, pauses, prayers—and
> it was like none. Shivering in the Camden Yards' chilly wind, I was
> caught between the quotidian and the sublime. Now my skepticism
> will have to share space with awe and, oddly, gratitude.[4]

It is a strange word, *gratitude,* particularly from the lips of someone who admits to being unhappy about some of the Catholic church's teachings, including those stressed heavily by John Paul II. But it is not inappropriate. John Paul II has certainly antagonized an important minority within the Catholic church's theological hierarchy and dismayed many lay Catholics, especially in the West, by his emphasis on the church's traditional opposition to artificial birth control, abortion, divorce and remarriage, female ordination, and the homosexual lifestyle. But he has somehow transcended his critics in the magnitude of his achievement as a pope and as a man. "There are only two popes formally called the Great, Leo [the First, 440–461] and Gregory [the First, 590–604]," explains Fr. Richard John Neuhaus, editor in chief of *First Things,* and a priest in the archdiocese of New York. He adds: "I fully expect that in the next century people will refer to John Paul II as 'the Great.' I think he is one of the handful of really outstanding occupants of the Holy See. It has to do with his personal qualities and the historical moment."[5]

The personal qualities are worth examining, and we shall do that. They are what indeed make him a Great Soul. But let's consider what Pope John Paul II has already accomplished.

There is now little argument over the judgment that Pope John Paul II played a decisive role—in the views of some, *the* decisive role—in the collapse of Communism in Europe in the 1980's. And if a scheduled visit to Cuba takes place in 1998, the pope is likely to play a role in the final abandonment of Communism there. During his first visit as pope to Poland in June 1979, within months of his taking office, he inspired his fellow countrymen with such a sense of excitement about his own

Christian philosophy of life and governance—a Christian philosophy—
that it highlighted for them how tawdry and indeed bankrupt the
philosophy of Communism had become in the three decades it had been
in power.

John Paul never called upon the Poles to resist their rulers, much less
to take up arms and revolt against them. But in every public statement
and appearance, whether in Poland or elsewhere, he seemed to convince
them of two things. First, Communism was not even authentically Polish.
Second, it was not invincible, though many in the world had come to
believe that it was.

Within fourteen months of John Paul's June 1979 Polish visit, when he
was seen in person by nearly one-third of the entire Polish people, Poland
was rocked by an unprecedented outburst of strike activity and demands
for government recognition of Solidarity, a labor union independent of
the Communist rulers. The troubles had first surfaced in the Baltic port
of Gdansk, when an unemployed electrician, Lech Walesa, had climbed
over the fence into the shipyard and taken over leadership of the strike.
Western reporters were astounded to see that the striking workers knelt
to pray and that many of them spoke glowingly of the pope. When he
signed an agreement with the government at the end of August to legalize Solidarity, Walesa playfully wielded a huge felt pen decorated with a
picture of John Paul II. The crumbling of Communism in Eastern Europe
was beginning, and the pope had set off the first dynamite blast.

John Paul II, of course, was not alone when he embarked on his
formidable spiritual and philosophical foray into the heartland of Soviet-
controlled Europe. Providence had assembled, it seemed, an unusually
strong and vigorous assemblage of Western political power throughout
most of the 1980's decade. The United States had elected the most de-
terminedly anti-Communist president ever in Ronald Reagan. Britain
was governed by a prime minister, Margaret Thatcher, whom even the
Soviets had dubbed "the iron lady" for her tough foreign policy positions. Reagan's weapon of choice against the Soviet empire was American
military power, not so much in its actual use, but in its potential to deter
and contain adversaries. He built up the U.S. military and embarked on
a program to defend against strategic nuclear missiles (the so-called "Star
Wars" Strategic Defense Initiative). And he brought revolution, or
counter-revolution as Communists would call it, to the backyard of

Communist or pro-Soviet regimes from Central America to South Africa. Thatcher backed him totally, and resolutely articulated European support for American efforts.

Meanwhile, John Paul suspended in public some of his misgivings about the moral and political weaknesses of the West. He also clamped down firmly on any Catholic theological support for revolution around the world, the so-called "liberation theology," and deployed the formidable global resources of the Catholic church in a duel between moral conviction and Communist power.

The duel assumed entirely unexpected proportions after 1981, when the Polish authorities imposed martial law on their anarchic country and arrested Walesa and his Solidarity lieutenants. For a while, they seemed more alarmed by the threat of Soviet invasion than by foreign disapproval or the possibility that their own system would ultimately collapse. When labor leader Walesa was under house arrest, the pope's encouragement to him—both public and private—and his skillful and flexible diplomacy with the Polish government were decisive in leading to the final, peaceful retreat from power of Poland's Communist rulers. Once the dike of Communist control was breached in Poland, the floodwaters of change quickly engulfed the rest of Eastern Europe.

Poland, under martial law and as tense as a violin string in the 1980's, frightened her Eastern European neighbors and caused some nervousness in the West. What if the Soviets lost patience with diplomacy and threats altogether, and invaded Eastern Europe once again? Three times in three decades—East Germany in 1953, Hungary in 1956, and Czechoslovakia in 1968—Soviet troops had poured across their own borders to suppress the people of their neighboring states who wanted change. What if they did the same in Poland?

Here was another of the pope's extraordinary achievements in the breakup of the empire. During a delicate and tense period in East-West relations, from 1985 to 1991, when Moscow might have reacted against unwanted change in violent and frightening ways, John Paul cooed softly and gently in Moscow's direction. Soviet reformer Mikhail Gorbachev had come to power in 1985 and launched policies of restructuring his country from top to bottom called *perestroika*. It certainly looked more attractive than the old Soviet ways, but what if it backfired? What if Kremlin reactionaries rejected any alteration in their system out of fear of losing power altogether?

In defusing this potential time bomb, the pope was decisive. His non-confrontational, behind-the-scenes overtures to Moscow and his repeated assurances that he was not trying to destroy the Soviet system found a sympathetic hearing from Gorbachev himself. The pope's respectful attitude, publicly and privately, to people with whose views he did not agree at all, was a major factor in this development. Gorbachev had come to a belief in something he often called "universal human values," a sort of consensus of human rights that Communists previously had never admitted believing in. At the climax of the 1980's decade, after all of the Communist regimes of Eastern Europe (except Romania, which was to collapse in a hail of gunfire at the end of the year) had been overturned without violence, Gorbachev, in December 1989, met with John Paul II in the Vatican.

It was truly a historic meeting, the first time a Soviet leader had ever called upon a pope. John Paul brought to bear on the Soviet leader the full power of his intellect, his breadth of human insight, and his ability to convey respect to whomever he was speaking. "We have changed our attitude," said Gorbachev after his meeting with the pope was over. "Moral values that religion generated and embodied for centuries can help in the renewal of our country too."[6] No Soviet leader prior to Gorbachev could have made this remark. But no other pope in modern times could have led him to do so.

The pope was later to deny publicly any role of his own in Communism's collapse, though he has said that it showed "the finger of God," and that it was a "miracle." But Gorbachev himself had no such doubts. "Everything that happened in Eastern Europe in these last few years," he wrote in 1992, "would have been impossible without the presence of this pope and the important role—including the political role—that he played on the world stage."[7]

What Gorbachev may only have dimly glimpsed was how seamlessly integrated John Paul's views were across the entire spectrum of human life: spiritual, physical, economic, and political. Many Catholics and others have disagreed with them, sometimes with intensity. But it has always been much harder to deny his passionate interest in almost every aspect of human life and the human condition. "Whether one agrees with his positions or not," Leo D. Lefebure, a professor at the University of St. Mary of the Lake, Mundelein, Illinois, wrote in *Christian Century*, a generally liberal Catholic periodical, "he is one of the few world leaders to possess a deeply considered religious and philosophical perspective on human existence."[8] The *Economist*, a British weekly news magazine that is strongly conservative, but sometimes critical of the papacy, observed: "His convictions sum to a world-view of a depth and consistency that no other world leader can match. This is the source of the moral authority that is the pope's only real power."[9]

THE DEFENSE OF THE HUMAN PERSON

How does one measure moral authority and its impact on world events? There are few agreed-upon criteria. But if it cannot be measured, it can certainly be recognized. It would not be an exaggeration to say that Pope John Paul II almost single-handedly saved the Roman Catholic Church from an internal deep divisiveness that, had it continued, might have led to irreparable long-term erosion of its integrity and cohesion as a major global institution. At the same time, especially in the Third World, the pope brought a self-confidence and sense of hope to the dioceses at the front line of Catholic Christendom's encounter with the non-Christian world. This both invigorated efforts at evangelism and often propelled Roman Catholic prelates as far apart as Indonesia and Sudan into major social and political roles within their own societies. In the United States, the Catholic hierarchy bemoaned the decline in priestly calling. But in Kenya, to name but one nation that has responded to the pope's leadership, so many young men have come forward as candidates to the still-all-male Catholic priesthood that seminaries and educational institutions have been hard-pressed to keep up with the new Catholic zeal.

Meanwhile, John Paul universalized the Catholic church by promoting to cardinal the most geographically and culturally diverse group of Catholic leaders in history. By the end of 1996 he had named no fewer than 100 of the 120-member college of cardinals, two-thirds of them from Third World nations, and half of the world's 4,200 bishops. In doing so, he took care to appoint prelates who were overwhelmingly supportive of his own doctrinal conservatism. The impact of these appointments will be felt within Catholicism for years to come, no matter who John Paul's eventual successor is.

John Paul has thought long and hard about the coming Third Millennium's significance for the entire Christian world. With his "New

Evangelization" thrust as the focus of Catholic Christian activities in the entire 1990's decade, he has ensured that the Catholic church will enter the twenty-first century brimming with zeal about the relevance of the message of Christ to the world as a whole. Above all, John Paul's Catholicism is not the "smells and bells" caricature of narrowness and intolerance that Protestants have often traditionally attributed to the Church of Rome, but a Catholicism of warmth and openness to all biblically based, orthodox Christian traditions. It is inconceivable, for example, that any previous pope would have called Billy Graham his "brother" (see page 8).

Far more than any previous pope, indeed to an extent that exceeds the travel of all the previous popes of history combined, this pope has taken his message around the world. In fact, it has been one of my great disappointments as a journalist that, as of writing this book, I have never seen the pope in person. In the first eighteen years of his papacy, he had traveled more than 580,000 miles—farther than journeying to the moon and back—and visited an incredible 112 countries, several of them multiple times. By 1996, the crowds his presence created exceeded in size anything known in history, including those drawn to the crusades of Billy Graham. In the year 1995, in Manila, an estimated four million people turned out to see him in person, probably the single largest crowd ever assembled in history to view one individual.

One of John Paul's ambitions, he has said, has been to visit every nation on earth where there is a Catholic presence. But John Paul has also gone to nations no other pope might even dare to enter—Islamic-controlled Sudan, for example, or Bosnia. He has been surprisingly open to the leaders of other religions, welcoming even Buddhism's highest leader, the Dalai Lama, to a pan-religious gathering in Assisi, Italy, in 1986. But he has never stepped back from declaring his core conviction that his own Christian faith is truth itself, a truth that will be universally recognized once there is a genuinely free market for religious ideas around the world. He has bluntly challenged governments within the Islamic world to be as open to the Christian witness—by permitting Christian worship and church-building—as predominantly Christian societies have been to the Islamic message.

No other pope has done so much to mend the often sorrowful historical record of Catholicism's—and Christendom's as a whole—relations with the Jewish people. John Paul, on April 12, 1986, became probably the first pope to enter the synagogue in Rome since the apostle Peter did so himself more than nineteen hundred years earlier. In 1994, he invited a Jewish conductor, Gilbert Levine, to conduct in the Vatican a solemn concert on behalf of victims of the Holocaust of World War II. Seated next to him was not just the president of Italy, Luigi Scalfaro, but Rome's chief rabbi, Elio Toaff.

He greeted within the Vatican a group of Holocaust survivors on the fiftieth anniversary of the Warsaw Ghetto Uprising. He has been outspoken in demanding that the Catholic church confess its past crimes against Jews and repent of them. He established diplomatic relations with the state of Israel at the end of 1993, against the recommendations of some advisers who have long wanted the Catholic church to play a role in some future scheme for the internationalization of Jerusalem. When the first Israeli ambassador to the Holy See presented his credentials in September 1994, the pope said that Israel and the papacy had "joined forces to oppose every form of intolerance, in whatever form it is expressed. Most particularly," he added, "they are vigilantly working together to oppose all anti-Semitism, aware that we have recently been forced to observe some deplorable manifestations of it."[10] Even today, the most frequent Vatican visitor is his childhood Jewish friend Jerzy Kluger, a Polish businessman who lives in Rome. Kluger still addresses John Paul as "Lolek," the Polish diminutive for Karol.

Of all our Great Souls, the pope is surely the most universal in the range of his experience, the extent of his travels and interests, the breadth of his conception of life. If there is one phrase that has capsulated his entire worldview within the framework of total commitment to Jesus Christ, it is "human dignity."

Long before he became pope, long before he became even a cardinal, John Paul arrived at the conviction that the roots of the extraordinary brutality of the twentieth century—some of which he experienced firsthand as a young man—lay in a spreading contempt for individual human life, for individual human dignity. The murders committed under Nazism or Communism, or interethnic violence in our own day, John Paul believes, all stem from an unwillingness even to see other human beings as people, much less as creatures whose inherent value derives from being created by God Himself. "The human person," he writes in the papal encyclical *Centesimus Annus* (On the Hundredth Anniversary) "receives from God its essential dignity, and with it the capacity to transcend every social order so as to move towards truth and goodness."[11]

John Paul's writings, sermons, homilies, and interviews are filled over and over with references to "the defense of the human person and the safeguarding of human dignity." He has expressed deep concern over the impact on modern societies of "a culture of death," a utilitarian, materialistic attitude toward life itself that he believes could become the cutting edge of a terrible new assault upon human life, comparable perhaps to the Holocaust of World War II. The issue, he believes, is not just abortion, destructive and immoral though he considers this to be. Rather, it is the slighting of human life inherent when unborn babies are dehumanized as "fetuses" and there is a casual social tolerance of their physical elimination. Casualness about abortion, he believes, is a slippery slope that leads inexorably down to euthanasia, and from there to concepts like "quality of life" that might in the future come to determine whether the old, the handicapped, or the weak are permitted by society to continue living at all.

The issue is not just a moral or even theoretical one, he insists, nor a topic confined to "religious" or "philosophical" discussions. It is vital to the survival of democracy itself. "It is one thing," he told the United Nations in 1995, in perhaps the most powerful moral discourse that organization has ever heard, "to affirm a legitimate pluralism of 'forms of freedom,' and another to deny any universality or intelligibility to the nature of man or to the human experience. . . . Modern totalitarianism," he adds, "has been, first and foremost, an assault on the dignity of the person, an assault which has gone even to the point of denying the inalienable value of the individual's life."[12]

Without a sense of the universal value of human beings, of a universal moral law that applies to all cultures, the pope argues, what protection will there be from coercion and brutality in the future against regimes intent on imposing their ideology or struggle for power upon their own citizens and those around them? In his major encyclical, *Evangelium Vitae* (The Gospel of Life), the pope explains:

> It is therefore urgently necessary, for the future of society and the development of a sound democracy, to rediscover those essential and innate human and moral values which flow from the very truth of the human being and express and safeguard the dignity of the person: values which no individual, no majority and no state can ever create, modify or destroy, but must only acknowledge, respect, and promote.[13]

The moral authority that the pope brings to these positions, compelling a hearing even from those normally in strong disagreement with them, is very plainly derived from something other than the office of the papacy. There are kings and queens, not to mention superpower presidents, who possess wealth and power a thousand times greater than the combined resources of the Vatican and its global parish. Yet none would gain the respectful hearing that the pope has come to be assured of wherever he goes. That "rare authority," according to the Catholic periodical *Commonweal*, derives from several factors: his "personal sanctity and self-discipline, his honest regard for 'the other,' his travels to every part of the globe . . . [his] sophisticated philosophical thinking, married to an outspoken faith."

The magazine names as the "most compelling" of John Paul's attributes "the richness of his personal experience." Indeed John Paul II was student, poet, actor, playwright, quarry laborer, parish priest, youth leader, university professor, bishop, and church prelate, all before becoming pope. Each of these positions provided the future pope with a rich and diverse insight into human life under many guises. But one attribute above all has been the lodestar of the pope's extraordinary passage through life and his achievement as pontiff of his church. That is, quite simply, his prayer life, or the "personal sanctity" referred to by *Commonweal*.[14]

There is not a single biography or recollection of John Paul as a child or a student or a laborer or a priest or even a bishop that does not bring up, sooner or later, his profound private spiritual walk. Even as pope he has been described as spending at times up to seven hours a day in prayer, barely credible though this may seem for the leader of the world's largest single religious organization. "The testimony is universal that prayer, more than food or liquid, is the sustaining force of this Pope's life," *Time* declared in its cover story honoring him as 1994's "Man of the Year."[15]

Pope John Paul II is at prayer in his private chapel by 6:15 A.M., at times prostrate on the floor, at times actually groaning in the travail of intercession. During moments of "down time" amid the panoply of solemn public appearances, he again and again closes his eyes, tightens his facial muscles in concentration, sometimes shades his eyes with his hand, and withdraws to that inner, sealed room of his soul where he communicates with God. "Prayer," he has said, "is a conversation" with God. But it also means "contact with God," he says, a subtle difference. Without "a deep experience of prayer," he told a group of American Catholic bishops in 1993, "growth in the moral life will be shallow."[16]

"When I was young," John Paul confided after becoming pope, "I thought that prayer could be—should be—only in thankfulness and adoration. A prayer of supplication seemed to be something unworthy. Afterwards, I changed my opinion completely. Today I ask very much."[17] Nor are these requests on his own behalf. The prie-dieu—or small kneeling desk—in the papal private chapel contains each day a big stack of yellow-colored "intentions"—a prayer list—submitted to him by the rich and the poor, the great and the insignificant. He is serious about all requests for prayer.

Some papal biographers, or journalists writing about the papacy, don't seem to know how to cope with prayer, probably because they have never experienced it at more than the superficial level—if at all—in their own lives. So they resort to the word *mystical* to describe the pope's spiritual life. But "mystical" is entirely misleading. It implies something almost psychic, paranormal, or on a level beyond the purview of ordinary people. The pope has a profound spiritual life, but the prayer component of it is as normative and central as that in the life of any mature Christian.

By the criteria of some papal biographers, millions of Americans, evangelical Protestants, high church Protestants, and Catholics also have a "mystical" prayer life. The truly remarkable thing about the pope's prayer life has nothing to do with mysticism, and everything to do with consistency. It did not spring up within him in response to the demands of the papacy. On the contrary, it grew up with him from a very early age. If prayer today is distinct evidence of a divine calling upon the pope, then that calling was evident almost from his earliest years.

POETRY, THE THEATER, AND AN "APPRENTICE SAINT"

Karol Jozef Wojtyla was born in Wadowice, a small town some thirty miles southwest of the Polish town of Krakow, on May 18, 1920. He was the third child of Karol Wojtyla, an officer in the Polish army, and Emilia Kaczorowska, the daughter of a Krakow upholsterer, himself of Lithuanian background. The pregnancy was difficult and probably tense: Emilia's second child, Olga, had died in infancy, and Karol's elder brother, Edmund, was already thirteen at the time of Karol's birth.

The yellow stone house where Wojtyla was born, on what is today

Koscielna (Church) Street, has long since become a museum visited annually by hundreds of thousands of visitors. In fact, the Wojtylas' second-floor apartment was directly across the narrow street from Wadowice's main Catholic church, Our Lady of Perpetual Help. The apartment was not owned by the Wojtylas, but rather rented, in fact, from a prosperous Jewish merchant named Chaim Balamuth. The adjoining apartment in Rynek Street, No. 2 (the name before it became Church Street), was itself rented by a Jewish family called Beer.

Regina Beer—or "Ginka"—as she was called, was two years older than Karol, a beautiful young girl whose family miraculously escaped the Holocaust and moved to Israel before World War II broke out. The Jewish population of Wadowice, a city of some twenty thousand at the time of Karol's birth, was high, perhaps amounting to 20 to 30 percent of the total population. Though anti-Semitism certainly existed in Poland during Karol Wojtyla's infancy and childhood, it was apparently little in evidence in Wadowice.

Wojtyla's family were deeply devout Catholics. From an early age, "Lolek," as his mother affectionately called Karol, using the diminutive form of the name, was taught to dip his fingers into an urn of holy water before entering and leaving his apartment, and cross himself. His mother read the Bible to him from when he was very young, and apparently wanted him to be a priest, according to neighbors. "You will see, my Lolus [an alternative diminutive form of Lolek] will become a great person," she is reported to have said.[18] Morning prayers were recited at a small altar in the parlor, the church feasts were all observed, and the Bible was also read by the family in the evenings.

At the age of six, Lolek began attending the local grammar school, located on the second floor of Wadowice's district court building. From the beginning he earned excellent grades, especially in Polish language, religion, arithmetic, drawing, singing, sports and exercise, application, and behavior. He was an athletic boy, and enjoyed playing with other boys in the town, as well as spending time with his father and his mother, who was becoming increasingly ill.

The first of three major family tragedies fell upon little Lolek when he was still only eight: his mother died of an inflammation of the heart muscle and kidney. Edmund, his elder brother by thirteen years, was already away at the university, so it fell to the elder Karol, Lolek's father, now living on a slim pension from the Polish army, to bring up the young lad. The two continued to live in the second-floor apartment, Karol senior doing the cooking and house-cleaning and the two of them sharing a bedroom.

The "Lieutenant," as Lolek's father was known around the town, was a respected citizen of deep personal integrity who helped Karol study German by himself while still in school, and would at times play a makeshift game of soccer with his son in the apartment's parlor. It was a warm and affectionate relationship. But his mother's death clearly affected Lolek deeply, clothing the boy in a seriousness some thought went beyond his years.

At ten, Lolek enrolled in the Wadowice boys' school, the town's official public high school, rather than the church school to which he could have gone. His father evidently believed that the education he received there would be of a higher standard. Lolek had developed the habit of attending Mass daily at the parish church before running to the school. Around this time, too, he became an altar boy at the church. There his religion teacher, Father Kazimierz Figlewicz, took an early interest in his charge, giving him supervisory responsibilities over the other boys.

In 1930, when he was still eleven, Karol senior took Lolek for the first time on a pilgrimage to Czestochowa to pray before the image of the Black Madonna, the *Queen of Poland,* as the famous painting of the Virgin Mary was known. The young boy was deeply stirred by this firsthand encounter with deep Polish devotionalism. He returned two years later with a group from his school.

His brother, Edmund, graduated in 1930 from the School of Medicine at Krakow's Jagiellonian University. A popular, charming twenty-four-year-old, he got on well with the young Lolek and sometimes took him on hikes in the countryside during his brief breaks from college studies. The two of them would occasionally dribble a soccer ball through the streets of Wadowice. But Edmund, too, was to become a tragic childhood loss for the young Wojtyla boy. In December 1932, he died after contracting scarlet fever from a patient he had been treating at the hospital where he was an intern. He was just twenty-six years old. Lolek was later to confide to the French journalist Andre Frossard: "My brother's death probably affected me more deeply than my mother's because of the peculiar circumstances, which were certainly tragic, and because I was more grown up."[19]

Nonetheless, young Karol continued to live with his father and enjoy both a warm friendship and a growing Catholic piety. They got up at 6:00 A.M., breakfasted together, attended Mass together, and then Karol would run off to school. This would end at 2:00 P.M., allowing time for Karol to play with his friends. Then there would be church again in the evening, homework, supper, and a stroll, perhaps, with the Lieutenant.

His father, meanwhile, took a keen interest in supervising Karol's spiritual growth. Whenever Karol helped serve Mass as altar boy in the church, his father would be there to attend the service. Father and son would often be seen kneeling together in prayer at the altar rail by others who came and went into the church. Karol himself got into the practice of punctuating his entire day with different times of prayer. He would disappear into his room at home for a brief period on his knees even after completing a homework assignment.

But important as a growing personal devotionalism was in Karol's life, it was hardly the sum of his activities. Several of his high school classmates were Jewish. One of his closest friends, and a neighbor, was Jerzy Kluger—still a friend—son of the president of Wadowice's Jewish community. Karol became familiar with the Jewish feasts, noticing the Sukkoth (Feast of Tabernacles) booths set up in the courtyard of the apartment building each autumn. One year, Karol was even taken to the town synagogue by his father on Yom Kippur to hear a particularly talented young Jewish singer sing the Kol Nidre. He and Jerzy played soccer together, and both were very good at the sport, Karol in particular as a goalie.

In light of the horrors of the World War II Holocaust in Poland, and of the ambivalent (at best) attitude in later years by many Poles to the Jews who lived among them, it might be surprising how comfortably integrated many Jews and Poles in fact were, in some parts of Poland, before World War II. There is little doubt that Pope John Paul's intuitive admiration and respect for Judaism and the Jewish people are, in large measure, the products of his childhood friendships.

At fifteen, Karol joined the Marian Sodality, a nationwide brotherhood of young Catholics who wished to develop special veneration for the Virgin Mary. The sodality's chapter was similar to the one that first attracted Mother Teresa. For young Karol, it was surely the beginning of a lifelong, intense sense of closeness to the Virgin Mary that has characterized John Paul's overall Christian piety. Six months after joining, he was elected president, and he was reelected the following year.

Protestants in general, and evangelical Christians in particular, have always had an especially difficult time with this aspect of Catholic piety.

Veneration can appear suspiciously close to worship, and, Evangelicals feel, if Jesus Himself is not made the central focus of Christian commitment, the worship that results can be close to idolatry. Yet in Karol Wojtyla's case, it has never seemed that his Marian piety has detracted from his insistence on placing Jesus Christ at the very center of the Christian life, and indeed of the life of the world.

Karol, entering his teenage years, was earnest about his faith, but apparently was never priggish or offensive in his piety. He continued to play soccer, laugh with friends, even go to the movies from time to time with his father. He was a "normal" teenager, even if quieter, more reflective, and much less brash than most teenagers in the West—and perhaps also in Poland—would be today. His friends were conscious that he didn't get into fights, and he never used the bad words typically bandied about by teenagers in all cultures. Though nothing was said, people noticed this, and tended to clean up their language in his presence.

The young man's consistent piety was obvious to all who knew him. Friends asked him during his second-last year in high school, "Do you want to become a priest?" *"Non sum dignus,"* he replied in Latin: "I am not worthy." Doubtless, this was a sincere self-appraisal. But the real reason he replied in this way was that he really didn't want to become a priest. Karol Wojtyla had discovered the theater.

He was about fourteen when he first began to act in plays performed at the Wadowice high school. It was not just acting that drew him to the theater; it was the words and ideas expressed by some of the great Polish playwrights and poets. After school hours there were dramatic readings from Poland's great literary masters, small chamber music recitals, and poetry recitations. Karol eagerly took part in as many of these events as he could. In his spare time, also, he was delving into Poland's great romantic and patriotic authors—men like Adam Mickiewicz, whose commitment to human rights in the nineteenth century was far in advance of the general standards of the day. In his 1848 *Manifesto for a Future Slav State Constitution,* he even pronounced equality of citizenship for Jews, a progressive idea that was rare in its time. Karol read and memorized the poetry of Juliusz Slowacki, one of whose poems, "The Slavic Pope," prophetically proclaimed:

> Amid the discord God rings
> An enormous bell

For the Slavic Pope
The throne is open.
This one will not flee the sword,
Like that Italian.
Like God, he will bravely face the sword,
For him, world is dust . . .
Look, here comes the Slavic Pope,
A brother of the people.[20]

Karol not only acted in the historical, romantic dramas that the Wadowice Theater Circle performed, he directed, stage-managed, produced, and helped organize the frequently patriotic, sometimes classical works that the group most liked to put on. Karol had a fine acting and reciting voice and by all accounts a superb memory. At one point, he stood in for a fellow student who, at the last minute, was unable to perform, preparing and completing memorization of the part in just two days. The theater became his out-of-school obsession. He joined school expeditions to Krakow to see performances there. As his voice deepened and his physique developed in later teenage years, many began to believe that he would devote his life to the theater in some form or other.

The theater exerts a pull on its devotees, whether mere spectators of drama or actors themselves, that is very difficult for others to comprehend. Acting moves the mind to an altogether different plane from the ordinary, for it is always a right-brain, creative activity, no matter how tedious the practices and rehearsals can sometimes be. I toyed with acting as an undergraduate, even touring Israel once in a production of *Romeo and Juliet* (a very young, undergraduate Michael York was Romeo). There are few personal creative experiences to compare with knowing that an audience is being moved to an entirely new level of experience by the combination of great drama, great words, and at times, great acting.

With Karol Wojtyla, however, the obsession with acting became a door through which other influences entered his life. A powerful new mentor was Mieczyslaw Kotlarczyk, a brilliant cultural figure in Wadowice. Kotlarczyk was a former professor of Polish literature, and a man whose commitment to the theater was no mere fascination with the glamour of acting. The founder of his own theater group in Wadowice, the Amateur University Theater, he believed intensely in the power of the spoken word in drama, in contrast to, for example, ornate stage sets and dramatic stage movements. Also a teacher in the Carmelite Fathers' high school in Wadowice, Kotlarczyk was a deep believer in the theater as a vehicle for conveying Christian ideas in the profoundest way. His single-minded devotion to theater, his seriousness, his intellectual brilliance, and his warm encouragement of Karol drew them together in many long conversations.

Perhaps Karol felt comfortable confiding his ideas and aspirations to someone much older than he was—nineteen years older in this case—because of his close and warm relationship with his brother before Edmund's tragic death. Karol now found himself drawn to the intellectually powerful, but down-to-earth and analytical poems of Cyprian Norwid. Like Mickiewicz, he was a nineteenth-century Polish poet, but unlike the author of "The Slavic Pope," he was a man who stressed the need to focus on the concrete and what could be experienced in person, at first hand. One of Norwid's works, which Karol memorized and read aloud at school in a recitation contest, was "Promethidion." Norwid's ideas on the redeeming effect of work on human creativity have found their way into the mature writings, including the encyclicals, of the adult Karol Wojtyla as Pope John Paul II.

Words, poetry, powerful human motivating ideas; the impact of drama; the nature and role of Poland as a nation; the Polish Christian legacy—all of these surged together as Karol drew to the end of his high school years in Wadowice. His high school exam marks were outstanding, and he received the highest grades in Polish, Latin, Greek, German, history, Polish current affairs, philosophy, and physical education. To indicate how demanding the high school standard of Latin was at the time, students were required to speak Latin fluently for forty minutes in response to the first question on the exam, then speak for a further fifteen minutes in response to the second question. Ever since then, Karol Wojtyla's command of Latin (which was, until Vatican II, a prerequisite for Catholic priesthood) has been considered phenomenal. Not surprisingly, the future pope was selected as class valedictorian among forty-two fellow students when his high school graduation formally took place May 27, 1938.

His selection, made in advance of the end of the school year, had a providential consequence. On May 6, three weeks before graduation, the then archbishop of Krakow, Adam Sapieha, arrived at the school to pay an official visit to the student body. Karol was asked to give the welcoming speech. Sapieha was stunned by Karol's poise, eloquence, and diction. Had he considered entering the seminary? he asked Wadowice's parish priest, Father Edward Zacher. Karol himself requested permission to answer the question. He said he wanted to attend the university to study Polish literature and philology. "A pity," Sapieha responded. The question came up later in a conversation among the faculty of the school. Once again, Sapieha expressed disappointment. Just six years later, that sense of regret had vanished as Sapieha found himself, under the terrifying conditions of the Nazi occupation of Poland, supervising a clandestine seminary for prospective Polish priests. Among his charges at that time: Karol Wojtyla.

In order to attend the university at all, Karol and his father had to move physically to Krakow in August 1938. The city, which miraculously survived the Nazi occupation during World War II largely intact, had long been known as a royal city, and had been the seat of Poland's Jagiellonian Dynasty (1386–1572), after which the university was named. It was a culturally rich and diverse town of about a quarter of a million people at the time, with a large Jewish population. Even today, the sense of a cultivated, civilized city permeates the streets and squares that lie in the shadow of the cathedral or the university. The two Wojtylas occupied a small apartment—two rooms, a kitchen, and a bathroom—in the basement of a two-story house not far from Krakow's Vistula River. The apartment was entered by a door underneath the staircase that led to the second story of the building.

Karol entered the university's philosophy faculty (in European universities, the word *faculty* approximates to the American term "department"). He took on an extremely heavy academic load, selecting courses in Polish language, drama, novelistic literature, even Old Church Slavonic (the language of the Russian Orthodox Church), and an introduction to Russian literature. He chose to attend lectures outside the regular university courseload, too, including one dealing with the Christian ethics of Max Scheler, a German philosopher whose work was later to be the topic of Karol's second academic dissertation.

As he had at high school in Wadowice, Karol filled his nonstudy hours with activities that must have left him little time even for sleep. He recited poetry he had written at a public poetry reading within weeks of arriving in Krakow, he became active in a variety of intellectual and cultural circles among the students, and he began serious literary compositions of his own: cycles of lyric poetry, plays, plans for major dramatic works. He still tended to be a loner, avoiding parties, attending Mass daily, and on the first Friday of each month going to Wawel Cathedral, overlooking the Vistula, for confession. On one occasion, as a practical joke, his classmates placed a note on his desk that read, "Karol Wojtyla, Apprentice Saint."

Looking back, it seems astonishing now that life could have proceeded so normally, even tranquilly, in Poland such a short time before the vol-cano of World War II and Nazi violence spewed forth upon the country. It was not as though warning signs of the forthcoming eruption hadn't been plentiful. Any European, whether in the Western or Eastern parts of the Continent, would have observed with misgivings the rise to power of Hitler in Germany in 1933, and the reoccupation by the Germans of the officially demilitarized Rhineland in 1936. The Germans had also blatantly used the Civil War in Spain the same year as a testing ground for newly developed warplanes and other weaponry.

At some point, Karol's father must surely have discussed the military implications of these developments with his son. By early 1938, the writ-ing was more than obviously on the wall—at least in retrospect—that terrible things might be in store for Europe. With the Anschluss of March 1938, when Karol Wojtyla was in his last months of high school, Austria was incorporated with brutal swiftness into the Third Reich, and Hitler rode in triumph through the streets of Vienna where he had spent his youth as an impoverished art student.

Next, Czechoslovakia felt Hitler's wrath. Nestled between Austria and Germany, with Poland to its east, Czechoslovakia gave the impression on the map of being an intruder in a totally Third Reich–dominated chunk of Europe. Hitler's excuse for moving against Czechoslovakia was as con-venient as it was transparent: Nazi-invented complaints by the large minority population of ethnic Germans living in the Sudetenland, the western part of Czechoslovakia, that they were an oppressed minority ruled by tyrannical Slavs.

An actual German invasion of Czechoslovakia was barely averted in the spring of 1938 by an uncharacteristic display of British and French diplo-matic resolution. In the developing crisis, it suddenly dawned on ordinary British and French citizens, as air-raid shelters were dug, gas masks were handed out, and the first prewar mobilizations occurred, how close war had come to them, and how frightening it looked. By the autumn, the mood in both London and Paris had turned against continuing to confront Hitler.

When British prime minister Neville Chamberlain returned from meetings with Hitler in Munich at the end of September 1938, he was cheered resoundingly by fellow Britons at London's Heston Airport. "Peace in our time," he had proclaimed, waving an umbrella and a piece of paper with Hitler's signature on it.

By the spring of 1939, the obviousness of this delusion had become clear to all of Europe. At Munich, the Nazis had acquired the Sudetenland for Germany. In March 1939 they felt strong enough to march in and occupy the entire country without a shot being fired. Czechoslovakia ceased to exist. Shamefully, even Poland had gorged like a hyena on the dismembered country, acquiring from the Munich agreement several hundred miles of Czech territory in Silesia.

In Krakow, especially at the Jagiellonian University, where Karol Wojtyla was quietly pursuing his studies, a deep polarization seemed to be setting in among the students. Though there were frequent anti-German demonstrations, ultra-Nationalists among the students, brandishing strong anti-Semitic slogans, had begun to assume a prominence in some campus organizations. Karol, who had been deeply hurt when a neighboring Jewish family in Wadowice had left Poland for Palestine because of a sense of rising anti-Semitism in Poland, deeply disliked the new, quasi-fascist tendencies among some of his fellow students, as all of his contemporaries from this period attest.

Karol, however, did not become an activist in any organization, and continued his studies and activities much as he would have done had all Europe been at peace. Despite the brutal example of Czechoslovakia, many Poles appeared to believe that their million-man army, along with assurances of support from Britain and France if Hitler attacked, would protect their nation from the insatiable territorial appetite of the Nazis.

On the morning of September 1, 1939, this final item of Polish self-deception was obliterated for good. As Karol Wojtyla walked to his monthly Friday morning confession before Mass, German bombers were already subjecting Krakow to a nightmarish assault, the first major air raid of World War II. A few miles to the West, German mechanized divisions were already pushing through ill-prepared Polish defenses in a pincer-movement on Warsaw itself.

The Wawel Cathedral to which Karol climbed the steep steps was deserted. Krakow's citizens had scurried away to shelters, or at least off the

streets as the spreading cacophony of sirens and exploding bombs enveloped the city. Only Father Kazimierz Figlewicz was there to say the Mass.
As Karol's confessor and the man who had made him an altar boy a few
years earlier, he now knew the young Wojtyla well. Despite the crashing
of bombs, the rattling of windows, and a sense that it was the beginning
of the end of everything they had ever known about Poland, Figlewicz
insisted on the celebration of Mass as though it were peacetime. Karol
Wojtyla unhesitatingly participated.[21]

A QUARRY, A RHAPSODIC THEATER, AND A "TRUE PATH"

The war devastated Poland far sooner than any Pole, even in his worst
nightmare, could have possibly imagined. Five days after the initial bombing on September 6, the Germans had occupied Krakow. Then, from the
east, Soviet armies entered to complete the dismemberment of the country (under the Hitler-Stalin Pact of 1939, the nation was to be divided
between them). By November 2, the country was officially divided between the Germans and the Soviets.

Karol Wojtyla's immediate concern was to ensure a livelihood for himself and his father, still living in their basement apartment near the Vistula.
He registered at the university once more, November 2, but four days
later the Nazis rounded up 186 Jagiellonian University professors to attend a meeting in Krakow, then arrested and deported them. Though some
were later released after international pressure, others died in concentration camps. The university ceased to function.

Meanwhile, the Nazis were seizing young men for forced labor to
maintain the German war machine. For a few months, Karol avoided this
by getting a job as a delivery boy for a Krakow restaurant. By October
1940, though, even this menial occupation had become dangerous. He was
a healthy-looking young man who could have been taken in any number
of sweeps by the authorities through the city in the perpetual search for
more forced labor recruits.

Through friends, he managed to secure a job as a manual worker in
the Zakrzowek Quarry of the Solvay chemical plant. Large limestone
blocks were quarried to provide a component of caustic soda, an ingredient in explosives. Since the work was considered essential for the German
war effort, workers were given a special pass that ensured their protection

from forced-labor sweeps, along with additional food rations because of the demanding nature of the labor.

Each day Karol walked to the plant across open fields, often in the freezing cold, at first helping to lay railroad track from the quarry. Then, for a while, he was put to work actually breaking up the limestone with a pickax. Later, he was placed in charge of the explosives inside one of the plant's buildings, a location that provided warmth and shelter and an opportunity to read—and to pray.

Pray, indeed, he did: on rising early in the morning, during his walk to work across the fields, in moments stolen from the routine of work, and then again on return from the plant at night. Some of the workers made fun of his piety, but most behaved respectfully toward him. In the evening hours, he was able to pray with someone—his own father.

Away from the drudgery of Solvay, Karol poured himself into two pursuits. These had run parallel during his high school days and had intersected with each other, but in the end they finally could not be compatible with each other. One of them was his beloved theater. He had written large amounts of poetry early in 1939, including a fine hymn in Polish, "Magnificat," the Latin name for the traditional song of worship of the Virgin Mary in the Bible when the angel Gabriel informs her that she will bear the Christ.

Now, during the war, he wrote three plays, *David, Job,* and *Jeremiah,* all of them later published in Poland. He also threw himself into a dangerous form of cultural resistance to the Nazis, an underground theater group called the Rhapsodic Theater. Meeting for rehearsals on Wednesdays and Sundays in the Wojtyla basement apartment and in other private homes, a small handful of spirited Poles determined to keep alive their country's national and spiritual traditions in defiance of the Nazis' plans to eliminate these from history. They performed Slowacki's *King-Spirit* and Wyspianski's *Wesele.* The performances themselves were closely guarded secrets, the audiences never amounting to more than some fifteen people. Altogether, between the formation of the Rhapsodic Theater in 1941 and the war's end, the group put on twenty-two different productions.

The second pursuit was not defined in professional terms, yet it grew unselfconsciously out of Karol's very nature: his continuing search for a larger role in his life of God, of prayer, of living for a purpose that was wholly consecrated to his Maker. In some measure, the tragedies of bereavement in his early childhood had reinforced an intuitive spiritual longing within him. His mother's death followed by his brother's had forced him to ask the kind of questions about loss and suffering that few people encounter so starkly before they are grown.

In February 1940, at a weekly discussion at Karol's parish church, St. Stanislaw Kostka, not far from his apartment on Tyniecka Street, he met a quiet, short, gray-haired man of unimpressive appearance and somewhat stilted speech. His name was Jan Leopold Tyranowski, and he was a tailor. This rather lonely profession gave him ample time for quiet and private meditation, for prayer—and as it turned out—for discipling in a unique way young men on an intense spiritual journey.

Tyranowski, at the request of some Salesian fathers, had become involved in a program called the "Living Rosary" that would help young Poles, under wartime conditions, walk a disciplined, spiritual, Catholic life and sharpen their overall spiritual appetite. He began by recruiting a group of fifteen men, selecting them carefully after observing them at prayer gatherings, church discussion groups, or during Mass. He would meet with them in his cramped, second-story apartment in groups to share his insights into living the spiritual life at a far deeper level than they were familiar with. He gave them assignments to fortify their self-discipline: daily prayer times, Bible readings, periods of meditation; and he asked them to keep a close spiritual diary of their efforts in these areas. "Every moment must be put to use," he would say, and Karol used that wisdom to fuel his own phenomenal energy throughout the rest of his life. Once a week, each of them would meet individually with Tyranowski. He became their mentor, spiritual adviser, and confidant.

He became especially close to Karol, whose sometimes melancholic spiritual temperament rendered him receptive to Tyranowski's thoughts on two great figures of Catholic mystical literature, St. Teresa of Avila and her slightly younger contemporary, St. John of the Cross. Karol had already absorbed something of Polish mystical Christian thought in the poetry of Mickiewicz, but now he seemed ready for the more distilled encounters of intense prayer and spiritual meditation written about, often in exquisite Spanish poetry, by St. John of the Cross.

Walking by the River Vistula, or meeting in Tyranowski's apartment, Karol learned from Tyranowski the paradoxical truth of Christian spiritual life that suffering can be an entrance-gate to deep spiritual joy and to a sense of extraordinary closeness to God. It does not have to be seen at all, as Protestants have sometimes believed it to be, evidence of divine displeasure. St. John of the Cross is famous for his profound insights into the process by which God gradually purges His most serious followers of the areas of their lives that are obstacles to true divine union with Him. In one of his most famous works, *The Dark Night*, St. John explains that the "dark night" of the Christian life—when any sense of God's blessing or presence seems completely absent and the heavens feel closed to the soul's entreaties—is actually a means for "an inflow of God into the soul. This purges the soul of its habitual ignorances and imperfections, natural and spiritual, and which the contemplatives call infused contemplation or mystical theology."[22]

After he had become pope, John Paul reflected publicly on the impact Tyranowski had had on him. He was, the pope said,

> one of those unknown saints, hidden like a marvelous light at the bottom of life, at a depth where night usually reigns. . . . In his words, in his spirituality and in the example of a life given entirely to God alone, he represented a new world that I did not yet know. I saw the beauty of the soul opened up by grace.[23]

It was a year after meeting Tyranowski that Karol suddenly found himself needing more grace than ever before. He had experienced personal family tragedy twice. Now came his final, and surely the most devastating one, the death of his beloved father in February 1942 at the relatively young age of sixty-two. The Lieutenant had fallen ill and, as the night of Nazi occupation grew steadily darker over Poland, had seemed to lose his desire to live much longer. Six weeks later, when Karol was taking food over to his father with Maria Kydrynska, the wife of one of Karol's best friends, he discovered his father dead in their apartment from a heart attack.

Despite his earlier bereavements, the loss of his father bore in on his soul more heavily than anything that had happened to him so far in his life. But it did not discourage him in his continuing spiritual quest, as it might have scores of others. Instead, it seemed to harden the growing conviction that, no matter what his earlier misgivings had been, he was inexorably being called to a life totally consecrated to God through the church itself. "I gradually became aware of my true path," he said later.

I was working at a plant and devoting myself, as far as the terrors of
the occupation allowed, to my taste for literature and drama. My
priestly vocation took shape in the midst of all that, like an inner fact
of unquestionable and absolute clarity. The following year [1942], in
the autumn, I knew that I was called.[24]

The decision might, in retrospect, have appeared inevitable, but it was
not easy to defend to his closest friends. His drama mentor from Wadowice,
Mieczyslaw Kotlarczyk, had managed to make his way to Krakow in 1942.
With his father gone, Karol was only too happy to allow Kotlarczyk and
his wife to stay with him. Kotlarczyk was now active in the Rhapsodic
Theater, but in the fall of 1942, Karol asked him for no further roles in the
theater's productions. He explained that they would interfere with his
pathway to the priesthood.

Kotlarczyk, keenly aware that Karol's dramatic gifts were still in their
ascendancy, believed the decision was a mistake. So did other colleagues
from the group. However, Polish writer Mieczyslaw Malinski, who became a priest in Krakow at the same time as Karol, and knew the young
man well, commented insightfully on the influence of both Karol's men-
tors on him. "If Kotlarczyk taught Karol that good must be achieved
through beauty," he said, "Tyranowski would tell him that 'priesthood is
an even shorter way to make people good.'"[25]

The priesthood won. Through intermediaries, Karol's decision was
conveyed to Archbishop Sapieha on Wawel Hill in Krakow. The prelate
had already become deeply involved in the resistance effort against Nazi
rule, issuing Jews with baptismal certificates to protect them from arrest,
and providing a steady stream of information about Krakow and his diocese, through trusted Vatican couriers, to Rome itself.

He had also decided that it was a priority for the church to build up a
new, young priesthood, despite the German ban on all seminary teaching
or ordinations of priests, to fill the gap in church ranks already caused by
the war. By May of 1945, a total of 1,932 of Poland's priests, 850 monks, and
289 nuns had either been murdered directly by the Nazis or had died in
imprisonment under unspeakable conditions. When the war came to an
end, Sapieha grasped early on, Poland would desperately need a new generation of priests equipped to fill the gaps in the church's ranks.

Karol had wanted to go straight into the meditative Polish religious order, the Discalced Carmelites, an order that consciously sought to pursue the spiritual pathway pioneered by St. John of the Cross. But Bishop Sapieha, whose permission was in any case required for all Polish men in the Krakow archdiocese who sought holy orders, would have none of it. Karol, he said, should walk the road of the parish priest. This, he insisted, and in the larger church as a whole, was where his gifts would be most needed. In fact, Sapieha turned down Karol Wojtyla's request to join the Carmelites on two more occasions, the last one in 1949. What he wanted of Karol right away was for him to join a select, completely secret corps of young men who had been accepted by Sapieha for clandestine training in the Catholic priesthood.

Most of the students did not even know who the others were. They would meet with designated theology teachers one-on-one in private homes. They were instructed to pursue their studies in their free time when not performing ordinary, secular jobs. Karol liked to take the night-shift in the Solvay plant, where he was now permitted to work in the chemical factory. It was quieter than the normal day shift, and it permitted him both to pray and to study for long, uninterrupted periods.

His secret seminary life had been in process for more than a year when he came within a hair's breadth of death. On his return from an afternoon shift at Solvay on February 29, 1944, a German truck rounding a corner at high speed struck him and threw him to the ground, causing his head to hit the edge of the sidewalk. Just then, a woman on a passing streetcar spotted the body on the street, jumped off, and ran over to him. He looked quite dead. By utter chance, a German military staff car happened to drive by at the same time. For some reason, the officer within it ordered the driver to stop, got out, examined Karol to see whether he was still alive, then flagged down a passing Polish vehicle and ordered it to take the injured young man immediately to the hospital. Karol never discovered who the German good Samaritan was, but he did later write to thank his Polish benefactor.

Karol suffered a heavy concussion and remained unconscious for nine hours. But he had suffered no lasting damage, and after two weeks in the hospital, he spent a further few weeks convalescing in a friend's home. The incident probably sobered him in a number of ways. It may also have prepared him for the most frightening ordeal so far of life under German occupation.

By July of 1944, the war was accelerating out of Germany's favor. The Western Allies had finally established a second front in Europe, invading

Normandy on D-Day, June 6, 1944. The Russians, already on Polish soil, were squeezing the Germans back toward their own homeland. Soviet troops had even advanced to the Vistula River opposite Warsaw. Convinced that liberation was just days away, the Polish resistance in the capital rose up on August 1 and heroically, but futilely, fought to break free from the Nazi yoke. Watching the fighting through binoculars from the other side of the river, Soviet Major General Radzievskii, on Stalin's orders, did nothing to aid the Poles. Stalin wanted a Poland stripped of any national heroes who might challenge his own postwar order for Eastern Europe.

Faced with the challenge in Warsaw, the jittery occupiers believed similar uprisings might break out at any moment in the rest of Poland. Thus, on August 6, 1944, they conducted the most draconian security sweep through Krakow of the entire war. German troops, shouting and smashing down doors where necessary, combed downtown Warsaw, rounding up thousands of young men and boys. As the din grew closer, it was clear that the house where Karol and the Kotlarczyks had their basement apartment was about to be raided. Paralyzed with fear, Jan Kotlarczyk sat immobile at a table in the living room. In his own room, Karol went down on his knees and began to pray, and then stretched himself prone on the floor, his arms spread-eagled as he called out to God.

The prayers, clearly, were answered. For some reason, the Germans had failed to notice, or in their haste had forgotten about, the door that led down to where Karol and his two guests waited in silent immobility for the angels of probable death either to come upon them or to pass by. They passed by. And the trucks drove off.

Krakow was stunned and silent after this Nazi locust raid on the remaining boys and young men. Bishop Sapieha now realized that the lives of his underground seminarians would be in deadly peril if they continued with their normal secular jobs. He thus, through a priest, ordered them all to report to the bishop's palace on Wawel Hill. A Polish woman walked several yards in front of Wojtyla through the streets to the archbishop's residence, watching at each intersection for German patrols. Once inside, Karol found himself with six other clandestine seminarians. "I am your rector," Sapieha now told them. "We shall put our trust in God's providence. No harm will befall us."[26] The seminarians, he said, should remain inside the bishop's palace for the remainder of the war, or at least until the Germans left the city. For additional safety, they should all also wear the priestly cassock within the confines of the building. The lessons went on, meanwhile, with the seminarians sleeping on metal beds on the first floor of the palace.

By mid-January 1945, the Germans had finally retreated from Krakow, loaded down with plunder from a city so attractive that it was sometimes called "the Polish Florence." Miraculously, they did not raze it to the ground, as they had Warsaw, and only a limited amount of damage was done as the Nazi rearguards retreated and the Soviet troops rode in triumph into the traumatized town. The seminarians were able to reemerge from hiding and pursue their studies for the priesthood in the building originally designed for this purpose, which had been occupied by German troops during the war.

In April 1945, Karol became an assistant instructor in theology at the reopened Jagiellonian University, all the while continuing a heavy load of studies for his new vocation. One course in particular, a moral theological study of "the right to life," was to have a deep impact on his personal philosophy. But he was still deeply drawn to the Carmelites and the contemplative life. He deepened his studies of St. John of the Cross, even learning Spanish in order to read the great mystical author in the original language.

By November of 1946, Sapieha was eager to push Karol out beyond Poland itself to enlarge his knowledge of the world and to deepen his already impressive academic studies. He had shortened the preparation time just for Karol by six months, and ordained him November 1 a priest of the Roman Catholic Church.

November 1 was All Saints' Day, and it also coincided with the return to Krakow of the ashes of Poland's Auschwitz victims. Ordinarily, Karol Wojtyla would have begun, just as all recently ordained priests would normally do, a period as a parish priest in some obscure parish, a sort of spiritual boot camp for young ordinands. But Sapieha, who had first sensed both profound spirituality and enormous gifts in Karol when the lad was still in high school, had more ambitious plans. On November 15, 1946, he dispatched him to Rome for eighteen months of postgraduate studies at the Pontifical Angelicum University, a Dominican college. There were few regular airline services anywhere in Europe at this time. The only reliable way for transcontinental travel was by train. It was thus from Krakow to Paris, and thence from Paris to Rome, that the brilliant, earnest, but already deeply seasoned young man set out on the next major pathway of his life.

ROME AND THE ROAD TO THE PAPACY

After the deprivations and terrors of Poland under the Nazis, it is hard to imagine what impact the first encounter with Western Europe had upon Karol Wojtyla. Poland, sadly, had exchanged one totalitarian conqueror, Germany, for another, a Soviet-backed domestic variety of Communism, known in Poland as the United Workers Party. Though ravaged by the war almost as much as Poland, most of the nations of Western Europe, especially once the U.S.-initiated Marshall Plan kicked in during 1947–48, began to make a swift economic recovery. One of the few Poles to live for an extended period in the West just after the war, Karol noted in a Polish Roman Catholic weekly in 1949 that the Western half of the Continent was "an ocean of consumer goods, stores, restaurants, automobiles," along with "unemployed people, children begging, and empty churches on Sunday."[27] Even at this stage of his life, Karol Wojtyla was unimpressed with the rich fruits of material prosperity when they were apparently accompanied by a deep spiritual poverty.

In Rome, he explored the city and fell in love with it, learned a fluent, though heavily accented Italian, and became familiar with the major Catholic institutions. He learned about the subtly different national and cultural streams within the Roman Catholic Church, as well as about many peculiarly Roman aspects of church function. While in Rome and attending the university, Karol resided at the Belgian College, a small residence run by Belgian nuns and accommodating some twenty-two seminarians, or young priests. It was cold in winter and very hot in summer, and conditions were primitive. When Karol arrived the college still lacked showers. But after wartime Poland, it must have seemed both liberating and energizing to the young man. Along with other students of the Belgian College, he took part in a small private audience with Pope Pius XII in 1947. Meanwhile, he improved his French and got a good head start at learning conversational English from American fellow students.

But for all of the glamour and excitement of Rome, Karol never wavered in his deep personal daily devotionalism. He prayed each morning at a parish church in a working-class area of Rome. His academic program was focused on work toward a doctorate on the work of St. John of the Cross. But for Karol Wojtyla, the riches of Christianity's devotional and even mystical traditions were no mere academic hobby. In March 1947, he and a Polish friend drove to a church near Naples, the San Giovanni Rotondo, where a saintly Capuchin monk, Father Francesco Forgione Pio, heard the confessions of thousands of worshipers on a regular basis.

Padre Pio was characterized by the regular appearance on his hands, feet, and sides of the signs of the stigmata, or Christ's wounds from the Crucifixion, a phenomenon associated most famously in Catholic church history with St. Francis of Assisi. A popular legend, on which neither John Paul II nor the Vatican has ever commented, holds that Padre Pio prophesied to the young priest in 1947 that he would be pope, and indeed that he would be an assassin's target. Whether the ancient monk said anything of the sort to Karol Wojtyla may never be known for sure, but something of lasting significance appears to have happened to Karol Wojtyla during his short visit. On the thirtieth anniversary of his receiving the "tonsure" (the very first step toward ordination as a priest) in the archbishop's palace in Krakow in the fall of 1947, Karol Wojtyla returned to San Giovanni Rotondo for three days of prayer and reminiscences. By that time, he had already become a cardinal.

There was one episode in Karol's life that further enhanced his comprehension of the challenge facing the gospel in the discouraged, deeply secular environment of Europe in the late 1940's. Once again, at the perceptive request of Bishop Sapieha, Karol spent the summer vacation months from Rome investigating the worker-priest movement in France and Belgium. The movement had sprung up in response to a growing sense that the Catholic church was simply losing touch with modern workers in the aftermath of World War II. With his own background as a manual worker and his intuitive sympathy for the working man, Karol responded warmly to the experiments in liturgy and pastoral work he encountered in Marseilles, Paris, and Brussels. "Catholic intellectual creativity alone will not transform the society," he later wrote.[28] He was already reaching toward an understanding of the gospel as something other than a rubber stamp for any existing social order. He would remain fiercely opposed to Marxism throughout his life; however, he did not believe that society would gradually solve its multifold problems through the simple expedient of adopting capitalism wholesale.

By the following summer, in 1948, Karol's dissertation on St. John of the Cross at the Angelicum had been accepted with the highest possible grades. It was time for him to return to Poland, and he did so, once again by train, in June 1948. Already, events in Eastern Europe had moved more swiftly—and more negatively—than he had probably foreseen. After conquering Germany and the remainder of Eastern Europe, Joseph Stalin seemed at the apogee of his global influence. One by one, the facade of democratic rule collapsed in the countries of Europe behind the "Iron Curtain."

In February 1948, the Communists seized control of Prague, Czechoslovakia, in a coup. Later in the spring, Soviet forces were to close off access to the western sector of occupied Berlin, setting in motion what became known as the Berlin Airlift. In Poland, the Communists, through their official party, the Polish United Workers Party, were tightening up on all segments of national life that posed a threat to their desire for total hegemony over society. The church, inevitably, was high on the list of targets.

Karol was immediately assigned to a remote rural parish for the requisite hands-on encounter of a traditional Polish parish priest. Sapieha dispatched him to the village of Niegowic, some thirty miles east of Krakow, for seven months. Just twenty-eight years old, in a parish that lacked sewage, running water, or electricity, Karol bumped head-on into the pastoral problems of simple, ordinary people weighed down by the pressures of work and family.

Even today, there are parts of the Polish countryside that are extraordinarily untouched by civilization despite the heavy pollution that has scarred much of the land. Poland has the largest remaining tracts of the great European primeval forests, in which European bison today still wander unbothered by the hurrying human world. I personally spent a little time in the Polish countryside during my period as a correspondent in Eastern Europe and was amazed to watch ancient horse-drawn carts pulling farmers' produce along the sides of main roads as trucks, buses, and passenger cars whizzed by.

Karol Wojtyla was certainly not a stranger to primitive conditions, though even he, with his experience of Western Europe behind him, must at times have blanched or chuckled at the uncomfortable quaintness of it all. Yet he took his confessional duties with the utmost seriousness, writing to a friend about the importance, amid all of the trivial, mechanical aspects of parish work, of maintaining a deep prayer life. "In the absence of deep inner life," he wrote, "a priest will imperceptibly turn into an office clerk, and his apostolate will turn into a parish office routine, just solving daily problems."[29] Karol even brought glimpses of the intellectual world into the tedium-filled lives of the local peasantry, organizing a drama circle in the parish, and putting on plays with student actors.

In 1949, back at Jagiellonian University, he completed studies for a master's degree in theology, and just a few weeks later, for a doctorate in sacred theology on the basis of an expanded version of his Angelicum University dissertation. He was now reassigned to an urban parish, St. Florian's, in Krakow. There he quickly developed a circle of cultured, well-educated Catholic friends and contacts, continuing in his spare time a demanding schedule of writing. He produced poems, plays, and essays during this period. He also enlarged his reading in every possible direction.

None of these activities, though, detracted from a deeply involved parish schedule. Karol began conducting hiking trips for young people around the region's mountains and lakes, talking to them in great detail about the challenges they were facing in their lives. Priests were not permitted by the Communists to conduct church meetings outside of their parishes, so Karol traveled in mufti with his young charges, men and women, hearing them speak with a frankness unusual in the presence of a priest about sexual temptations and about the struggles of being spiritual in a harshly materialistic and highly controlled society. They talked, joked, and sang deep into the night around campfires, and Karol conducted Mass each morning.

He also took his students to the theater, played chess with them, and had them bring their parents to church-organized functions. Yet after two years, in 1951, he was asked to leave the parish church to work full-time on his second doctoral dissertation, a complex study of Christian ethics focusing on the work of a German philosopher named Max Scheler (1874–1928).

He continued, despite all of his other activities, to write poetry and plays, essays and scholarly studies. In one of his best-known dramatic works from this period, "Brother of Our God," the protagonist is a historical figure, Brother Albert, a young Pole who began serving the very poor in Krakow around the turn of the century. What is striking about the play is that it is an early example of John Paul's conviction that every human being has a right to a basic level of living decency. One character in the play, not identified by name, addresses the homeless huddled down in a filthy hovel of a shelter: "Don't be afraid!" he tells them in a booming voice. This foreshadows the very words John Paul II later spoke to the crowds in St. Peter's Square the day of his installation as pope.

"Don't be afraid!" was advice that every priest in Poland needed in the early 1950's. Though the regime permitted the church to conduct its fundamental pastoral work, along with seminary education, from 1951 onward, pressures had tightened. The Korean War in 1950 had brought East-West tensions to a dangerous pitch, and even Stalin's death in March 1953 failed to stem a rising tide of persecution against Poland's Catholic hierarchy. In September 1953, the country's primate, Stefan Wyszynski, was arrested and held under house arrest for three years, not being released until the dramatic political changes in Poland in 1956.

In 1954 the authorities closed the Jagiellonian University in Krakow, interrupting Karol's popular courses there, but not at all his teaching functions as a whole. He now crisscrossed the country, conducting seminars and giving lectures from Lublin's Catholic University to Katowice, Czestochowa, and, of course, in Krakow itself. He looked the part of an eccentric professor: thick, horn-rimmed spectacles, purple beret, frayed—though clean—cassock, shapeless shoes, dark-green overcoat apparently made from material not originally designed for overcoats. He joked with his students, listened to their problems, sometimes lent them money. And he prayed. Constantly. Before lectures, between lectures, or after lectures—on his knees in the chapel.

Two years after the itinerant, phenomenally demanding teaching schedule, in 1956 he was appointed chairman of the Faculty of Ethics at the Catholic University of Lublin. He often returned to Krakow in a tedious, twelve-hour train shuttle, spending part of the evening writing, then falling asleep, then standing in silent morning meditation or prayer in the train's corridor. His energy, his discipline, his creativity, his interest in everything from the work of physicians to the latest developments in science, were certainly attracting the attention of thoughtful members of Poland's church hierarchy. Yet in retrospect, there was no indication whatsoever of the role he would subsequently play in the disintegration of Communism in Eastern Europe.

In 1956 Poland came perilously close to experiencing the nightmarish invasion by Soviet troops that crushed the Hungarian uprising in

November of the same year. The Poles avoided it by bringing to power a formerly disgraced Communist leader, Wladyslaw Gomulka. He was determined that his nation would conduct business in its own manner even though it would remain politically loyal to Moscow and the Warsaw Pact alliance. Primate Wyszynski was released within a week of Gomulka's coming to power in October 1956.

It may have been Wojtyla's mere youth—he was only in his mid-thirties—and his uninvolvement in the administrative affairs of Poland's church that kept him out of any political trouble throughout the upheavals of the 1953–56 period. But just as Archbishop Adam Sapieha in 1946–51 had presided like a guardian angel over Karol's early career as a priest, it was now the job of his successor, Archbishop Eugeniusz Baziak, to act as an instrument of providence. Against diocesan expectations, Baziak put Karol's name forward to replace one of Krakow's suffragan (auxiliary) bishops who had died early in 1958. Karol was still very young, just thirty-eight, had no administrative experience at all, and only a truncated career as a parish priest. The nomination had to be signed by the pope in Rome, Pius XII, then approved by the Polish primate Wyszynski. On September 28, 1958, Karol was ordained suffragan bishop of Krakow in a solemn ceremony in the cathedral on Wawel Hill. He selected as his official motto *"totus tuus"* ("all yours") that he had taken from a Breton saint, Louis Marie Grignon de Montfort, whose works he had read in the night hours as a laborer at the Solvay chemical plant during the war. When he became pope, he was to sign each right-hand page of every manuscript he wrote with the words *totus tuus*.

He had been diligent, self-sacrificing, and bold in his work with young people, but not at all "political" in the sense of cultivating contacts high in the Vatican, or even in the state, hierarchy. Once he was a suffragan bishop, however, he began an astonishingly swift rise through the ranks not just of the Polish hierarchy but of the worldwide Catholic church. When he had been just a priest and a professor, he undoubtedly irritated the Communist authorities from time to time, but they did not seem to regard him as a threat to the regime. But once he began conducting the enormous schedule of church contacts and meetings with professionals, students, academics, and representatives of wide chunks of Polish society as an actual bishop, his visibility itself became a problem.

Within months of taking office, Wojtyla learned firsthand that, to defend his church against the pressures of the Communist authorities, he would have to practice both firmness and flexibility—and above all to know exactly when to use each. He discovered that he could accomplish much by taking the initiative when Catholic prelates hitherto had tended to wait until the regime acted. He developed a habit of fighting tooth and nail for every visible expression of the church's liturgical presence, even while not confronting the authorities on the fundamentals of whether they were a legitimate political authority in the first place.

Wojtyla ensured that processions, pilgrimages, celebration Masses, and memorial services all were conducted vigorously and with as massive a church presence as possible. He infused his clergy with a zeal for normal pastoral work, and he never stopped trying to enlarge the church's contacts with society as a whole. Sometimes this would take the form of special Masses for particular social groups. In 1969 he began the "Sacrosong Movement," an effort to bring church worship music in as contemporary form as possible to as wide a public audience as possible outside the church.

Above all else, what really transformed Karol Wojtyla from a gifted, but largely unknown Polish academic and middle-level prelate into a formidable figure on the Catholic church's global scene, was Vatican II. From its ceremonial beginnings in October 1962 until its concluding session in 1965, the Second Vatican Council (the first had been in 1869–70) was to set in motion changes within Catholicism more radical than anything that had happened to the church since the Reformation in the sixteenth century. Even today, many of those changes have been the very phenomena against which Karol Wojtyla, as Pope John Paul II, has taken a vigorous stand. There is little question, though, that Wojtyla approved of the basic thrust of *aggiornamento* (bringing up to date) that Pope John XIII, who launched Vatican II, sought to bring to the church's doctrine and practice. This, even if he had misgivings about the direction of the changes sought by some within the church.

From the very beginning of Vatican II in October 1962, Karol Wojtyla's reputation for intellectual brilliance and breadth of interest and experience spread rapidly. Not all of the Polish bishops officially invited had been permitted passports by the Polish government. In retrospect, Wojtyla's inclusion among the favored ones seems fortuitous. Wojtyla quickly emerged not just as the most gifted of the ten Poles who arrived in Rome, but as one of the most talented of the more than two thousand bishops present from all over the world.

He had done his homework well for the council, which was four years in preparation, and was well versed to speak out on a variety of issues. His knowledge of several languages—by this time German, Italian, Spanish, Polish, Russian, and English—in addition to his formidable command of Latin, enabled him to converse comfortably with leading Catholic bishops and cardinals from all over the world. But the future pope took a special interest in getting to know prelates from Third World countries, particularly Africa. He seemed to take an instant liking to the African bishops he encountered; it is possible that in Poland he had never once met a senior African Catholic figure.

Some critics of the papacy today like to attribute to John Paul II as pope a concerted effort to roll back the clock to pre–Vatican II church attitudes. John Paul II has certainly resisted fiercely some Catholic church trends that accelerated after Vatican II: liberation theology, for example, or the movement to try to relax the church's rules on sexual practice. It is also true that Wojtyla was firmly opposed to any tendency in the church to loosen its prohibitions against artificial birth control. But in several areas, there is no doubt that Wojtyla solidly backed the changes brought by Vatican II.

During the four years that the council met in Rome each autumn from 1962 to 1965, Wojtyla shuttled back and forth between Krakow and the Italian capital and played a role in important doctrinal formulations. On the subject of religious freedom, for example, he argued that the church could not morally demand religious freedom for itself if it denied it to others. He spoke strongly against any coercion of conscience by the church in any situation. He also, characteristically, balanced this high view of freedom with a cautionary note, pleading that, in the "Declaration on Religious Freedom," the church make it clear that freedom was not a mere entitlement to do whatever one pleased.

In one of the most historic Vatican II changes, Karol Wojtyla was a leading figure. This was the decision of the Catholic church, in the document on relations with non-Christian religions, *Nostra Aetate*, to absolve the Jewish people as a whole for responsibility for the crucifixion of Christ. That document, which was partly crafted by Wojtyla, said, "cannot be blamed on all the Jews living without distinction, nor upon the Jews of today."[30]

The decision was no mere theological afterthought; probably no Roman Catholic prelate in the world—other than Father Jean-Marie Lustiger, the Jewish-born future archbishop of Paris—had enjoyed closer relationships with Jews as a youth than Wojtyla. Certainly few, if any, of the assembled bishops believed with such passion in a cleansing of the often tragic story of Catholic attitudes toward the Jewish people. Wojtyla's role in this major innovation was of a piece with his role as pope in striving to do whatever he could for better Vatican-Jewish, and Vatican-Israeli, relations.

While Vatican II rolled forward in its stately, yet pathbreaking manner, Karol Wojtyla's career in the Polish Catholic church was experiencing yet another of its providential interventions. At issue was the next archbishop of Krakow. Wojtyla's earlier benefactor, Archbishop Eugeniusz Baziak, had died in June 1962, and it was up to the primate, Wyszynski, to nominate a replacement. Rome, naturally, had to sign off on it, in the form of the pope's own approval. But so did the Communist authorities in Warsaw. It was one of the unwritten rules of the curious coexistence of church and state in Poland that the regime could, in effect, veto an episcopal appointment. Providentially for Wojtyla, this is exactly what it proceeded to do for several months.

One reason was that Wyszynski was reluctant to nominate Wojtyla for the post of archbishop. Karol was still quite young, just forty-two, and there were several other Polish bishops of greater experience. Wyszynski was much older than Wojtyla. He may have dreaded having to cope with an intellectually gifted younger man in Poland's second most important diocese. Though there was no actual hostility between Wyszynski and Wojtyla, there was no comfortable chemistry, either. Even just before the conclave that was to elect Karol Wojtyla as Pope John Paul II in 1978, Wyszynski had made it plain that he neither wanted nor expected to see the cardinals select a Pole to fit the shoes of the Fisherman.

It was thus yet another of the ironies in the life of John Paul II that, just as a Nazi officer ensured that the future pope stayed alive in 1942, it was a senior Polish Communist who ensured that he became archbishop of Krakow in 1963. The man was Zenon Kiszko, the number two ranking apparatchik in the Polish United Workers Party (i.e., Communists) and the regime official able to veto the most senior Catholic church appointments. One by one, six of Wyszynski's nominations were turned down by Kiszko, who cannily assumed that if Wyszynski consistently refused to nominate Wojtyla, perhaps Wojtyla was someone the party could work with in the future. They knew the stubborn old primate only too well. He was a dyed-in-the-wool anti-Communist. As for Wojtyla, well, he had been forceful once or twice as suffragan bishop, and he was very energetic. But he was an intellectual, and moderately progressive in some of his views. Perhaps, Kiszko thought, he might be more amenable to working closely with the regime than any of Wyszynski's preferred choices.

Eventually, after the old primate's first six preferences were rejected, Wojtyla's name was submitted and accepted. Poland's Communists believed they had scored something of a coup in disappointing Wyszynski so deeply. Their judgment turned out to be incredibly wrong. It wasn't the only miscalculation the Communists made. In a top secret document of the Polish secret police from August 1967, after Wojtyla had already been made cardinal, the police concluded that Karol's politics were "his weaker suit," and that he lacked "organizing and leadership qualities."[31] The secret police, as I discovered again and again in Eastern Europe, were diligent and usually oppressive in their methods. But they could also be quite amazingly stupid in their analysis of people and events.

While the drawn-out process of finding a new Krakow archbishop was taking place in Poland, in Rome itself a far more important development had transpired, the election of a new pope. John XXIII died in June 1963, after an influential but short reign of just five years. His one great achievement had been Vatican II, but he had also moved the church to a more centrist position in the Cold War between the United States and the Soviet Union. His encyclical, *Pacem in Terris* (Peace on Earth), called for disarmament by the superpowers and a commitment by responsible global leaders to avoid war at all costs.

The new pope, Cardinal Montini, the archbishop of Milan, was an experienced Vatican diplomat. Just as Sapieha had been the guardian angel of Wojtyla's admission into the priesthood, Baziak of his elevation to bishop, and (unwittingly) the Communist Kiszko of his being appointed archbishop, so Montini, as Pope Paul VI, ensured that Wojtyla became a cardinal. And once cardinal, it was Paul VI's continuing favor that raised Wojtyla from a young, brilliant, but essentially obscure Polish prelate to that mysteriously vague, but to Italians, exquisitely exciting, status of *papabile*: roughly translatable as "in a position to be elected pope."

That, of course, was well into the future. But Wojtyla's course was set when he became Krakow's archbishop. In 1965, the regime finally caved in to incessant demands that it grant a construction permit for a church in

Nowa Huta, a barrackslike new town for workers in the steel industry outside Krakow. He had relentlessly held church services there in the cold, in the open air, in a makeshift chapel supposed to cater to twenty thousand people, never giving up his demand for a construction permit.

Characteristic of his unflinching commitment to principles he believed essential and integral to the Christian life was a firestorm of controversy he encountered in 1965 with some of the workers of the same Solvay plant where he had been a laborer in World War II. While in Rome he, other Polish bishops, and German bishops had come together in a remarkable mood of mutual reconciliation and of determination to set behind them the agonies of Polish-German relations over decades and centuries. Many Polish workers were outraged at this, to the satisfaction of the Polish Communists who attacked the Polish bishops' statement acknowledging that the Germans had suffered historically too. But Wojtyla stood his ground: The appeal to the German bishops, he said, was based on "the deepest principles of Christian ethics." Responding to a letter purportedly written by Solvay workers, he wrote:

> When we worked together during the occupation, we had much in common—and, in the first place, respect for man, his conscience, his personality, and his social dignity. I had learned this in great measure from Solvay workers—but I do not find this basic principle contained in your letter.[32]

"IT IS GOD'S WILL"

Vatican II had ensured a very high visibility for Wojtyla among Catholic prelates worldwide. His talents and his diplomatic skills were now seen by the Vatican as major attributes to be called upon for the church's larger purposes. Wojtyla had first met Paul VI in 1964, and the pope of that day had reminisced about his Vatican diplomatic service in Poland. He was deeply impressed by Wojtyla's experience as a worker. A second audience with Paul VI took place in April 1967. Less than six weeks later, Wojtyla was named a cardinal, and what became an increasingly warm friendship between the Pole and the Italian began to gather momentum.

Partly because of his work on Vatican committees, and partly because Paul VI repeatedly wanted to confer with him, Wojtyla visited Rome numerous times for meetings with the pope between 1967 and Paul's death in 1978. In the years between 1973 and 1975, Wojtyla had eleven private audiences with the pope, an exceptionally high number for someone not resident in Rome.

Paul VI leaned on Wojtyla in other ways too. As the controversy over Vatican attitudes toward birth control bubbled to a head in the 1960's, Paul VI for a time seemed uncertain which way to move. Some of the more progressive cardinals and bishops urged him to relax the absolute Catholic ban on artificial means of contraception. There was no justification for it, they said, even in the Bible. In fact, the commission appointed by Pope John XXIII to reexamine the issue of artificial birth control had actually submitted a report to Pope Paul VI in June 1966 recommending that the Catholic church end the ban on its usage.

For some reason, Wojtyla had been unable to attend the concluding meeting of the commission, of which he was a member. Instead, he organized an intensive study of the whole question of artificial contraception within the diocese in Krakow and forwarded his thoughts to the Vatican in writing. Two years later, these ideas found their way into the text of Paul VI's encyclical *Humanae Vitae*, the decisive papal declaration that the Vatican would remain opposed to birth control except by the "natural method." Wojtyla's insistence on preserving the ban on birth control was part of his ever growing conviction that the human person was so sacred that anything interfering with its conception—not to mention the coming to full term of a conceived child—was a serious moral crime against God's most beloved of all creatures, the human being.

During the 1960's in Krakow, Karol Wojtyla stayed clear of political ferment and the wilder cultural protests that had seeped into Eastern Europe from the West. But he did take some major initiatives with long-term consequences. He continued, for example, to reach out to the Jewish community. In 1969 he became the first Catholic cardinal ever to visit the synagogue in the Kasimierz district of Krakow.

The same year, he began the first of his major world travels. He had visited Egypt, Jordan, and Israel in 1963, but had otherwise never been out of Europe. He now traveled to the United States and Canada, broadening his social skills—he discovered the dubious merits of the cocktail party—and learning firsthand about the complexities of America's own Catholic scene. He was not happy with a lot of what he saw: the almost stupefying luxury in living standards compared with what Poland still had, the crassness of much of the popular culture, the tendency of American Catholics to be far more skeptical about official church doctrines and policies than most Polish Catholics. Many of Wojtyla's impressions, some of them perhaps too harsh, have surfaced in comments and homilies over the years since then.

But there were encounters with different parts of global Catholicism, too. Wojtyla was in Australia, New Zealand, and Papua New Guinea in 1973, and these trips gave him further opportunities to meet with Catholic prelates and important figures from a vast variety of countries, not just from the Oceanian region. He was introduced to Mother Teresa for the first time at the Melbourne Eucharistic Conference that year. In 1975, foreshadowing his restless papal curiosity about the entire world, he invited to Krakow prelates he had met from Africa and Asia. He was responsible for the first visit to Poland by an African cardinal, that of Paul Zoungrana of Upper Volta (now Burkina Faso) in 1975. Karol Wojtyla was, perhaps without realizing it, preparing himself for the future task of managing the full global dominion of the church of Rome. But he was also acquiring the insatiable appetite for travel that has become the very hallmark of his papacy.

Men of lesser discipline of prayer, of lesser humility, lacking the deep scars of personal suffering imposed through early family loss, untempered by the humiliations and terrors of an enemy occupation, might have settled comfortably into a life of glamour, travel, and moderate fame. But Wojtyla's unbridled commitment to his own vision of the church, no longer just in Poland, but worldwide, was plainly visible in the entire character of the man. For one thing, it had caught the eye of the reigning Pope Paul VI.

A pope, it is said, often contrives to secure the appointment of his own successor. There is nothing mysterious in this: A dead pope is a dead pope, but the papacy is an institution nearly two thousand years old. Cardinals certainly believe that the Holy Spirit guides the choice of each successor to the Holy See. But they also believe there are signs along the way, hints and nudges about a handful of prelates who have somehow earned the trust and favor of a living pope in a manner indicative of special quality.

In February 1976, Paul VI invited Karol Wojtyla to preside over the annual weeklong Lenten spiritual exercises of the Roman Curia. To address a gathering of some one hundred of the most powerful people in the Roman Catholic Church, including the pope, for several days in a row in St. Matilda's Chapel in the Vatican, would have been an unusual honor for any Catholic priest. To do so as a cardinal from Poland, in the Italian language, moreover, was an exceptional honor. Perhaps more than anything in Wojtyla's life so far, it provided the Vatican's top leadership with an opportunity to examine close-up a man who was emerging as one of the most intellectually gifted figures in the entire Roman Catholic Church. He was widely regarded as pleasant of temperament and warm in his relations with people. He was also known to be a man of deep prayer habits. Wojtyla prayed and studied earnestly, with less than three weeks' notice, at a retreat in the Tatry Mountains of his native land. His "Meditations," subsequently published as a book, *A Sign of Contradiction*, expounded his thoughts on the nature of the contemporary world. The domain of Marxism-Leninism, still regnant in Eastern Europe, was one of "autocracy," he said. Western capitalism itself, he added, was often also the source of "economic imperialism." As for those who wanted to impose abortion and birth control on humanity, he added, all who were against this trend, including Pope Paul VI, were "in the front line in a lively battle for the dignity of man."[33]

There is little doubt that the high church officials of the Curia were deeply impressed by both what they had heard and what they saw. Wojtyla had succeeded in displaying not just a command of intellectual concepts inherent in the Christian philosophy of life, but a spiritual personality that seemed integrated with those concepts in a remarkable way. Furthermore, he displayed this combination of attributes at a time of deep upheaval in East-West relations around the world: the defeat of the United States in Vietnam in 1975 and the collapse of Laos and Cambodia that year to Communist forces.

The West, including Italy, was reaping the consequences of the generational and cultural conflicts of the 1960's: divorce rates higher than ever before, the legalization of abortion in the United States (*Roe v. Wade* in 1973), the toppling of dictatorial regimes in Spain and Italy, and, for a while, the threat of Communist governments taking over those countries. Without being political, Wojtyla seemed to dig deep into the resources of Christian thought and morality in a way that suggested the infusion of a new energy into the Catholic church worldwide.

Even so, when Paul VI finally died after a long struggle with prostate cancer on August 7, 1978, Wojtyla's name was not high on the list of papal cardinals who entered the conclave in the Sistine Chapel to select his successor. The Italian cardinals, still dominating the selection process and indeed the Vatican in general, ensured during the balloting that another of their own became pope: Albino Luciani of Venice, a pious, pastorally minded man who seemed warm of heart and eager to steer the papacy back to more pastoral waters after the controversies of Paul VI's years. But Luciani, Pope John Paul I, died of heart failure after just thirty-two days in office, the shortest reign of any previous pope.

Once more, the cardinals were summoned to Rome for a conclave. This time, the mood was tense not simply because of the crisis of such a short papal reign, but because there was no longer any consensus on another candidate. The options seemed so wide open that, for the first time, the assembled prelates took the possibility of a foreign pope seriously.

The first four ballots during October 15, 1978, produced a deadlock. The Italians couldn't come up with any name of their own that the majority of the cardinals would support. Overnight, the possibility of a foreign-born pope being elected began to evolve into a probability. Wojtyla now realized that his own candidacy was being pushed by an impressively diverse coalition of non-Italians, including Cardinals Konig of Vienna, Krol of Philadelphia, Suenens of Belgium, Vicente Enrique y Tarancon of Spain, and Lorscheider of Brazil.

It is remarkable that Wojtyla's backers included both conservatives and relative liberals among the cardinals. Instinctively, these cardinals recognized that Wojtyla could not be pigeonholed into some neat political or ideological category. He was sophisticated about politics—after all, he had often outwitted as cardinal of Krakow his own country's seasoned Communist apparatchiks—but all his life he seemed more drawn to the contemplative aspects of the Christian faith and to Christianity's impact upon culture. He was no friend to Communism; neither was he a man who thought capitalism, in and of itself, provided all of humankind's answers. Jerzy Turowicz, the editor of Krakow's Catholic intellectual (and hence inherently anti-Communist) weekly magazine *Tygodnyk Powszeczny*, has said simply of Wojtyla: "He is not a leftist; he's not a rightist; and he's not a nationalist either."[34]

By the morning of the conclave's second day, the tide was moving decisively in Wojtyla's favor. As the vote-counting in the eighth ballot approached half the number needed to be elected—two-thirds plus one—Wojtyla was sitting bolt upright. He had been writing furiously, but now he put his pencil aside. According to Cardinal Konig, he was "red in the face." Then he held his head in his hands. Finally, as the count approached the requisite figure of 94, he resumed writing. He was preparing the remarks he was to make as pope-elect. Cardinal Villot, the chamberlain of the conclave, approached him and asked in Latin: "In accordance with canon law, do you accept?"

"It is God's will," Wojtyla replied. "I accept."[35] Then, to honor his short-lived predecessor John Paul I, who had died after just thirty-two days in office, he selected the name John Paul II.

It was a few days later that the electrifying scenes of John Paul II's installation were played out in St. Peter's Square. "He has won the Romans," wrote Andrew M. Greeley in his journal, and later in his book *The Making of the Popes*.[36] Suddenly, not just Rome, but the entire Catholic church had a leader of obvious physical vigor, personal self-confidence, brilliant intellect, deep spirituality, and determination to make an enormous mark on the world.

And make a mark, he did. From his very first papal trip overseas, John Paul showed that there was not going to be any time of papacy-in-training. In January 1979, he traveled to the Dominican Republic and Mexico, encountering crowds estimated to total three million people in each country. Even aboard the papal jet he broke protocol, wandering back into the journalists' segment of the plane like a savvy politician, taking questions first from the seats along one side of the aircraft and then from the other. When his plane alighted at Santo Domingo, capital of the Dominican Republic, he inaugurated a practice that at first astonished onlookers, but came to characterize all of his subsequent foreign travels until the 1990's, when he became physically too weak to do it: He knelt down and kissed the ground, indicating his sense of a papal visit as a visit of Christian service and respect, not as a celebrity arrival.

He did the same thing on landing in Mexico City, even though Mexico's prickly church-state relations forbade any official government welcoming ceremonies. But it was in Puebla, Mexico, that the new steel of papal authority showed through the warmth and charm of this son of Poland. Addressing the Conference of Latin American Bishops (sometimes abbreviated to CELAM, after the Spanish abbreviation), he faced head-on the challenge to both traditional orthodox doctrine and ecclesiastical authority posed by the newly emergent liberation theology. In both Protestant and Catholic guises, this interpretation of Christian social activism and Scripture used the Marxist analysis of class struggle as a starting point for a highly politicized, even revolutionary approach to existing societies. The liberation theologians, he said, without naming any of them, "make an effort to show Jesus as politically committed, as someone who fought against Roman domination and the powerful, indeed as someone implicated in class struggle." But this was completely wrong, he insisted. "This notion of a political Jesus, a revolutionary, the subversive from Nazareth, is not in harmony with the church's teaching."[37]

John Paul was to maintain this formidable and, at times, confrontational approach to dissident doctrine throughout his papacy. In the 1980's, for example, he ordered the suspension of Cardinal Charles E. Curran, a moral theologian, from a teaching position at Washington's Catholic University because of Curran's nontraditional teachings on marriage and sexual behavior. He also imposed a year's teaching silence on Leonardo Boff, a prominent liberation theologian, and Hans Kung, a prominent Swiss theologian who had publicly questioned several orthodox Catholic beliefs. These moves were unexpectedly forceful. They stirred up a hornet's nest of opposition from hundreds of Catholic academics in universities around the world who felt that the principle of freedom of thought was being threatened. In 1989, some four hundred of them signed the "Cologne Declaration," complaining that the Vatican was now requiring "blind obedience" to traditional doctrinal positions.

But John Paul was in fact navigating a narrow, and at times treacherous, pathway: acknowledging the right of freedom of thought on the one hand, and on the other resisting a tendency, inside and outside the church, to idolize freedom for its own sake, irrespective of truth. "Certain currents of modern thought," he wrote in one of his most important encyclicals, *Veritatis Splendor* (The Splendor of Truth), in 1993,

> have gone so far as to *exalt freedom to such an extent that it becomes an absolute, which would then be the source of values.* This is the direction taken by doctrines which have lost the sense of the transcendent or which are explicitly atheistic.[38] [emphasis in original]

John Paul believes that freedom must never be viewed as an end in itself, but always as a means to approach truth. "Freedom is not simply the absence of tyranny or oppression," he told an audience of the world's diplomats at the United Nations General Assembly in 1995, in perhaps the greatest single speech of his papacy. He went on:

> Nor is freedom a license to do whatever we like. Freedom has an inner "logic" which distinguishes and ennobles it: *Freedom is ordered to the truth*, and is fulfilled in man's quest for truth and in man's living in the truth. Detached from the truth about the human person, freedom deteriorates into license in the lives of individuals, and in political life, it becomes the caprice of the most powerful and the arrogance of power. Far from being a limitation upon freedom or a threat to it, reference to the truth about the human person—a truth universally knowable through the moral law written on the hearts of all—is, in fact, the guarantor of freedom's future.[39] [emphasis in original]

Above all, John Paul argued that the "magisterium," as Catholics call the authoritative voice of their church's leaders, must be faithful to the traditions of the Christian faith handed down by earlier generations, and to Scripture itself.

One of the most prolific popes in the history of the papacy, John Paul II's first encyclical was published in March 1979, less than five months after he became pope. By the end of 1996 he had published eleven more encyclicals. His entire literary output, including his youthful poetry and his mature philosophical and spiritual writings, amounts to some 150 volumes. Yet the first encyclical, called *Redemptor Hominis* (The Redeemer of Mankind), in many ways sums up the essence of John Paul's entire thought as pope and helps explain the subsequent course of his papacy. "The redeemer of mankind, Jesus Christ, is the center of the universe and history," he declares. It is the church's duty, he says in the encyclical, not just to introduce ordinary people to Christ, but to honor at all times the unique individuality of every human being in his or her personhood.

Indeed "human dignity" and "personhood" crop up again and again in John Paul's writings and sermons, whether he is writing about differing economic and social systems, as in *Centesimus Annus* (On the Hundredth

Anniversary, 1991) or about the protection of human life, as in *Evangelium Vitae* (The Gospel of Life, 1995). He has written:

> The root of modern totalitarianism is to be found in the denial of the transcendent dignity of the human person who, as the visible image of the invisible God is therefore by his very nature the subject of rights which no one may violate—no individual, group, class, nation, or State.[40]

John Paul clearly favors the free market system of economics over socialism, but he also speaks out strongly against the frequent cruelty of market forces that are unsoftened by considerations of basic human decency.

His opposition to abortion is based not merely on the belief that fetuses are human beings and that abortion is thus the actual taking of human life, but that population programs that include abortion as specific options lead to a devaluing of the entire concept of life itself. In July 1993, preparing for a trip to the United States, and in particular a visit to the World Youth Day in Denver, Colorado, he decried what he called "a culture of death, often presented as the civilized achievement of new rights, but which, in fact, lays a trap for human life by preventing it through abortion from being born, or by extinguishing it through euthanasia."[41]

In frankly criticizing some of the trends of modern mass culture, particularly in the developed world, John Paul has always sought to move beyond mere negative commentary. Thus in *Evangelium Vitae*, he says Christians together "must build a new culture of life," a project that he believes is "also rooted in the Church's mission of evangelization. The purpose of the Gospel, in fact," he adds, citing Pope Paul VI, his predecessor, "is to transform humanity from within and to make it new." Though some might assume that John Paul, as a European from a deeply Catholic country, is unappreciative of the extraordinary richness of global culture, he hardly misses an opportunity to express the opposite. Just as every human being is precious in God's sight, he told the United Nations in 1995, so nations must universally respect the cultures of other nations, for

> every culture is an effort to ponder the mystery of the world and in particular of the human person: it is a way of giving expression to the

transcendent dimension of human life. The heart of every culture is its approach to the greatest of all mysteries: the mystery of God.[42]

MIRACLE IN ST. PETER'S SQUARE

The role of the Christian message, John Paul believes, is not to force change on non-Christian cultures by imposing values and fashions on them from the outside, much less from above. But, as he adds, "like the yeast which leavens the whole measure of dough (cf. Matt. 13:33), the Gospel is meant to permeate all cultures and give them life from within, so that they may express the full truth about the human person and about human life."[43]

As John Paul's spokesman, Joaquin Navarro-Valls has put it, John Paul's goal as pope has been nothing less than the establishment of a completely Christian alternative to the humanistic philosophies of the twentieth century such as Marxism, structuralism, and atheistic ideas of post-Enlightenment. Those ideas, Navarro-Valls added, "were simply among the tools of the age. Wojtyla said no, we have something new, we don't have to copy. Let us humbly build a new sociology, a new anthropology, that is based on something genuinely Christian."[44]

Though John Paul did not voice these views as bluntly as his spokesman expressed them at the outset of his papacy, no journey that he made as pope made it clearer what his goal was than his first visit as pontiff to Poland in June 1979. Moscow tried desperately to stop the visit, understanding well what it might lead to. Soviet Communist Party general secretary Leonid Brezhnev, in fact, phoned his Polish counterpart, Edward Gierek, and urged him to announce that John Paul II couldn't come because the pope had taken ill. "Comrade Leonid, I cannot do that," Gierek sensibly replied. "I must receive John Paul II."[45]

Gierek did receive the pope, awkwardly, because for nine ecstatic days all of Poland became euphoric about their returned native son. An estimated ten million Poles, nearly a third of the population, flocked to wherever in the country they could catch a glimpse of the pope, whether meeting with ordinary Poles or celebrating the Mass. The authorities were so alarmed at the galvanizing effect John Paul's presence was having on their populace that they ordered the television cameras not to pan across the crowds and show the huge throngs.

But the damage was done. Some have denied any connection between the sense of exultation created in Poles by John Paul's visit in June 1979 and the sudden emergence of the Solidarity free trade union in Gdansk in August of the following year. Certainly there would have been labor troubles in Poland no matter who had been pope at the time. But would the results have been anything like what they turned out to be if John Paul had not carefully nurtured the events in his own country throughout the 1980's decade? It doesn't seem likely.

Well before Solidarity's existence, however, Moscow's intelligence organizations were already becoming worried about the direction in international relations that the pope was taking. He certainly was not a fiery anti-Communist as a predecessor, Pius XII, had been in the 1930's and 1940's. In fact, he spoke about the defects of capitalism in terms of which some Communists might even approve. What he clearly did not believe in was the status quo. His immediate predecessor, Paul VI, had nurtured a steady, quiet process of seeking points of commonality with the materialist regimes that were often cruelly suppressing Catholics across Eastern Europe.

This approach was similar to the *Ostpolitik* first articulated by former West German chancellor Willy Brandt. The idea was to seek a concession here, a tidbit there from the Communist regimes entrenched in Eastern Europe, but never to challenge them directly. John Paul was far too sophisticated to mount an overt ideological crusade against Communism in his own continent. But in his sermons, in his writings, in his conversational remarks with everyone, he made it clear that he did not expect these regimes to last at all.

Alarmed by both the Polish visit in June and by the degree to which John Paul's papacy was reinvigorating the entire Catholic church, the Soviet KGB launched a top secret six-point campaign in November 1979 to "work against the policies of the Vatican in relation to the socialist states." KGB agents were instructed to spread disinformation about the pope including the idea, for example, that his policies and ideas were actually harmful to the Catholic church. The plot was as nonsensical as it was likely to fail. By the time KGB agents around the world had received their instructions, John Paul's dashing style and his global travels had raised his popularity to new heights.

Everywhere he went he could be seen kissing babies or dazzling young people with his charm. His public appearances had the timing and drama associated with a skilled stage performance. More important, he knew exactly in what direction he wanted the Catholic church, Christendom in general, and indeed the whole world, to go. What must have angered the Kremlin's leaders more than anything was the intense interest John Paul took in the developing labor union events in Poland from 1980 onward. It was as though the Vatican were all but egging on the gradual dismembering of state socialism in the country.

Did Moscow therefore, through its Bulgarian allies and proxies, actually encourage the Turkish fanatic, self-described "international terrorist" Mehmet Ali Agca, to pull the trigger of a 9 mm pistol at short range from the pope in St. Peter's Square in May 1981? There has never been totally convincing proof, either, of Moscow's complicity or its lack of connection with the assassination attempt. There was clearly a Bulgarian connection of some kind or other. In the past, the Bulgarians had been known to carry out overseas assassinations of pesky political opponents. What about Moscow? Certainly Moscow had an interest in not seeing the pope continue to shake the very foundations of its empire in Eastern Europe. But would it go so far as to encourage, even if quite tacitly, an attempt on the life of the pope?

Ali Agca himself has given contradictory responses to all of these questions. When John Paul himself visited him for twenty minutes in his Roman prison cell in December 1983, there was whispering between the two even as the pope was making it clear he personally forgave his would-be assassin. "The pope knows everything," Agca said cryptically after the meeting. But if he does, he is certainly not saying publicly who he thinks was behind the attempt to kill him. That Agca pulled the trigger is beyond doubt. That he had once previously threatened harm against the pope is also known. But that was in 1979, before Solidarity came into existence. Agca could as easily have been working for a militant Islamic organization or, because of his own bizarre anarchist motives, for the intelligence services of any particular country.

In a sense, of course, the issue is moot, though historically intriguing: The Soviet Union is no more, Bulgaria is no longer Communist, and the pope's global influence seems not a whit lessened by the evil effort to snuff out his life.

Looking back, it is astonishing that John Paul not only recovered swiftly from the bullet wound, but after a few months' convalescence resumed his activities with as much energy as ever. The bullet missed his aorta by a few millimeters, and he attributed his survival to divine intervention. "One hand fired and another hand guided the bullet," he said later.[46] As it happened, May 13, the day of the assassination attempt, was the anniversary of one of the first apparitions of the Virgin of Fatima, an event in 1917 when three Portuguese shepherd children said they had witnessed an appearance of the Virgin Mary.

In one of the three prophecies the children said they had heard, it was predicted that Russia would eventually be reconverted—presumably from the atheism of Marxism-Leninism—after spreading "errors" all over the world. It is highly unlikely that the shepherd girls could have predicted six months in advance the Bolshevik Revolution that was to sweep Lenin and the Communists to power in November 1917.

John Paul's survival of his assassination attempt seemed to confirm for him that his papacy had indeed been marked for great events. Throughout the 1980's, indeed, he was at the center of the unfolding drama of the collapse of Communism in Eastern Europe first, and then, in 1991, of the Soviet Union itself. Much has been made, especially in the recent and well-informed biography, *His Holiness,* by former Watergate reporter Carl Bernstein and Italian journalist Marco Politi, of John Paul's close connections with the Reagan White House during the climactic final years of the Cold War.

Although the pope clearly was briefed on the situation in Poland at different times by senior members of the Reagan administration, from CIA Director Bill Casey to National Security Advisers Richard Allen and then William Clark, it is unlikely that Washington-Vatican cooperation extended much beyond the exchange of information. The pope, after all, had his own excellent sources inside Poland and Eastern Europe through the Catholic church itself. Besides, though Reagan and the pope surely admired each other in different respects, and indeed shared the same total conviction that Communism would eventually fall, any resemblance between the two men stopped there. Reagan believed in America's destiny as the bulwark of freedom against Communism all over the world. His preferred weapon in the struggle was always American power and American national will.

John Paul didn't believe in power at all—he had been a victim of power under the Nazis—but in the invincible superiority of moral truth and Christian faith over the forces of atheism and cynicism. After Reagan had left office, it was George Bush who felt the weight of John Paul's dismay at the use of military force to solve international problems. In January 1991, just before Operation Desert Storm launched the American and Coalition forces against Saddam Hussein's Iraq, John Paul decried the up-coming conflict as "a defeat for all humanity." It was necessary for man-kind as a whole, he told diplomats accredited to the Holy See, to "proceed resolutely toward outlawing war completely."[47]

The pope was instrumental in keeping alive the flame of Solidarity's spirit of defiance against state power in Poland after the Polish govern-ment declared martial law in December 1981 and banned the labor union. He maintained clandestine contact with Walesa, then under house arrest, for the first few years of martial law, and insisted on being allowed to visit him in a remote government-controlled location during a papal visit in 1983. He was very careful. He never openly criticized Poland's military strongman, General Wojciech Jaruzelski, and in fact he held his fellow Pole in some respect as a man of integrity.

There is little doubt that John Paul's deft handling of Jaruzelski, his cautious and nonconfrontational dealings with the Soviet Union in the 1980's, along with his uncompromising championship of real human rights, helped defuse Poland's crisis. By 1987, after a meeting with the pope that the general was to describe as "historic," the tide began to turn in Eastern Europe. The following year, Solidarity was legalized once more, and in 1989 it took the most dramatic step to date of any country in Eastern Europe by electing a non-Communist prime minister in a free election.

John Paul, meanwhile, had also weakened the appeal of Nicaragua's leftist Sandinista in Latin America as a whole by declaring liberation the-ology itself anathema and affirming that he had no sympathy whatever for Marxist solutions to global social problems. When he first visited Managua in 1983, he publicly wagged his finger in a reception line at Trappist monk and Sandinista minister of culture Ernesto Cardenal for not quitting the priesthood before joining his country's leftist government. In 1985, he officially defrocked Cardenal and three other leftist Nicara-guan priests. The Sandinistas, of course, were eventually voted out of office in 1990 in a free election. The populace had grown tired of their authoritarian and hectoring ways.

Throughout the 1980's and 1990's, John Paul waged a relentless struggle against any population control program that included abortion. In 1994, he even tangled politely but firmly with the Clinton administration, which the Vatican held responsible for the agenda at the International Conference on Population and Development in Cairo, Egypt. At first, the conference all but explicitly supported a universal right to abortion. After some tense weeks of negotiation, the Cairo conference backed away from its original, more radical program.

How can one briefly describe John Paul II? For one thing, he is a man of action. Few popes in history, by their intelligence, skillful diplomacy, and consistent championship of the moral high ground in politics have had such a profound impact on the politics of their day. Not one, on a more mundane note, has been so physically active as John Paul, who even as pontiff continued to swim, hike, and ski. No pope in modern times has captured the affections of so many people who do not, at heart, agree with him on many issues.

Paradoxically, polls in the United States have consistently shown that vast numbers of American Catholics disagree with the pope on major doctrinal issues, even though they regard his papacy itself as a major success. This is particularly true with Catholic women, many of whom deeply resent John Paul for his continuing refusal to consider the ordination of women to the priesthood.

A *Washington Post*/ABC News poll in September 1995 found that 93 percent of Catholics believe one can practice artificial birth control and continue to be a good Catholic, while a further 85 percent think one could divorce and remarry and still remain a good Catholic. John Paul, of course, has resolutely fought against these two beliefs from the beginning of his reign as pope—and, indeed, throughout most of his adult life. Yet in a separate poll taken by *U.S. News & World Report* at almost exactly the same time, 86 percent of Catholics thought John Paul was doing a good job as pope. In effect, many Catholics have agreed that John Paul II has had one of the most profound impacts of any single individual on the entire contemporary world during his papacy, even though they can't agree with the issues on which he has the strongest convictions.

What Catholics and many other Christians have clearly discerned in John Paul II is a moral authority of such rarity in the modern world that they are unsure even how to explain it.

It has many components. One is John Paul's integrity as a person. This was honed in the hardest of times, during the tensions and dangers of life under Nazi occupation during World War II. It was refined during the personal anguish of the early loss of all of his closest family members, and during his struggles as priest and bishop against the political oppression and cultural mockery of his country's atheistic authorities.

But perhaps the most significant component of John Paul II's character is his commitment to human dignity as the essence of moral behavior. For a Christian, the source of all human dignity is always God Himself, for it is the Bible that says unequivocally that humans are made in God's image, and that we are commanded not just to be civil to our neighbors, but to love them. For John Paul II, the very heart of all human rights, in all cultures and civilizations—Christian or not—is the dignity of the human person.

Rights based on this concept, he told the United Nations in 1995, are not "abstract points." Forms of culture and of freedom may differ, he said, but there is a "universal moral law written on the human heart." People, he said, recognize this even when they are well aware of cultural differences among themselves and among the nations of the world. John Paul II may be one of the last major leaders of this century asserting without qualification the absolute objectivity of moral values and of the inherent dignity of the human condition.

Billy Graham has said of Pope John Paul II, certainly with accuracy, that he will "go down in history as the greatest of our modern popes. He's the strong conscience of the whole Christian world." I respect that judgment, but for me it doesn't go far enough. I am not a Roman Catholic, and I certainly share many of the Protestant reservations about some aspects of Catholic doctrine and some forms of Catholic devotionalism. Yet it is my view that Pope John Paul II, in his profound spiritual depth, his prayer life, his enormous intellectual universe, his compassion and sympathy for the oppressed, and above all in his vision of how Christians collectively are supposed to live, is the greatest single Christian leader of the twentieth century. When he is gone, he may well be viewed, quite simply, as one of the most exemplary figures in all of Christian history.

CHAPTER 6

ELIE WIESEL: REMEMBRANCE

"My goal is always the same: to invoke the past as a shield for the future;
to show the invisible world of yesterday and through it, perhaps on it,
erect a moral world where men are not victims and children never
starve and never run in fear."

—ELIE WIESEL
A Personal Response [1]

IN 1988, I WAS INVOLVED in an effort among journalists in Washington and New York to respond to the plight of a fellow reporter—a prisoner, in fact. Associated Press correspondent Terry Anderson had been held captive in Beirut since March 1986 by a pitiless Islamic militant group. In New York, a group of us had gone to visit UN Secretary General Javier Perez de Cuellar in the hope of learning what more might be done to shake Terry and his fellow hostages loose. Ever vigilant about the plight of even single victims of militancy and fanaticism, Elie Wiesel came to the meeting. It was my first face-to-face encounter with his commanding moral presence.

He was slight in build, modest, shy in demeanor. His face was thin, the forehead a plowed field of neatly spaced creases. His eyes were extraordinarily melancholy even when he smiled, which he did readily enough. He was fastidiously courteous—a man ready to listen, ready to respond, but impatient of the trivial or the superficial. Though he was physically light, weighing perhaps 150 pounds, everyone around him was aware of a weightiness about him. In part, of course, we felt his status as a Nobel laureate, as the voice of the Holocaust's survivors, as humanity's conscience in the face of the twentieth century's relentless violence. But there was something else.

It was as if a burden of remembrance lay upon him, borne for those six million who did not survive.

The words we exchanged were brief; I do not even recall them. But he graciously signed an autograph in my reporter's notebook "For Abigail," my then eleven-year-old daughter. Later we spoke by phone and met again, to discuss his life, his views, and his thoughts on a variety of topics.

This time, it was the voice that struck me. There was certainly a trace of a French accent, the product of his teenage years and young manhood in Paris. But there was also something conspicuously central European, too, an insistence of the consonants, a reminder of his childhood Romanian, Hungarian, and Yiddish. Above all, when Wiesel speaks, he does so quietly, even when addressing a large audience. Interlocutors must listen intently to what Wiesel is saying in order to catch his words. He seems at times to be rationing them before he speaks.

This quietness is appropriate. By the time he was fifteen, Elie Wiesel had heard the spoken cacophony of hell itself. Shouts, screams, grunts, groans, and imprecations in a score of tongues had roared and clattered around his teenage head. He had been in the Auschwitz and Buchenwald concentration camps, a forced, horrified eyewitness to the greatest collective crime in human history, and had somehow survived.

For a decade, Wiesel remained silent about that hideous inferno of souls, above all of Jewish souls—the "Event," as he often prefers to describe it. When he did begin to speak and found his literary and personal voice, it was quiet, measured, sparse in vocabulary. To describe great evil powerfully, Wiesel seems to have intuited, the foulness must first be distilled, then laid out quietly before readers or hearers. Hatred is a perpetually raised voice. Wiesel's response through his writings, lectures, articles, and crusades on behalf of global human decency and the moral power of humanity is offered calmly. Above all else, with carefully ordered words, he always speaks of remembrance.

It is hard for us today to grasp how difficult it has been for the world to come to terms with the Holocaust. The very word was rare in daily usage until, in 1960, Wiesel himself first employed it in the *New York Times Book Review* to describe what happened to Europe's Jews under Hitler in World War II. Today the word is universally recognized to mean the great crime against the Jewish people, the demented dream of an Austrian neo-pagan. Hitler was assisted by some who called themselves Christians and showed circumstantial evidence of Christianity (baptism as infants, occasional churchgoing, enjoyment of Christmas carols); his purpose was to eliminate the entire Jewish race from the earth. After various television miniseries (*Holocaust, The Winds of War, War and Remembrance*) and a host of movies, above all *Schindler's List*, the enormity of what happened during 1939–45, but especially after 1942, became evident to people everywhere.

There are still some countries, mostly in the Islamic world, that refuse to give serious credence to this particular aspect of history, doubtless fearing that knowledge of the Jewish plight then might lessen government-encouraged animosity toward Israel now. There is a stubborn corps of revisionist holdouts in the U.S. and elsewhere who flatly deny that the Holocaust occurred. But now there is a new problem, the discounting of the event through use of the term "Holocaust" in non–World War II contexts. "Now I'm sorry. It's been so trivialized and vulgarized," Wiesel told *Time* in an interview many years ago. "Today one must ask, 'Do you mean the show or the event?'"[2]

Trivialization may be the common curse of a mass culture. Our world seems to pride itself on the ability to change television channels without leaving the couch, and would rather not hear any news that is tragic, much less that suggests a deep weakness in the human race. What Wiesel has accomplished, though, is unlikely ever to be buried in trivia. In 1958, he produced a book in France, *La Nuit*, that was to alter profoundly the common understanding in the West of what had happened to the Jews of Europe. It took Hitler's starchy, bureaucratic term "Final Solution" (i.e., a deliberate decision to murder all of the Jews who could be reached by the Germans) and turned it into the searing literature of truth. It stunned the French, for it opened for them an insight into twentieth-century evil that even their own experience with the Nazis during the 1940–44 Occupation had not revealed.

Two years after its publication in France, it appeared as an English edition in the U.S., *Night*. Until then almost the only broadly known personal recollection of Hitler's insanity against the Jews was *The Diary of Anne Frank*. *The Diary* was and is a powerful document, for it is a peep into the world of moral madness as seen through the eyes of a young girl when she and her family were still fugitives hiding out in Holland. But *Night* plunges readers headfirst into the cauldron of Nazi wickedness, through the eyes of an adolescent boy torn from his Romanian home and transported with his family into Auschwitz in railroad cattle cars. Wiesel's book is only 109 pages in its current paperback form,[3] but what it lacks in length it makes up for in sustained moral power. Here is a passage that sums up what Wiesel accomplished both in *Night* and in his subsequent works:

> Never shall I forget that night, the first night in camp, which has turned my life into one long night, seven times cursed and seven times sealed. Never shall I forget that smoke. Never shall I forget the little faces of the children whose bodies I saw turned into wreaths of smoke beneath a silent blue sky.
>
> Never shall I forget those flames which consumed my faith forever.
>
> Never shall I forget that nocturnal silence which deprived me, for all eternity, of the desire to live. Never shall I forget those moments which murdered my God and my soul and turned my dreams to dust. Never shall I forget these things, even if I am condemned to live as long as God Himself. Never.[4]

When Wiesel first offered the book to New York publishers in the late 1950's, it was turned down flat by twenty of them. It was too sad, said some. Nobody wanted to read about such things, said others. As for the author, he was an unknown Romanian Jewish refugee from Nazi Germany working in New York for an Israeli newspaper. "We don't want one-book authors," said yet another publisher. "He probably won't write anything else."[5]

New York publishers are sometimes wrong. To date, Wiesel has written some thirty-five books, including novels, essays, plays, a cantata, lengthy interviews, and a volume of memoirs. In the process, he has become not just a distinguished novelist, man of letters, observer of the world scene, and chronicler of unspeakable evil. As both a writer and a person he has forced people to look more closely at the nature of human evil.

Wiesel has never stopped asking why people are indifferent to the suffering of different human communities when such suffering is deliberately and malevolently imposed on them by others. He championed the cause of Soviet Jews when few in the U.S. or the rest of the world paid any attention to their plight. He spoke up for the condition of Biafrans in Nigeria's grueling civil war in 1967–70. He pleaded for the Misquito Indians of Nicaragua, the victims of apartheid in South Africa, Cambodian refugees from the Khmer Communist killing fields, the Bosnians under siege in Sarajevo. Often he has gone to remote places of privation with food and medicine. Other times he has gathered teenagers who have been traumatized by wars and hatred in strife-filled locations like Northern Ireland, the Middle East, or the Balkans. He did this in Venice in 1995.

But it was not as an organizer of human relief that Wiesel was the voice heard around the world. It was as an advocate of the human conscience. I Ic had become, said the Norwegian Nobel Prize chairman when Wiesel was named 1986's winner of the Prize for Peace, "a messenger to mankind," someone who spoke up for "peace, atonement, and human dignity."

In 1987, within months of being awarded the Nobel, Wiesel founded the Elie Wiesel Foundation for Humanity, an organization dedicated to bringing people together, to examining what constitutes fanaticism or hatred. It is a measure of his stature as this "messenger to mankind" that when his foundation organized a conference in Oslo in 1990 to examine the nature of hate around the world, participants who showed up included French President François Mitterand, former U.S. president Jimmy Carter, president of Czechoslovakia (and former dissident) Václav Havel, and just-released South African political prisoner Nelson Mandela. What did they see in Wiesel? Not just a Jew who had reflected profoundly on the crime of all crimes against the Jews, but a man who wanted to give back to the world the insights into the human condition he had gained in that reflection.

He has at least twice spoken out publicly in the presence of U.S. presidents on issues that have burned within his own conscience. In 1985, at a White House ceremony, he politely but firmly asked the incumbent U.S. president, Ronald Reagan, not to visit in West Germany a military cemetery where soldiers from the Nazi SS had been buried. Reagan went ahead with his plans anyway, for reasons we shall look at in the pages that follow. In 1993, at the opening of the U.S. Holocaust Memorial Museum in Washington, Wiesel challenged another incumbent president, Bill Clinton, not to permit America to stand idly by as the Balkans bled to death. Clinton anguished publicly over this, dithered for another two years, and finally committed America to sending troops into Bosnia to enforce a cease-fire.

Wiesel achieved his moral stature not by what he organized, but by what he continually brought to remembrance through his writings. He has been called "the spiritual archivist of the Holocaust." But *archivist* is a dry and dusty word. It implies someone who merely compiles information, in this case, information about the Holocaust. What has preoccupied Wiesel throughout his adult life is not the assemblage of facts but the function within civilization of human memory itself. "To be a Jew is to remember," he has said. "[The French philosopher Jean-Paul] Sartre used to say that human beings are condemned to be free. I would paraphrase that and say, we are condemned to save the world with our memories. The question is: How? In other words, how do we manage to humanize destiny?"[6]

That is a question to which no human being, and certainly no society in general, can give a definitive answer. Wiesel has nevertheless attempted to force people from widely different backgrounds and faiths to think about the question for themselves. Many of his books are novels, semibiographical stories that deal with situations he became familiar with as both a Holocaust survivor and a foreign correspondent covering major world news. But in both the novels and his nonfiction writings there are profound moral dilemmas, questions about humankind, about God, and about the nature of evil wrenched from situations that never provide simple answers. "I attach more importance to questions than to answers," he has said. "For only the questions can be shared."[7]

But the questioner's experience can be shared by only a tiny, and indeed dwindling, group of people. A question about the solar system might be banal when posed by an average astronomy student. When it is offered by someone who has walked on the surface of the moon, it has more substance. Thus, by analogy, so it is with Wiesel. Questions posed about evil by someone who lived in the very center of its most orgiastic form command more attention than the same queries posed by others.

His questions are piercing: Where was God during the Holocaust? Can Jews ever again think of God in the same terms as they did before Auschwitz? Can Christians? Could God be both all-powerful and all-merciful and permit such atrocities to be committed against His own people? How could the Holocaust take place in one of the most educationally and culturally "advanced" nations of Europe? Why were most Germans, at least nominally Christian, so unwilling or unable to counter Hitler's anti-Semitic rantings even before the Final Solution was embarked upon? What role did Christian theological objections to the Jews play in the climate that led to Hitler? Why was the Vatican silent when the Jews were rounded up for death and the pope knew full well what was happening? What does the behavior of so-called Christians have to say about the Christian claim that Jesus was and is the Messiah long awaited by the Jews? When will the Messiah come?

"Through his writings," Wiesel's biographer, Robert McAfee Brown, writes,

> Wiesel has kept his conscience, and ours, finely tuned. It is danger-
> ous to read him, for he shows us things we would rather not see and
> are often infinitely clever in avoiding. But it is important to read him,
> for we must see those things, lest we repeat them ourselves.[8]

What is extraordinary about Wiesel is not that he writes incessantly about the Holocaust. He does not. Indeed, *Night* is his only work, and it is a very brief one, that describes his own vision of hell once he had de-scended into it. His other novels and writings allude to the Event or to its consequences in the lives of individuals and of nations. He deals with political activity in *Dawn* (1960), suicide in *The Accident* (1961), madness in *The Town Beyond the Wall* (1962), faith in *The Gates of the Forest* (1964), and the Jewish return to Zion in *A Beggar in Jerusalem* (1968).

Wiesel has said that he sees all of these works as fanning out from the terrible human reality that is contained in his first book, which of course is not fiction at all, but an autobiography. What Wiesel has somehow achieved is a continuity of moral memory in both his life and his writings that confronts people with the reality of human evil. In that sense, Wiesel is a Great Soul above all because of his understanding of remembrance and of the role that it plays—and must always play—in the civilizing, or as he would say, the "humanizing" of the human condition.

"Remembering is a noble and necessary act," Wiesel told his Nobel Peace Prize audience when he delivered his acceptance lecture in December 1986.

> The call of memory, the call to memory, reaches us from the very
> dawn of history. No commandment figures so frequently, so insis-
> tently, in the Bible. It is incumbent upon us to remember the good
> we have received, and the evil we have suffered. New Year's day, Rosh
> Hashana, is also called Yom Hazikaron, the day of memory. On that
> day, the day of universal judgment, man appeals to God to remem-
> ber: our salvation depends on it. If God wishes to remember our
> suffering, all will be well; if He refuses, all will be lost. Thus, the

rejection of memory becomes a divine curse, one that would doom us to repeat past disasters, past wars.[9]

"Ani maamin ve eviat ha Meshiah" ("I believe in the coming of the Messiah"), Wiesel learned to pray as a little boy in Romania, reciting the prayer of Maimonides, the ancient Jewish sage from Spain. He still believes in that. But he does so through the thick veil of remembrance.

A SHTETL CALLED SIGHET

Elie Wiesel was born in Sighet, a small, predominantly Jewish town in the Transylvanian region of Romania, on September 30, 1928. He himself has called the town a *shtetl*, which is Yiddish for a "Jewish small town." With a population of some twenty thousand, Sighet was physically closer to Budapest in Hungary (165 miles) than to Bucharest (200 miles), and in 1940 it was ceded to Hungary under Nazi coercion, only to be handed back to Romania in 1944 under pressure from the advancing Soviets.

Wiesel's parents were Shlomo and Sarah Wiesel, deeply devout and observant Jews. His father ran a small store in the town and was not at home much. Elie looked up to him and admired him deeply, but felt a certain distance from him. "I never really knew my father," he has said. "It hurts to admit that, but it would hurt even more if I deluded myself. The truth is I knew little of the man I loved most in the world, the man whose merest glance could stir me."[10] Saturday, the sabbath, or *shabbat* in Hebrew, was the only day of the week he spent much time with his father, and he loved to go with him to the synagogue. Father and son would go hand in hand to the services, but if another worshiper came to greet Shlomo, the father would drop his son's hand. "Did my father have any idea how much that hurt?" he asked himself later on.[11]

Elie seems to have felt emotionally much closer to his mother, and even her brief absences from home to serve in the family store for a few hours appear to have left him feeling lonely, even rejected. "I search my mind for my earliest memory and I see a little boy siting on his bed, calling for his mother," he has written. "I would count the minutes that I was separated from my mother."[12] He had two elder sisters, Hilda and Bea, both of whom were to survive Auschwitz along with him (though he was separated from them the entire time of his imprisonment) and a little sister, Tsiporah, who perished in the gas chambers, along with Elie's mother. The entire family had a special affection for the sweet-natured little girl, whom they nicknamed Tsipouka. Her loss seems to have left a hole in Wiesel's heart bigger than most of the others.

The other member of Elie's family who had a profound impact on the young boy as he grew up in Sighet was Dodye Feig, his maternal grandfather. A farmer and a Hasid, Feig was held almost in reverence by the Jews of the region. He actually lived in a small rural community a few hours' walk from Sighet, but he was known far beyond it.

The Hasidic movement of Judaism had been founded in the mid-eighteenth century by Israel ben Eliezer, later to be known as Baal Shem Tov (Master of the Good Name). Hasidism was and is a pietistic movement that sought to counter the more formalistic Jewish tradition of rabbinical teaching and legal observances with a spontaneous life of prayer and worship from the heart. Piety, it stressed, was superior to learning; all human beings could come closer to God if they had a warm and trusting heart, regardless of their knowledge or ignorance. Hasidism from its inception has stressed fervor, spontaneity, sometimes shouting and dancing, as forms of legitimate worship. Today, Hasidic Jews in both Israel and other countries—including especially the U.S.—are easily recognizable through their wearing of long side-curls, beards, large black or sometimes fur hats, and frock-coat-length suits.

Hasidic Jews have tended to be more open to mystical interpretations of their faith, and, indeed, to belief in the miraculous powers of *tzaddikim*, or pious holy men supposedly able both to intercede in prayer with God more effectively than other Jews and at times able to effect healing cures. Wiesel did not see his grandfather often, but the times he spent with him had a powerful impact upon the young boy's life. "People loved him for his kindness," Wiesel has written.

> Whenever he came to spend Shabbat with us, the holy day would become double holy. Dressed in his silk caftan and shtreimel [a wide-brimmed fur hat worn by Hasidim] he would linger on our doorstep to welcome with song the angels who protect the children and the joys of Israel; and he would sing with so much love and so much conviction that I would hear a rustling of wings above my head. He radiated happiness, and so did I.[13]

Today, though he does not dress as a strict Hasidic Jew, Wiesel often describes himself as "a Hasid." The self-description is revealing, for it shows a side of the man that, while in no way critical of traditional Jewish learning as a vehicle of personal piety, does not regard even biblical and rabbinical knowledge in and of itself as its sole vehicle.

Elie's mother hoped that he might be a learned rabbi with a strong secular education. His first school in Sighet introduced him almost magically to the joys of the Hebrew language and the Hebrew Bible. "When I read the first word [of Genesis] aloud—Breshit, 'in the beginning'—I felt transported into an enchanted universe," he has written. The teacher himself seemed to share the same enchantment and imparted to his charges a deep reverence for the Hebrew written word. "'It was with the twenty-two letters of the aleph-beth that God created the world,' said the teacher, who seemed very old at the time to the young Elie, but probably was just a midde-aged man. 'Take care of them and they will take care of you.'"[14] Elie devoured books, both sacred and secular, with a zeal that isolated him from his classmates. He did not play soccer or other sports. In fact, he would bribe his peers for their approval by handing over to them both his school lunch and gift items from his family whenever they came his way.

Then something happened at the age of eight that seemed to set him apart in his mother's eyes and awoke within his own mind the sense that there might be something special about his future. A venerable Jewish Hasid, Rabbi Israel of Wishnitz, came to Sighet, in effect to hold court among his followers. Families came to him for counsel and to receive some sort of blessing from his presence. Elie was left alone in conversation with the white-bearded man for several minutes. He does not recall what was said. But when his mother went in by herself to speak with the rabbi, she came out distraught and in tears. Not until years later did Wiesel learn that the devout old man had prophesied that Elie would become *gadol b'Israel* (literally "a great man in Israel," but meaning a great man among the Jewish people), but that neither he nor Wiesel's mother would live to see that day.

In Sighet, life revolved around the Sabbath, which started well before sundown on Friday afternoon. Stores closed, people prepared their houses and the shabbat meal and scurried to make preparations for the meticulously observed day of rest and worship. These were precious and intimate times for Jewish families, whether rich or poor. "When I shall have

forgotten everything else," Wiesel wrote, "my memory will still retain
the atmosphere of holiday, of serenity pervading even the poorest houses;
the white tablecloth, the candles, the meticulously combed little girls, the
men on their way to synagogue."[15]

The Wiesel family was not at all wealthy: When cherries were bought
to be eaten at home, for example, each member of the family would receive just ten. Yet the family prepared a cauldron of soup in the yard for
beggars each Wednesday, market day, so that no one approaching the house
for help would go away hungry. "I'd rather feed someone whose pockets
are full than send someone away on an empty stomach," Wiesel's father
told him. What he meant was that he worried less about being taken advantage of than failing to extend charity when it was truly needed. For
Wiesel, memories of these precious and reverent times with his family,
enjoying traditional Jewish shabbat services, seem to have become a filter
through which much of his observation of both the world at large and of
Jewish life in general have been viewed. "I left Sighet," he wrote later, "but
it refuses to leave me."[16]

Anti-Semitism was a fact of life throughout most of Eastern Europe
in Wiesel's childhood, even before Hitler ravaged the entire Continent
with his particular bacillus of hatred and murder. It is true that in Poland
and perhaps other countries there were instances of deep mutual respect
between individual neighbors within the Jewish and the Gentile communities—the case of the young Karol Wojtyla is worth recalling—but it was
not the overall pattern.

In Romania, young men, even Wiesel's non-Jewish classmates, sometimes donned masks on the eve of Christmas and Easter and wandered
the streets in search of some lone Jew to insult or beat up with whips. The
Jews of Sighet accepted such adversities within the normal patina of Jewish life. "If drunks insulted us, cursing us for having 'profaned the Host,'
'poisoned the wells,' or 'killed the Lord,' it was only natural, to be expected," Wiesel wrote later. Yet he would often ask himself, Why do they
hate us? Why do they persecute us?[17]

Not all of the Christians of Sighet behaved this way. An extraordinary
exception was their Romanian maid, Maria, who spoke Yiddish as well as
Romanian and was well versed in Jewish ways. Later, she risked her life in
an effort to protect the Wiesels from deportation to Germany. But Wiesel
himself had no understanding of or, indeed, interest in Christianity at the

time, as he has openly acknowledged. He did not know that Christianity had actually grown directly out of Judaism, or that the God whom Christians worshiped through Jesus Christ was actually the God also of Abraham, Isaac, and Jacob: the God of Israel.

THE DISTANT RUMBLING OF THE NIGHT

By the time Wiesel was ten, traditional Christian anti-Semitism had given way to a much darker threat, the rise of Nazism in Germany. The West's betrayal of Czechoslovakia in 1938 had introduced the word *Munich* into the common vocabulary of fear and betrayal. As refugees from Czechoslovakia in 1938, and then a year later from Poland, began to rumble in carts into those European countries where Jews were still at least nominally free, the approaching tsunami of destruction began to cast its shadow even on the orderly life of the shtetl.

Many simply could not believe that the Germans, who had been so civilized in World War I in contrast to the brutal and traditionally anti-Semitic Russians, could possibly have absorbed a culture of death into their nation. Many Jews, faced with the approaching rumble of war, retreated into a haven of messianic expectation. "Of course, we all awaited the Messiah," Wiesel wrote. "It would all work out in the end. A little patience." His mother was quite specific as she rocked him to sleep at night. The Messiah would come and save the Jews from the anti-Semites. The ancient fears of Jews of their host nations would once and for all be stilled.

But the fears got worse. Polish refugees had already arrived in the town exhausted and grief-stricken, with horrifying tales of the brutality of the invading and occupying Germans. In 1940, after the Hungarian-speaking portion of Transylvania in which Sighet was located was handed over to Hungary, Jews who could not document their Hungarian citizenship were handed over to Nazi-held Polish Galicia, there to be swallowed up by the thrashing Nazi death machine. Amazingly, one Jew escaped, Moshe the Beadle, as he has become known in all of Wiesel's writings. He was in fact a real person, named Moishele. He told of Jewish deportees to Poland being slaughtered and buried naked in ditches, and of the insane brutality of the German occupiers.

But nobody believed him. Surely he had become mad, everyone said.

The Germans couldn't possibly behave in that manner. Wiesel listened to Moishele's tales wide-eyed and fascinated, but equally skeptical.

Life, meanwhile, somehow went on its appointed rounds in Sighet, even as war crept ever closer. France fell in 1940 and soon the entire continent lay prostrate under the Nazi heel. Wiesel went through the traditional Jewish passage to adulthood, the bar mitzvah, when he was thirteen. He was eagerly drawn to the Bible as a source of knowledge and wisdom, and indeed filled notebooks with commentaries on his readings. But as the teenage years drew upon him, he also found himself torn by conflicting and agonizing needs. At one level, his awakening sexuality was torturing him with fantasies derived from looking at movie posters or eyeing a passing pretty girl on the street. At another level, his intense desire for spiritual purity was drawing him ever deeper into Jewish mysticism. "To purify my spirit I resorted to prayer," he wrote, "a common and sometimes effective device."[18]

Prayer, in fact, and an intense desire for closeness to God, were consuming more and more of Wiesel's life. "I was so obsessed with God that I forgot his creation," he wrote. "Was it Ernest Renan who wrote that the Greeks had reason, the Romans power, and the Jews the sense of God? I sought God everywhere."[19] As he buried himself in Jewish books, he found himself more and more attracted to the Kabala, the mystical Jewish tradition that has at times veered directly into the occult. For this reason, though the Kabala has introduced the idea, embraced by the Hasidic tradition, that God can be approached directly in a personal experience, it has at times been vigorously resisted by Orthodox rabbis as potentially heretical, pantheistic, and indeed demonic. Partly out of fear of what the Kabala could do in a person's life, a tradition grew that Jews should be initiated into it by someone who himself was an initiate. In theory, this would protect a student from taking wrong and possibly dangerous directions within Kabalistic mysticism.

Wiesel's curiosity about the mystical, and indeed the occult, was no mere vicarious fascination, though teenage interest in the forbidden and the dangerous may well have contributed to his interest. An important strand of Kabalistic tradition held that through the conjuring of certain names and phrases, the Messiah Himself could be induced to come to earth sooner than was planned. Wiesel plunged into works on astrology, parapsychology, hypnotism, and magic in Hebrew, Aramaic, and Hungarian. But he took a more decisive step too. He found a Kabalist in Sighet whom he simply identifies as Kalman. This man, for Wiesel a "master of mysticism," was himself an initiate and agreed, after persuasion, to meet with Elie and two companions of the same age to follow the pathway into the power of divine mysteries.

According to Wiesel, the four of them met frequently in 1943 and 1944, sometimes "every evening." They fasted twice a week during the day to prepare themselves for the mystical journey, and devoured every Kabalistic text they could lay their hands on that would, supposedly, aid them in their dangerous journey. Wiesel's father and others in the town became alarmed at what was happening. "Eschatology was a forbidden domain, a minefield," Wiesel admits, looking back. "One did not trifle with the fundamental mysteries of Creation and annihilation with impunity."[20]

Indeed not. After six months of intensive study, repetition of incantations, and ascetic exercises, the oldest of the three students, Yiddele, fell inexplicably ill. He lost his power of speech, his will to live, and subsided into what seemed to be a near-catatonic state. Psychologists and neurologists were consulted, prayers were said, but to no avail. Yiddele never recovered. After another interval, the second student, Sruli, fell ill, with similar symptoms.

Yet Wiesel, obstinate and obsessed with speeding the arrival of the Messiah, continued. After several months, he and Kalman were clearly entering a dangerous zone of occult practice, even though their motives were admirable: They wanted to speed up the coming of the Messiah to save the Jews of Europe. On the night of Tishah-b'Ab (a day of fasting in memory of the destruction of the temple) 1943, Wiesel went to Kalman's house and stayed up all night with him in study and repetition of Kabalistic incantations. It turned into a night of crisis and terror. "I felt a terrible force pulling at me," Wiesel recalls,

> dragging me down one precipice, then another. Near four in the morning I thought I saw a being with a hidden face chained to an enormous dead tree. As in the tale of Rabbi Joseph dell Reina [a Kabalistic initiate of the fifteenth century], a thousand dogs were baying, spitting flames, but the being remained motionless, his head supporting the heavens. 'It's him!' I cried. 'Master, it's him! Let's free him!'

> I awoke drenched in sweat, delirious, unable to tell dream from real-
> ity, not knowing who, or where, I was. My master sat on the floor in
> apparent despair, his body racked by sobs, hitting his head against the
> wall. At that moment I felt madness lurking, menacing us both. . . .[21]

Wiesel says that he was sure that had the Germans not entered Sighet
the following spring in 1944, he would have suffered the same fate as his
two comrades. "Thus it was the killers who 'saved' me," he says now
with deep irony. "Woe unto me, it is to them that I owe the fact that I
was spared."[22]

But "spared" for what?

It was on March 19, 1944, Wiesel says, that the first sinking sense of
what was about to happen to the Jewish community of Sighet came upon
the citizens of the shtetl. A man burst into the synagogue with the news
that the Germans had crossed the Romanian frontier and were beginning
to occupy the country. It was true. German officers and soldiers had entered the town.

At first they seemed to behave politely, making their beds and giving candy to the children. The attitude of most of Sighet's Jews was
straightforward: How could these people possibly be planning anything wicked? Only one man countered the overall sense of calm with
a shrillness that jarred on everyone's nerves: Moshe the Beadle. At the
Wiesel's Passover Seder a few days after the German arrival, he offered to share with Shlomo Wiesel and the rest of the family the terrible secrets of Nazi atrocities that he had personally seen in Poland.
He was forbidden to speak. No one wanted to hear this sort of news,
whether it was truthful or not.

Before long, the Germans ordered the Jews of the town to wear a yellow star on their clothing. It was the beginning of the process of first
identifying, then isolating, then rounding up the townsfolk who were Jews.
Jewish stores and businesses were closed and Jews were not permitted to
travel. Hungarian gendarmes added to the population's misery by raiding
private houses and confiscating precious items. Finally, two ghettos were
created for the town, a larger one in which the majority of the Jews were
to live, and a smaller one a distance away. Homes that had belonged to
families for generations had to be abandoned. There was desperate talk
among some of attempting to escape to Palestine. Wiesel himself even

believed that the Messiah would come and lead the Jews in a triumphant final battle there against Gog and Magog.

But in the end, nobody wanted to do anything truly radical. After all, "reliable" Jewish sources had indicated that the only inconvenience would be the process of relocation to some point "in the East." It is astonishing that, two years after it was known by the Allies what Hitler had already undertaken against the Jews who were under his control, there was no systematic effort by the British or the Americans to warn the remaining parts of Europe's Jewish community as a whole.

Early in May 1944, two high-ranking German officers came into town. One of them, Wiesel believes, may have been Adolf Eichmann himself, the notorious administrator of the "Final Solution" to eliminate the Jews by mass execution. In 1962, when Wiesel, by then a journalist, was attending in Jerusalem the trial of Adolf Eichmann, he became convinced that he recognized him from some previous encounter. It could only have been in Sighet or in Auschwitz itself.

Events began to accelerate. Street by street, the larger makeshift ghetto was now being abandoned as the Germans ordered Jews to march in groups to locations where they could be put on board cattle cars leading out of Romania. Not a person suspected that the cattle cars would not lead to comfortable relocation camps but to the factory of death itself.

As the sun climbed higher in the sky in May, assigned groups of Jews were ordered to assemble in the street and await the command to move out on foot. They were not permitted to move into the shade or return even briefly to their homes for final errands. The Wiesel family, including little Tsipouka, tried to provide some refreshment by moving among the families assigned for transportation with pitchers of water and other refreshments. As the large ghetto emptied rapidly, there was a sharp knock on the shuttered and sealed window of the house where the Wiesels were staying, at the edge of the ghetto. To open the window or not? They hesitated for a moment, then laboriously pried the shutters open, only to find no one there.

The following night, they heard the knock again. This time, they saw who it was: Maria, the Wiesel's Christian maid. She had somehow found her way through the barbed wire and other obstacles intended to seal the ghetto off completely from the rest of the community. Even in broad daylight she had ignored the strict prohibitions against entry into the ghetto by outsiders and arrived loaded down with cheese, fruit, and eggs for the family. But now her mission was different, urgent, and surely the last time she would have an opportunity to spend any time with the family that had treated her so well.

Maria had an appeal to make. Would they come with her to a hut in the mountains where they could all stay and be safe? There was room enough for everyone, she said, and she knew a way they could safely use to reach the hut. There were no Germans in the area where the hut was, nor any of their supporters among the Hungarian or Romanian population.

It was surely an appealing option. By May 1944, the sound of artillery fire just a dozen or so miles away in the hills could be heard, a sign of the advancing Soviet army. To have hidden out in the countryside until the Germans themselves were pushed out of Romania would certainly have ensured the safety of the Wiesels. The family discussion must have been anguished and tense as Maria waited for their response, but in the end, they decided not to go. Maria begged them to come with her. But they responded as a family: Families should stay together and the whole Jewish community should stay together. After all, no one had yet heard the names Auschwitz, or Dachau, or Bergen-Belsen, or Ravensbrück. Maria may not have known, but she probably guessed, as a handful of European Christians did, what would happen to the Jews when they fell into Hitler's hands. "If other Christians had acted like her, the trains rolling toward the unknown would have been less crowded. . . . It was a simple and devout Christian woman who saved her town's honor."[23]

On May 16, 1944, the Wiesels and the last remaining Jews of the larger Sighet ghetto were moved out, temporarily at first to a smaller ghetto, but then, inevitably, to the railroad station. There the transports of death were waiting, the cattle cars bringing into Auschwitz from the farthest corners of Europe at times as many as ten thousand Jews a day. The Wiesels, along with hundreds of others, boarded the train in early June. The cattle cars were sealed, and one person in each car was arbitrarily told that he was in charge: If anyone should somehow escape, he would personally be shot. Toilet facilities consisted of a bucket concealed behind a makeshift cloth to preserve a modicum of privacy. The deportees were jammed so tightly, about eighty to each car, that breathing itself was difficult. The stench of human waste, sweat, and fear hung over everyone. Only those near the windows had any access to fresh air, offering those lucky enough to be next to them glimpses of the rolling Transylvanian hills slipping past. Most slept standing up, since it was only by taking turns that any could sit down at all.

"REMEMBER IT FOREVER. ENGRAVE IT ON YOUR MINDS. YOU ARE AT AUSCHWITZ."

The deportees had been under the impression that they would be relocated to a camp somewhere in Hungary. But when the train stopped at a station on the Hungarian-Czech border, it became obvious that this was not the case at all. In the middle of the third night, one of the prisoners, a woman called Mrs. Schächter who had apparently lost her mind early in the journey after being separated from her husband, suddenly let out a piercing scream. "Fire! I can see a fire! I can see a fire!" As everyone awoke from their dozing, or even from a deep sleep in a standing position, those near the window tried to see if there was anything out there. The sky was black. People tried to calm her. But she went on, screaming and moaning for a long time. "Jews, listen to me!" she begged them, as Wiesel has described the scene in his novel *Night*, "I can see a fire! There are huge flames! It is a furnace!"[24] Now fear was replaced by anger and young people began to hit her, and then to try to gag her.

What had she "seen"? No one in Sighet—except perhaps Moshe the Beadle—had even heard of Auschwitz or the crematoria there whose flames, gushing out of tall chimneys, consumed every day the living and the dead, even small children thrown in alive by the SS guards like offerings to an insatiable Moloch. Looking back, Wiesel was to write, "It was as though she were possessed by an evil spirit which spoke from the depths of her being."[25] "Life in the cattle cars was the death of my adolescence," Wiesel wrote later.[26] He was only fifteen.

On the fourth day, the train finally stopped at a station with barbed wire, visible through the windows, stretching into infinity: Auschwitz, or Oswiecim, in Polish, located within Poland, but under the absolute control of the military guardians of the Third Reich. It was a gigantic combination of three camps—sometimes referred to as Auschwitz 1, Auschwitz 2, and Auschwitz 3—where Jews, gypsies, oppositionists, Catholic priests, but above all Jews and more Jews were brought daily for extermination. Some deaths took place within minutes of arrival in the gas chambers of Auschwitz-Birkenau, the destination of the trains, as pellets of Zyklon B gas were dropped through a roof aperture onto the floor. Others came within months as conditions of slave labor wore men and women by the thousands into sickness or death. On the station platform of Auschwitz-Birkenau, a curt order from German officers determined instantly the life expectancy of each cattle-car-load of new arrivals. Men to the left, women to the right. For the last time, Wiesel caught a glimpse of his mother and little Tsipouka as they were marched off to the gas chambers.

As the men were ordered to head off in groups of five to the center of a large square, Wiesel found himself approaching a black-clad SS officer with a monocle in one eye and a conductor's baton in one hand. "How old are you?" he asked Wiesel. "Eighteen," the youth replied, obeying the instruction of another prisoner not to reveal his real age. He responded to further questions that he was a farmer and that he was in good health. Unbeknownst to them, Wiesel and his father had just been spared selection by the infamous Dr. Joseph Mengele, the Nazi physician whose medical experiments have made his name synonymous with the diabolical perversion of medical science for evil experiments.

But the ordeal of the first day's entry into a living purgatory, a tribulation never before known even in the tragedy-spotted history of the Jews, was still not over. The slow march in groups of five now headed toward a ditch from which flames were roaring skyward. Through the whirls of heat haze Wiesel then saw something that has seared his memory for life: truckloads of children and babies being dumped into the inferno. Someone in the slowly marching crowd started reciting the Kaddish, the Jewish prayer for the dead. Were they reciting it in advance, so to speak, for themselves? That was the impression Wiesel left in *Night*, whose most famous passage, cited at the beginning of this chapter: "Never shall I forget that night, the first night in camp," begins just after this description of his family's arrival in Auschwitz.[27] Those words are now inscribed on the wall of one of the exhibit floors of the U.S. Holocaust Memorial Museum in Washington, D.C.

For eight months Wiesel and his father somehow survived as slave laborers in Auschwitz, moving from one camp to another in the huge Auschwitz complex, mercifully being spared the more arduous work like hauling gassed or other dead bodies to the crematoria (one young man had to throw his own father's cadaver into the furnace), enduring shouts, threats, beatings, the shaving of all body hair, roll calls, and a calorie intake that in a few months reduced a healthy man to a living skeleton. On his arm, as on the arms of all the concentration camp prisoners, was his SS-supplied number, A-7713. "Remember this," an SS officer told the new arrivals at one point.

> Remember it forever. Engrave it into your minds. You are at Auschwitz. And Auschwitz is not a convalescent home. It's a concentration camp. Here, you have got to work. If not, you will go straight to the furnace. To the crematory. Work or the crematory—the choice is in your hands.[28]

Wiesel did remember it forever, did engrave it upon his mind. Some forty-two years later it was because he took to heart the words of an SS officer, in a way that evil man had never intended, that he won the Nobel Peace Prize.

Why was it that Wiesel survived and thousands of fellow Jews from his own town perished? "Logically I shouldn't have survived," he has written. "Sickly, timid, fearful, and lacking all resourcefulness, I never did anything to stay alive." He did not want to die, yet neither he nor his father consciously thought that they would somehow live through until liberation. "Was it the will to testify—and therefore the need to survive—that helped me through? Did I survive in order to combat forgetting?" He admits today that he does not know, that he certainly had no sense of special mission or calling at the time other than to stay close to his father.[29]

One day, along with thousands of inmates, he was forced to watch the public execution of three other prisoners who had been caught after the Gestapo discovered a stock of arms being prepared for an eventual uprising. Two of the men were adults, the third a teenage boy. There had been several public hangings that Wiesel had been forced to watch with the other prisoners, but this one was different. The boy had a delicate-looking face, and after the three chairs on which the doomed men had been standing with their nooses on were kicked over, the lad was so light that he twitched and tossed under the rope for perhaps half an hour. One by one, the assembled prisoner-witnesses had to march by the scene. The boy's eyes were still alive when it became Wiesel's turn to pass beneath him.

"Where is God now?" a man behind Wiesel asked. "Where is He now?"

Wiesel felt a voice inside him answer. "Here He is—He is hanging here on this gallows. . . ."[30]

For many Jews in Auschwitz that thought came to them in blinding rushes, not as piety (God suffering as a human being), nor as a poetic reflection of man's inhumanity to man. Wiesel found himself the youngest witness to an amazing "trial" one evening in which three fellow concentration camp inmates, rabbinical scholars, actually "sued"—to use Wiesel's own words—God. They asked Him to answer why He had allowed such indescribable suffering to happen to His own people. Later, Wiesel developed this profound and anguished questioning in a play, *The Trial of God*, which transposes the "trial" he himself witnessed to a Jewish community in Shamgorod, the Ukraine, after an actual pogrom in 1649.

Wiesel's faith in God while in Auschwitz was stretched and torn perhaps more than is possible to happen to a person without that person becoming an atheist. But even the inmate scholars who "tried" God and found Him "guilty" proceeded to pray after their meeting. Wiesel himself, along with others in the camp, would sacrifice his desperately needed sleep in order to observe Jewish prayers morning and evening in one of the Auschwitz blocks. "Yes, we practiced religion even in a death camp," he wrote. "I said my prayers every day." It was only later that a true crisis of trust in God arose in his heart.[31]

As the months dragged on, Wiesel's father, Shlomo, grew weaker. The cruel winter of 1944–45 came on, and with it more deaths in the camp from starvation or exhaustion. In January, Wiesel was faced with a terrible personal dilemma. He was weak with fever and a dangerously swollen knee. If he went into the infirmary to report it, he might be treated humanely and the knee cured. But he might also be sent off without pity to Birkenau, that part of Auschwitz where the gas chambers were.

He took his chance and was actually treated kindly by an inmate doctor who told him he would live. After an operation, his knee swiftly recovered and his fever left him.

By then it was January 1945 and the Nazi regime was approaching its death throes. Russian armies were just a few miles away, though to the inmates they seemed impossibly slow in liberating the camp. Chaos began to mount as the SS made the decision to evacuate as many of the living prisoners as they could to the West, out of Poland into the heart of Germany. On the night of January 19, block by block, the prisoners were ordered out into the snowy night, swollen grotesquely from their skeletal size by layer after layer of extra clothing, whatever they could find to keep out the night cold. They marched for hours, the SS guards methodically shooting anyone who could not keep up, anyone who dropped out of line for even a few seconds. All through the night the survivors shuffled mechanically onward, braced to endure the fatigue and cold by the period reports of rifles and small arms finishing off their comrades.

The journey west, some of it by train, but most of it on foot, went on for several days until the surviving inmates stumbled into another concentration camp in the heart of Germany, Buchenwald, not far from the elegant town of Weimar. It was here, on January 29, that Elie's father Shlomo finally died of dysentery, starvation, and exhaustion. He and Elie had somehow stuck together for the seven months they had been in Auschwitz and had even survived the nightmarish evacuation to the West. But though he was seriously ill, the medical staff considered him too far gone to bother trying to keep alive. Even in his last few hours, animal-like neighbors on the boarded bunks stole from him the last crumbs of bread and soup. At night he was still barely alive, but by dawn, when Wiesel awoke he had died and they already had dragged his body away. "I did not weep," Wiesel wrote in *Night*, "and it pained me that I could not weep. But I had no more tears."[32]

In a strange no-man's-land between life and death, Elie Wiesel somehow went through the motions of living between the end of January and the end of the Buchenwald nightmare. Early in April, the SS began evacuating the camp, some ten thousand prisoners moved each day, none of them surviving. On April 10, Wiesel found himself in the twenty thousand remaining. Evacuation of all was promised for the following day. Then it suddenly happened. On the morning of April 11, an underground movement, that had existed in the camp long before the Auschwitz evacuees arrived, rose up and attacked the SS. By noon, the camp was free. Early in the evening, the first American military units had also arrived. They were stunned, horrified, and disgusted by what they saw. One sergeant was so outraged he both wept and cursed at the sight. For the surviving Jews, Wiesel wrote, the curses on his lips became "holy words."[33]

Wiesel was seriously ill with intestinal problems almost immediately after liberation from Buchenwald, probably the result of extreme hunger and privation followed by precipitate eating. After he had spent several days in the former SS hospital of the camp, he had recovered enough to make an important decision: where to go next.

THE TALMUD AND THE LEFT BANK

As far as he knew, his entire family had been wiped out. He had personally watched his father's life slip away. He had seen his mother and Tsipouka being led off to the gas chambers. There had been no word from Bea and Hilda, his elder sisters, and each new list of survivors brought into Buchenwald from other parts of the defeated Reich turned up no reference to them. Some men from Sighet proposed that the survivors make their way back to Romania, at least partly to experience the joy of tormenting their former persecutors among the non-Jews. But Wiesel had no desire to join them. Instead, he found himself part of a group of some four hundred orphaned children headed for Belgium. At the last minute, with the intervention of France's new leader, General de Gaulle, the train was diverted to France instead.

The orphans ranged in age from around five to the late teens. Prematurely aged, still numb with the trauma of their experience, they watched as Frenchmen and -women came to the stations en route and offered them bread, café au lait, and cookies. Still fiercely observant of kosher rules, Wiesel turned down the hot meals offered.

From 1945 until 1947, Elie was in various homes in France organized by a Jewish group, the Children's Rescue Society (O.S.E. after the French initials) learning French, getting used to normal life in a free society, and trying to discover who he was and what he wanted to do. He remained devoutly orthodox in his Judaism, saying his prayers every day and attending synagogue. But the innocence of his early Sighet years had been burned up forever by Auschwitz. From now on, his faith had to fight its way into his heart through a barrage of inner questions Wiesel posed to his God, and through a curtain of non-Jewish ideas.

From 1947, after O.S.E. moved some of its charges to the Paris suburbs, Wiesel was able to study French seriously with François Wahl, a French tutor only slightly older than he was, who lived in Paris. The two of them read French classic writers like Racine and Pascal, and Wahl took him to the Comédie-Francaise where Wiesel could see French classic plays performed. In the summer, he earned some extra money as a camp counselor for the younger children in O.S.E. camps. He directed the O.S.E.

home's choir, becoming infatuated with young girls in the chorus one after another, yearning for female companionship, but also tormented by a yearning to remain physically and spiritually pure. He found himself overcompensating for his shyness and his desire by barking harshly at the very females in the choir to whom he secretly wanted to be close.

A chance photograph of Wiesel with other young orphans in a French newspaper brought him back in contact with his sisters. His eldest sister, Hilda, who had married another camp survivor, had moved to Paris to live. She had seen Elie's picture in a newspaper article about the orphans and contacted the orphanage director. The following day she and Elie met in Paris and embraced in mutual anguish. She told him that Bea, Elie's other sister, was also alive, but was still living in a Displaced Person's Camp in Kassel, Germany.

With French identity papers confirming that he was still stateless, Wiesel traveled by train back into Germany, now a defeated and profoundly despondent land. He was astonished that the former rulers of Europe had adopted so readily the role of the vanquished. Staying in a German home one night before visiting Bea, Wiesel, tormented by sexual desire, but even more determined to be spiritually honorable, turned down the sexual advances of a German war widow in her thirties. The price of one night of her offered services was ten cigarettes and two Hershey bars.

Back in France, and still under the care of the O.S.E., Wiesel for two years fell under the spell, the influence, and finally the educational training of one of the most mysterious and extraordinary men he was ever to meet. He was a Jew, and the name he gave people was simply Shushani, though he had not been named Shushani at birth. He was a diminutive, shabbily dressed little man with a large head and a tiny hat atop it, and dusty glasses. He never said anything about who he was or how he had come to be in France, not to mention where he had been brought up. He had hung around the shabbat services at the O.S.E. home outside Paris where Wiesel had moved, saying little or nothing, but evidently noticing everything.

One day, as Wiesel was returning to the home by train from Paris, Shushani was sitting in the same compartment. As though he had known Wiesel for years, he began to question him about the book he was reading. Wiesel shyly revealed that he was preparing a talk on Job for a forthcoming meeting at the home. Shushani began to talk about Job, and Wiesel began to grasp what a startlingly brilliant and insightful mind he was.

Over the next year and a half, Shushani talked frequently with Wiesel and other Jewish students at the home.

His appearance, as if from nowhere, and his equally mysterious origins, at first frightened Wiesel a little. But as he came to know him and derive immense insights into the entire world of learning, especially Jewish learning, from him, the encounter appears to have had a profound impact on the young man.

Shushani was a Talmudic scholar, originally from Lithuania, and he spoke Yiddish with a strong Lithuanian lilt. His name, Wiesel discovered later, was Mordechai Rosenbaum. He appeared to have memorized the entire Babylonian and Jerusalem Talmuds, knew Sanskrit, the Greek and Latin classics, and innumerable modern languages. To demonstrate his genius to Wiesel, like a juggler showing off new tricks, he once learned Hungarian in two weeks. One evening, he lectured to the orphans at the O.S.E. home at Taverny for four hours straight simply on the very first verse of the book of Isaiah.

He passed himself as a rabbi, but no one knew where he had acquired his learning, or even, at the time, where he was from. He never seemed to be reading a book. For some reason, though, he imparted to Wiesel huge chunks of his knowledge and understanding, as though grasping intuitively that Wiesel among few others was capable of absorbing it all. He was absolutely silent about his roots, his past, even his close relatives, if any of them were alive. Once, when Wiesel was rash enough to ask him a personal question, Shushani angrily closed off any further discussion of it. Only later, piecing together morsels of information from others who had bumped into him in different parts of the world, did Wiesel learn his real name or from where he originally came.

There was something deeply mysterious to Wiesel about Shushani and his sudden appearance. For a moment, the youth wondered if there was something of the infernal supernatural about him. He wrote indecipherable manuscripts in an unknown script—some of which Wiesel apparently owns—and in 1965 he died in Montevideo, Uruguay. Why had he gone there? No one seemed to know. Where did he get money to live on? No one was sure about that, though it was rumored that famous professors in France paid huge sums of money to be instructed by him.

"I am increasingly convinced," Wiesel has written in his *Memoirs*, "that he must be considered one of the great, disturbing figures of our tradition.

He saw his role as that of agitator and troublemaker. He upset the believer by demonstrating the fragility of his faith; he shook the heretic by making him feel the torments of the void." The effect of Shushani's genius and teaching on Wiesel seems to have been incalculable. "What I know is," Wiesel writes today, "that I would not be the man I am, the Jew I am, had not an astonishing, disconcerting vagabond accosted me one day to inform me that I understood nothing."[34]

In 1948, at the age of nineteen, Wiesel managed to enroll in the Sorbonne, Paris's premier university, in the Faculty of Letters. There he plunged even more deeply into the French classics, philosophy both ancient and modern, the existentialist thought of Jean-Paul Sartre, then in his heyday, and the ideas of Martin Buber. He was thirsty for knowledge and understanding of the world, but his deep ingestion of the Jewish worldview from an early age helped stave off the more extreme ideas of the contemporary French intelligentsia.

He lived the life of an impoverished student, inhabiting a dingy cubicle room far from his place of study and having to decide each day whether to take the metro home or spend the money on a sandwich. Sometimes his sister Bea would send him condensed milk or cookies, or Hilda in Paris would invite him to eat with her and her husband. But the income of her husband, a portrait artist, was barely enough to feed the two of them, much less a famished teenage student. Hilda, for her part, didn't seem to grasp just how precarious the physical existence of Elie had become.

Most of the time he was desperately poor, in fact close to destitution. At one point he fell seriously ill after consuming a can of sardines without bread. The lack of nutrition also subtly affected his mental health. For several weeks he was despondent to the point of contemplating suicide. He thought that he might conceivably die of starvation. He lost his desire to accomplish anything in life and he sensed that the dead, those countless fellow Jews who had perished in the camps, were beckoning to him to come and join them. The only thing that seemed to be utterly solid in his mind was his memory, the rocklike certainty of his knowledge of all that had taken place.

Elie Wiesel had taken a kind of private vow after his liberation from Auschwitz: For ten years he would write nothing at all about what he had experienced. He had come to an understanding of the role memory played in both a person's individual life and in civilization's survival. But he was also mystically frightened of the power of words themselves, a fear possibly aggravated by Shushani's terrifying lessons. He told himself that if he were to enjoy writing, there would be many, many topics to write about before he brought himself around to the Event itself. Let ten years go by first.

Europe, meanwhile, was not standing still. The vacuum of power and legitimacy left in all of the countries that had been controlled by the Nazis had attracted new, and often alarming political currents. Defining what Winston Churchill in 1946 first called the Iron Curtain in the Soviet-controlled sector of Eastern Europe, whole nations were slowly sinking into the quicksand of Stalinist terror. Between 1947 and 1949, the noose of Soviet Communist control drew ever tighter. And there were ugly outbreaks in some Eastern European countries of officially sponsored anti-Semitic propaganda.

Meanwhile, in the Middle East, the race to establish a Jewish state had also captured the imagination of Europe as episodes like the journey of the *Exodus,* a ship filled with Jewish would-be immigrants to Palestine, was turned back in 1947 by the patrolling British navy. Wiesel had earnestly tried to emigrate to Palestine immediately after liberation from Buchenwald, and again later, when he was at the orphanage homes in France. Each time his lack of known relatives in the future Israel had resulted in a rejection of his application to travel there. Frustrated at his inability to take part in the dramatic events surrounding the partition of Palestine and the emergence of the state of Israel, in 1947 he naively rang the bell of the Jewish Agency in Paris and asked if he could join the Haganah, the underground army of the Jews of Palestine. The door was slammed in his face.

He had more luck with a letter to a weekly Yiddish-language paper that was the organ of the Irgun, a Palestine-based Jewish militant organization. Irgun was at serious odds with the Haganah over tactics on how to deal with the British mandatory authorities responsible for running Palestine. After the establishment of Israel, adherents of the Irgun were to form the main opposition in the Israeli Knesset, or Parliament, until former Irgun leader Menachem Begin's Likud Party won the elections of 1977. Those who had been with the much larger Haganah generally identified with Israel's Labor Party, led in recent years by Yitzhak Rabin (assassinated in 1995) and Shimon Peres.

Wiesel's patriotic and pompous letter, as he himself described it, secured him an interview with a secretive Irgun agent in Paris named Joseph. On the spot he was given a job with the Irgun organ, *Zion in Kampf* (Zion's Struggle), translating Hebrew materials into Yiddish. He had felt vaguely guilty for not having been part of any underground resistance movement in the camps.

Now, he believed, he had a chance to "redeem" himself. The $60 a month or so that the job paid seemed like a fortune to Wiesel then. Even better, he had glimpses of himself as a glamorous foreign correspondent. He was, after all, now a "journalist." He wrote: "I felt privileged, important, and useful. Though I was in no danger, I thought of my situation as problematic, and somewhat heroic: militant journalist, fighter for Jewish freedom. I was very young and very enthusiastic and in search of a cause."[35]

The cause, of course, was Israel, or the future Israel, as it was to be. Events in Palestine itself were reaching a crisis point. On May 14, 1948, David Ben-Gurion declared the independence of Israel, precipitating a deadly battle between Jewish forces and troops from five Arab states who sought to strangle the new nation at birth. In Paris, Wiesel could scarcely contain his excitement. But he was in anguish over the incident of the ship *Altalena,* an Irgun-organized boat that arrived on the shores of Palestine with both one thousand refugees from Displaced Person camps and a large supply of arms and ammunition.

The Palmach, the forces of Israel's provisional government, fired on the ship June 24, 1948, off the Israeli coast near Tel Aviv, killing many people and preventing its landing. Ben-Gurion's supporters later said that they feared the Irgun might have been landing the weapons not to supply their own forces in the independence war, but preparatory to a coup attempt against the provisional government. It is one of history's great and tragic ironies that one of the young Palmach officers who fired on fellow Jews aboard the *Altalena* was future prime minister Yitzhak Rabin, who later lost his own life at the hands of a fellow Jew.

In 1949, after the Irgun had closed its offices in Paris, Wiesel traveled to Israel for the first time, as a correspondent for the French newspaper *L'Arche* aboard a boat filled with new immigrants. Outside Tel Aviv, he was shocked at the sight of the beached *Altalena,* on whose hull an angry activist had written the words "Herut [the Irgun's political party], you will end like the Altalena."[36] He crisscrossed Israel for several months, grieving that, for the first time perhaps since the time of King David, all of the Jews had been driven out of the Old City, now under the control of Jordan.

Wiesel was also deeply saddened by the contemptuous treatment in Israel of many of the survivors of the Holocaust once they settled there. "Six hundred thousand of us defeated six well-equipped Arab armies," Wiesel remembers the conversation often going. "Six million of you let yourselves be led like lambs to the slaughter."[37] Wiesel felt it was impossible to explain to the sometimes arrogant Israeli-born Jews exactly how it had all happened. He was also saddened that school textbooks said very little about the Holocaust.

Before returning to Paris, he secured a job as Paris correspondent for *Yediot Ahronot*, then the smallest and most financially strapped of all the Hebrew language dailies. His initial pay was $50 a month, less than he had received while working for the Irgun organ, and so little that he was frequently hungry. He scraped along with translation work here and there to augment his meager income. Journalistically, though, it was a time of excitement and, in a way, intellectual intoxication for a young man in France. The political left was powerful and conspicuous, with frequent demonstrations against the various governments that, in the 1950's, came and went with inexhaustible frequency. Wiesel immersed himself deeply in the French intellectual avant-garde writers of the day: Sartre, Malraux, Camus, and Valery.

In the process, he was broadening his view of religious experience too. Could holiness exist outside of religious commitment? What were the limits of responsibility for both man and God? And why was there still virtually no literature describing exactly what had happened during the Holocaust?

He traveled to a variety of interesting places in the early 1950's. In Morocco, he searched for one of the few Jewish communities in the Arab world that had not been expelled or attacked at the time of Israel's independence. In Spain he encountered a man who was amazed that Jews were still alive and whose ignorance seemed nothing short of startling to Wiesel. He invited Wiesel to his home and then solemnly showed him a rare parchment heirloom, in Hebrew, that had been passed down from father to son in his family. With difficulty, Wiesel interpreted it for the Spaniard. It was by one Moshe ben Abraham, calling upon his descendants to remember his origins. Standing in front of Wiesel was the ancient Jew's direct descendant, a man completely ignorant of his origins.

Wiesel then became involved in one of the most intensely emotional controversies facing both Israel and world Jewry in the early 1950's: Should the newly created, and desperately impoverished Jewish state accept reparations payment from the government of West Germany? Intensive Israeli–West German negotiations had taken place in Belgium in 1952 and had led to some of the most politically dangerous and violent political demonstrations in Jerusalem of Israel's history.

He made a brief trip for *Yediot* to both Bonn and the concentration camp of Dachau, and he returned to Paris depressed. There had been little reference to the predominantly Jewish origin of the Dachau victims. "In Hitler's day Jewish life had been in danger," he recalled in his *Memoirs*. "Now it was Jewish memory that was at risk."[38] But Providence seemed to force that very issue ever more persistently at him. A short time later, he was asked to be a simultaneous interpreter at the 1953 Geneva meeting of the World Jewish Congress. One of the hottest items on the agenda was the forthcoming Israeli–West German talks.

Technically, Wiesel was not functioning as a reporter at the meeting. But when a furious argument broke out at one of the meeting's sessions, he heard words from Nahum Goldmann, the congress president, that he could scarcely believe and that forced him to resign as an interpreter and resume his reportorial functions. A rabbi present asked if the delegates could say the Kaddish for the victims of the German assault upon the Jews. Goldmann grew impatient and retorted: "Which will profit Israel more, the Kaddish or German financial compensation?"[39] Outraged by what he had heard, Wiesel quickly resigned his job, then cabled to Tel Aviv a passionate account of the meeting.

The next day, a storm breaking over his head, Goldmann called a press conference and flatly denied that he had said the words Wiesel had attributed to him. Wiesel was put in an impossible position. If he stood up to acknowledge that he had personally heard them while performing as an interpreter, he would severely embarrass the man who had hired him for the job. If he kept silent, his own reputation would be at risk. He kept silent, but later asked the rabbi who had requested the Kaddish to confirm the request and Goldmann's response. The rabbi dutifully confirmed in a written statement to Wiesel that Goldmann had said exactly what he was quoted as saying. But Wiesel had been hurt by Goldmann's flat-out denial of the story.

MEETING WITH FRANÇOIS MAURIAC

Wiesel traveled to Canada briefly, where his sister Bea had emigrated and was working at the Israeli Embassy in Ottawa. He also secured a visa to

India, whose traditions of Hindu mysticism seemed powerfully close to some of Wiesel's own spiritual searching since childhood.

He believed that all religions had similar origins, and he wanted to know if Hinduism could teach him things he was still eager to know about life. But he came away disheartened by India's caste system and by the appalling misery of the very poor that he saw on the streets of India's cities. He wondered how "a civilized state like India could tolerate such misery and agony." He was not satisfied by the smiles and shrugs in response that he received from Indians he talked to about this.

The Hindu doctrine of reincarnation seemed to him a complete contradiction of the Jewish requirement that human beings were under obligation to respond to the sufferings of others. He also disliked the opposition of Mahatma Gandhi, the ascetic Hindu leader of India's independence struggle, to Jewish immigration to Palestine before Israel was established. On one level, he felt drawn to India: He was fascinated by its culture's speculation about mystical topics. But on another level, the experience alienated him. In the end, he decided, the Indian concept of God was too different from his Jewish understanding. "I returned from India even more Jewish than before," he said later.[40]

Another long trip Wiesel took in early 1954 was to Brazil, where he investigated reports that the Catholic church had persuaded impoverished Jewish immigrants in Israel to convert to Catholicism in return for a small cash reward and passage by ship to Brazil. On talking to the indigent passengers in third class who had actually accepted the offer, Wiesel asked them how they could abandon their Jewish faith after so many of their ancestors had died rather than renounce it. Life was too hard in Israel, they replied. Besides, they had merely made a promise to convert.

What was a promise? Stepping no doubt outside the normal bounds of a reporter's activity by becoming part of the story, Wiesel contacted various Jewish communities on the ship's route down the South American coast. He did this to ensure that when the immigrants were finally permitted off the ship in Brazil, they would be taken care of by the local Jewish community, and not by Roman Catholic priests.

En route, Wiesel, meanwhile, was putting together a long manuscript in Yiddish. It was as if the need to relate the Auschwitz experience, perhaps in anticipation of the end of the ten-year vow of silence, was beginning to bubble up within him. He spent much of the time aboard the ship in his cabin doing nothing but writing. "I wrote to testify," he said later, "to stop the dead from dying, to justify my own survival. I wrote to speak to all those who were gone."[41]

When he landed in Buenos Aires, a Jewish publisher asked if he could take a look at the tatty manuscript Wiesel was clutching. It was already several hundred pages long. Reluctantly, Wiesel agreed. He was certain that nothing would come of it and yet he had handed over the manuscript, his only copy, to someone else. In December of the following year, he received a package in the mail from South America. What he had written, *Un Di Velt Hot Geshvign* (And the World Remained Silent), came back to him now as a book. He was immensely relieved. Though the original manuscript had been 862 pages long and the book that came out of it had been cut down to 245 pages in Buenos Aires, what he had written had not been lost for all time. He never did, however, get back his original manuscript.

The turning point of Wiesel's life as a writer and journalist was 1954, and it occurred in a totally unexpected way. For France, it was a time of immense, perhaps even catastrophic trauma. After fighting for years to contain the Vietminh rebellion in Vietnam, led by Ho Chi Minh and the Communists, the cream of the French army found itself bottled up in a valley in the northern part of Vietnam called Dien Bien Phu in 1954. As the Communists poured in thousands of rounds of shells and dug infantry trenches ever closer to the French headquarters, the French army resistance collapsed. It spelled not just the end of France's imperial era in Indochina but in many ways the decisive departure of the country from the front ranks of world military power.

In France itself, there was a prolonged political crisis. Into power swept Pierre Mendès-France, a liberal Jewish politician who promised to end the French involvement in Indochina within thirty days of taking office. International talks on the future of Indochina took place in Geneva, incidentally setting up the unstable regional environment that led to America's own tragic involvement in Vietnam and Laos a generation later. For Wiesel, though, the tense French political situation was a reporter's dream, especially because Mendès-France was Jewish. From *Yediot Ahronot,* the instructions to him were clear: Get to Mendès-France for an interview at all costs.

He tried every means he knew to approach the man, including an almost comical on-again-off-again arrangement through a mysterious Israeli envoy, Joseph Givon, who seemed to know everyone in the world from General de Gaulle to Mao Tse-tung. One day, providentially, as he thought, he attended a reception at the Israeli Embassy in Paris and ran into France's most recent Nobel laureate for literature, François Mauriac. *At last*, Wiesel thought to himself, *a chance to get to Mendès-France*. Mauriac and he were known to be very close. Affably, Mauriac agreed to an interview with the young reporter and set a day and a time. A devout Roman Catholic whose behavior during the German occupation had been impeccable, he was used to being interviewed on his past, on literature, and on events in contemporary French political life. He was an expert on this too. He didn't know that Wiesel only wanted to use him as a slingshot to get to Mendès-France.

Wiesel showed up nervous and chain-smoking at the appointed time at Mauriac's Paris apartment. The older man was gracious and quickly put Wiesel at his ease. Instead of sitting back to receive the reporter's questions, though, he began to speak with ever greater passion about his favorite topic, Jesus Christ. He spoke warmly about his feelings toward Israel, toward the Jews in general, a people, he said who had been martyrs throughout history. For Mauriac, Wiesel noticed with some irritation, it was as though everything in creation had some connection to Jesus.

"Every reference led back to him," Wiesel wrote in one of his earliest accounts of the meeting. "Jerusalem? The eternal city," Wiesel describes Mauriac as continuing, "where Jesus turned his disciples into apostles. The Bible? The Old Testament, which thanks to Jesus of Nazareth, succeeded in enriching itself with a New Testament. Mendez-France? A Jew, both brave and hated, not unlike Jesus a long time ago. . . ."[42] As for Jesus, Wiesel wrote later, "when [Mauriac] spoke his name, his smile seemed to turn inward. Once started, he had no wish to change the subject."[43]

The monologue, however eloquent and fascinating it was, finally triggered something off in Wiesel. All of his anger at Christian anti-Semitism over the centuries, his own accumulated grief from Sighet, Auschwitz, and Buchenwald, suddenly boiled over. He closed his notebook and stood up angrily. "Sir," he said to the still-seated Mauriac,

> You speak of Christ. Christians love to speak of him. The passion of Christ, the agony of Christ, the death of Christ. In your religion, that is all you speak of. Well, I want you to know that ten years ago, not very far from here, I knew Jewish children every one of whom

suffered a thousand times more, six million times more, than Christ on the cross. And we don't speak about them. Can you understand that, sir? We don't speak about them.[44]

Mauriac went pale. He said nothing, but still seated on the sofa with a woolen blanket around him, he gazed back at Wiesel, as if expecting to hear more. But Wiesel was already on the way out, closing the apartment door after him and pressing the buzzer for the elevator.

The door behind him quietly opened again, and there was Mauriac, gently taking Wiesel's arm and asking him to come back into the apartment once more. After they had both sat down without saying anything else, Mauriac began to weep, still looking at Wiesel, but engulfed in grief. For a long time the tears simply streamed down his face. Wiesel began to feel remorse for his own rudeness and harshness.

Wiesel wanted to apologize, but Mauriac wouldn't let him. Instead, he wanted to know everything about Wiesel's experience, his parents, the trains, the camps. He asked why Wiesel had not written all of this down. Wiesel told him about his vow to remain silent for ten years. Mauriac wanted to know about this too. Then, escorting him back to the elevator, he told the much younger man, "I think that you are wrong. You are wrong not to speak. . . . Listen to the old man that I am: one must speak out—one must also speak out."[45]

This encounter had a profound impact on both men. For one thing, it was the beginning of a friendship of immense mutual respect between two strong-minded writers who disagreed profoundly on matters totally essential to each—for Mauriac, his absolute Christian commitment, for Wiesel, his absolute Jewish one—yet who valued infinitely the core of human integrity and human dignity in each other. Until Mauriac's death in 1970, the two wrote deeply felt letters to each other, and once Wiesel had moved to the U.S., he paid a visit to the old man every time he was in Paris.

Mauriac never "made any attempt to proselytze" Wiesel, to use Wiesel's own words, yet he succeeded in conveying to Wiesel, at a deeper level than perhaps any other Christian had been able to, the possibility of both loving Jesus deeply and loving the Jews deeply too. "It was because he loved Jesus that he defended Jews," Wiesel was to write in his *Memoirs*, "because he suffered at Jesus's suffering, that he strove to assuage ours. But I came to understand that only later."[46]

"The fact is that, practically, I owe Francois Mauriac my career," Wiesel has said. "He was a Christian, and we were very close friends. Had it not been for Mauriac, I would have become or remained an obscure writer, a journalist."[47] "I owe him a lot," Wiesel freely admits about Mauriac. "I don't know how I would have fared without Mauriac. He kept a watchful eye on my literary efforts."[48] Very specifically, it was to Mauriac that Wiesel first sent the manuscript of *Night* in its first French edition (*La Nuit*), a year after their first meeting. It was to become the launching pad of Wiesel's rapid rise to international fame as a writer.

During the early 1950's, Wiesel returned to Israel from Paris as often as he could after his first visit in 1949, getting to know the country better and watching as the young state coped with the struggles of surviving amid a hostile Arab sea and absorbing hundreds of thousands of Jewish refugees from other parts of the Middle East. His reputation as an energetic and intelligent reporter and his occasional scoops had turned him into something of a celebrity within *Yediot*. He was now the paper's chief foreign correspondent. Yet Paris did not seem the right place any longer to cover news relating to Israel and to the world Jewish community in general. Other cities were becoming much more important as news generators. At the top of the list was New York. During a visit to Israel of several weeks in 1955, Dov Judkowski of *Yediot Ahronot* suggested he now move to New York. He would receive the then impressive salary of $160 a month.

Despite the glamorous-sounding title of "Chief Foreign Correspondent" and the New York byline, the transfer across the Atlantic was a major challenge for Wiesel. French had become his second language, and he had mastered it. He knew English well, but he could not write in it as fluently or as concisely as French. In addition, he was starting in a gigantic, strange city very much on the bottom rungs of the journalistic ladder.

A friend secured him a desk in the press room at the UN—an excellent base, as it turned out, to cover both international events as they occurred through the eyes of the UN, and other events in America. He learned some useful foreign reporters' tricks of those days. For example, he would traipse across midtown Manhattan in the evening to pick up the early editions of the *New York Times*. He continued to write for *Yediot Ahronot* until the Yiddish-language *Jewish Daily Forward* hired him. He lived the life of a busy, undomesticated bachelor in the Master Hotel at 103rd Street and Riverside Drive, sixty blocks north of the UN and on the other side of town.

He was lonely too. In France he had embarked on fleeting romances with some of the former fellow "orphans" in the O.S.E. home in Taverny. In 1955, he was in love for several months with an American student, "Kathleen," who was beautiful and intelligent, but not Jewish. There were problems in this from the start: She wanted to sleep with him very early on, and he didn't. Besides, something seemed to gnaw at Wiesel inside. He wanted a wife with whom he could share deep philosophical and religious convictions. He and Kathleen broke up painfully in 1955 in Paris. One of the few close female friends he seems to have spent time with was Aviva, the secretary of his *Yediot* publisher in Israel. He had met her on his various visits to Israel, and during her own rare trips to New York they would do things together.

One likely reason for his continued bachelorhood in a lonely foreign city may well have been an encroaching spiritual crisis in his life. His visit to Israel in 1955 had found him, for the first time in his life since, perhaps, bar mitzvah, not saying his morning prayers. He had met there the "young" Rebbe (the title denotes a Hasidic master) of Wishnitz, the son of the charismatic old man whose prophecies about Elie Wiesel at the age of eight had so frightened Wiesel's mother. Now, with the younger man, he suddenly grasped how far his years of study in Paris and as a journalist had taken him from his devout Hasidic roots. By the following year, 1956, he was no longer attending synagogue at all except on the Jewish High Holidays or the Yizkor service (a service in memory of the dead). There was no Shushani to talk all this out with. He was feeling within himself a profound sense of protest against divine justice, and against injustice. He was, in short, sinking into a deep religious crisis.[49]

"I AM ONE WHO PRAYS"

Then Providence, suddenly and with enormous pain, intervened. Wiesel was crossing New York's Seventh Avenue at 45th Street one evening on the way back from the *New York Times* with his copy of the paper. It was a stifling hot July evening in 1956, and he was planning to see a movie with Aviva, who was passing through New York on vacation from Israel. Suddenly, his world fell apart. A taxi slashed into him from behind, scooping him up and sending him tumbling, "like a figure in a Chagall painting," almost an entire block to 44th Street. He lay between consciousness and coma for twenty minutes until an ambulance finally arrived and rushed him to a hospital. En route, he gave precise instructions to Aviva on whom to tell about the mishap and who should cover for him journalistically. Then he collapsed. It took a ten-hour operation to reconstruct his shattered left side.

What effect did this brush with death have on Wiesel? He had certainly faced far more terrifying physical dangers almost daily at Auschwitz. But both a new sense of proportion about life and a new sense of time came into Wiesel's life. He has said that he dislikes the American term "killing time." "Every minute should be used, everything should be used," he now insists.[50] Perhaps he was beginning to grasp just why it was he had mysteriously survived Auschwitz. Why he had earned the lifelong friendship of one of the most powerful literary figures in France. And why, in the end, he had survived what could so easily have been a final, fatal encounter in midtown New York.

From 1956 onward, Wiesel seemed to acquire a new sense of urgency in his writing. Now the reporting seemed to take second place in his professional life to writing novels that derived their characters and their moral settings from the consequences of the Event. *Night*, as we shall see below, finally appeared in the U.S. in 1960. But in the four years after that, a veritable stream of writing poured from Wiesel's pen: *Dawn* (1961), *The Accident* (1961), *The Town Beyond the Wall* (1962), and *The Gates of the Forest* (1964). After the accident, Wiesel marshaled the first four hours of his day, from 6:00 A.M. until 10:00 A.M., into an almost sacrosanct permanent reserve for serious writing. He was to keep this schedule methodically for the rest of his working life.

Meanwhile, even in a wheelchair and on crutches, Wiesel was deeply absorbed by the two great world crises that captured global attention in the fall of 1956: the tragically abortive attempt of Hungary's freedom fighters to throw off the Soviet yoke, and the Anglo-French-Israeli attack on Egypt at almost exactly the same time. In the hospital, encased in a body cast, Wiesel managed to gather around him reporting colleagues from the UN who filled him in on the rising Middle East tensions. Egypt's passionately pan-Arabist leader, Gamal Abdel Nasser, had nationalized the Suez Canal in 1956, provoking the British and the French in the fall to a military expedition against Egypt in which the Israelis also became secretly involved.

U.S. president Eisenhower forced the British and the French to withdraw from Egypt and, together with the UN, put immense pressure on Israel to withdraw also from the Sinai Peninsula that Israel had occupied during the fighting. By the time Israel's then foreign minister Golda Meir arrived in New York to negotiate a way out of the crisis early the following year, Wiesel had resumed active reporting but was hobbling about the UN on crutches. Taking pity on him, and impressed by his perfect command of modern Hebrew, Golda astonished her aides by permitting Wiesel to go through her briefing papers at the end of each day in her suite at the Essex House, where the Israeli delegation was staying. He became a confidant to her and they remained very good friends for several years.

Other reporting opportunities came by Wiesel: a visit to Cuba in 1960, shortly after Castro came to power; the Bay of Pigs fiasco in 1961; the Cuban Missile Crisis of 1962; and, indeed, the assassination of JFK itself. But one of the most emotionally draining and philosophically challenging of all Wiesel's assignments was to cover the trial of Adolf Eichmann in Jerusalem in 1962.

The architect and administrator of Hitler's Final Solution against the Jews, Eichmann had slipped out of Germany in the chaos of its collapse at the end of World War II and fled to Argentina. There he lived an inconspicuous life until Israeli commandos caught up with him in 1960, kidnapped him off the street, and flew him clandestinely back to Jerusalem for trial. The trial took place in Jerusalem's Beit Haam, an auditorium where, by coincidence, I arrived the following summer to perform in the Oxford undergraduate production of *Romeo and Juliet*. We youthful actors changed in Eichmann's former cell, above the auditorium, a spacious area complete with personal toilet, but deliberately lacking any furnishings that could serve Eichmann as a tool for his own self-destruction. Eichmann was already dead, but the accoutrements of his final days on earth were still in place.

Watching Eichmann taking notes quietly and professionally every day for many hours during the trial, protected from the possibilities of all extrajudicial violence against him by a bullet-proof glass enclosure, Wiesel was profoundly unnerved. There was something frightening about Eichmann. "Why did he inspire such fear in me?" Wiesel wrote later. "Is there an ontological evil unrelated to action?"[51] It disturbed Wiesel, above all, that Eichmann was casually considered "sane." "For me," Wiesel wrote later, "there could be no common ground with him. We could not inhabit the same universe or be governed by the same laws."[52]

Wiesel, in the end, does not appear to believe there is a source of evil independent of the human race or even independent of God. He does not, for one thing, believe in original sin, as Christians do. In a televised conversation with New York's Cardinal O'Connor in 1989, he made it clear he thought that, for God to be God, He must be in "every thought, in every tear, in every joy. And in evil. It's up to us to redeem that evil," he added. "But if I say that God is not everywhere, God is not God."[53] What Wiesel clearly does believe about wicked acts committed deliberately today is that the perpetrators so often feel they must link those acts to Nazism. The phenomenon of skinheads is one example he cites. Though Wiesel may not believe in evil as a moral category independent of God as Christians do, his face-to-face experience with Nazi evil seems to have provided him with a moral gyroscope of good and evil behavior that virtually anyone with a developed conscience could agree with.

Meanwhile, in 1958, *Night* had finally appeared in France to immense critical acclaim. Wiesel briefly returned to France to help lend publicity to the book. It was very much Mauriac's contribution that it had been published at all, and that when it was published, it was a major literary event. Despite the French success, New York publishers were as wary at first of the topic and the manuscript, now in English, as the French had been. Finally, Hill and Wang agreed to publish it, in a version even shorter than the French edition. Mauriac's foreword was included. In it, he acknowledged his tears of remorse toward Wiesel for his insensitivity to the young writer. He should, he said, have spoken of God's grace, of how the very stumbling block to Wiesel's own faith was the cornerstone of his own. But, Mauriac concluded, "I could only embrace him, weeping."[54]

The book received an almost instant and unanimous critical success when it appeared in the U.S. in 1960. Overnight, it transformed Wiesel from a foreign correspondent who wrote occasional books into a major literary and philosophical figure in his own right. That, of course, was a mixed blessing. "The moment you achieve visibility," he says, "you become a target, and often there are more arrows than compliments." When the first negative review of *Night* was brought to his attention, Wiesel says he felt a childish desire to go out, buy all of the available newsstand copies, and burn them.[55]

The very power of *Night*, its unflinching exposure to the public eye of the greatest evil ever attempted on a single people, aroused jealousy and opposition in some quarters. After Wiesel's fourth book and third novel, *The Town Beyond the Wall*, appeared in 1962, the year of Eichmann's trial, a Belgian radio reporter asked Wiesel, "How much longer are you going to wallow in suffering?"[56] Others, less crudely, indicated a similar impatience. "Are you ever going to stop writing about the Jewish tragedy?" he was now being asked, in different forms, in both France and the U.S. Wiesel's response, then and now, was the same: "Even if I wrote on nothing else, it would never be enough; even if all the survivors did nothing but write about their experiences, it would still not be enough." But the complaints did not stop there. Other, nastier rumors were bandied about that Wiesel and others were "making a fortune off the Holocaust," as if any amount of money in the universe could compensate for the murder of mothers, sisters, loved ones, and millions of fellow Jews.[57]

The dilemma for Wiesel and others who have written about the Holocaust extensively has never stopped being cruel. Should a writer refrain from writing about tragedy and evil simply because readers would pay to read him and he might thus indirectly prosper from the crimes of others? For Wiesel, the response to this question was always clear. He had survived and others hadn't. He above all owed them the responsibility to keep alive the memory of the evil that they had experienced. It is interesting that today he regards the most wicked of all anti-Semites to be those who are the historical revisionists, who deny that the Holocaust ever happened.

In 1964, for the first time in twenty years, Wiesel returned to Sighet. He found homes abandoned and sealed up, synagogues mostly closed and no trace of the vibrant Jewish life that had existed before World War II. But he did come across in one of the few still-open synagogues a store of Jewish holy books that had been moved there, probably after being discovered in abandoned homes. Among them, to his amazement, were Bible commentaries he himself had written in Sighet at the age of thirteen or fourteen.

The following year, 1965, he traveled for the first time to the Soviet Union, deeply concerned about the condition of Jews there and the absence, hitherto, of more than token protest on their behalf in the West. He went during the High Holy days to Moscow, Leningrad, Kiev, and Tbilisi, meeting Jews in all of these cities. He watched Hasidic Jews dance on the streets of Moscow. He learned about Jewish samizdat literature and the groping attempts of a largely secularized generation of Jews to come to terms with their cultural and religious heritage. When his account of the visit, *The Jews of Silence*, came out in 1968, it helped galvanize a worldwide movement to protect Soviet Jewry from the regime's restrictions on Jewish cultural and religious life and to open the doors, if possible, for emigration to Israel.

But Wiesel's book stirred up more than Jews in the West. When Wiesel returned to Moscow a year later, after his book had appeared, he narrowly escaped arrest at Sheremetyevo Airport on leaving the country. He had to be spirited off to the Israeli Embassy by Israeli security officials. Only after the intervention of General de Gaulle, contacted by François Mauriac, was he able to leave the country unhindered a few days later.

The following year, 1967, he felt an impassioned need to fly to Israel shortly after the Six-Day War broke out in early June. Since there had been a news blackout from Israel, the only war news was coming from Arab capitals, and it was uniformly assertive of great victories by the Arab armies over the Jewish state. Wiesel wondered if, once again, Jews were about to be crushed, this time together with the sovereign state of Israel. If that was the case, he wanted to be there as a witness to it.

He caught one of the last El Al flights into Tel Aviv and as quickly as he could, found transportation to Jerusalem. There in the ancient Jewish capital, he arrived to discover that the Old City, previously occupied by Jordanian forces, was now in Jewish hands. He found himself rushing with thousands of other Israelis, running as fast as he could, to the Western Wall, Judaism's holiest site. Israeli paratroopers had barely completed snatching it from Jordanian troops and there was still sporadic sniper fire around the city.

No Jews had been permitted to pray at the Western Wall since the end of Israel's War of Independence in 1948, and no Jews had even been permitted by the Jordanians to live in the eastern half of Jerusalem under their control. Wiesel noticed an old man muttering to himself in the general euphoria of Israel's full control over its historic capital. The old man asked Wiesel, "Do you know how we managed to defeat the enemy? Six million Jewish souls prayed for us."

"Who are you?" Wiesel asked.

"I am one who prays," said the old man.[58]

Wiesel later wrote in his journal, in Yiddish, "It is in Jerusalem that our people have been initiated into what our mystics call *aliya neshama*, or ascension of the collective soul."[59]

While he was still absorbing the roller coaster of emotions over the war, the sickening feelings of fear followed by exultant joy at the victory, Wiesel was already planning in his mind what he knew must be his next book, *A Beggar in Jerusalem*, which was published in 1968. The book moves nervously back and forth between different styles in an effort to capture the kaleido-scope of feelings Jews had in responding to the restoration to them of their ancient capital. It is probably Wiesel's most emotionally intense effort to articulate the supercharged feelings of a Diaspora Jew toward the capital city of his ancient homeland at a time of dramatic historical change. In the Yiddish-language travel journal that Wiesel kept during this visit to Israel, he remarked on the "moral and perhaps mystical dimension" of Jerusalem's return to the Jews. But he also found himself disturbed by something. The Arab children in the newly conquered Arab cities of the West Bank showed fear whenever they saw Wiesel and other Israelis. "For the first time in my life, children were afraid of me," he wrote.[60]

MESSENGER TO HUMANKIND

He returned to the U.S. via Paris. From 1968 onward, recognition, prizes, and honors began to flow to Wiesel in great numbers. His first honorary doctorate had been awarded to him in New York from the Jewish Theological Seminary, on the very day the Six-Day War broke out. (He has since received some seventy-five honorary doctorates.) Now juries on both sides of the Atlantic were recognizing his achievements as a writer. In 1968 he was awarded the Prix Médicis in Paris, one of France's top literary awards, for *A Beggar in Jerusalem*.

His growing fame as a writer finally enabled him to concentrate on the other thing in addition to writing that he has always loved doing, teaching. From 1972 to 1976 he was Distinguished Professor of Judaic Studies at the City University of New York. From 1978 onward, he has served as the Andrew W. Mellon Professor of Humanities at Boston University, though he continues to live primarily in New York on the Upper East Side.

He had, meanwhile, ended his bachelorhood in 1969 by marrying Marion Erster Rose, a woman of Austrian descent who was to become the translator of all of Wiesel's subsequent books. She was divorced, and had one daughter, Jennifer, from her previous marriage. After they were married, they had one more child, a son, Shlomo Elisha. Fluent in five languages, and thoroughly literate, she matched Wiesel in his interest in literature and the arts. Yet she also had stories of her own childhood in Vienna and her flight from the Nazis through Europe to Switzerland. In a sense, she matched Wiesel also in his European roots.

As he continued to write and speak out in the 1970's and later, Wiesel began to enlarge the focus of his concern for oppressed ethnic groups. He traveled to Central America to draw attention to the issue of the mistreatment of the Misquito Indians of Nicaragua. He saw the consequences of apartheid close-up in South Africa. He was shocked by the suffering of Biafrans in the Nigerian civil war that ended in 1970. And he continued to speak out on behalf of Jews of the Soviet Union.

And of course, he continued to write: Plays, novels, essays, appeals, and a cantata flowed from his pen. By the mid-1970's he had in many ways come to symbolize not just a Jewish survivor of the Holocaust or even a moving exponent of Jewish identity and legacy. He had succeeded in universalizing as a global human horror a specific one, committed by one people against another, in this case, the Jews. For Wiesel, Auschwitz was not simply a blot upon German history but a blot on the whole of human history. If the human race did not continue to remember what it signified, he was convinced it was in terrible danger of repeating the crime, if not against the Jews, then against some other defenseless people.

Some observers have compared Wiesel to the biblical figure Job, a man who does not hesitate to argue with God about what he believes are immense divine injustices against him. But given Wiesel's desire that the experience of the Holocaust be a message to all the nations, not at all just to the Jews or to their persecutors, then, as Robert McAfee Brown suggests, he is closer to the prophet Jeremiah. In fact, Wiesel has written about Jeremiah in his book *Five Biblical Portraits*. His characterization of Jeremiah in many respects is a characterization of the calling he believes is his own. He writes:

> The prophet of Israel has become the prophet to all nations. He now
> understands—and makes others understand—that Israel's destiny affects
> everyone else's. What happens to Judah will eventually happen to Babylon,

then Rome, and ultimately to the entire world. And so the most Jewish of
the Jewish prophets becomes the most universal among them.[61]

"Jewish history lies at the center of history," Wiesel has written. "Whatever the world may try to do to us it will do to itself."[62] It may well have been
because of Wiesel's universal interest in the human condition as well as
because of his preeminent role in memorializing the Holocaust that President Jimmy Carter asked him to head the U.S. Holocaust Memorial Council
in 1978. Not especially interested in administration and uncertain about the
council's task, Wiesel was at first reluctant to accept the job. Carter, though,
had prepared well for his White House meeting with him. In the Oval Office, he presented Wiesel with aerial photographs of Auschwitz taken by
U.S. reconnaissance aircraft during World War II. He then asked Wiesel to
explain the different parts of the photograph. Carter's strategy was effective: Wiesel agreed to take the job and was chairman for six years. His dream
during this time was to create a museum that would be both a memorial
and an educational entity.

For the first few years, Wiesel and members of the council traveled to
different locations to observe what had been done to commemorate the
destruction of Europe's Jews during World War II. Nothing shocked him
as much as the visit the group took to Babi Yar in the Ukraine in 1979.
Here, in 1941, more than 100,000 Jews and Ukrainian civilians had been
mowed down in one of the most brutal mass murders performed by the
Nazis in their conquered territories. The Soviets had erected a memorial
at Babi Yar, but on seeing it firsthand, Wiesel said he found it "huge, ugly,
blasphemous." One simple reason for his outrage was that there was no
mention of the huge proportion of victims who were Jewish.

In 1980, with a group of human rights activists from several faith backgrounds, Wiesel traveled to Thailand. They hoped to deliver twenty truckloads of medical supplies to Cambodia. That country had endured the
ravaging onslaught of the Pol Pot regime, fanatical French-trained Communists who became responsible for the infamous "killing fields." They
had ruled for three and a half years, from 1975 to 1979, when the Vietnamese invaded Cambodia and drove the regime from power.

Though thousands died during the Vietnamese onslaught, thousands more
had taken the opportunity of their country's internal chaos to permanently
flee Cambodia across the border to Thailand. Wiesel and his companions were

unable to deliver their medical supplies into Cambodia, but they spoke through loudspeakers across the border. "I came here because nobody came when I was there," he declared simply.[63] "There" was Auschwitz. But it was also Cambodia's "killing fields," or later, Bosnia, or Rwanda.

Wiesel's sense of obligation to Jews, especially to those who had died in the Holocaust, never lessened even as he enlarged the tent of his concern to speak out against injustice and oppression in many different parts of the world. In 1982 he dropped his French publisher, *Le Seuil*, after its chief, Michel Chodkiewicz, accused the Israelis of genocide by their invasion of Lebanon. Chodkiewicz, a convert to Islam, refused to retract or correct the comment, so Wiesel left until he was succeeded in the job by a different executive.

In April 1985, Wiesel was the guest of honor at a White House ceremony to honor him with the Congressional Gold Medal of Achievement, one of America's highest civilian awards, and one later to be awarded to Billy Graham.

It was not a harmonious occasion. A storm of controversy had blown up over the just-announced itinerary of a forthcoming visit to West Germany by President Ronald Reagan. One of the places the Germans wanted to show Reagan was a military cemetery at Bitburg, where, in addition to regular German World War II soldiers, Nazi Waffen SS officers had been buried. Many American Jews were outraged. Turning from his podium to President Reagan during the White House ceremony, Wiesel looked the president in the eye and said, "That place [Bitburg], Mr. President, is not your place. Your place is with the victims of the S.S. . . . . The issue here is not politics, but good and evil."

Reagan looked resolutely back at Wiesel and did not comment. And he did not back down from the decision to visit Bitburg. Officials from his administration made the case that, unpleasant though it was that the cemetery contained SS soldiers (which they had apparently not known about when the location was first broached), West Germany's leader, Helmut Kohl, a staunch ally of the U.S. at a crucial period of the Cold War, would suffer major political embarrassment if Washington asked for the itinerary to be altered. Reagan, although he did not reveal it at the time, was shaken by the incident.

Yet moral issues often announce themselves in unexpected places. When the most prestigious award of all came Wiesel's way, the Nobel

Peace Prize in 1986, one of the groups that had lobbied energetically for it in the very year of the Bitburg controversy was seventy members of the German Parliament, or Bundestag. Wiesel's name had been nominated several times earlier before the Peace Prize announcement in October that year. The German parliamentary support was clearly a central factor in the selection of Wiesel for the prize. Wiesel, said the Nobel Committee's chairman Egil Aarvik in Oslo, was "one of the most important spiritual leaders and guides in an age when violence, repression and racism continue to characterize the world. Wiesel is a messenger to mankind: his message is one of peace, atonement, and human dignity."

In December 1986, the Wiesels traveled as a family to Oslo for the award ceremony and the delivery of Wiesel's official Nobel lecture. Aarvik introduced Wiesel with the comment that the aim of the writer's lifework had not been to gain sympathy for the victims or survivors of the Holocaust, but "to awaken our conscience. Our indifference to evil makes us partners in the crime. . . .The fight for freedom and human dignity— whether in Latin America, Asia, Europe, or South Africa—has become his life's purpose."[64] Aarvik went on:

> I doubt whether any other individual, through the use of such quiet speech, has achieved more or been more widely heard. The words are not big and the voice which speaks them is low. It is a voice of peace we hear. . . .Truly, prisoner A-7713 has become a human being once again, a human being dedicated to humanity.[65]

Wiesel, in his lecture, spoke eloquently on the issue of remembrance. But he also publicly criticized the South African system of apartheid and the imprisonment there of Nelson Mandela. He mentioned the house arrest in the Soviet Union of physicist Andrey Sakharov, and of the Soviet prohibition on emigration for many Soviet Jews who wished to go to Israel. He spoke of Job ("Job, our ancestor. Job, our contemporary. His ordeal concerns all humanity").

And he spoke of God. "Where was God in all this?" he asked his distinguished audience, referring to the Holocaust. In Wiesel's first novel, *Night*, a voice in the crowd had described God as the victim of a hanging along with three executed victims of the Nazis. But Wiesel has emphatically rejected the so-called "death of God" theology. No one, Jewish or Christian, who came out of the Holocaust, he has said, could subscribe to that. So where was God in Auschwitz?

In his *Memoirs*, Wiesel describes one of many meetings with the Lubavitcher rebbe Menachem Mendel Schneerson, a man of prodigious intellectual abilities and reputed spiritual power in the Hasidic community. Once again, the topic of God and Auschwitz came up. Could one love God without faith in Him? Wiesel asked the rebbe. Schneerson replied that faith had to precede everything else. Wiesel persisted. "Rebbe," he asked, "how can you believe in God after Auschwitz?"

After a long, long pause, the rebbe responded, "How can you not believe in God after Auschwitz?"[66]

Carol Rittner, director of the Elie Wiesel Foundation for Humanity, has herself reflected on Wiesel's understanding of an all-powerful God amid a totally evil environment. She writes:

> While Wiesel rejects the very notion of "God is dead," he challenges Jews and non-Jews alike to confront the real difficulty, which he maintains is not to live in a world without God, but to choose to live in a world with God, even while facing the evil, the suffering and the mystery of the Holocaust.[67]

For Wiesel, his childhood in Sighet was a time of a passionate desire on his part to know God. "I existed to glorify God and to sanctify his Word," he says. "I existed to link my destiny to that of my people, and the destiny of my people to that of humanity."[68] Coming from his Hasidic background, he believes that "everything must be translated in spiritual terms, which means into quest for truth. We are here to search for truth about God, about human beings, about life."[69]

Truth has been the central ingredient in Solzhenitsyn's pathway as a writer. It is the plumb line for Pope John Paul II as to how freedom should be ordered. For Wiesel, truth is an absolutely indispensable ingredient in the understanding of God in the context of Auschwitz. The Auschwitz experience did not destroy Wiesel's faith in God, but for him it raised deeply painful questions about both God's power and His love. He seems uncertain whether he will ever have satisfactory answers, though he believes that it is the Jewish duty always to address God with even very troubling questions. "I have risen against His justice," he says, "protested His silence and sometimes His absence, but my anger rises up within faith and not outside it."[70]

In a 1974 lecture to Stanford University, Wiesel said flatly that he did not consider that there was such a thing as Jewish theology, because "God wants man to be concerned with human things, not with godly things. . . . Jewish theology is human relations."[71] Yet Cardinal Jean-Marie Lustiger, the archbishop of Paris, who was born a Jew and has always affirmed his Jewish roots despite his acceptance of the Catholic faith in childhood, says of Wiesel, whom he greatly admires, "He is one of the great theologians of the century." How can this be? "Whoever questions and even challenges God," Lustiger explains, "all the while desiring to obey His Word and listening to His silence, that person is a theologian."[72]

For Wiesel, questions about God are inseparable also from questions about Jewishness. And Jewishness, Wiesel insists, is itself inseparable from the most fundamental questions about human existence. "The Jews are God's memory and the heart of mankind," he said in an interview with a Catholic journal. "We do not always know this, but the others do, and that is why they treat us with suspicion and cruelty. Memory frightens them. Through us, they are linked to the beginning and the end. By eliminating us they hope to gain immortality."[73]

One of the most terrible lessons of Auschwitz, in Wiesel's view, is that what the world will do today to the Jews, it will do tomorrow to itself. "This, perhaps, may be our mission to the world," he adds, "we are to save it from self-destruction."[74] "To be a Jew is to remember," Wiesel has said in many different ways. To be a Jew,

> is to be a human being. If there is one word I would like to imprint on everything I do, it is the word "humanize." . . . In *Messengers of God*, I said that the mission of the Jew was not to make the world Jewish but to humanize it, to make it a warmer, more hospitable, more human, more welcoming world.[75]

In *humanize* and *human dignity* there are resonances connecting Wiesel in his moral grasp of the human condition with John Paul II. This is true, although Wiesel would certainly not wish anyone to read into his insights any connection with Catholicism.

But what could he do with the insights that, providentially or not, had fallen to him in the years since Auschwitz? Within months of receiving the Nobel Prize, Wiesel had created his own humanitarian foundation to explore ways of investigating some of the most intractable problems facing the human race: the persistence of hatred, the traumatization of ever more generations of young people in the ethnic conflicts of their parents.

In 1988, the Elie Wiesel Foundation for Humanity gathered together seventy-five Nobel laureates in Paris to propose fresh principles, policies, and strategies to meet the twenty-first century. Two years later, he assembled another group of Nobel laureates, philosophers, and former political prisoners for a conference in Oslo called "The Anatomy of Hate: Resolving Conflict Through Dialogue and Democracy." Along with Václav Havel and Nelson Mandela were Günter Grass, the erstwhile host to Solzhenitsyn, South African novelist Nadine Gordimer, and even Tiananmen democracy movement leaders Chai Ling and Li Lu.

The impressive gathering, not surprisingly, failed to come to any consensus on what causes hatred. But it sparked an eerily prophetic warning from German Günter Grass on the folly of Western Europe's reckless armes trades with much of the world. Grass singled out Iraq. "Specifically, through shipments from West Germany," Grass said, "Iraq is in a position to hit targets with long range missiles equipped with chemical warheads and possibly nuclear ones as well."[76]

It was true. Just three years later, during the Gulf War, Iraqi Scud missiles were sent crashing into the suburbs of Tel Aviv and other spots in Israel. Mercifully, there were no chemical warheads on these missiles, but the foreign-supplied chemicals, inadvertently exploded by the conquering Coalition forces at the end of the war, led to long-term health problems for many American veterans of the Gulf War.

Wiesel would not remain silent. He spoke up again and again on behalf of political prisoners like the Chinese hero of the 1978 Democracy Wall movement, Wei Jingsheng; of Western hostages like journalist Terry Anderson, held by Islamic radical groups in Lebanon; and of ethnic minorities persecuted or bullied in many different parts of the world. But no issue seemed to galvanize him more urgently than the "ethnic cleansing" carried out by Serbian, Croatian, and even Bosnian Muslim forces in the former Yugoslav republic of Bosnia-Herzegovina. Just as he had confronted Reagan in the White House over a forthcoming presidential visit to West

Germany, so he brought up his concerns about Bosnia in another public setting where a U.S. president was close by him.

It happened in April 1993 at the formal inauguration of the U.S. Holocaust Memorial Museum in Washington. As the founding chairman of the committee that put together the museum, Wiesel was the main speaker. He reminded his audience again of the crushing failure of the Western Allies during World War II to stop the suffering and murder of the Jews of Europe even after it had become clear what Hitler's plans were for them. "By 1943, nearly 4 million Jews . . . had already perished," he said. "The Pentagon knew. The State Department knew. The White House knew. . . . Ask yourselves," he went on, "how could murderers do what they did and go on living? Why weren't the railways leading to Birkenau bombed by Allied bombers. . . . And why was there not public outcry, indignation and outrage?"

Then Wiesel, without warning, turned and looked at President Clinton, who was the most important of all the guests there. Respectfully, and carefully, he warned, "And Mr. President, I must tell you something. I have been in the former Yugoslavia last fall. I cannot sleep since what I have seen. As a Jew I am saying that. We must do something to stop the bloodshed in that country. People fight each other and children die. Why? Something, anything, must be done."[77]

Clinton didn't flinch, as Reagan hadn't when a similar, conscience-provoking question had been put to him by Wiesel back in 1985. But he certainly didn't look comfortable. Wiesel's words, he told reporters on leaving the ceremony, had been "a challenge to all of us."

Wiesel's lobbying on behalf of the victims of ethnic cleansing in Bosnia did not stop with a public appeal to President Clinton. Early in 1993 he lunched with senior State Department officials to discuss what the U.S. was doing and should be doing in the former Yugoslavia. He told Undersecretary of State Peter Tarnoff and State Department Counsel Timothy E. Wirth that the mass killings of Muslims by Serbs absolutely demanded outside intervention. Tarnoff was not impressed. According to Richard Johnson, former head of the State Department's Yugoslavia desk, who was present at the luncheon, Tarnoff told Wiesel that the moral stakes of the political credibility of the Clinton presidency were more important than the issue of Bosnia. Of course intervention could be tried in Bosnia, Tarnoff said, but what if it failed?

Wouldn't that be a disaster for the liberal agenda of the current Demo-cratic administration?[78]

Wiesel didn't think so. In September 1993 he participated in an appeal to NATO signed by one hundred prominent former leaders, Nobel laure-ates, and others, asking for NATO air strikes against Bosnian Serb military targets. It was not until 1995 that this appeal bore fruit and Serb positions were indeed bombed by NATO. But it was also not until December 1995, after thousands of Bosnian Muslims had been tortured, killed, or driven from their homes, that American, British, French, and other NATO troops intervened in Bosnia decisively enough to bring an end to the killing. Present in the White House when the intervention decision was an-nounced, Wiesel declared that he supported it "with pride and pleasure."[79]

Prominence and fame may be gratifying in many ways, but along with the warm public approval they have brought Wiesel pain and anxiety. Like other Great Souls, he has received several death threats, particularly after he has publicly spoken up on behalf of Israel. The hard-core pro-Nazi histori-ans who have tried to pretend that the Holocaust never took place have denounced him bitterly in articles that crop up regularly on the Internet.

Some of his harshest critics have come from within the ranks of the Jew-ish community itself. Simon Wiesenthal, the famous Nazi-hunter, bitterly com-plained in an unpublished interview with a New York journalist that he had expected to share the Nobel Peace Prize in 1986 with Wiesel, but that the lobbying of Wiesel's friends had been too powerful for him. In fact, the antipathy between the two men had other causes as well. Wiesel had praised a book that criticized Wiesenthal for allegedly covering up the SS connections of former Austrian president Kurt Waldheim.[80]

Other attacks have been no less harsh. Martin Peretz, editor in chief and chairman of the *New Republic*, made some snide comments about Wiesel in 1988 for taking to task in public those in the American Jewish community who criticized Israel for the methods it was using to suppress the Palestinian *intifadeh,* or uprising, on the West Bank and in Gaza. "L'histoire, c'est moi [history, that's me] has always been his favorite theme," Peretz wrote.[81] Others have been unhappy with Wiesel for writ-ing about the Holocaust in a way that appears to set it aside from other historical events altogether.

If the Holocaust has been Wiesel's benchmark of evil in the sufferings endured by Jews throughout history, the reestablishment of Israel has seemed to him an almost miraculous benchmark of God's faithfulness. He dislikes any public criticism of Israel precisely because the country represents so much of the Jewish hope for him. "Within the life I have had I have seen so many Jews humiliated," he says, "that I cannot bring myself to humiliate Israel, except for the fanatics, who are obscene."[82] "I think the secularists were wrong when they wanted to have a nation like all others," he has also said. "They were wrong because Israel cannot be a nation like all others."[83] It troubles Wiesel that Israel's behavior has not always been exemplary toward other nations. He is especially troubled by the existence of Jews within Israel who are as much "fanatics" in their inhumanity to Israel's presumed foes, particularly toward the Arabs under Israeli political control.

REFLECTING ON THE PROBLEM OF EVIL

What remains unique about Wiesel is his powerful moral vision of what the Holocaust meant: for the Jews who suffered and died in it, for the Nazi killers who perpetrated it, for the Christians who were unconscionably ambivalent about denouncing it, for those who survived it. Some critics in Israel and the U.S. have been disturbed by Wiesel's insistence on the uniqueness of the Event. They consider his viewpoint to be "mystical" because it implies almost a supernatural element of wickedness in what happened. Indeed, Wiesel has described the Holocaust as "a mutation on a cosmic scale."

But what is a "mutation" in relation to human behavior? We are talking, after all, about willed evil. Many Jews are not comfortable with the notion of a personal source of evil—Satan—despite the fact that the concept is entirely biblical (see the book of Job, for example). The cliché "The Devil made me do it" has, of course, been overused to the point of absurdity.

Yet Wiesel's profound reflection on the source and the implementation of evil has in some ways brought his perspective on the reality of human wickedness closer to the Christian view. This view holds that wicked human behavior can be attributed indeed to "the world" (fascination with power and fame) and "the flesh" (i.e., greedy human appetites), but also, quite literally, to "the devil."

Christians have always believed that some evil acts throughout human history have been influenced by, if not at times actually directed by, the demonic agents of a personal source of evil, i.e., the devil, or Satan. When all of the common sociological explanations for anti-Semitism in Europe have been offered, what does explain Hitler's rise to power? Uniformly, Germans who joined adoring, almost worshiping crowds who showed up to listen to Hitler have spoken of his "charisma," his "magnetism," his "presence." Could all of these attributes be explained away merely as natural shoots watered by Europe's longtime subterranean lake of anti-Semitism?

As Wiesel himself has often pointed out, Hitler's single-mindedness in desiring, planning, and executing the Holocaust against the Jews went beyond the rational. At a time when rail transportation was desperately needed for the German war effort, when the Allies had already created a second front in Europe by landing on the beaches of Normandy, priority was routinely given to the cattle cars carrying Jews into Auschwitz from the rest of Europe. This made no practical or military sense at all. It was irrational. But perhaps it wasn't just "madness."

Many people, particularly Christians, would consider that almost everything Hitler did in the political arena was demonic in origin. Several books have documented Hitler's fascination with the occult and with the symbols of occultic paganism.[84] Some of Hitler's closest associates seemed to notice when a peculiar kind of oratorical power—mesmerizing in its effect on audiences—would come upon the führer at times during his speeches. From a Christian worldview, it would make sense to attribute such moments to direct demonic influence.

Indeed, Hitler attracted to his cause people with similarly murderous intentions vis-à-vis the Jews. One of these was the Grand Mufti of Jerusalem, Haji Amin al-Husseini, who traveled to Germany during World War II, met with Hitler, and warmly encouraged the Nazi leader in all of his wartime actions, including what became known as the "Final Solution." Haji Amin was the mastermind of an Arab revolt against both the British Mandatory authorities in Palestine and the Jews who had already migrated there earlier as part of the Zionist dream. There is a letter to Haji Amin from Hitler's foreign minister, Joachim von Ribbentrop, promising in 1942 that Germany would lend its support to Arab objectives to destroy the "Jewish National Home in Palestine."[85]

Wiesel, a complex man, is probably not comfortable with a "demonic" interpretation of the origins of evil. His belief that there is no such thing as Jewish theology is based on the view, as we have seen, that theology is "human relations," and that God doesn't want people to be concerned with "godly things." He has said that beneath every mask that evil wears there is something in common: indifference.

But indifference is a passive quality, not an active one. If there is indeed a devil, then he is surely not passive in what he does. A student of the Bible might say that the Jewish Torah, the Law, explicitly demonstrates the supernatural power of God. At the same time it actually condemns any contact with other sources of occult supernatural power or knowledge, for example, through sorcery, witchcraft, divination, or spiritism (see Lev. 19:31).

As a youth in Sighet, Wiesel saw at first hand the tragic effect of involvement in the occult on two of his friends. He himself admits that it was indirectly the arrival of the Germans that spared him from a similar fate. It is surprising that he has confronted the nature of human evil more insightfully and powerfully than virtually anyone alive, and yet has shied away from the logical conclusion that human behavior may at times be subject to forces over which it has no control at all: radically evil forces.

Christians should respect Wiesel's reluctance to listen sympathetically to some of the Christian perspectives on the Holocaust. The subterranean lake of European anti-Semitism that we have already mentioned was certainly fed, for centuries, by waters of both Catholic and Protestant theological anti-Semitism. Even if Hitler himself was an occultic neo-pagan, and no more a Christian than Stalin was (Stalin had actually attended Orthodox seminary), some of the bureaucrats and officials who carried out the Holocaust went to Catholic confession or Protestant Communion and considered themselves Christian, as Wiesel notes.

Any Jew has the right to ask why Pope Pius XII was silent before World War II and during the Holocaust, or why so few German pastors or priests spoke up against the spreading virus of Nazi hatred. A strong outside protest might have delayed, or even undermined, the devastation. Jews are amply justified in asking Christians to speak very humbly about their faith in light of what some bearing the name of Christ didn't do to ward off the Event, and what others—far worse—actually did to accomplish it.

Wiesel over the years has mellowed toward Christians, at least in part because of his friendship with Mauriac. In America, many Christians, both liberal and evangelical, have been deeply moved by his writing and have written to him to express their appreciation of him. But his childhood years certainly plowed in his mind deep furrows of suspicion toward Christians.

In Sighet, he grew up in an atmosphere of anxiety for Jews, well before the Nazis. "As a child," he says simply, "I lived in fear."[86] He would cross the street rather than walk in front of a church. He admits that he knew absolutely nothing about the Christian faith and indeed had no desire to know. "At school I sat with Christian boys of my age," he says, "but we didn't speak to one another. At recess we played separated by an invisible wall. I never visited a Christian schoolmate at his home. We had nothing in common."[87]

He did not even know that Christianity and Judaism shared the same biblical roots, the same belief in eternity, the same worship of the same God. "All I knew of Christianity," he wrote, "was its hate for my people."[88] That may be an unfair characterization of Christianity as a faith, but it is an honest reflection of what many Jews have encountered in daily life from "Christians," especially before and during Christian holidays like Christmas and Easter.

Mauriac may have been the first truly committed Christian who reached out humbly and in love to Wiesel without making an apology for his faith. Wiesel remained grateful to him even when the two disagreed, as they sometimes did (for example, over General de Gaulle's remark that Israelis were "a self-assured and dominating people," a remark to which Wiesel objected because it seemed to be a demeaning characterization of Jews in general). In his *Memoirs*, Wiesel cites some excerpts from fascinating conversations with Mauriac over the differences between the two men on the Christian and the Jewish views of God, Jesus, and faith itself. One of them reads:

Mauriac: How did you manage it?

Wiesel: Manage what?

Mauriac: To survive.

Wiesel: I don't know.

Mauriac: It was God. God's will. The Lord chose you.

Wiesel: No, don't say that.

Mauriac: Don't you believe in God?

Wiesel: Yes, I do.

Mauriac: It was your faith that saved you.

Wiesel: Don't say that, I beg you.

Mauriac:	Faith can offer support and comfort. It can be a kind of nourishment, a higher nourishment. Faith embodies life and life's power. Perhaps it was faith that made you strong.
Wiesel:	Strength had nothing to do with it.
Mauriac:	Or God?
Wiesel:	Not God either.
Mauriac:	Then what?
Wiesel:	I don't know.[89]

"The difference between the Jew and the Christian today," Wiesel has said, "is that we are still waiting for the Messiah to come. At the same time, we don't know what the Messiah is or who he is."[90] Wiesel at one point said that it was Christianity itself that "died" at Auschwitz and that what Christians had done over the centuries in the name of Christ had caused deep dishonor to accrue to that name itself. But, again, he has softened the harsher edges of his criticism of the Christian faith over the years, and he is courteous and gentle today with Christians even when there is disagreement with them. He has also been openly critical of his own faith for ignoring Christians because, by believing in Jesus, the first Christians—who were, of course, Jewish—became from the Jewish point of view "heretics."[91]

Interestingly, he doesn't accept that a Jewish person can believe that Jesus is the Messiah, and yet remain Jewish. "Where I come from," he says, "and from where I stand, one cannot be Jew and Christian at the same time. Jesus was Jewish, but those who claim allegiance to him today are not."[92] It is important to respect this position, even while not necessarily agreeing with it. Does a Jewish person after all cease to be Jewish by being a Buddhist, a Hindu, or even an atheist? There are growing numbers of Jews who do indeed believe that Jesus is the Messiah and vociferously continue to assert their Jewishness. They insist that they remain Jews.

But Christians should be careful not to take issue noisily with Wiesel or with other Jews over this. For hundreds of years, "conversion" to Christianity was never an option, but an obligation imposed by supposedly Christian regimes on Jewish communities on pain of death. The word "conversion" has a deeply painful ring to it for many Jews. Perhaps only a Jew himself should be allowed to address this issue. The French cardinal

Jean-Marie Lustiger, who is archbishop of Paris, was born a Jew, and continues to insist that he is still ethnically Jewish. He has put it this way:

> I can bear the night into which Israel was plunged only by sharing
> the night into which the Messiah willingly entered in order to open
> to all the Way of Life and to bring forth the light of the world, the
> light of Resurrection, a light more dazzling than all the suns. When
> I believe this, I do not consider myself separated before God from
> Elie Wiesel, whom I love as a brother.[93]

It is certainly a tribute to Lustiger that he should make this generous and inclusive remark as a believer in Jesus to Wiesel, who regards belief in Jesus as Messiah to be incompatible with true Jewishness. But it is a tribute to Wiesel, too, that he has allowed the logic of human generosity to overcome deeply painful experiences from early in his life.

To his fingertips, Wiesel is not just a man who remembers the Event and who writes about it, but a man who stands almost trembling before the power of words—for both good or ill. "Be careful of words," Wiesel quotes a learned rabbi as saying. "They're dangerous. Be wary of them. They beget either demons or angels. It's up to you to give life to one or the other."[94] Hitler and Stalin imbued words with death, and Wiesel saw at first hand the consequences of speech that had been marinated in hatred and violence.

"To write is to plumb the unfathomable depths of being," Wiesel has said.[95] "I don't believe in art for art's sake," he has noted elsewhere (unconsciously echoing Solzhenitsyn's view of the moral calling upon all writers). "For me literature must have an ethical dimension. The aim of the literature I call testimony is to disturb."[96]

But it should not merely disturb. . . . Rather, it should provoke, chasten, and compel the reader to face things in life he or she would probably rather pretend did not exist. Throughout his life as a writer and as a concerned citizen of both the United States and the world, Wiesel has never stopped tugging at people by the corner of their jackets. He has never ceased asking, imploring, or even demanding their attention to the atrocities that human beings, in the very depths of their wicked capabilities, continue to commit against other human beings.

What authority does Wiesel have to do this? He has the authority of a man who has risked death threats and disfavor for reminding the world of what it would rather forget. He has the authority of someone who has come into his calling—the calling to ward off future evil by calling to mind the monstrous forms it took in the recent past. And he has the authority of an eyewitness, the survivor of unspeakable evil.

Elie Wiesel is the youngest of the Great Souls, and perhaps the most sobering of them all. Billy Graham has pointed us toward salvation. Nelson Mandela has challenged us to forgive. Aleksandr Solzhenitsyn has required of us truth. Mother Teresa has epitomized love. Pope John Paul II has reminded us of the God-given gift of human dignity. Elie Wiesel is a Great Soul because of another reminder, the terrible truth about the human capacity for evil and our need never to forget it.

All have been gifts to our century, indeed to our millennium. As we face the next one, they are bright lights to all of us, illuminating the uncertain pathway ahead.

NOTES

INTRODUCTION

1. C. S. Lewis, *The Abolition of Man* (New York: The Macmillan Publishing Company, 1947).
2. The late Professor Donald W. Treadgold, formerly chairman of the History Department at the University of Washington, conducting a course on "The Influence of the West on Russia and China."
3. *Webster's Third New International Dictionary* (Chicago: Encyclopaedia Britannica, 1971), I, 994.
4. *Roget's International Thesaurus* (New York: Harper & Row Publishers, 1977), 979,6.
5. *Webster's Third New International Dictionary*, III, 2176.
6. Daniel Boorstin, *The Image: A Guide to Pseudo-Events in America* (New York: Atheneum, 1987), 57–58.
7. Ibid.
8. James W. Wilson, *On Character* (Washington, D.C.: AEI Press, 1995), 42.
9. See especially William J. Bennett, *The Book of Virtues: A Treasury of Great Moral Stories* (New York: Simon and Schuster, 1993) and Gertrude Himmelfarb, *The Demoralization of Society: From Victorian Virtues to Modern Values* (New York: Random House, 1994).
10. Ibid., 208.

CHAPTER ONE
Billy Graham—Salvation

1. Two books have powerfully detailed the extent of this persecution: Paul Marshall and Lela Gilbert's *Their Blood Cries Out* (Dallas: Word, 1997) and Nina Shea's *In the Lion's Den* (Nashville: Broadman & Holman, 1997).

2. Joe Treen, "America's Crusader," *People*, October 7, 1991, 117.
3. Billy Graham Evangelistic Association, Internet.
4. Nancy Gibbs and Richard H. Ostling, "God's Billy Pulpit," *Time*, November 15, 1993, 72.
5. Grant Walker, "Charles Atlas with a Halo: America's Billy Graham," *Christian Century*, April 1, 1992, 336.
6. Interview by author with Graham, "Preachers, Politics, and Temptation," *Time*, May 28, 1990, 14.
7. Billy Graham Evangelistic Association, Internet.
8. William Martin, *A Prophet with Honor: The Billy Graham Story* (New York: William Morrow and Company, 1991), 491.
9. "Preachers, Politics, and Temptation," 14.
10. Martin, *A Prophet with Honor*, 61.
11. Ibid., 59.
12. Ibid., 58–59.
13. John Pollock, *To All the Nations: The Billy Graham Story* (New York: Harper & Row Publishers, 1985), 12.
14. Martin, *A Prophet with Honor*, 60.
15. Ibid.
16. Ibid., 61.
17. Pollock, *To All the Nations: The Billy Graham Story*, 13.
18. Ibid., 12.
19. Martin, *A Prophet with Honor*, 62.
20. Ibid.
21. The description by a contemporary of nineteenth-century revival meetings, Thomas Low Nichols, is cited in John Warwick Montgomery, *The Shaping of America* (Minneapolis: Bethany Fellowship, 1976), 168.
22. Pollock, *To All the Nations*, 15.
23. Ibid.
24. Martin, *A Prophet with Honor*, 63.
25. Ibid., 64.
26. Ibid.
27. Ibid., 68.
28. Ibid., 70.
29. Ibid., 73.
30. Ibid.
31. Pollock, *To All the Nations*, 21.
32. Ibid., 23.
33. Martin, *A Prophet with Honor*, 75.
34. Pollock, *To All the Nations*, 23.
35. Martin, *A Prophet with Honor*, 75–76.
36. Pollock, *To All the Nations*, 24.
37. Ibid., 25.
38. Martin, *A Prophet with Honor*, 79.
39. Pollock, *To All the Nations*, 27.
40. Ibid., 26.
41. Ibid., 27.
42. Ibid., 29.
43. Martin, *A Prophet with Honor*, 83.
44. Ibid., 95.

45. Billy Graham, *Just As I Am: The Autobiography of Billy Graham* (New York, Harper-Collins Publishers, 1997), 97.
46. Martin, *A Prophet with Honor*, 451.
47. Pollock, *To All the Nations*, 35.
48. Ibid., 36.
49. Martin, *A Prophet with Honor*, 98–99.
50. Ibid., 101.
51. Ibid., 125.
52. Ibid., 105.
53. Graham, *Just As I Am*, 651.
54. Martin, *A Prophet with Honor*, 111.
55. Pollock, *To All the Nations*, 42.
56. Martin, *A Prophet with Honor*, 112.
57. Ibid., 115.
58. Pollock, *To All the Nations*, 48.
59. Martin, *A Prophet with Honor*, 120.
60. Pollock, *To All the Nations*, 49.
61. Martin, *A Prophet with Honor*, (illustration pages) 160–61.
62. Ibid., 168.
63. Ibid., 170.
64. Ibid., 173.
65. Ibid., 172.
66. Ibid., 235.
67. Ibid.
68. William Martin, "Fifty Years with Billy," *Christianity Today*, November 13, 1995, 22.
69. Ibid., 22–70.
70. Martin, *A Prophet with Honor*, 223.
71. William Martin, "Fifty Years with Billy," 21.
72. Martin, *A Prophet with Honor*, 175.
73. Ibid., 182.
74. Ibid., 181.
75. Graham, *Just As I Am*, 236.
76. Miller, Merle. *Plain Speaking: An Oral Biography of Harry S. Truman* (Berkley Publishing Corporation, 1973), 363.
77. Billy Graham, *Peace with God* (Revised and Expanded edition, Minneapolis: Grason Publishing, 1984).
78. Graham, *Just As I Am*, 400.
79. Jeffrey L. Sheler, "After the Legend," *U.S. News & World Report*, May 3, 1993, 72.
80. Martin, *A Prophet with Honor*, (illustration pages) 320–21.
81. Ibid., 349.
82. Ibid., 283.
83. Richard Nixon, *The Memoirs of Richard Nixon* (New York: Grosset and Dunlap, 1978), 293.
84. Ibid., 428.
85. Charles Hirshberg, "The Eternal Crusader," *Life*, November 1994, 110.
86. Joe Green, "America's Crusade," *People*, October 7, 1991, 120.
87. Interview by author with Graham, *Time*, May 28, 1990, 13.
88. Graham, *Just As I Am*, 454.
89. Ibid., 442.
90. Martin, *A Prophet with Honor*, 423.

91. Gustav Niebuhr, "Billy Graham: Loyal to Longtime Friend in Triumph and Defeat," *Washington Post*, April 28, 1994, A12.

92. Nancy Gibbs and Richard H. Ostling, "God's Billy Pulpit," 78.

93. Graham, *Just As I Am*, 538.

94. Interview with author, "Preachers, Politics, and Temptation," 13.

95. Martin, *A Prophet with Honor*, 593.

96. *Time*, May 28, 1990, 13.

97. Martin, *A Prophet with Honor,* 515.

98. Ibid.

99. "Graham in Moscow: What Did He Really Say?" *Christianity Today*, June 18, 1982, 12.

100. Martin, *A Prophet with Honor*, 616.

101. Ibid., 507.

102. Ibid., 588.

103. Interview with author, *Time*, May 28, 1990, 13.

104. Martin, *A Prophet with Honor*, 301.

105. Billy Graham, *A Biblical Standard for Evangelists* (Minneapolis: World Wide Publications, 1984), 33.

CHAPTER TWO
Nelson Mandela—Forgiveness

1. Nelson Mandela, *Long Walk to Freedom* (New York: Little, Brown and Company, 1994), 540.

2. Arthur Miller, "Talking with Mandela: The Measure of the Man," *The Nation*, February 11, 1991, 151.

3. Cited in *World Press Review*, January 1995, 10, from *The London Observer*.

4. Conversation with the author, January 25, 1995.

5. Richard Stengel, "The Making of a Leader," *Time*, May 4, 1994, 36.

6. Miller, "Talking with Mandela: The Measure of the Man," 153.

7. Meg Greenfield, "A Lesson in Dignity," *Newsweek*, April 8, 1996, 84.

8. "Nelson Mandela," *People*, December 31, 1990, 77.

9. Cited by Anthony Lewis, "The Essential Mandela," *New York Times*, June 22, 1990, A27.

10. Rev. Jesse Jackson, "What Nelson Mandela Told Me," *Ebony*, May 1990, 186.

11. Robin Petersen, "Parable of the Kingdom," *Christian Century*, January 17, 1996, 36.

12. Mandela, *Long Walk to Freedom*, 453.

13. Michael Cassidy, *A Witness Forever* (London: Hodder & Stoughton, 1995), 125.

14. Ibid., 12.

15. Ibid., 17.

16. Ibid., 19.

17. Ibid., 30.

18. Ibid., 32.

19. Ibid., 33.

20. Ibid., 37.

21. Ibid., 45.

22. Ibid., 61.

23. Ibid., 74.

24. Ibid., 84.

25. Ibid., 98.
26. Ibid., 104–5.
27. Ibid., 105.
28. Ibid., 122.
29. Ibid., 126.
30. Ibid., 137.
31. Ibid., 141.
32. Fatima Meer, *Higher than Hope: The Authorized Biography of Nelson Mandela* (New York: Harper & Row, 1990), 141.
33. Mandela, *Long Walk to Freedom*, 142.
34. Ibid., 150.
35. Ibid., 152.
36. Ibid., 163.
37. Ibid., 181.
38. Ibid., 133.
39. Ibid., 136.
40. Ibid., 138.
41. Ibid., 186.
42. Ibid., 188.
43. Ibid., 202.
44. Ibid., 206.
45. Ibid., 212.
46. Ibid., 227.
47. Ibid., 246.
48. Ibid., 264.
49. Ibid., 274.
50. Richard Stengel, "The Making of a Leader," *Time*, May 4, 1994, 36.
51. *The New York Times*, June 10, 1990, A6.
52. Mandela, *Long Walk to Freedom*, 275.
53. Ibid., 286.
54. Ibid., 298.
55. Ibid., 320.
56. Ibid., 320–21.
57. Ibid., 321.
58. Ibid., 322.
59. Ibid., 328.
60. Ibid.
61. Ibid., 349.
62. Ibid., 402.
63. James Gregory, *Goodbye Bafana: Nelson Mandela, My Prisoner, My Friend* (London: Headline Book Publishing, 1995), 13.
64. Ibid., 331–32.
65. Mandela, *Long Walk to Freedom*, 424.
66. Ibid., 457.
67. Ibid., 458–59.
68. Ibid., 463.
69. Ibid., 479.
70. Scott McLeod, "Mandela: Free at Last?" *Time*, February 5, 1990, 28.
71. Ibid., 27.
72. Ibid.

73. Maureen Dowd, "Mandela Declines to Rule Out Force," *New York Times*, June 26, 1990, A14.

74. Emma Gilbey, *The Lady: The Life and Times of Winnie Mandela* (London: Vintage, 1993), 145.

75. Mandela, *Long Walk to Freedom*, 533.

76. *A Witness Forever*, 168.

77. Ibid., 191.

78. Mandela, *Long Walk to Freedom*, 540.

79. "Fifteen Days that Shook the World," *Ebony*, August 1994, 88.

80. Inaugural Address, Historical Speeches Homepage, Internet.

81. Suzanne Daley, "Mandela Broadens Limits for Apartheid-Era Amnesty," *New York Times*, December 14, 1996, A4.

CHAPTER THREE
Aleksandr Solzhenitsyn—Truth

1. "The Homecoming," BBC-Frontline Production, 1995 (a documentary of Solzhenitsyn's return to Russia in 1994).

2. Margaret Shipiro, "Solzhenitsyn Returns to New Russia, Writer Ends 20 Year Exile, Seeking Ways Out of 'Our Quagmire,'" *Washington Post*, May 28, 1994, A1.

3. Quoted in Paul Gray, "Russia's Prophet in Exile," *Time*, July 24, 1989, 56.

4. David Remnick, "The Exile Returns," *New Yorker*, February 14, 1994, 70.

5. Solzhenitsyn interview with Bernard Levin, PBS Program, *FiringLine*, 1970.

6. Malcolm Muggeridge, on William F. Buckley's *FiringLine*, April 1976.

7. David Remnick, "The Exile Returns," 104.

8. Michael Scammell, *Solzhenitsyn: A Biography* (New York: W. W. Norton and Company, 1984), 42.

9. Ibid., 58.

10. Ibid., 81.

11. Aleksandr Solzhenitsyn, *The Gulag Archipelago* (New York: Harper & Row Publishers, 1973), Vol. I, Part 1, 19.

12. Solzhenitsyn, *The Gulag Archipelago*, Vol. 1, Part 1, 183.

13. Robert Conquest describes the process in great detail in *The Great Terror* (New York: The Macmillan Company, 1968), 138–40.

14. Scammell, *Solzhenitsyn*, 153.

15. Ibid., 230.

16. Ibid., 238.

17. Ibid., 245.

18. Cited in Scammell, *Solzhenitsyn*, 254.

19. Solzhenitsyn, *The Gulag Archipelago: 1918–1956. An Experiment in Literary Investigation* (New York: HarperCollins, 1992), Vol. III, Part 5, Chapter 5, 105.

20. Ibid., 106.

21. Ibid., 615.

22. Scammell, *Solzhenitsyn*, 344.

23. Aleksandr Solzhenitsyn, *The Oak and the Calf* (New York: Harper & Row, 1980), 4.

24. Alekxandr Solzhenitsyn, *Invisible Allies* (Washington, D.C.: Counterpoint, 1995), 35.

25. Cited in Scammell, *Solzhenitsyn*, 400.

26. Solzhenitsyn, *Invisible Allies*, 34.

27. Cited in Scammell, *Solzhenitsyn*, 448.
28. Ibid., 449.
29. Aleksandr Solzhenitsyn, *"Matryona's House" and "We Never Make Mistakes": Two Short Novels* (New York: W. W. Norton & Company, 1971), 138.
30. Scammell, *Solzhenitsyn*, 421.
31. Cited in Michael Scammell, *The Solzhenitsyn Files* (Carol Stream, IL: Edition Q, Inc., 1995), 23.
32. Solzhenitsyn, *The Oak and the Calf*, 103–4.
33. Scammell, *The Solzhenitsyn Files*, 10.
34. Scammell, *Solzhenitsyn*, 574.
35. Solzhenitsyn, *The Oak and the Calf*, 145.
36. Scammell, *Solzhenitsyn*, 575.
37. Cited in Scammell, *Solzhenitsyn*, 581.
38. Ibid., 602.
39. Scammell, *The Solzhenitsyn Files*, 20.
40. Cited in Scammell, *Solzhenitsyn*, 643.
41. Citation from Andrei Sakharov, *Memoirs* (New York: Alfred A. Knopf Inc., 1990), in *Time*, May 21, 1990, 52.
42. Ibid.
43. Scammell, *Solzhenitsyn*, 553.
44. Solzhenitsyn, *Invisible Allies*, 197.
45. Ibid., 198.
46. Edward E. Ericson Jr., *Solzhenitsyn and the Modern World* (Washington, D.C.: Regnery Gateway, 1993), 54.
47. Scammell, *Solzhenitsyn*, 676.
48. Ibid., 681.
49. Ibid., 741.
50. Scammell, *The Solzhenitsyn Files*, 203–9, passim.
51. David Remnick, "The Exile Returns," 73.
52. Cited in Joseph Epstein, "Why Solzhenitsyn Will Not Go Away," *Commentary*, November 1996, 205.
53. Scammell, *The Solzhenitsyn Files*, 285.
54. Scammell, *Solzhenitsyn*, 829–31.
55. Solzhenitsyn, *The Oak and the Calf*, 396.
56. Ibid., 408.
57. Ibid., 451.
58. Scammell, *Solzhenitsyn*, 863.
59. Ericson, *Solzhenitsyn and the Modern World*, 81.
60. Aleksandr Solzhenitsyn, *Nobel Lecture in Literature, 1970*, 165.
61. David Remnick, "The Exile Returns," *New Yorker*, February 14, 1994, 101.
62. Aleksander Solzhenitsyn, *Warning to the West* (New York: Farrar, Strauss and Giroux, 1976), 41.
63. Ibid., 115.
64. Ibid., 119.
65. Remnick, "The Exile Returns," 99.
66. Ibid., 102.
67. Ronald Berman, ed., *Solzhenitsyn at Harvard* (Washington, D.C.: Ethics and Public Policy Center, 1980), 5.
68. Ibid., 13.
69. Ibid., 66–67.

70. Interview with author, "Russia's Prophet in Exile," *Time*, July 24, 1989, 56.
71. Ibid.
72. Paul Klebnikov, "An Intervew with Aleksandr Solzhenitsyn," *Forbes*, May 9, 1994, 122.
73. Interview with author, Moscow, October 1995.
74. Ibid.

CHAPTER FOUR
Mother Teresa—Compassion
1. Mother Teresa of Calcutta, *My Life for the Poor* (New York: Ballantine Books, 1985), 101.
2. Ibid., 102.
3. Interview of author with Mother Teresa, July 22, 1975.
4. Malcolm Muggeridge, *Something Beautiful for God: Mother Teresa of Calcutta* (San Francisco: Harper and Row, 1971), 18.
5. Prince Michael of Greece, "All the Lives We Touch," *Parade*, August 11, 1996, 5.
6. Telephone conversation with the author, August 2, 1996.
7. Cited in *The Nobel Prize* (Stockholm: Imprimerie Royale, 1979), 38.
8. Ibid., 34.
9. Ibid., 35.
10. Ibid., 36.
11. Cited in Kathryn Spink, *The Miracle of Love: Mother Teresa of Calcutta, Her Missionaries of Charity, and her Co-workers* (San Francisco: Harper and Row, 1981) .
12. Lush Gjergji, *Mother Teresa: Her Life, Her Works* (New Rochelle, NY: New City Press, 1991).
13. Ibid.
14. Ibid., 14.
15. Ibid., 16.
16. Cited in Mother Teresa, *Loving Jesus* (Ann Arbor: Servant Publications, 1991), 138.
17. Gjergji, *Mother Teresa*, 14.
18. Eileen Egan, *Such a Vision of the Street: Mother Teresa—The Spirit and the Work* (Garden City, NY: Doubleday & Co., 1985), 7.
19. Mother Teresa, *Loving Jesus,* 138.
20. Gjergji, *Mother Teresa*, 22.
21. Ibid., 22–23.
22. Ibid., 73.
23. Ibid.., 23–24.
24. Ibid., 25.
25. Ibid., 28.
26. Ibid.
27. Cited in Egan, *Such a Vision of the Street*, 18.
28 Gjergji, *Mother Teresa*, 31.
29 Ibid., 33.
30. Mother Teresa, *Loving Jesus*, 141.
31. Gjergji, *Mother Teresa*, 31.
32. Ibid., 36.
33. Ibid.
34. Egan, *Such a Vision of the Street*, 25.
35. Mother Teresa, *Loving Jesus*, 142.
36. Egan, *Such a Vision of the Street*, 25.

37. Gjergji, *Mother Teresa*, 38.

38. Ibid., 39.

39. Egan, *Such a Vision of the Street*, 30.

40. Ibid., 29–33.

41. Spink, *The Miracle of Love*, 23.

42. Mother Teresa, *My Life for the Poor* (New York: Ballantine Books, 1985), 14–15.

43. Egan, *Such a Vision of the Street*, 38.

44. Ibid.

45. Ibid., 42.

46. Address of Mother Teresa to National Prayer Breakfast, Washington, D.C., February 4, 1994.

47. Templeton Award Speech, 1973, cited in Spink, *The Miracle of Love*, 241.

48. Egan, *Such a Vision of the Street*, 64.

49. Ibid., 67.

50. Muggeridge, *Something Beautiful for God*, 44.

51. Address to National Prayer Breakfast, February 4, 1994.

52. Ibid.

53. Edward W. Desmond, "A Pencil in the Hand of God," *Time*, December 4, 1989, 11.

54. Egan, *Such a Vision of the Street*, 43.

55. Ibid., 44.

56. Gjergji, *Mother Teresa*, 65–66.

57. Ibid., 61.

58. *Nobel Prize Speeches*, 232.

59. Gjergji, *Mother Teresa*, 67.

60. Address to National Prayer Breakfast, February 4, 1994.

61. Ibid.

62. Mother Teresa, *My Life for the Poor*, 67.

63. Spink, *The Miracle of Love*, 69.

64. Egan, *Such a Vision of the Street*, 18.

65. Ibid., 120.

66. Ibid., 130.

67. Ibid., 106.

68. Ibid.

69. Ibid., 205.

70. Ibid., 352.

71. *The Nobel Prize*, 37–38, passim.

72. Ibid., 224.

73. Ibid., 221–23, passim.

74. The text, as recited by the Co-Workers of Mother Teresa on a daily basis, is as follows: "Lord, make me a channel of Thy peace, that where there is hatred I may bring love; that where there is wrong, I may bring the spirit of forgiveness; that where there is discord, I may bring harmony; that where there is error, I may bring truth; that where there is doubt, I may bring faith; that where there is despair, I may bring hope; that where there are shadows, I may bring light; that where there is sadness, I may bring joy.

Lord, grant that I may seek to comfort rather than to be comforted; to understand than to be understood; to love than to be loved; for it is by forgetting self that one finds; it is by dying that one awakens to eternal life. Amen." Cited in Muggeridge, *Something Beautiful for God*, 151.

75. *Nobel Prize Speeches*, 224.

76. Egan, *Such a Vision of the Street*, 356.

77. "People: Faces of the Decade," *Time*, January 1, 1990, 88.

78. Jim Twoey, in conversation with the author, August 16, 1996.

79. Gjergji, *Mother Teresa*, 57.

80. Ibid., 57–58.

81. Egan, *Such a Vision of the Street*, 266.

82. George M. Anderson, S.J., "A Woman of Peace: An Interview with Eileen Egan," *America*, February 10, 1996, 20–21.

83. Letter from Mother Teresa to Judge Lance Ito, January 18, 1992, displayed in Christopher Hitchens, *The Missionary Position: Mother Teresa in Theory and Practice* (New York: Verso Press, 1995), 67.

84. Egan, *Such a Vision of the Street*, 363.

85. "Soviet Peace Group Is Host to Mother Teresa," *Washington Post*, August 21, 1987.

86. Egan, *Such a Vision of the Street*, 344.

87. Hitchens, *The Missionary Position*, 48.

88. Cited in *Biblical Discernment Ministries*, Internet, August 1996.

89. Desmond, "A Pencil in the Hand of God," 11.

90. Cited in Egan, *Such a Vision of the Street*, 343.

91. Hitchens, *The Missionary Position*, 41.

92. Telephone conversation with the author, August 2, 1996.

93. *Nobel Prize Speeches*, 225.

94. Gjergji, *Mother Teresa*, 71.

CHAPTER FIVE
Pope John Paul II—Human Dignity

1. Carl Bernstein and Marco Politi, *His Holiness: John Paul II and the Hidden History of Our Time* (New York: Doubleday, 1996), 181.

2. Celestine Bohlen, "Pope's Tremor Is All but Confirmed As Parkinson's," *New York Times*, October 13, 1996, A3.

3. Paul Gray, "Empire of the Spirit," *Time*, December 26, 1994–January 2, 1995, 53.

4. Jennifer Bradley, "Baltimore Diarist: Indulgences," *New Republic*, October 30, 1995, 50.

5. Conversation with author, July 27, 1996.

6. *Life*, January 1990, 136.

7. Cited in Tad Szulc, *Pope John Paul II: The Biography* (New York: Scribner's, 1995), 415.

8. Leo D. Lefebure, "John Paul II: The Philosopher Pope," *Christian Century*, February 15, 1995, 170.

9. "The Pope: A See Change," *Economist*, April 29, 1995, 25.

10. Szulc, *Pope John Paul II*, 455.

11. John Paul II, *On the Hundredth Anniversary of Rerum Novarum* (Boston: St. Paul Books & Media), 55.

12. John Paul II, Speech to the UN General Assembly, October 5, 1995.

13. John Paul II, *The Gospel of Life* (Boston: St. Paul Books & Media, 1995), 116.

14. "The Pope at the U.N.," *Commonweal*, October 25, 1995, 5.

15. John Elson, "Lives of the Pope," *Time*, December 26, 1994–January 2, 1995, 64.

16. Jeffrey L. Sheler et. al, "Keeping Faith in His Time," *U.S. News & World Report*, October 9, 1995, 73.

17. Szulc, *Pope John Paul II*, 19.

18. For the details of John Paul's childhood, see Szulc, *Pope John Paul II*, and Bernstein, Polti, *His Holiness*, especially 60–83 and 18–44 respectively.

19. Bernstein, Politi, *His Holiness,* 27.
20. Cited in Bernstein, Politi, *His Holiness*, 38.
21. Bernstein, Politi, *His Holiness*, 47.
22. St. John of the Cross, *The Collected Works of St. John of the Cross* (Washington, D.C.: ICS Publications, 1991), 401.
23. Bernstein, Politi, *His Holiness*, 52.
24. Szulc, *Pope John Paul II*, 118.
25. Ibid., 112.
26. Bernstein, Politi, *His Holiness*, 67.
27. Sheler, "Keeping Faith in His Time," 75.
28. Szulc, *Pope John Paul II*, 148.
29. Ibid., 161.
30. Ibid., 233.
31. Ibid., 244.
32. Ibid., 234–35.
33. Ibid., 262.
34. Bernstein, Politi, *His Holiness*, 119.
35. Szulc, *Pope John Paul II*, 280.
36. Cited in Charles Mortiz, ed., *Current Biography* (New York: H. W. Wilson Company), 1979.
37. Bernstein, Politi, *His Holiness*, 209.
38. Pope John Paul II, *The Splendor of Truth* (Boston: Pauline Books & Media, 1993), 48.
39. John Paul II, "Building the Culture of Freedom," speech to UN, October 5, 1995, cited in *American Purpose,* Winter 1995, Volume 9, Numbers 4, 5.
40. *Centesimus Annus,* 64.
41. Kenneth L. Woodward, "Mixed Blessings," *Newsweek*, August 16, 1993, 40.
42. John Paul II, "Building the Culture of Freedom," 4.
43. Ibid., 150.
44. *Time*, December 26, 1995, 65.
45. Kenneth L. Woodward, "Life, Death and the Pope," *Newsweek,* April 10, 1996, 63.
46. Bernstein, Politi, *His Holiness*, 294.
47. "State of the Union," *America*, February 23, 1991, 196.

CHAPTER SIX
Elie Wiesel—Remembrance

1. Cited in Robert McAfee Brown, *Elie Wiesel: Messenger to All Humanity* (Notre Dame: University of Notre Dame Press, 1989), 109.
2. *Time*, March 18, 1985, 79.
3. Elie Wiesel, *Night* (New York: Bantam Books, 1986).
4. Ibid., 32.
5. Elizabeth Devereaux, "'A commitment to memory' fuels the Nobel laureate's work, including his latest novel," *Publisher's Weekly,* April 6, 1992, 39.
6. Carol Rittner, "An Interview with Elie Wiesel," *America,* November 19, 1988, 397 and 400.
7. Charles Mortiz, ed., *Current Biography* (New York: H. W. Wilson Company, 1986).
8. Brown, *Elie Wiesel*, 254.
9. Elie Wiesel, "Hope, Despair, and Memory," Nobel Lecture, December 11, 1986, cited in *The Nobel Prize* (Stockholm: Imprimerie Royale, 1986), 322.

10. Elie Wiesel, *Memoirs: All Rivers Run to the Sea* (New York: Alfred A. Knopf), 1.
11. Ibid., 4.
12. Ibid., 10.
13. Elie Wiesel, *A Jew Today* (New York: Random House, 1978), 68.
14. Wiesel, *Memoirs*, 10.
15. Wiesel, *A Jew Today*, 8.
16. Wiesel, *Memoirs*, 32.
17. Ibid., 19.
18. Ibid., 21.
19. Ibid., 33.
20. Ibid., 36.
21. Ibid., 40.
22. Ibid.
23. Ibid., 69–70.
24. Wiesel, *Night*, 22.
25. Ibid., 23.
26. Wiesel, *Memoirs*, 75.
27. Wiesel, *Night*, 31.
28. Ibid., 36.
29. Wiesel, *Memoirs*, 79–80, passim.
30. Ibid., 62.
31. Ibid., 82.
32. Wiesel, *Night*, 106.
33. Wiescl, *Memoirs*, 97.
34. Ibid., 130.
35. Ibid., 165.
36. Ibid., 180.
37. Ibid., 183.
38. Ibid., 202.
39. Ibid., 206.
40. Ibid., 229.
41. Wiesel, *Memoirs*, 239.
42. Wiesel, *A Jew Today*, 17–18.
43. Wiesel, *Memoirs*, 266.
44. Wiesel, *A Jew Today*, 18.
45. Ibid., 19.
46. Wiesel, *Memoirs*, 266.
47. Henry James Cargas, *Conversations with Elie Wiesel* (South Bend, IN: Justice Books, 1992), 33.
48. Wiesel, *Memoirs*, 267.
49. Ibid., 293.
50. Cargas, *Conversations with Elie Wiesel*, 33.
51. Ibid., 348.
52. Cited in Brown, *Elie Wiesel*, 211.
53. Elie Wiesel and John Cardinal O'Connor, *A Journey of Faith* (New York: Donald I. Fine Inc., 1990), 8.
54. Wiesel, *Night*, xi.
55. Wiesel, *Memoirs*, 322.
56. Ibid., 332.
57. Ibid., 333.

58. Ibid., 388.
59. Ibid., 389.
60. Ibid., 391.
61. Cited in Brown, *Elie Wiesel*, 16.
62. Elie Wiesel, *Against Silence: The Voice and Vision of Elie Wiesel* (New York: Holocaust Library, 1985), Vol. I, 330.
63. Cited in Brown, *Elie Wiesel*, 130.
64. *The Nobel Prize*, 32.
65. Ibid., 33–37.
66. Wiesel, *Memoirs*, 403.
67. Rittner, "An Interview with Elie Wiesel," 397.
68. Cited in Brown, *Elie Wiesel*, 115.
69. Rittner, "An Interview with Elie Wiesel," 398.
70. Wiesel, *Memoirs*, 84.
71. Cited in Brown, *Elie Wiesel*, 141.
72. Cardinal Jean-Marie Lustiger, "The Absence of God? The Presence of God? A Meditation in Three Parts on *Night*," *America*, November 19, 1988, 402–3, passim.
73. Cited in *America*, November 19, 1988, 36.
74. Cited in Brown, *Elie Wiesel*, 134.
75. Rittner, "An Interview with Elie Wiesel," *America*, November 19, 1988, 398.
76. Report of conference by the Elie Wiesel Foundation for Humanity, New York, 1991, 7.
77. Henry Allen, "Holocaust Museum Dedicated With Hope," *Washington Post*, April 23, 1993, 1.
78. Daniel Williams, "Ex-official Accuses U.S. of Being Soft on Serbs," *Washington Post*, February 4, 1994, 24.
79. White House, Press Release, December 13, 1995.
80. Beth Landman and Deborah Mitchell, "Intelligencer: A Bitter Battle over Nobel Pursuit," *New York*, 1996.
81. Martin Peretz, "Cambridge Diarist," *The New Republic*, April 25, 1988, 43.
82. Bill Marx, "Monument Man," on Internet, Phoenix Media/Communication Group, December 14–21, 1995.
83. Cargas, *Conversations with Elie Wiesel*, 15.
84. See for example, Jean-Michel Angebert, *The Occult and the Third Reich* (New York: Macmillan Publishing Company, Inc., 1974).
85. Cited in Benjamin Netanyahu, *A Place Among the Nations: Israel and the World* (New York: Bantam Books, 1993), 417.
86. Cited in Brown, *Elie Wiesel*, 167.
87. Elie Wiesel, *From the Kingdom of Memory* (New York: Schocken Books, 1990), 138.
88. Elie Wiesel, *A Jew for Today* (New York: Random House, 1978), 5.
89. Wiesel, *Memoirs*, 270–71.
90. Cargas, *Conversations with Elie Wiesel*, 17.
91. Ibid., 47.
92. Wiesel, *Memoirs*, 271.
93. Lustiger, "The Absence of God? The Presence of God?", 405–6.
94. Cited in Brown, *Elie Wiesel*, 45.
95. Wiesel, *Memoirs*, 321.
96. Ibid.